The Founding of the State of Israel

The Founding
of the State
# of Israel

Other books in the At Issue in History series:

The Founding of the State of Israel

Mitchell Bard, *Book Editor*

Daniel Leone, *President*
Bonnie Szumski, *Publisher*
Scott Barbour, *Managing Editor*

 **AT ISSUE IN HISTORY**

GREENHAVEN
PRESS®

San Diego • Detroit • New York • San Francisco • Cleveland
New Haven, Conn. • Waterville, Maine • London • Munich

LIBRARY OF CONGRESS CATALOGING-IN-PUBLICATION DATA

The founding of the state of Israel / Mitchell Bard, book editor.
    p. cm. — (At issue in history)
Includes bibliographical references and index.
ISBN 0-7377-1349-6 (pbk. : alk. paper) — ISBN 0-7377-1348-8 (lib. : alk. paper)
    1. Palestine—History—1917–1948. 2. Palestine—Politics and government—1917–1948. 3. Zionism—Government policy—Great Britain—History. 4. Jewish-Arab relations—History—1917–1948. I. Series.
DS126.F68 2003
956.94'04—dc21   2002034683

Printed in the United States of America

Contents

Chapter 2: Partition and War: The Birth of Israel

Chapter 3: Looking Back at the Creation of Israel

Foreword

Historian Robert Weiss defines history simply as "a record and interpretation of past events." Both elements—record and interpretation—are necessary, Weiss argues.

> Names, dates, places, and events are the essence of history. But historical writing is not a compendium of facts. It consists of facts placed in a sequence to tell a connected story. A work of history is not merely a story, however. It also must analyze what happened and *why*—that is, it must interpret the past for the reader.

For example, the events of December 7, 1941, that led President Franklin D. Roosevelt to call it "a date which will live in infamy" are fairly well known and straightforward. A force of Japanese planes and submarines launched a torpedo and bombing attack on American military targets in Pearl Harbor, Hawaii. The surprise assault sank five battleships, disabled or sank fourteen additional ships, and left almost twenty-four hundred American soldiers and sailors dead. On the following day, the United States formally entered World War II when Congress declared war on Japan.

These facts and consequences were almost immediately communicated to the American people who heard reports about Pearl Harbor and President Roosevelt's response on the radio. All realized that this was an important and pivotal event in American and world history. Yet the news from Pearl Harbor raised many unanswered questions. Why did Japan decide to launch such an offensive? Why were the attackers so successful in catching America by surprise? What did the attack reveal about the two nations, their people, and their leadership? What were its causes, and what were its effects? Political leaders, academic historians, and students look to learn the basic facts of historical events and to read the intepretations of these events by many different sources, both primary and secondary, in order to develop a more complete picture of the event in a historical context.

In the case of Pearl Harbor, several important questions surrounding the event remain in dispute, most notably the role of President Roosevelt. Some historians have blamed his policies for deliberately provoking Japan to attack in order to propel America into World War II; a few have gone so far as to accuse him of knowing of the impending attack but not informing others. Other historians, examining the same event, have exonerated the president of such charges, arguing that the historical evidence does not support such a theory.

The Greenhaven At Issue in History series recognizes that many important historical events have been interpreted differently and in some cases remain shrouded in controversy. Each volume features a collection of articles that focus on a topic that has sparked controversy among eyewitnesses, contemporary observers, and historians. An introductory essay sets the stage for each topic by presenting background and context. Several chapters then examine different facets of the subject at hand with readings chosen for their diversity of opinion. Each selection is preceded by a summary of the author's main points and conclusions. A bibliography is included for those students interested in pursuing further research. An annotated table of contents and thorough index help readers to quickly locate material of interest. Taken together, the contents of each of the volumes in the Greenhaven At Issue in History series will help students become more discriminating and thoughtful readers of history.

Introduction

For the Jewish people the founding of Israel represented nothing less than a miracle, the rebirth of their independent homeland, from which they were driven two thousand years earlier. It was all the more significant due to its timing, coming just a few years after the Holocaust, the most cataclysmic event in Jewish history. For Arabs, Israel's founding was something else entirely. Rather than a miracle it was (and continues to be) viewed as a disaster that led to the dispersion of hundreds of thousands of Palestinian Arabs and the insinuation of an unwanted Jewish outpost in the Arab and Muslim heartland.

The modern history of Israel is one defined primarily by conflict as the Jews fought the imperial rulers of their homeland—the British—the native inhabitants of the area, and the surrounding Arab nations for the right to reestablish their nation. The Arabs did everything in their power to prevent the Jews from achieving their national aspirations and, to this day, most have not given up the struggle to reverse what happened in 1948 when Israel's statehood was formally declared.

A Long History

It may appear that the Jews suddenly showed up in the Middle East in the twentieth century and demanded to have a state of their own, but this is not accurate. The Jewish people have maintained a connection to their ancestral homeland for more than thirty-seven hundred years. In fact Jews trace their claim to the land of Israel to the biblical promise made by God to Abraham to make his descendants a great nation in the land between the Nile and Euphrates (Genesis 12: 1–2). For people with deep religious convictions, this biblical connection is enough. For those more concerned with history and politics, though, this is not a convincing argument for the Jewish people's right to the land. But the biblical promise is not the only basis for the Jewish people's claim. They can also point to the fact that

12

they created the first independent nation in the region of the Promised Land around 1000 B.C. when the twelve Jewish tribes that emerged from slavery in Egypt united to form the world's first constitutional monarchy.

Throughout the following centuries, the Jews continued to maintain a presence in the region, although they were conquered and exiled by various powers, including the Assyrians, the Babylonians, the Greeks, and the Romans. After Muhammad died in 632 his followers marched out of Arabia and proceeded to create a great empire stretching across the Middle East (including Palestine) and North Africa and into Spain. It is at this point, at the earliest, that Arabs can make any claim to the land of Israel. For thirteen hundred years the Muslims ruled the region, but they never established any political entity in Palestine. In fact for most of Muslim history the area was considered a backwater and was largely neglected.

The Rise of Zionism

Throughout the centuries, Jewish communities grew and contracted depending on the degree of tolerance of the rulers. Under Muslim rule, large numbers of Jews were not allowed to return to the land, and the rulers made sure that those who did live under their governments remained powerless. When the Ottoman Turks conquered the area in the sixteenth century, they treated the Jews with relative tolerance and the community slowly began to grow. In the nineteenth century more Jews, particularly those who were orthodox, began to establish communities in Israel.

At the same time the situation in much of the Christian world was bad for the Jews—and growing worse. Throughout centuries of Christian expansion Jews had experienced varying degrees of anti-Semitism. By the mid-nineteenth century several Jewish thinkers began to conclude that there was no way to eradicate this hatred and that the only way to insure Jewish safety and survival was to establish a homeland where the Jews would control their own destiny. The belief that the Jews were a nation like any other, and that they had a right to self-determination in their homeland, became known as Zionism.

Zionism came in a variety of "flavors." For example, practical Zionists focused their efforts on settling the land. Religious Zionists believed the Jewish homeland should be based on Jewish law. Socialist Zionists were interested in establishing a just society. Messianic Zionists thought that establishing a Jewish state would help to usher in the messianic age. A small minority of Jews, though, based on their view that the Messiah had to come first before the Jews could return to their homeland, adopted an anti-Zionist position.

Many of these positions were theoretical or philosophical. But a Viennese journalist named Theodor Herzl set out to implement the creation of a Jewish state and founded what may be called political Zionism. For Herzl the key to independence was to win international backing and legal recognition for a Jewish state. Herzl founded the World Zionist Organization, which held its first conference in Basel, Switzerland, in 1897, and announced the goal of the Zionist movement was the creation of a Jewish state in Palestine.

Some people believed the situation for Jews was so perilous that it was important to establish a haven to protect them immediately, no matter where. Herzl initially joined in this view and negotiated with the British who, at one point, intimated they might be prepared to allow the Jews to establish their state in Uganda. The idea of settling anywhere other than the land of Israel caused a rift in the Zionist movement in 1903.

The Uganda plan never got very far. Herzl was persuaded that he had made a mistake and, after having considered this alternative as a temporary solution, joined the overwhelming majority in the organization that insisted the only place for a Jewish state was in the Promised Land.

Waves of Immigrants

Jews had longed to return to their homeland throughout the centuries, and the timing for finally doing so became ripe in the late nineteenth and early twentieth centuries. The new political Zionist movement encouraged many to return home, and the persecution of Jewish communities in various parts of the world forced others to seek a safe haven. In addition the Muslim empire was slowly crumbling, and the Turkish rulers were gradually losing their ability to prevent the building of a Jewish community in Israel.

While Herzl was politicking, attacks on Jews in Russia helped provoke large-scale immigration to Palestine. This was one of a series of waves of immigration. The first wave

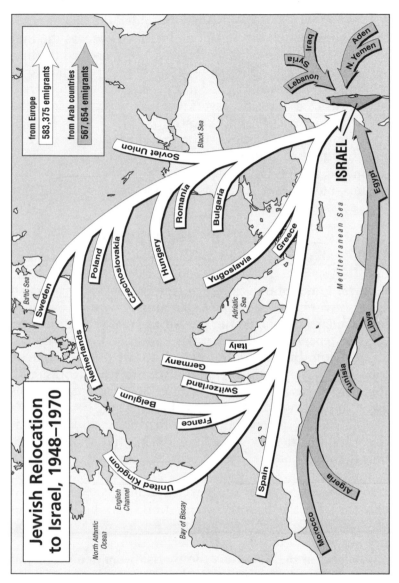

Jewish Relocation to Israel, 1948–1970

of about twenty thousand Jews had come in the 1880s, also provoked by anti-Semitism abroad. This is referred to as the First Aliyah. The word *aliyah* literally means "to go up" and is applied to Jews who move to Israel because they are viewed as moving closer to God.

After a new series of pogroms in Russia at the beginning of the twentieth century, a second wave of forty thousand immigrants arrived between 1904 and 1914. These were many of the socialist Zionists who founded the first agricultural collectives known as kibbutzim (Degania was the first in 1909). These settlers started newspapers, created the first self-defense organization to protect themselves from Arab marauders, and revived the Hebrew language (which had been restricted to use in prayers and now was adopted as the everyday method of communication).

The native Arabs viewed the growing presence of Jews in what they considered their homeland with growing alarm. Sometimes their opposition was voiced in political forums, but other times it was expressed in violence against the Jewish pioneers.

The Balfour Declaration

By the end of the Second Aliyah World War I had broken out. By this time Herzl had died and been replaced as the political leader of the Zionist movement by a Russian-born Englishman named Chaim Weizmann. A chemist by training, Weizmann lobbied the British to support the creation of an independent Jewish state in Palestine. On November 2, 1917, the British notified the Zionists, in a letter from foreign secretary Arthur James Balfour to Lord Rothschild, that the proposals they had submitted were acceptable. This came to be known as the Balfour Declaration.

The main reason the British made the declaration at that time was that they needed to bring the United States into the war. They believed American Jews had a great deal of influence on U.S. foreign policy and that they would use it to pressure the American government to enter the war in exchange for the Balfour Declaration. The United States did join the fight with Britain, but for its own reasons and not because of the Jews or the declaration.

As part of the war effort the British were determined to defeat the Turks and dismantle the Ottoman Empire. To do this they believed they needed the help of the Arabs in Arabia. They secretly negotiated with one of the key leaders of the Arabs, Hussein ibn Ali. The British promised to give Arabs independence in conquered Turkish territories if ibn Ali led his people in a revolt against the Ottoman Empire. He agreed, and his forces helped the British win the war in the Middle East.

Great Britain and France (which had also fought the Turks) emerged as the major powers in the Middle East after the collapse of the Ottoman Empire. While they had promised the Arabs independence in most of the Middle East, the British and French had left Palestine out of the areas pledged to become sovereign Arab territory. They also had decided that nations must be able to sustain themselves before becoming autonomous, and they determined that the Arabs were not yet ready. To help nations prepare for independence the great powers devised the mandate system. Though in truth, Britain and France hoped to maintain control over the Middle East for their own purposes.

The British Mandate

When the San Remo Conference that followed the end of World War I convened on April 24, 1920, France and Great Britain implemented a secret agreement they had made during the war to divvy up the Ottoman Empire. France was given the mandate for Syria, and Great Britain was given the mandate for Iraq and Palestine. The mandate for Palestine, which included the Balfour Declaration, was formalized by the League of Nations on September 23, 1922.

The British recognized that the mandates contradicted their agreements with the Arabs; consequently, they made every effort to placate the Arab leaders by installing them as puppet rulers over territories under their control. Britain created an entirely new province by severing almost 80 percent of historic Palestine east of the Jordan River and calling it Transjordan (now called Jordan).

Many Jews were furious about the mandate, especially after Transjordan was lopped off from what they believed to be their homeland. Still, most Zionists were happy because the mandate included the Balfour Declaration, and the international community's recognition of the mandate was viewed as giving their goal even greater political legitimacy.

At the end of World War I the Jewish population was still only about 90,000, compared with 600,000 Arabs. After the war the Third Aliyah, stimulated largely by the Russian Revolution, brought another 40,000 Jews to Palestine. This group helped develop the country, draining malarial swamps and building towns. During this period the underground military defense force known as the Haganah was created, as was the first Jewish labor union movement, the Histadrut.

With official sanction of the mandate the Jews began to place a higher priority on developing the structure for a state—including a political body to make decisions for the community, expansion of rural and urban development, and most important, the expansion of the population. In the 1920s, the goal of increasing the Jewish population was again aided by a combination of anti-Semitism and economic hardship, this time primarily in Poland. The Fourth Aliyah was the result, bringing in about 80,000 more Jews, mostly from the middle class, who subsequently helped build the economy of Palestine.

A final large wave of 250,000 immigrants arrived in the decade from 1929 to 1939. This group, which included many professionals who helped build towns and industry, came as a result of the persecution of Jews by German chancellor Adolf Hitler.

Arabs Revolt

The Arab population of Palestine was extremely unhappy about the waves of Jewish immigrants, whom they saw as foreigners invading their country and stealing their land. They complained bitterly—first to the Turks and then to the British mandatory authorities. The Zionists made some efforts to negotiate with the Arabs and to find a way to coexist, but they were not successful. The Arabs turned to violence, instigated largely by the religious leader known as the Mufti of Jerusalem, Haj Amin el-Hussaini.

Beginning in 1921 the Mufti provoked the first of several riots against the Jews in an effort to force the British to terminate the Balfour Declaration and restrict Jewish immigration. A second major riot, in 1929, led to the massacre of Jews from the ancient town of Hebron, the place where Jewish patriarchs were believed to be buried. Jews who survived were forced to leave the city and would not return for more than four decades (Jews reestablished a presence in the city several years after Hebron was captured by Israeli forces in the Six-Day War of 1967). In 1936 a more sustained revolt, lasting three years, was mounted by the Arabs.

Each time the Arabs rioted the British launched an investigation. Commissions went to Palestine and heard Arab complaints that the Jews were stealing their land and driving them out of Palestine. In fact, all the land the Jews owned was purchased, usually at exorbitant prices, from wealthy landowners who lived outside Palestine. Moreover, the commissions usually found that the Arabs benefited from the Jewish settlement because it improved the standard of living in the country by enhancing the economy and providing better health care. Consequently, it actually stimulated Arab immigration into Palestine. Though the commissions essentially found the Arab claims groundless, they still recommended, in a series of "white papers," that Jewish immigration be curtailed in the hope of pacifying the Arabs. This tactic did not work.

Dividing Palestine

In 1937 a British commission led by former secretary of state Lord Earl Peel was sent to Palestine to investigate. The commission came to the conclusion that the best solution to the problem was to divide the country into two states, an Arab state and a Jewish state. It seemed logical that if two people were fighting over one land, it should be divided between them. The Arabs rejected the plan, known as the Peel Plan. They would never share "their" land with the Jews. The idea divided the Jews. Many were willing to accept the compromise solution, but others believed they were entitled to a state in all of Palestine. The British shelved the plan.

In the meantime one Zionist, Vladimir Jabotinsky, viewed Peel's partition idea as another step away from the Balfour Declaration. He insisted that the Jews should still get a state in all of historic Palestine—including the part that had been sliced away to create Transjordan. He argued that the British would never fulfill their promise to create a homeland and that the Jews would have to fight to achieve their aspirations. Toward that end, some of his followers split off from the Haganah, which had functioned purely as a self-defense force. They created a more militant organization known as the Irgun, which began to take offensive actions against the Arabs and later the British.

With the failure of the Peel Plan, the British resorted to their usual policy of restricting Jewish immigration, but this did nothing to assuage the anger felt by the Arabs, and their revolt continued into 1939. That year Jewish immigration more than doubled as Jews sought to flee Nazi Germany and what would become a world war began with the German invasion of Poland.

The British then issued a white paper announcing that the new government policy was to establish an Arab state in Palestine within ten years. Furthermore, Jewish immigration would be limited to no more than seventy-five thousand immigrants over the following five years, and none would be allowed after that without Arab permission. The declaration was a complete abandonment of the Balfour promise. Worse yet it severely restricted immigration in the short run and put the long-term decision in the hands of the Arabs at the very moment when the need for Jews to escape from Europe was growing more urgent.

The Jews Declare War

The Jews were torn. As the war in Europe expanded to a world war and the fate of the Jews became more precarious, the Jews in Palestine were determined to fight Hitler. At the same time, they could not tolerate the repudiation of the Balfour Declaration. The leader of the Jewish community, David Ben-Gurion, announced, "We must assist the British in the war as if there were no White Paper and we must resist the White Paper as if there were no war."

Many Jews joined the fight against the Nazis. They also reaffirmed their commitment to the establishment of a Jewish state at a meeting of Zionists at the Biltmore Hotel in New York in 1942. At the same time the Jews in Palestine did everything they could to illegally smuggle immigrants into the country. As the news of the Holocaust began to seep out, this effort became imperative. The British were equally determined, however, to prevent more Jews than were allowed according to their quota from entering Palestine, thereby dooming thousands, perhaps millions, to death at the hands of the Nazis.

Jews in Palestine fighting the British also became more militant. Another splinter group known as the Stern Gang (after its founder Avraham Stern) began to terrorize the British and assassinated one of their government officials in Cairo in 1944. The violent attacks by the Irgun and the Stern Gang were condemned by Jewish leaders in Palestine, who still used the Haganah primarily as a defensive force to protect Jewish communities from attacks by Arabs. The violence nevertheless escalated, with the most dramatic attack being the bombing of the King David Hotel by the Irgun in 1946. A part of the hotel was used as a headquarters for the British military, and the Irgun had issued warnings that it would be blown up. The British ignored the warnings and failed to evacuate the building. As a result, ninety-one people were killed, including fifteen Jews. The attack, like many others by the small, radical paramilitary groups, caused outrage among the British and consternation within the mainstream Jewish community, which condemned all such terrorist attacks.

When World War II ended, the British made it clear that they would not implement the Balfour Declaration. They also continued to severely restrict Jewish immigration, preventing the now stateless Jewish survivors of the Holocaust from going to their homeland. A number of ships carrying immigrants were turned back or sunk or their passengers arrested and imprisoned on Cyprus. The most famous case was that of the *Exodus*, a ship that left France July 11, 1947, carrying forty-five hundred immigrants. The British navy challenged and boarded the ship, killing three Jews. The immigrants were forcibly transported back to Germany in British ships.

The British people became increasingly distraught about

the events in Palestine, where mandatory authorities were unable to keep order. Arabs continued attacking the Jews, and now the Jews were increasingly fighting back. This had never particularly upset people in England because English citizens had remained largely above the fray; however, Jews were now increasingly attacking British targets. The Haganah had turned offensive but still was focusing on military targets. The militants, however, were humiliating and sometimes murdering British soldiers in response, they said, to what the British were doing to the Jews.

By February 1947 the British government had had enough and decided to turn the question of what to do with Palestine over to the United Nations (UN). The expectation was that the UN would fail to resolve the issue and leave it to the British to do what they wanted. At that point the British expected to be able to take whatever measures were necessary to pacify the country. The British tried to insure this outcome by specifying that the Jews and Arabs had to agree on any proposed solution—something they knew would be impossible.

As had occurred many times before, the UN sent a delegation, the UN Special Committee on Palestine (UNSCOP), to investigate the cause of the conflict between Jews and Arabs and listen to their respective positions. The majority of the delegates came to the same conclusion that the British Peel commission had arrived at almost exactly a decade earlier, namely, that the only fair way to resolve the dispute was to divide Palestine into both an Arab and Jewish state.

The UN adopted a resolution partitioning Palestine on November 29, 1947. The Arabs rejected the partition, insisting that they were entitled to all of Palestine, and subsequently went to war to prevent its implementation. Their publicly declared aim was to destroy the Jewish state. Since that date only two Arab states, Egypt and Jordan, have abandoned that goal and made peace with Israel. The other Arab states officially remain at war with Israel.

The Jews were also not enthusiastic about the partition resolution. They believed the Jewish homeland had already been partitioned once when the British created Transjordan. They were now being asked to accept statehood in an area a fraction of the size of the original Promised Land. Though they were offered about 60 percent of the territory of Palestine, most of that was the infertile land of the Negev desert region. Furthermore, the UN plan called for the internationalization of Jerusalem, which meant the Jews had to give up the place that had been their ancient capital and the focal point of their connection to the Holy Land for centuries. From a practical standpoint it meant the isolation of one hundred thousand Jews living in the city who were to be surrounded by the Arab state that was to encircle the internationalized area.

Despite what Zionists viewed as an unsatisfactory offer, they decided to accept the plan because it meant the establishment of a Jewish state with the backing of the international community. The Jews knew they would have to fight the Arabs to keep the area they had been allotted, but they believed that once the state was established they could build it and make it strong.

The conflict between Jews and Arabs did not begin or end with the founding of the state of Israel on May 14, 1948. Since then Israel has fought several wars with its neighbors and has experienced internal conflict as Palestinians in Israeli-occupied territories have engaged in violent uprisings. Because both sides fervently believe they have the right to call the disputed territory their home, the ongoing conflict has proven frustratingly resistant to international peacemaking efforts. Thus, over fifty years after its occurrence, the founding of the state of Israel remains a contentious event.

Chapter 1

Debating the Promise of a Jewish Homeland

1

The Jews Need a National Home in Palestine

Richard Gottheil

During the nineteenth century, a number of Jewish thinkers came to the conclusion that anti-Semitism was ineradicable and that the only hope of Jewish survival in the long run was the creation of a Jewish homeland. For most Jews, the only possible home for the Jews was the land of Israel, believed to have been promised by God, where the ancient Jewish nation had once flourished. The movement to establish a Jewish national home in Palestine was know as Zionism. In the following speech, originally delivered in November 1898, Richard Gottheil outlines the goals of Zionism. Gottheil argues that the assimilation of Jews in existing nations is not a practical goal due to the persistence of anti-Semitism. He concludes that the well-being of the Jewish people can only be guaranteed through the creation of a nation in their historic home of Palestine. Gottheil was a professor of Semitic languages and Rabbinical Literature at Columbia University in New York and president of the American Federation of Zionists.

I know that there are a great many of our people who look for a final solution of the Jewish question in what they call "assimilation." The more the Jews assimilate themselves to their surroundings, they think, the more completely will the causes for anti-Jewish feeling cease to exist. But have you ever for a moment stopped to consider what assimila-

Richard Gottheil, "The Aims of Zionism," speech, November 1, 1898, New York.

tion means? It has very pertinently been pointed out that the use of the word is borrowed from the dictionary of physiology. But in physiology it is not the food which assimilates itself into the body. It is the body which assimilates the food. The Jew may wish to be assimilated; he may do all he will towards this end. But if the great mass in which he lives does not wish to assimilate him—what then? If demands are made upon the Jew which practically mean extermination, which practically mean his total effacement from among the nations of the globe and from among the religious forces of the world,—what answer will you give? And the demands made are practically of that nature.

I can imagine it possible for a people who are possessed of an active and aggressive charity which it expresses, not only in words, but also in deeds, to contain and live at peace with men of the most varied habits. But, unfortunately, such people do not exist; nations are swayed by feelings which are dictated solely by their own self-interests; and the Zionists in meeting this state of things, are the most practical as well as the most ideal of the Jews.

There is no place where that which is distinctively Jewish in [the Jew's] manner or in his way of life is à la mode.

It is quite useless to tell the English workingman that his Jewish fellow-laborer from Russia has actually increased the riches of the United Kingdom; that he has created quite a new industry,—that of making ladies' cloaks, for which formerly England sent £2,000,000 to the continent every year. He sees in him some one who is different to himself, and unfortunately successful, though different. And until that difference entirely ceases, whether of habit, of way, or of religious observance, he will look upon him and treat him as an enemy.

An Especial Disadvantage

For the Jew has this especial disadvantage. There is no place where that which is distinctively Jewish in his manner or in his way of life is *à la mode*. We may well laugh at the Irishman's brogue; but in Ireland, he knows, his brogue is at home. We may poke fun at the Frenchman as he shrugs his shoulders and speaks with every member of his body. The Frenchman feels that in France it is the proper thing so to do. Even the Turk will wear his fez, and feel little the worse for the occasional jibes with which the street boy may greet it. But this consciousness, this ennobling consciousness, is all denied the Jew. What he does is nowhere *à la mode*; no, not even his features; and if he can disguise these by parting his hair in the middle or cutting his beard to a point, he feels he is on the road towards assimilation. He is even ready to use the term "Jewish" for what he considers uncouth and low.

We believe that [a Jewish national] home can only naturally . . . be found . . . in Palestine.

For such as these amongst us, Zionism also has its message. It wishes to give back to the Jew that nobleness of spirit, that confidence in himself, that belief in his own powers which only perfect freedom can give. With a home of his own, he will no longer feel himself a pariah among the nations, he will nowhere hide his own peculiarities,—peculiarities to which he has a right as much as any one,—but will see that those peculiarities carry with them a message which will force for them the admiration of the world. He will feel that he belongs somewhere and not everywhere. He will try to be something and not everything. The great word which Zionism preaches is conciliation of conflicting aims, of conflicting lines of action; conciliation of Jew to Jew. It means conciliation of the non-Jewish world to the Jew as well. It wishes to heal old wounds; and by frankly confessing differences which do exist, however much we try to explain them away, to work out its own salvation upon its own ground, and from these to send forth its spiritual message to a conciliated world.

But, you will ask, if Zionism is able to find a permanent home in Palestine for those Jews who are forced to go there as well as those who wish to go, what is to become of us who have entered, to such a degree, into the life around us, and who feel able to continue as we have begun? What is to be our relation to the new Jewish polity? I can only answer: Exactly the same as is the relation of people of other nationalities all the world over to their parent home. What becomes of the Englishman in every corner of the globe? What becomes of the German? Does the fact that the great mass of their people live in their own land prevent them from doing their whole duty towards the land in which they happen to live? Is the German-American considered less of an American because he cultivates the German language and is interested in the fate of his fellow-Germans at home? Is the Irish-American less of an American because he gathers money to help his struggling brethren in the Green Isle? Or are the Scandinavian-Americans less worthy of the title Americans, because they consider precious the bonds which bind them to the land of their birth, as well as those which bind them to the land of their adoption?

Nay! It would seem to me that just those who are so afraid that our action will be misinterpreted should be among the greatest helpers in the Zionist cause. For those who feel no racial and national communion with the life from which they have sprung should greet with joy the turning of Jewish immigration to some place other than the land in which they dwell. They must feel, for example, that a continual influx of Jews who are not Americans is a continual menace to the more or less complete absorption for which they are striving.

The Zionist Position

But I must not detain you much longer. Will you permit me to sum up for you the position which we Zionists take in the following statements:

We believe that the Jews are something more than a purely religious body; that they are not only a race, but also a nation; though a nation without as yet two important requisites—a common home and a common language.

We believe that if an end is to be made to Jewish misery and to the exceptional position which the Jews occupy,—which is the primary cause of Jewish misery,—the Jewish nation must be placed once again in a home of its own.

We believe that such a national regeneration is the fulfillment of the hope which has been present to the Jew throughout his long and painful history.

We believe that only by means of such a national regeneration can the religious regeneration of the Jews take place, and they be put in a position to do that work in the religious world which Providence has appointed for them.

We believe that such a home can only naturally, and

without violence to their whole past, be found in the land of their fathers—in Palestine.

We believe that such a return must have the guarantee of the great powers of the world in order to secure for the Jews a stable future.

And we hold that this does not mean that all Jews must return to Palestine.

This, ladies and gentlemen, is the Zionist program. Shall we be able to carry it through? I cannot believe that the Jewish people have been preserved throughout these centuries either for eternal misery or for total absorption at this stage of the world's history. I cannot think that our people have so far misunderstood their own purpose in life, as now to give the lie to their own past and to every hope which has animated their suffering body.

Bear with me but a few moments longer while I read the words which a Christian writer puts into the mouth of a Jew. "The effect of our separateness will not be completed and have its hightest transformation, unless our race takes on again the character of a nationality. That is the fulfillment of the religious trust that molded them into a people, whose life has made half the inspiration of the world. . . . Revive the organic centre; let the unity of Israel which has made the growth and form of its religion be an outward reality. Looking toward a land and a polity, our dispersed people in all the ends of the earth may share the dignity of a national life which has a voice among the peoples of the East and the West—which will plant the wisdom and skill of our race so that it may be, as of old, a medium of transmission and understanding. Let that come to pass, and the living warmth will spread to the weak extremities of Israel. Let the central fire be kindled again, and the light will reach afar. The degraded and scorned of the race will learn to think of their sacred land, not as a place for saintly beggary to await death in loathsome idleness, but as a republic, where the Jewish spirit manifests itself in a new order founded on the old, purified, enriched by the experiences which our greatest sons have gathered from the life of the ages. A new Judea, poised between East and West—a covenant of reconciliation. The sons of Judah have to choose, that God may again choose them. The Messianic time is the time when Israel shall will the planting of the national ensign. The divine principle of our race is action, choice, resolved memory. Let us help to will our own better future of the world—not renounce our higher gift and say: 'Let us be as if we were not among the populations,' but choose our full heritage, claim the brotherhood of our nation, and carry into it a new brotherhood with the nations of the Gentiles. The vision is there; it will be fulfilled."

These are the words of the non-Jewish Zionist, George Eliot. We take hope, for has not that Jewish Zionist said: "We belong to a race that can do everything but fail."

2
Early Promises of Arab Independence

Husayn ibn 'Ali and Henry McMahon

The central figure in the Arab nationalist movement at the time of World War I was Husayn ibn 'Ali, who was appointed by the Turkish Committee of Union and Progress to the position of Sherif of Mecca in 1908. As Sherif, Husayn was responsible for the custody of Islam's shrines in the Hejaz (later Saudi Arabia) and, consequently, was recognized as one of the Muslims' spiritual leaders. In July 1915, Husayn sent a letter to Sir Henry McMahon, Britain's High Commissioner for Egypt, informing him of the terms for Arab participation in the war against the Turks. The letters between Husayn and McMahon that followed, excerpted below, outlined the areas that Britain was prepared to cede to the Arabs in exchange for their assistance. The Husayn-McMahon correspondence conspicuously fails to mention Palestine. The British argued the omission had been intentional, thereby justifying their refusal to grant the Arabs independence in Palestine after the war. McMahon himself later said he had never promised that Palestine was included in the promises he made. Nevertheless, the Arabs held then, as now, that the letters constituted a promise of independence in Palestine for the Arabs.

Translation of a letter from Sherif Husayn of Mecca to Sir Henry McMahon, His Majesty's High Commissioner at Cairo, July 14, 1915

Whereas the whole of the Arab nation without any exception have decided in these last years to accom-

Henry McMahon and Husayn ibn 'Ali, "The Hussein-McMahon Correspondence," www.jewishvirtuallibrary.org, 1915–1916.

plish their freedom, and grasp the reins of their administration both in theory and practice; and whereas they have found and felt that it is in the interest of the Government of Great Britain to support them and aid them in the attainment of their firm and lawful intentions (which are based upon the maintenance of the honour and dignity of their life) without any ulterior motives whatsoever unconnected with this object;

And whereas it is to their (the Arabs') interest also to prefer the assistance of the Government of Great Britain in consideration of their geographic position and economic interests, and also of the attitude of the above-mentioned Government, which is known to both nations and therefore need not be emphasized;

Subject to the above modifications, Great Britain is prepared to recognize and support the independence of the Arabs.

For these reasons the Arab nation sees fit to limit themselves, as time is short, to asking the Government of Great Britain, if it should think fit, for the approval, through her deputy or representative, of the following fundamental propositions, leaving out all things considered secondary in comparison with these, so that it may prepare all means necessary for attaining this noble purpose, until such time as it finds occasion for making the actual negotiations;

Firstly—England will acknowledge the independence of the Arab countries, bounded on the north by Mersina and Adana up to the 37th degree of latitude, on which degree fall Birijik, Urfa, Mardin, Midiat, Jezirat (Ibn 'Umar), Amadia, up to the border of Persia; on the east by the borders of Persia up to the Gulf of Basra; on the south by the Indian Ocean, with the exception of the position of Aden to remain as it is; on the west by the Red Sea, the Mediterranean Sea up to Mersina. England to approve the proclamation of an Arab Khalifate of Islam.

Secondly—The Arab Government of the Sherif will acknowledge that England shall have the preference in all economic enterprises in the Arab countries whenever conditions of enterprises are otherwise equal.

Thirdly—For the security of this Arab independence

and the certainty of such preference of economic enterprises, both high contracting parties will offer mutual assistance, to the best ability of their military and naval forces, to face any foreign Power which may attack either party. Peace not to be decided without agreement of both parties.

Fourthly—If one of the parties enters into an aggressive conflict, the other party will assume a neutral attitude, and in case of such party wishing the other to join forces, both to meet and discuss the conditions.

Fifthly—England will acknowledge the abolition of foreign privileges in the Arab countries, and will assist the Government of the Sherif in an International Convention for confirming such abolition.

Sixthly—Articles 3 and 4 of this treaty will remain in vigour for fifteen years, and, if either wishes it to be renewed, one year's notice before lapse of treaty is to be given.

Consequently, and as the whole of the Arab nation have (praise be to God) agreed and united for the attainment, at all costs and finally, of this noble object, they beg the Government of Great Britain to answer them positively or negatively in a period of thirty days after receiving this intimation; and if this period should lapse before they receive an answer, they reserve to themselves complete freedom of action. Moreover, we (the Sherif's family) will consider ourselves free in work and deed from the bonds of our previous declaration which we made through Ali Effendi.

Translation of a letter from McMahon to Husayn, August 30, 1915

To his Highness the Sherif Hussein.

(After compliments and salutations.)

We have the honour to thank you for your frank expressions of the sincerity of your feeling towards England. We rejoice, moreover, that your Highness and your people are of one opinion—that Arab interests are English interests and English Arab. To this intent we confirm to you the terms of Lord [Horatio] Kitchener's [British Secretary of War] message, which reached you by the hand of Ali Effendi, and in which was stated clearly our desire for the independence of Arabia and its inhabitants, together with our approval of the Arab Khalifate when it should be proclaimed. We declare once more that His Majesty's Government would welcome the resumption of the Khalifate by an

Arab of true race. With regard to the questions of limits and boundaries, it would appear to be premature to consume our time in discussing such details in the heat of war, and while, in many portions of them, the Turk is up to now in effective occupation; especially as we have learned, with surprise and regret, that some of the Arabs in those very parts, far from assisting us, are neglecting this their supreme opportunity and are lending their arms to the German and the Turk, to the new despoiler and the old oppressor. . . .

Friendly reassurances. Salutations!

(Signed) A.H. McMAHON.

Translation of a letter from Husayn to McMahon, September 9, 1915

To his Excellency the Most Exalted, the Most Eminent—the British High Commissioner in Egypt; may God grant him Success.

With great cheerfulness and delight I received your letter dated the 19th Shawal, 1333 (the 30th August, 1915), and have given it great consideration and regard, in spite of the impression I received from it of ambiguity and its tone of coldness and hesitation with regard to our essential point.

It is necessary to make clear to your Excellency our sincerity towards the illustrious British Empire and our confession of preference for it in all cases and matters and under all forms and circumstances. The real interests of the followers of our religion necessitate this.

Nevertheless, your Excellency will pardon me and permit me to say clearly that the coolness and hesitation which you have displayed in the question of the limits and boundaries by saying that the discussion of these at present is of no use and is a loss of time, and that they are still in the hands of the Government which is ruling them, &c., might be taken to infer an estrangement or something of the sort.

As the limits and boundaries demanded are not those of one person whom we should satisfy and with whom we should discuss them after the war is over, but our peoples have seen that the life of their new proposal is bound at least by these limits and their word is united on this.

Therefore, they have found it necessary first to discuss this point with the Power in whom they now have their confidence and trust as a final appeal, viz., the illustrious British Empire.

Their reason for this union and confidence is mutual interest, the necessity of regulating territorial divisions and the feelings of their inhabitants, so that they may know how to base their future and life, so not to meet her (England?) or any of her Allies in opposition to their resolution which would produce a contrary issue, which God forbid.

For the object is, honourable Minister, the truth which is established on a basis which guarantees the essential sources of life in future.

Yet within these limits they have not included places inhabited by a foreign race. It is a vain show of words and titles.

May God have mercy on the Khalifate and comfort Moslems in it.

I am confident that your Excellency will not doubt that it is not I personally who am demanding of these limits which include only our race, but that they are all proposals of the people, who, in short, believe that they are necessary for economic life.

Is this not right, your Excellency the Minister?

In a word, your high Excellency, we are firm in our sincerity and declaring our preference for loyalty towards you, whether you are satisfied with us, as has been said, or angry.

With reference to your remark in your letter above mentioned that some of our people are still doing their utmost in promoting the interests of Turkey, your goodness (lit. "perfectness") would not permit you to make this an excuse for the tone of coldness and hesitation with regard to our demands, demands which I cannot admit that you, as a man of sound opinion, will deny to be necessary for our existence; nay, they are the essential essence of our life, material and moral.

Up to the present moment I am myself with all my might carrying out in my country all things in conformity with the Islamic law, all things which tend to benefit the rest of the Kingdom, and I shall continue to do so until it pleases God to order otherwise.

In order to reassure your Excellency I can declare that the whole country, together with those who you say are submitting themselves to Turco-German orders, are all waiting the result of these negotiations, which are dependent only on your refusal or acceptance of the question of the limits and on your declaration of safeguarding their religion first and then the rest of rights from any harm or danger.

Whatever the illustrious Government of Great Britain finds conformable to its policy on this subject, communicate it to us and specify to us the course we should follow. . . .

Translation of a letter from McMahon to Husayn, October 24, 1915

I have received your letter of the 29th Shawal, 1333, with much pleasure and your expressions of friendliness and sincerity have given me the greatest satisfaction.

I regret that you should have received from my last letter the impression that I regarded the question of the limits and boundaries with coldness and hesitation; such was not the case, but it appeared to me that the time had not yet come when that question could be discussed in a conclusive manner.

I have realised, however, from your last letter that you regard this question as one of vital and urgent importance. I have, therefore, lost no time in informing the Government of Great Britain of the contents of your letter, and it is with great pleasure that I communicate to you on their behalf the following statement, which I am confident you will receive with satisfaction:

The two districts of Mersina and Alexandretta and portions of Syria lying to the west of the districts of Damascus, Homs, Hama and Aleppo cannot be said to be purely Arab, and should be excluded from the limits demanded.

With the above modification, and without prejudice of our existing treaties with Arab chiefs, we accept those limits.

As for those regions lying within those frontiers wherein Great Britain is free to act without detriment to the interest of her ally, France, I am empowered in the name of the Government of Great Britain to give the following assurances and make the following reply to your letter:

1. Subject to the above modifications, Great Britain is prepared to recognize and support the independence of the Arabs in all the regions within the limits demanded by the Sherif of Mecca.

2. Great Britain will guarantee the Holy Places against all external aggression and will recognise their inviolability.

3. When the situation admits, Great Britain will give to the Arabs her advice and will assist them to establish what may appear to be the most suitable forms of government in those various territories.

4. On the other hand, it is understood that the Arabs have decided to seek the advice and guidance of Great Britain only, and that such European advisers and officials as may be required for the formation of a sound form of administration will be British.

5. With regard to the vilayets of Bagdad and Basra, the Arabs will recognise that the established position and interests of Great Britain necessitate special administrative arrangements in order to secure these territories from foreign aggression, to promote the welfare of the local populations and to safeguard our mutual economic interests.

I am convinced that this declaration will assure you beyond all possible doubt of the sympathy of Great Britain towards the aspirations of her friends the Arabs and will result in a firm and lasting alliance, the immediate results of which will be the expulsion of the Turks from the Arab countries and the freeing of the Arab peoples from the Turkish yoke, which for so many years has pressed heavily upon them. . . .

(Signed) A.H. McMAHON.

Translation of a letter from Husayn to McMahon, November 5, 1915

I received with great pleasure your honoured letter, dated the 15th Zil Hijja (the 24th October, 1915), to which I beg to answer as follows:

1. In order to facilitate an agreement and to render a service to Islam, and at the same time to avoid all that may cause Islam troubles and hardships—seeing moreover that we have great consideration for the distinguished qualities and dispositions of the Government of Great Britain—we renounce our insistence on the inclusion of the vilayets of Mersina and Adana in the Arab Kingdom. But the two vilayets of Aleppo and Beirut and their sea coasts are purely Arab vilayets, and there is no difference between a Moslem and a Christian Arab: they are both descendants of one forefather.

We Moslems will follow the footsteps of the Commander of the Faithful Omar ibn Khattab, and other Khalifs succeeding him, who ordained in the laws of the Moslem Faith that Moslems should treat the Christians as they treat themselves. He, Omar, declared with reference to Christians: "They will have the same privileges and submit to the same duties as ourselves." They will thus enjoy their civic rights in as much as it accords with the general interests of the whole nation.

2. As the Iraqi vilayets are parts of the pure Arab Kingdom, and were in fact the seat of its Government in the time of Ali ibn Abu Talib, and in the time of all the Khalifs who succeeded him; and as in them began the civilisation of the Arabs, and as their towns were the first towns built in Islam where the Arab power became so great; therefore they are greatly valued by all Arabs far and near, and their traditions cannot be forgotten by them. Consequently, we cannot satisfy the Arab nations or make them submit to give us such a title to nobility. But in order to render an accord easy, and taking into consideration the assurances mentioned in the fifth article of your letter to keep and guard our mutual interests in that country as they are one and the same, for all these reasons we might agree to leave under the British administration for a short time those districts now occupied by the British troops without the rights of either party being prejudiced thereby (especially those of the Arab nation; which interests are to it economic and vital), and against a suitable sum paid as compensation to the Arab Kingdom for the period of occupation, in order to meet the expenses which every new kingdom is bound to support; at the same time respecting your agreements with the Sheikhs of those districts, and especially those which are essential.

> *When the Arabs know the Government of Great Britain is their ally . . . , then to enter the war at once will . . . be in conformity with the general interest of the Arabs.*

3. In your desire to hasten the movement we see not only advantages, but grounds of apprehension. The first of these grounds is the fear of the blame of the Moslems of the opposite party (as has already happened in the past), who would declare that we have revolted against Islam and ruined its forces. The second is that, standing in the face of Turkey which is supported by all the forces of Germany, we do not know what Great Britain and her Allies would do if one of the Entente Powers were weakened and obliged to make peace. We fear that the Arab nation will then be left

alone in the face of Turkey together with her allies, but we would not at all mind if we were to face the Turks alone. Therefore it is necessary to take these points into consideration in order to avoid a peace being concluded in which the parties concerned may decide the fate of our people as if we had taken part in the war without making good our claims to official consideration.

4. The Arab nation has a strong belief that after this war is over the Turks under German influence will direct their efforts to provoke the Arabs and violate their rights, both material and moral, to wipe out their nobility and honour and reduce them to utter submission as they are determined to ruin them entirely. The reasons for the slowness shown in our action have already been stated.

5. When the Arabs know the Government of Great Britain is their ally who will not leave them to themselves at the conclusion of peace in the face of Turkey and Germany, and that she will support and will effectively defend them, then to enter the war at once will, no doubt, be in conformity with the general interest of the Arabs. . . .

Translation of a letter from McMahon to Husayn, December 14, 1915

(After customary greetings and acknowledgment of previous letter.)

I am gratified to observe that you agree to the exclusion of the districts of Mersina and Adana from boundaries of the Arab territories.

I also note with great pleasure and satisfaction your assurances that the Arabs are determined to act in conformity with the precepts laid down by Omar Ibn Khattab and the early Khalifs, which secure the rights and privileges of all religions alike.

In stating that the Arabs are ready to recognise and respect all our treaties with Arab chiefs, it is, of course, understood that this will apply to all territories included in the Arab Kingdom, as the Government of Great Britain cannot repudiate engagements which already exist.

With regard to the vilayets of Aleppo and Beirut, the Government of Great Britain have fully understood and taken careful note of your observations, but, as the interests of our ally, France, are involved in them both, the question will require careful consideration and a further communication on the subject will be addressed to you in due course.

The Government of Great Britain, as I have already informed you, are ready to give all guarantees of assistance and support within their power to the Arab Kingdom, but their interests demand, as you yourself have recognised, a friendly and stable administration in the vilayet of Bagdad, and the adequate safeguarding of these interests calls for a much fuller and more detailed consideration than the present situation and the urgency of these negotiations permit.

We fully appreciate your desire for caution, and have no wish to urge you to hasty action, which might jeopardise the eventual success of your projects, but, in the meantime, it is most essential that you should spare no effort to attach all the Arab peoples to our united cause and urge them to afford no assistance to our enemies.

It is on the success of these efforts and on the more active measures which the Arabs may hereafter take in support of our cause, when the time for action comes, that the permanence and strength of our agreement must depend.

Under these circumstances I am further directed by the Government of Great Britain to inform you that you may rest assured that Great Britain has no intention of concluding any peace in terms of which the freedom of the Arab peoples from German and Turkish domination does not form an essential condition.

As an earnest of our intentions, and in order to aid you in your efforts in our joint cause, I am sending you by your trustworthy messenger a sum of twenty thousand pounds.

(Customary ending.)

(Signed) H. McMAHON.

Translation of a letter from Husayn to McMahon, January 1, 1916

We received from the bearer your letter, dated the 9th Safar (the 14th December, 1915), with great respect and honour, and I have understood its contents, which caused me the greatest pleasure and satisfaction, as it removed that which had made me uneasy. . . .

As regards the northern parts and their coasts, we have already stated in our previous letter what were the utmost possible modifications, and all this was only done so to fulfill those aspirations whose attainment is desired by the will of the Blessed and Supreme God. It is this same feeling and desire which impelled us to avoid what may possibly injure the alliance of Great Britain and France and the agreement made between them during the present wars and calamities; yet we find it our duty that the eminent minister should be sure that, at the first opportunity after this war is finished, we shall ask you (what we avert our eyes from today) for what we now leave to France in Beirut and its coasts.

I do not find it necessary to draw your attention to the fact that our plan is of greater security to the interests and protection of the rights of Great Britain than it is to us, and will necessarily be so whatever may happen, so that Great Britain may finally see her friends in that contentment and advancement which she is endeavouring to establish for them now, especially as her Allies being neighbours to us will be the germ of difficulties and discussion with which there will be no peaceful conditions. In addition to which the citizens of Beirut will decidedly never accept such dismemberment, and they may oblige us to undertake new measures which may exercise Great Britain, certainly not less than her present troubles, because of our belief and certainty in the reciprocity and indeed the identity of our interests, which is the only cause that caused us never to care to negotiate with any other Power but you. Consequently, it is impossible to allow any derogation that gives France, or any other Power, a span of land in those regions.

I declare this, and I have a strong belief, which the living will inherit from the dead, in the declarations which you give in the conclusion of your honoured letter. Therefore, the honourable and eminent Minister should believe and be sure, together with Great Britain, that we still remain firm to our resolution which [British administrator Ronald] Storrs learnt from us two years ago, for which we await the opportunity suitable to our situation, especially in view of that action the time of which has now come near and which destiny drives towards us with great haste and clearness, so that we and those who are of our opinion may have reasons for such action against any criticisms or responsibilities imposed upon us in future.

Your expression "we do not want to push you to any hasty action which might jeopardise the success of your aim" does not need any more explanation except what we may ask for, when necessary, such as arms, ammunition, &c.

I deem this sufficient, as I have occupied much of your

Honour's time. I beg to offer you my great veneration and respect.

Translation of a letter from McMahon to Husayn, January 25, 1916

We fully realise and entirely appreciate the motives which guide you in this important question, and we know well that you are acting entirely in the interests of the Arab peoples and with no thought beyond their welfare.

We take note of your remarks concerning the vilayet of Baghdad, and will take the question into careful consideration when the enemy has been defeated and the time for peaceful settlement arrives.

As regards the northern parts, we note with satisfaction your desire to avoid anything which might possibly injure the alliance of Great Britain and France. It is, as you know, our fixed determination that nothing shall be permitted to interfere in the slightest degree with our united prosecution of this war to a victorious conclusion. Moreover, when the victory has been won, the friendship of Great Britain and France will become yet more firm and enduring, cemented by the blood of Englishmen and Frenchmen who have died side by side fighting for the cause of right and liberty.

In this great cause Arabia is now associated, and God grant that the result of our mutual efforts and co-operation will bind us in a lasting friendship to the mutual welfare and happiness of us all.

We are greatly pleased to hear of the action you are taking to win all the Arabs over to our joint cause, and to dissuade them from giving any assistance to our enemies, and we leave it to your discretion to seize the most favourable moment for further and more decided measures.

3

The British Promise a Home for the Jews in Palestine

Arthur James Balfour

During World War I the British believed that supporting the Zionist program would win them the gratitude of American Jews, who would then lobby their government to join Britain in the war. (The United States ultimately did join the war effort, though the Jews had little to do with the U.S. decision.) In 1917, the British declared their support for a Jewish homeland in the form of a letter from Lord Arthur James Balfour to Baron Edmond de Rothschild, the unofficial leader of British Jewry. This text became known as the Balfour Declaration. For the next forty years, the Zionists would fight for the implementation of the declaration.

Foreign Office
November 2nd, 1917
Dear Lord Rothschild,

I have much pleasure in conveying to you, on behalf of His Majesty's Government, the following declaration of sympathy with Jewish Zionist aspirations which has been submitted to, and approved by, the Cabinet.

"His Majesty's Government view with favour the establishment in Palestine of a national home for the Jewish people, and will use their best endeavours to facilitate the achievement of this object, it being clearly understood that nothing shall be done which may prejudice the civil and re-

Arthur James Balfour, "The Balfour Declaration," www.mfa.gov.il, Israel Ministry of Foreign Affairs, 1917.

ligious rights of existing non-Jewish communities in Palestine, or the rights and political status enjoyed by Jews in any other country."

I should be grateful if you would bring this declaration to the knowledge of the Zionist Federation.

Yours sincerely,

Arthur James Balfour

4

Palestine Should Not Become a Jewish State

Inter-Allied Commission on Mandates in Turkey

Following the peace process at the end of World War I, U.S. president Woodrow Wilson decided to send an Inter-Allied Commission on Mandates in Turkey to the former Turkish (Ottoman) empire to determine what type of political arrangement the inhabitants preferred. Due to French and British opposition, the commission ultimately consisted of only two people—the Americans Henry C. King and Charles R. Crane. As part of their report, known as the King-Crane Report, the authors weigh in against following the extreme Zionist program to create an independent Jewish state in Palestine. King and Crane insist that the creation of such a state would violate the civil and religious rights of the non-Jewish inhabitants of the region, who are overwhelmingly opposed to the Zionist program.

We recommend . . . serious modification of the extreme Zionist Program for Palestine of unlimited immigration of Jews, looking finally to making Palestine distinctly a Jewish State.

(1) The Commissioners began their study of Zionism with minds predisposed in its favor, but the actual facts in Palestine, coupled with the force of the general principles proclaimed by the Allies and accepted by the Syrians, have driven them to the recommendation here made.

(2) The Commission was abundantly supplied with literature on the Zionist program by the Zionist Commission

Inter-Allied Commission on Mandates in Turkey, "Recommendations of the King-Crane Commission on Syria and Palestine," www.jewishvirtuallibrary.org, August 28, 1919.

to Palestine; heard in conferences much concerning the Zionist colonies and their claims; and personally saw something of what had been accomplished. They found much to approve in the aspirations and plans of the Zionists, and had warm appreciation for the devotion of many of the colonists, and for their success, by modern methods, in overcoming great natural obstacles.

The non-Jewish population of Palestine—nearly nine-tenths of the whole—are emphatically against the entire Zionist program.

---

(3) The Commission recognized also that definite encouragement had been given to the Zionists by the Allies in Mr. Balfour's often quoted statement, in its approval by other representatives of the Allies. If, however, the strict terms of the Balfour Statement are adhered to—favoring "the establishment in Palestine of a national home for the Jewish people, it being clearly understood that nothing shall be done which may prejudice the civil and religious rights of existing non-Jewish communities in Palestine"—it can hardly be doubted that the extreme Zionist Program must be greatly modified. For a "national home for the Jewish people" is not equivalent to making Palestine into a Jewish State; nor can the erection of such a Jewish State be accomplished without the gravest trespass upon the "civil and religious rights of existing non-Jewish communities in Palestine." The fact came out repeatedly in the Commission's conference with Jewish representatives, that the Zionists looked forward to a practically complete dispossession of the present non-Jewish inhabitants of Palestine, by various forms of purchase.

Wilson's Principles

In his address of July 4, 1918, President Wilson laid down the following principle as one of the four great "ends for which the associated peoples of the world were fighting": "The settlement of every question, whether of territory, of sovereignty, of economic arrangement or of political relationship upon the basis of the free acceptance of that settlement by the people immediately concerned, and not upon the basis of the material interest or advantage of any other nation or people which may desire a different settlement for the sake of its own exterior influence or mastery." If that principle is to rule, and so the wishes of Palestine's population are to be decisive as to what is to be done with Palestine, then it is to be remembered that the non-Jewish population of Palestine—nearly nine-tenths of the whole—are emphatically against the entire Zionist program. There was no one thing upon which the population of Palestine was more agreed than upon this. To subject a people so minded to unlimited Jewish immigration, and to steady financial and social pressure to surrender the land, would be a gross violation of the principle just quoted, and of the peoples' rights, though it kept within the forms of law.

It is to be noted also that the feeling against the Zionist program is not confined to Palestine, but shared very generally by the people throughout Syria, as our conferences clearly showed. More than 72 per cent—1350 in all—of all the petitions in the whole of Syria were directed against the Zionist program. Only two requests—those for a united Syria and for independence—had a larger support. This general feeling was only voiced by the "General Syrian Congress," in the seventh, eighth and tenth resolutions of their statement.

Intense Anti-Zionism

The Peace Conference should not shut its eyes to the fact that the anti-Zionist feeling in Palestine and Syria is intense and not lightly to be flouted. No British officer, consulted by the Commissioners, believed that the Zionist program could be carried out except by force of arms. The officers generally thought a force of not less than fifty thousand soldiers would be required even to initiate the program. That of itself is evidence of a strong sense of the injustice of the Zionist program, on the part of the non-Jewish populations of Palestine and Syria. Decisions, requiring armies to carry out, are sometimes necessary, but they are surely not gratuitously to be taken in the interests of a serious injustice. For the initial claim, often submitted by Zionist representatives, that they have a "right" to Palestine, based on an occupation of two thousand years ago, can hardly be seriously considered.

There is a further consideration that cannot justly be ignored, if the world is to look forward to Palestine becoming a definitely Jewish state, however gradually that may take place. That consideration grows out of the fact that Palestine is "the Holy Land" for Jews, Christians, and Moslems alike. Millions of Christians and Moslems all over the world are quite as much concerned as the Jews with conditions in Palestine, especially with those conditions which touch upon religious feeling and rights. The relations in these matters in Palestine are most delicate and difficult. With the best possible intentions, it may be doubted whether the Jews could possibly seem to either Christians or Moslems proper guardians of the holy places, or custodians of the Holy Land as a whole. The reason is this: the places which are most sacred to Christians—those having to do with Jesus—and which are also sacred to Moslems, are not only not sacred to Jews, but abhorrent to them. It is simply impossible, under those circumstances, for Moslems and Christians to feel satisfied to have these places in Jewish hands, or under the custody of Jews. There are still other places about which Moslems must have the same feeling. In fact, from this point of view, the Moslems, just because the sacred places of all three religions are sacred to them, have made very naturally much more satisfactory custodians of the holy places than the Jews could be. It must be believed that the precise meaning, in this respect, of the complete Jewish occupation of Palestine has not been fully sensed by those who urge the extreme Zionist program. For it would intensify, with a certainty like fate, the anti-Jewish feeling both in Palestine and in all other portions of the world which look to Palestine as "the Holy Land."

The Commissioners feel bound to recommend that only a greatly reduced Zionist program be attempted.

In view of all these considerations, and with a deep sense of sympathy for the Jewish cause, the Commissioners feel bound to recommend that only a greatly reduced Zionist program be attempted by the Peace Conference, and even that, only very gradually initiated. This would have to mean that Jewish immigration should be definitely limited, and that the project for making Palestine distinctly a Jewish commonwealth should be given up.

There would then be no reason why Palestine could not

be included in a united Syrian State, just as other portions of the country, the holy places being cared for by an International and Inter-religious Commission, somewhat as at present, under the oversight and approval of the Mandatory and of the League of Nations. The Jews, of course, would have representation upon this Commission.

5

A Jewish State
Will Hurt the Arabs

King Abdallah of Jordan

In 1921, Winston Churchill decided to reward one of the key
Arab leaders who helped Britain defeat the Ottoman Turks in
World War I, by taking nearly 80 percent of Palestine and creating an entirely new country and making their ally its king.
This is how Transjordan, later Jordan, came into being. Abdallah, the Arab leader who was installed as the monarch, had
a keen interest in the debate over what would happen to the remaining parts of Palestine, which he coveted for his kingdom.
Ultimately, during the war of 1948, his army would take control of most of what was to be the Arab state under the partition resolution. However, in 1934, long before his forces invaded the newly formed state of Israel, the king wrote to Sir
Arthur Wauchope, who was the British government's representative in the kingdom, to express his concerns about how
the Balfour Declaration and the immigration of Jews to Palestine was affecting the Arabs.

---

1. I understand from His Excellency the Colonial Secretary that His Majesty's Government has placed complete trust in the person of Your Excellency and that you are
the sole authority upon which it relies in the Palestine question. Appreciating as I do the gravity of this responsibility I
cannot conceal my pleasure at this news because of my confidence in the good understanding and firm bonds of friendship that exist between your honourable person and myself.
I am aware also that you have an unfettered love of justice

King Abdallah of Jordan, *My Memoirs Completed*, translated by Harold W.
Glidden. London: Longman, 1978. Copyright © 1978 by Longman Group, Ltd.
Reproduced by permission.

and a genuine discrimination for those things which link the interests of your noble government and people with the Arabs as opposed to others in the Near East.

With regard to the idea prevalent among us Arabs that the Jews in Great Britain enjoy a privileged position because some of their leaders occupy high posts in the government and in the House of Commons and thus are able to direct British policy along lines completely favourable to their own people rather than to others, I have learned also from His Excellency the Colonial Secretary[1] that this is not the case and that it is an erroneous belief. He has reassured me that on the contrary the British Government is not so influenced and that it follows a just course of action and one which is in accord with its national traditions.

For this and other reasons which I have already set forth I have deemed it fitting to write to Your Excellency on the subject of the Arab cause in Palestine, since any further delay would be reckoned as a grave disregard on my part of the national right of both the Arabs and their British friends.

2. The Arabs are greatly distressed because they perceive no concrete results from the reports of the British missions which in past years have been sent to Palestine to inquire into the true state of affairs there. This is in spite of the importance of their testimony and despite the truths contained in the White Paper[2] issued by former Colonial Secretary Lord Passfield.

Promises to Arabs Came First

3. The promises made to the Arabs during the World War were anterior to and more precise than the Balfour Declaration. It was these promises which moved a great many Palestinians—soldiers, officers, and civilians—to desert from the Turkish Army and rally to the banner of my father King Husayn in the Arab Revolt, during which its heroes fought side by side with the British forces. At that time the Zionists had absolutely no political position in Palestine and in no way constituted an element of its population.

4. The joint declaration issued in November 1918 by the two allied powers of Great Britain and France specifically stated that the Arabs would not be compelled to accept any

1. This probably refers to Sir Philip Cunliffe-Lister, who was Colonial Secretary from 9 November 1931 to 6 June 1935.   2. This was issued in 1930 as the result of an investigation into the causes of the disturbances of 1929.

form of government not agreeable to them. On the contrary, it was said that they would encourage the establishment of Arab national governments and that they would extend to them the assistance necessary for their consolidation and success. This declaration should be granted the importance it deserves and it should be taken into account when considering the carrying-out of the Balfour Declaration in Palestine.

The Arabs . . . see a manifest threat to their existence in the steady Jewish immigration into Palestine.

---

5. The Balfour Declaration provides that the Jews should have a national home in Palestine. The indications, however, are that *the Jews by various means and without opposition have been able to devise a programme for turning all of Palestine into a national home for the Jews.* If any impartial observer were to compare their position at the beginning of the immigration into Palestine with the great progress they have made up to the present in colonizing the country, *he would say that their success has been almost complete and that they will attain their goal in a few years.*

6. The Balfour Declaration lays down the condition that the interests of the Arab inhabitants are not to be harmed; in other words, that the interests of the Arabs are to be protected in their entirety. The Arabs, however, see a manifest threat to their existence in the steady Jewish immigration into Palestine accompanied by an influx of illegal arrivals in flagrant violation of this promise. In addition, the fears of the Arab political leaders are supported by the fact that the sale of land continues unrestricted and every day one piece of land after another is torn from the hands of the Arabs.

I know that this cannot be completely stopped even by the use of force. Nevertheless, I draw Your Excellency's attention to the difficult situation in which the Arabs find themselves in the face of the strong organization of the Zionists. In such cases it would be governments which would prevent the disappearance and submerging of a people. If these people possessed representatives in parliamentary or legislative bodies, they would be able to play their part in defending the people and countering the danger that threatens them.

7. Protection of the weak was one of the most honourable of the high aims for which the last World War was fought. What is more worthy of this noble principle than to remember it in times of peace in connection with the situation of the Palestine Arabs who made sacrifices in the war at a time when they were masters of their own country and without rivals for control of it?

Jews Bring Trouble

8. The Jewish immigration has brought to Palestine incompatible peoples of different principles and outlook from the Arabs, who have brought continual unrest and trouble to this peaceful and holy land. *Furthermore, Palestine has become a potential source of social danger the enormity of which will become apparent as soon as world peace is again disturbed;* this corruption will spread to the Arab countries in particular and to the Near East in general. I do not believe that the Government of Palestine would come to any different conclusion if it were to make a profound study of the situation; this is supported by the nature of certain clandestine Jewish groups the existence of which has been revealed by the law-courts.

The Jews have attempted and continue to attempt to go beyond the promises made in the Balfour Declaration.

---

9. The Jews have attempted and continue to attempt to go beyond the promises made in the Balfour Declaration and thereby have given rise in the minds of the Arabs to a fixed idea that *a Jewish state is being created which is masquerading under the name of the National Home.* The implications of this are causing fears to spread to the Arab countries outside of Palestine and to those persons in these countries who are in positions of important responsibility. The Jews have never given the slightest indication of their ability to amalgamate with the original Arab inhabitants of the country. I wish from the bottom of my heart that it were otherwise.

10. My experience leads me to believe that if the situation continues as it is, with unrestricted immigration and other things complained of by the Arabs, *it will lead to evil and terrible results in the near future.* I do not feel that at present sufficient thought is being given to this possibility; matters

are being dealt with on a day-to-day basis. As a result of this it is still said that there is room for new immigrants and that there is land which can be sold. Nevertheless, I hope that Your Excellency will join me in giving thought to the future we may face, and to the problems that may be most difficult to solve if immigration and the sale of land continue.

Your Excellency:

I lay before Your Excellency these matters which have disturbed the Arabs both in and out of Palestine. If I have told Your Excellency that the Muslim world is likewise disturbed by these events it is because I am quite certain that this is so. For this reason I have thought that I should draw Your Excellency's attention to these knotty problems which, with God's permission, I trust will be overcome by you.

I do not deny that Great Britain's interests have expanded in Palestine and the Arab countries since the war. But do you not feel, as I do, that in view of all this the continuation of the genuine friendship which the Arabs feel for your noble nation is an essential thing that must be nurtured and preserved?

Both in the past and in the present I have done all in my power to support these ties between the two nations. This is because I firmly believe that it is in the interest of the Arabs as well as the English to do so. I do not deny that my Arab people in Palestine have fallen into a number of political errors, but in my opinion this is all due to their overwhelming fear that their existence is being threatened. It is not to be expected, of course, that a people who are in such a state should preserve their normal balanced frame of mind or think as calmly as they ought to. For this reason their mistakes should be overlooked since the reasons for them are all too apparent.

I communicate to you in all frankness the fears of my Arab people in Palestine and I have summed them up in this memorandum to the best of my ability. It is my hope that you will consider this as an assistance from me to Your Excellency in the performance of the difficult duty which you have undertaken and will see it as motivated by sincere friendship for both my Arab people and my British friends.

Accept, Excellency, my highest esteem and my best greetings.

Your Excellency's sincere friend, 'Abdallah
Amman, 25 July 1934.

6

Britain Does Not Support a Jewish State in Palestine

British Government

In 1937, in response to Arab rioting, the British formed a commission to investigate the causes of the violence and formulate a possible resolution to the conflict between Jews and Arabs. The Peel Commission came to essentially the same conclusion the UN would a decade later; that is, the fairest solution would be to divide Palestine into two states, one Jewish and one Arab. Two years later, the British government issued a white paper that rejected the Peel Commission's partition plan on the grounds that it was not feasible. Instead, the government now proposed an independent state that would essentially be an Arab one, since it gave the Arabs veto power over Jewish immigration. The white paper was a complete repudiation of the Balfour Declaration and therefore vehemently opposed by the Zionists, who, from that point on, realized they could not rely on the British to support their national ambitions. The Arabs rejected the plan as well.

In the statement on Palestine, issued on 9 November, 1938, His Majesty's Government [Britain] announced their intention to invite representatives of the Arabs of Palestine, of certain neighboring countries and of the Jewish Agency to confer with them in London regarding future policy. It was their sincere hope that, as a result of full, free and frank discussions, some understanding might be

British Government, "British White Paper, 1939," www.yale.edu, June 1939.

reached. Conferences recently took place with Arab and Jewish delegations, lasting for a period of several weeks, and served the purpose of a complete exchange of views between British Ministers and the Arab and Jewish representatives. In the light of the discussions as well as of the situation in Palestine and of the Reports of the Royal Commission and the Partition Commission, certain proposals were formulated by His Majesty's Government and were laid before the Arab and Jewish delegations as the basis of an agreed settlement. Neither the Arab nor the Jewish delegation felt able to accept these proposals, and the conferences therefore did not result in an agreement. Accordingly His Majesty's Government are free to formulate their own policy, and after careful consideration they have decided to adhere generally to the proposals which were finally submitted to and discussed with the Arab and Jewish delegations.

The framers of the Mandate . . . could not have intended that Palestine should be converted into a Jewish state against the will of the Arab population.

The Mandate for Palestine, the terms of which were confirmed by the Council of the League of Nations in 1922, has governed the policy of successive British Governments for nearly 20 years. It embodies the Balfour Declaration and imposes on the Mandatory four main obligations. These obligations are set out in Article 2, 6 and 13 of the Mandate. There is no dispute regarding the interpretation of one of these obligations, that touching the protection of and access to the Holy Places and religious buildings or sites. The other three main obligations are generally as follows:

To place the country under such political, administrative and economic conditions as will secure the establishment in Palestine of a national home for the Jewish People. To facilitate Jewish immigration under suitable conditions, and to encourage, in cooperation with the Jewish Agency, close settlement by Jews on the Land.

To safeguard the civil and religious rights of all inhabitants of Palestine irrespective of race and religion, and, whilst facilitating Jewish immigration and settlement, to ensure that the rights and position of other sections of the population are not prejudiced.

To place the country under such political, administrative and economic conditions as will secure the development of self governing institutions.

The Royal Commission and previous Commissions of Enquiry have drawn attention to the ambiguity of certain expressions in the Mandate, such as the expression 'a national home for the Jewish people', and they have found in this ambiguity and the resulting uncertainty as to the objectives of policy a fundamental cause of unrest and hostility between Arabs and Jews. His Majesty's Government are convinced that in the interests of the peace and well being of the whole people of Palestine a clear definition of policy and objectives is essential. The proposal of partition recommended by the Royal Commission would have afforded such clarity, but the establishment of self supporting independent Arab and Jewish States within Palestine has been found to be impracticable. It has therefore been necessary for His Majesty's Government to devise an alternative policy which will, consistent with their obligations to Arabs and Jews, meet the needs of the situation in Palestine. . . .

Reinterpreting Balfour

It has been urged that the expression "a national home for the Jewish people" offered a prospect that Palestine might in due course become a Jewish State or Commonwealth. His Majesty's Government do not wish to contest the view, which was expressed by the Royal Commission, that the Zionist leaders at the time of the issue of the Balfour Declaration recognised that an ultimate Jewish State was not precluded by the terms of the Declaration. But, with the Royal Commission, His Majesty's Government believe that the framers of the Mandate in which the Balfour Declaration was embodied could not have intended that Palestine should be converted into a Jewish State against the will of the Arab population of the country. . . .

His Majesty's Government therefore now declare unequivocally that it is not part of their policy that Palestine should become a Jewish State. They would indeed regard it as contrary to their obligations to the Arabs under the Mandate, as well as to the assurances which have been given to the Arab people in the past, that the Arab population of

Palestine should be made the subjects of a Jewish State against their will. . . .

Creating a Palestinian State

His Majesty's Government are charged as the Mandatory authority "to secure the development of self governing institutions" in Palestine. Apart from this specific obligation, they would regard it as contrary to the whole spirit of the Mandate system that the population of Palestine should remain forever under Mandatory tutelage. It is proper that the people of the country should as early as possible enjoy the rights of self government which are exercised by the people of neighbouring countries. His Majesty's Government are unable at present to foresee the exact constitutional forms which government in Palestine will eventually take, but their objective is self government, and they desire to see established ultimately an independent Palestine State. It should be a State in which the two peoples in Palestine, Arabs and Jews, share authority in government in such a way that the essential interests of each are shared. . . .

The objective of His Majesty's Government is the establishment within 10 years of an independent Palestine State in such treaty relations with the United Kingdom as will provide satisfactorily for the commercial and strategic requirements of both countries in the future. The proposal for the establishment of the independent State would involve consultation with the Council of the League of Nations with a view to the termination of the Mandate.

The independent State should be one in which Arabs and Jews share government in such a way as to ensure that the essential interests of each community are safeguarded.

The establishment of the independent State will be preceded by a transitional period throughout which His Majesty's Government will retain responsibility for the country. During the transitional period the people of Palestine will be given an increasing part in the government of their country. Both sections of the population will have an opportunity to participate in the machinery of government, and the process will be carried on whether or not they both avail themselves of it.

As soon as peace and order have been sufficiently restored in Palestine steps will be taken to carry out this policy of giving the people of Palestine an increasing part in the

government of their country, the objective being to place
Palestinians in charge of all the Departments of Government, with the assistance of British advisers and subject to
the control of the High Commissioner. Arab and Jewish
representatives will be invited to serve as heads of Departments approximately in proportion to their respective populations. The number of Palestinians in charge of Departments will be increased as circumstances permit until all
heads of Departments are Palestinians, exercising the administrative and advisory functions which are presently performed by British officials. When that stage is reached consideration will be given to the question of converting the
Executive Council into a Council of Ministers with a con-
sequential change in the status and functions of the Palestinian heads of Departments.

His Majesty's Government make no proposals at this
stage regarding the establishment of an elective legislature.
Nevertheless they would regard this as an appropriate constitutional development, and, should public opinion in
Palestine hereafter show itself in favour of such a development, they will be prepared, provided that local conditions
permit, to establish the necessary machinery.

---

*The independent state should be one in which
Arabs and Jews share government in such a way
. . . that the essential interests of each
community are safeguarded.*

At the end of five years from the restoration of peace
and order, an appropriate body representative of the people
of Palestine and of His Majesty's Government will be set up
to review the working of the constitutional arrangements
during the transitional period and to consider and make recommendations regarding the constitution of the independent Palestine State.

His Majesty's Government will require to be satisfied
that in the treaty contemplated by sub-paragraph (6) adequate provision has been made for:

the security of, and freedom of access to the Holy
Places, and protection of the interests and property of the
various religious bodies.

the protection of the different communities in Palestine in accordance with the obligations of His Majesty's Government to both Arabs and Jews and for the special position in Palestine of the Jewish National Home.

such requirements to meet the strategic situation as may be regarded as necessary by His Majesty's Government in the light of the circumstances then existing. His Majesty's Government will also require to be satisfied that the interests of certain foreign countries in Palestine, for the preservation of which they are at present responsible, are adequately safeguarded.

His Majesty's Government will do everything in their power to create conditions which will enable the independent Palestine State to come into being within 10 years. If, at the end of 10 years, it appears to His Majesty's Government that, contrary to their hope, circumstances require the postponement of the establishment of the independent State, they will consult with representatives of the people of Palestine, the Council of the League of Nations and the neighbouring Arab States before deciding on such a postponement. If His Majesty's Government come to the conclusion that postponement is unavoidable, they will invite the co-operation of these parties in framing plans for the future with a view to achieving the desired objective at the earliest possible date. . . .

Limiting Jewish Immigration

Under Article 6 of the Mandate, the Administration of Palestine, "while ensuring that the rights and position of other sections of the population are not prejudiced," is required to "facilitate Jewish immigration under suitable conditions." . . .

But His Majesty's Government do not read either the Statement of Policy of 1922 or the letter of 1931 as implying that the Mandate requires them, for all time and in all circumstances, to facilitate the immigration of Jews into Palestine subject only to consideration of the country's economic absorptive capacity. Nor do they find anything in the Mandate or in subsequent Statements of Policy to support the view that the establishment of a Jewish National Home in Palestine cannot be effected unless immigration is allowed to continue indefinitely. If immigration has an adverse effect on the economic position in the country, it should clearly be restricted; and equally, if it has a seriously damaging effect on the political position in the country, that is a factor that should not be ignored. Although it is not difficult to contend that the large number of Jewish immigrants who have been admitted so far have been absorbed economically, the fear of the Arabs that this influx will continue indefinitely until the Jewish population is in a position to dominate them has produced consequences which are extremely grave for Jews and Arabs alike and for the peace and prosperity of Palestine. The lamentable disturbances of the past three years are only the latest and most sustained manifestation of this intense Arab apprehension. The methods employed by Arab terrorists against fellow Arabs and Jews alike must receive unqualified condemnation. But it cannot be denied that fear of indefinite Jewish immigration is widespread amongst the Arab population and that this fear has made possible disturbances which have given a serious setback to economic progress, depleted the Palestine exchequer, rendered life and property insecure, and produced a bitterness between the Arab and Jewish populations which is deplorable between citizens of the same country. If in these circumstances immigration is continued up to the economic absorptive capacity of the country, regardless of all other considerations, a fatal enmity between the two peoples will be perpetuated, and the situation in Palestine may become a permanent source of friction amongst all peoples in the Near and Middle East. His Majesty's Government cannot take the view that either their obligations under the Mandate, or considerations of common sense and justice, require that they should ignore these circumstances in framing immigration policy.

After [a] period of five years, no further Jewish immigration will be permitted unless the Arabs of Palestine are prepared to acquiesce in it.

In the view of the Royal Commission the association of the policy of the Balfour Declaration with the Mandate system implied the belief that Arab hostility to the former would sooner or later be overcome. It has been the hope of British Governments ever since the Balfour Declaration was issued that in time the Arab population, recognizing the advantages to be derived from Jewish settlement and development in Palestine, would become reconciled to the further growth of the Jewish National Home. This hope has not been fulfilled. The alternatives before His Majesty's Government are either (i) to seek to expand the Jewish National Home indefinitely by immigration, against the strongly expressed will of the Arab people of the country; or (ii) to permit further expansion of the Jewish National Home by immigration only if the Arabs are prepared to acquiesce in it. The former policy means rule by force. Apart from other considerations, such a policy seems to His Majesty's Government to be contrary to the whole spirit of Article 22 of the Covenant of the League of Nations, as well as to their specific obligations to the Arabs in the Palestine Mandate. Moreover, the relations between the Arabs and the Jews in Palestine must be based sooner or later on mutual tolerance and goodwill; the peace, security and progress of the Jewish National Home itself requires this. Therefore His Majesty's Government, after earnest consideration, and taking into account the extent to which the growth of the Jewish National Home has been facilitated over the last twenty years, have decided that the time has come to adopt in principle the second of the alternatives referred to above.

Many times and in many places in Palestine during recent years the Arab and Jewish inhabitants have lived in friendship together.

It has been urged that all further Jewish immigration into Palestine should be stopped forthwith. His Majesty's Government cannot accept such a proposal. It would damage the whole of the financial and economic system of Palestine and thus effect adversely the interests of Arabs and Jews alike. Moreover, in the view of His Majesty's Government, abruptly to stop further immigration would be unjust to the Jewish National Home. But, above all, His Majesty's Government are conscious of the present unhappy plight of large numbers of Jews who seek refuge from certain European countries, and they believe that Palestine can and should make a further contribution to the solution of this pressing world problem. In all these circumstances, they believe that they will be acting consistently with their Mandatory obligations to both Arabs and Jews, and in the manner best calculated to serve the interests of the whole people of Palestine, by adopting the following proposals regarding immigration:

Jewish immigration during the next five years will be at a rate which, if economic absorptive capacity permits, will bring the Jewish population up to approximately one third of the total population of the country. Taking into account the expected natural increase of the Arab and Jewish populations, and the number of illegal Jewish immigrants now in the country, this would allow of the admission, as from the beginning of April this year, of some 75,000 immigrants over the next five years. These immigrants would, subject to the criterion of economic absorptive capacity, be admitted as follows:

For each of the next five years a quota of 10,000 Jewish immigrants will be allowed on the understanding that a shortage one year may be added to the quotas for subsequent years, within the five year period, if economic absorptive capacity permits.

In addition, as a contribution towards the solution of the Jewish refugee problem, 25,000 refugees will be admitted as soon as the High Commissioner is satisfied that adequate provision for their maintenance is ensured, special consideration being given to refugee children and dependents.

The existing machinery for ascertaining economic absorptive capacity will be retained, and the High Commissioner will have the ultimate responsibility for deciding the limits of economic capacity. Before each periodic decision is taken, Jewish and Arab representatives will be consulted.

After the period of five years, no further Jewish immigration will be permitted unless the Arabs of Palestine are prepared to acquiesce in it. . . .

Controlling the Land

The Administration of Palestine is required, under Article 6 of the Mandate, "while ensuring that the rights and position of other sections of the population are not prejudiced," to encourage "close settlement by Jews on the land," and no restriction has been imposed hitherto on the transfer of land from Arabs to Jews. The Reports of several expert Commissions have indicated that, owing to the natural growth of the Arab population and the steady sale in recent years of

Arab land to Jews, there is now in certain areas no room for further transfers of Arab land, whilst in some other areas such transfers of land must be restricted if Arab cultivators are to maintain their existing standard of life and a considerable landless Arab population is not soon to be created. In these circumstances, the High Commissioner will be given general powers to prohibit and regulate transfers of land. These powers will date from the publication of this statement of policy and the High Commissioner will retain them throughout the transitional period.

The policy of the Government will be directed towards the development of the land and the improvement, where possible, of methods of cultivation. In the light of such development it will be open to the High Commissioner, should he be satisfied that the "rights and position" of the Arab population will be duly preserved, to review and modify any orders passed relating to the prohibition or restriction of the transfer of land. . . .

His Majesty's Government cannot hope to satisfy the partisans of one party or the other in such controversy as the Mandate has aroused. Their purpose is to be just as between the two people in Palestine whose destinies in that country have been affected by the great events of recent years, and who, since they live side by side, must learn to practice mutual tolerance, goodwill and cooperation. In looking to the future, His Majesty's Government are not blind to the fact that some events of the past make the task of creating these relations difficult; but they are encouraged by the knowledge that as many times and in many places in Palestine during recent years the Arab and Jewish inhabitants have lived in friendship together. Each community has much to contribute to the welfare of their common land, and each must earnestly desire peace in which to assist in increasing the well being of the whole people of the country. The responsibility which falls on them, no less than upon His Majesty's Government, to cooperate together to ensure peace is all the more solemn because their country is revered by many millions of Moslems, Jews and Christians throughout the world who pray for peace in Palestine and for the happiness of her people.

7

The United States Will Consult the Arabs and Jews on Palestine

Franklin D. Roosevelt

During World War II, the Palestine issue was of great interest to Jews around the world, and it was of particular concern to the British, who were the governing power. The situation in Palestine was of less interest, however, to the U.S. government, which was focused primarily on the war effort. President Franklin D. Roosevelt did not become involved in the issue and did not express an opinion on how to resolve the conflicting claims over Palestine. The one statement he did make is found in the following letter he wrote in response to a letter from the king of Saudi Arabia expressing concern about the Arabs in Palestine. After Roosevelt's death, partisans on both sides of the issue tried to use the letter to influence the policy of President Harry S. Truman, but the letter's content ultimately had no impact on Truman's decisions.

Great and Good Friend:
    I have received the communication which Your Majesty sent me under date of March 10, 1945, in which you refer to the question of Palestine and to the continuing interest of the Arabs in current developments affecting that country.

I am gratified that Your Majesty took this occasion to bring your views on this question to my attention and I have given the most careful attention to the statements which

Franklin D. Roosevelt, "Letter to the King of Saudi Arabia," April 5, 1945, *Documents on the Middle East*, edited by Ralph H. Magnus. Washington, DC: American Enterprise Institute for Public Policy Research, July 1969.

you make in your letter. I am also mindful of the memorable conversation which we had not so long ago and in the course of which I had an opportunity to obtain so vivid an impression of Your Majesty's sentiments on this question.

Your Majesty will recall that on previous occasions I communicated to you the attitude of the American Government toward Palestine and made clear our desire that no decision be taken with respect to the basic situation in that country without full consultation with both Arabs and Jews. Your Majesty will also doubtless recall that during our recent conversation I assured you that I would take no action in my capacity as Chief of the Executive Branch of this Government which might prove hostile to the Arab people.

It gives me pleasure to renew to Your Majesty the assurances which you have previously received regarding the attitude of my Government and my own, as Chief Executive, with regard to the question of Palestine and to inform you that the policy of this Government in this subject is unchanged.

I desire also at this time to send you my best wishes for Your Majesty's continued good health and for the welfare of your people.

Your Good Friend,
Franklin D. Roosevelt

8

The Arabs Demand Independence for Palestine

Anglo-American Committee of Inquiry

As the magnitude of the horror of the Holocaust became more widely known after World War II, greater pressure was exerted by Jews in Palestine and America to open the gates of Palestine to the survivors of Hitler's extermination campaign. The Jews demanded that the survivors be allowed to immigrate to Palestine, but the British remained unmoved and adamantly opposed to opening Palestine, in part because of the vehement opposition of the Arabs. In November 1945, a committee of American and British delegates was appointed to talk to the Jews and Arabs to determine their views on the immigration of Jews and the fate of Palestine. The Anglo-American Committee of Inquiry issued its report in April 1946. The following excerpt reveals that Arabs opposed the creation of a Jewish State and demanded independence.

The Arab case is based upon the fact that Palestine is a country which the Arabs have occupied for more than a thousand years, and a denial of the Jewish historical claims to Palestine. In issuing the Balfour Declaration, the Arabs maintain, the British Government were giving away something that did not belong to Britain, and they have consistently argued that the Mandate conflicted with the Covenant of the League of Nations from which it derived its authority. The Arabs deny that the part played by the British in freeing

Anglo-American Committee of Inquiry, "Report to the United States Government and His Majesty's Government in the United Kingdom," www.yale.edu, April 20, 1946.

them from the Turks gave Great Britain a right to dispose of their country. Indeed, they assert that Turkish was preferable to British rule, if the latter involves their eventual subjection to the Jews. They consider the Mandate a violation of their right of self-determination since it is forcing upon them an immigration which they do not desire and will not tolerate— an invasion of Palestine by the Jews.

The Arabs of Palestine point out that all the surrounding Arab States have now been granted independence. They argue that they are just as advanced as are the citizens of the nearby States, and they demand independence for Palestine now. The promises which have been made to them in the name of Great Britain, and the assurances concerning Palestine given to Arab leaders by Presidents Roosevelt and Truman, have been understood by the Arabs of Palestine as a recognition of the principle that they should enjoy the same rights as those enjoyed by the neighboring countries. Christian Arabs unite with Moslems in all of these contentions. They demand that their independence should be recognized at once, and they would like Palestine, as a self-governing country, to join the Arab League. . . .

In issuing the Balfour Declaration, the Arabs maintain, the British Government were giving away something that did not belong to Britain.

The suggestion that self-government should be withheld from Palestine until the Jews have acquired a majority seems outrageous to the Arabs. They wish to be masters in their own house. The Arabs were opposed to the idea of a Jewish National Home even before the Biltmore Program [a 1942 Zionist plan calling for Jewish control of all of Palestine] and the demand for a Jewish State. Needless to say, however, their opposition has become more intense and more bitter since that program was adopted.

The Arabs maintain that they have never been anti-Semitic; indeed, they are Semites themselves. Arab spokesmen profess the greatest sympathy for the persecuted Jews of Europe, but they point out that they have not been responsible for this persecution and that it is not just that they should be compelled to atone for the sins of Western peoples by accepting into their country hundreds of thousands of victims of European anti-Semitism. Some Arabs even declare that they might be willing to do their share in providing for refugees on a quota basis if the United States, the British Commonwealth and other Western countries would do the same.

Peel's Conclusions

The Peel Commission [a commission led by Robert Peel, calling for the partition of Palestine into separate Jewish and Arab States] took the view that the enterprise of the Jews in agriculture and industry had brought large, if indirect, benefits to the Arabs in raising their standard of living. Though a very large part of the Jewish purchases of land has been made from absentee landlords, many of them living outside Palestine, it is probable that many Arab farmers who have sold part of their land to the Jews have been able to make use of the money to improve the cultivation of their remaining holdings. The improvement of health conditions in many parts of the country, while due in part to the activities of Government and in part to the efforts of the Arabs themselves, has undoubtedly been assisted by the work of the Jewish settlers. It is also argued that the Jewish population has conferred substantial indirect benefits on the Arabs through its contribution to the public revenue. On the other hand, the Arabs contend that such improvement as there may have been in their standard of living is attributable solely to their own efforts, perhaps with a measure of aid at some points from the Administration. They assert that at least equal improvements have occurred in other Arab countries, and that the action taken by the Government to assist Jewish industry and agriculture has reacted unfavorably on the Arabs. Import duties for the protection of Jewish industries, for example, are said to have confronted Arab consumers with the necessity of buying high priced local products in place of cheaper imported goods. In any event the Arabs declare that, if they must choose between freedom and material improvement, they prefer freedom.

In exasperation at the disregard of their objection to Jewish immigration, the Arabs of Palestine have repeatedly risen in revolt. . . .

So bare an outline gives only an inadequate picture of the passion with which Arabs in Palestine and in neighboring countries resent the invasion of Palestine by a people which, though originally Semitic, now represents an alien civilization. . . .

Western Influence

It is not surprising that the Arabs have bitterly resented this invasion and have resisted it by force of arms. The Arab civilization of Palestine is based on the clan; leadership resides in a small group of influential families, and it is almost impossible for the son of an Arab fellah to rise to a position of wealth and political influence. Arab agriculture in Palestine is traditional, and improvement is hampered by an antiquated system of land tenure. The Arab adheres to a strict social code far removed from the customs of the modern world, and he is shocked by innovations of dress and manners which seem completely natural to the Jewish immigrant. Thus, the sight of a Jewish woman in shorts offends the Arab concept of propriety. The freedom of relations between the sexes and the neglect of good form as he conceives it violate the entire code of life in which the Arab is brought up.

The Arabs of Palestine are overwhelmed by a vague sense of the power of Western capital represented by the Jewish population.

The Arabs of Palestine are overwhelmed by a vague sense of the power of Western capital represented by the Jewish population. The influx of Western capital and the purchase of modern equipment for agriculture and industry excite in the minds of the Arabs a sense of inferiority and the feeling that they are contending against an imponderable force which is difficult to resist. This feeling is accentuated by the fact that they realize that the Jewish case is well understood and well portrayed in Washington and London, and that they have no means comparable in effectiveness of stating their side of the controversy to the Western World. They have particularly resented the resolutions in favor of Zionist aspirations, adopted respectively by the United States Congress and by the British Labor Party. Although the Arab States have diplomatic representation and five of them are members of the United Nations, the Arabs of Palestine feel nevertheless that they have not succeeded in making their case heard. . . .

Arab Nationalism

The period since the first World War has been marked by a rising wave of nationalism in all Arab countries. Palestinian Arabs share this sentiment, and they are strongly supported in their demand for independence and self-government by all the States of the Arab League. No other subject has occupied so much of the attention of the Arab League or has done so much to unite its membership as has the question of Palestine.

Those members of the Committee who traveled in the neighboring Arab countries found that hostility to Zionism was as strong and widespread there as in Palestine itself. . . .

Moreover the Governments of the neighboring States believe that a Zionist State in Palestine would be a direct threat to them and would impede their efforts towards a closer Arab union. The chief delegate of Syria at the General Assembly of the United Nations told the Committee in London that "Palestine in alien hands would be a wedge splitting the Arab world at a most vital and sensitive point." The same witness expressed the further fear of the Arabs that a Zionist State would inevitably become expansionist and aggressive, and would tend to enter into alliance with any Power which might, in the future, pursue an anti-Arab policy. "The Middle East," he wrote, "is a vital region in which all the Great Powers are interested. A Zionist State in Palestine could only exist with the support of foreign Powers. This would not only mean a state of tension between those foreign Powers and the Arab States, but also the grave possibility of dangerous alignments and maneuvers which might end in international friction at the highest level and possibly disaster."

Chapter 2

Partition and War: The Birth of Israel

1

Palestine Should Be Partitioned into Jewish and Arab States

UN Special Committee on Palestine

The British controlled Palestine after World War I and faced opposition from both Arabs and Jews living there. Both groups were demanding independence, the Arabs on the basis of their longstanding presence there and what they believed to be wartime promises from Britain for independence, and the Jews because of the Balfour Declaration's commitment to establishing a Jewish homeland in Palestine. Violence escalated through the years as Jews and Arabs attacked each other and British officials and installations. In February 1947 the British turned the question of what to do about Palestine over to the United Nations. The British fully expected the UN to be equally stymied by the conflicting demands and made it clear that they would accept only a UN solution that would be acceptable to both Arabs and Jews, knowing that this was impossible. The British thought the UN would be unable to satisfy the parties and then allow Britain to do as it pleased. The UN appointed a committee composed of representatives of eleven member nations. The Special Committee on Palestine (UNSCOP) went to Palestine and spoke to both sides. Afterward, they produced two reports, a majority and minority recommendation. The minority (India, Iran, and Yugoslavia), leaning toward the Arab position, proposed the creation of a single federal, or bi-national, state. They acknowledged, however, that such an arrangement would be unlikely to work because it would require the Arabs and Jews to cooperate and live together in the same nation. The majority (Canada, Czechoslo-

United Nations, "UN Special Committee on Palestine, Recommendations to the General Assembly," www.palestinecenter.org, September 3, 1947.

vakia, Guatemala, the Netherlands, Peru, Sweden, and Uruguay) recognized the irreconcilability of the two sides' claims and concluded the only solution was to create two states; to partition Palestine into a Jewish and Arab state. This excerpt from the UNSCOP report explains the thinking behind the partition recommendation.

---

1. The Committee held a series of informal discussions during its deliberations in Geneva as a means of appraising comprehensively the numerous aspects of the Palestine problem. In these discussions the members of the Committee debated at length and in great detail the various proposals advanced for its solution.

2. In the early stages of the discussions, it became apparent that there was little support for either of the solutions which would take an extreme position, namely, a single independent State of Palestine, under either Arab or Jewish domination. It was clear, therefore, that there was no disposition in the Committee to support in full the official proposals of either the Arab States or the Jewish Agency. It was recognized by all members that an effort must be made to find a solution which would avoid meeting fully the claims of one group at the expense of committing grave injustice against the other.

Partition is the only means available by which political and economic responsibility can be placed squarely on both Arabs and Jews.

---

3. At its forty-seventh meeting on 27 August 1947, the Committee formally rejected both of the extreme solutions. In taking this action, the Committee was fully aware that both Arabs and Jews advance strong claims to rights and interests in Palestine, the Arabs by virtue of being for centuries the indigenous and preponderant people there, and the Jews by virtue of historical association with the country and international pledges made to them respecting their rights in it. But the Committee also realized that the crux of the Palestine problem is to be found in the fact that two sizeable groups, an Arab population of over 1,200,000 and a

Jewish population of over 600,000, with intense nationalist aspirations, are diffused throughout a country that is arid, limited in area, and poor in all essential resources. It was relatively easy to conclude, therefore, that since both groups steadfastly maintain their claims, it is manifestly impossible, in the circumstances, to satisfy fully the claims of both groups, while it is indefensible to accept the full claims of one at the expense of the other.

The scheme satisfies the deepest aspiration of both [Jews and Arabs]: independence.

---

4. Following the rejection of the extreme solutions in its informal discussions, the Committee devoted its attention to the bi-national State and cantonal proposals. It considered both, but the members who may have been prepared to consider these proposals in principle were not impressed by the workability of either. It was apparent that the bi-national solution, although attractive in some of its aspects, would have little meaning unless provision were made for numerical or political parity between the two population groups, as provided for in the proposal of Dr. J.L. Magnes. This, however, would require the inauguration of complicated mechanical devices which are patently artificial and of dubious practicality.

5. The cantonal solution, under the existing conditions of Arab and Jewish diffusion in Palestine, might easily entail an excessive fragmentation of the governmental processes, and in its ultimate result, would be quite unworkable.

Two Plans Emerge

6. Having thus disposed of the extreme solutions and the bi-national and cantonal schemes, the members of the Committee, by and large, manifested a tendency to move toward either partition qualified by economic unity, or a federal-State plan. In due course, the Committee established two informal working groups, one on partition under a confederation arrangement and one on the federal State, for the purpose of working out the details of the two plans.

7. As a result of the work done in these working groups, a substantial measure of unanimity with regard to a number of important issues emerged, as evidenced in the forty-

seventh meeting of the Committee. On the basis of this measure of agreement, a drafting sub-committee was appointed to formulate specific texts.

8. In the course of its forty-ninth meeting on 29 August 1947, the Committee considered the report of the drafting sub-committee, and unanimously approved eleven recommendations to the General Assembly [and] a twelfth recommendation, with which the representatives of Guatemala and Uruguay were not in agreement. . . .

Plan of Partition with Economic Union Justification

1. The basic premise underlying the partition proposal is that the claims to Palestine of the Arabs and Jews, both possessing validity, are irreconcilable, and that among all of the solutions advanced, partition will provide the most realistic and practicable settlement, and is the most likely to afford a workable basis for meeting in part the claims and national aspirations of both parties.

2. It is a fact that both of these peoples have their historic roots in Palestine, and that both make vital contributions to the economic and cultural life of the country. The partition solution takes these considerations fully into account.

3. The basic conflict in Palestine is a clash of two intense nationalisms. Regardless of the historical origins of the conflict, the rights and wrongs of the promises and counter-promises, and the international intervention incident to the Mandate, there are now in Palestine some 650,000 Jews and some 1,200,000 Arabs who are dissimilar in their ways of living and, for the time being, separated by political interests which render difficult full and effective political co-operation among them, whether voluntary or induced by constitutional arrangements.

4. Only by means of partition can these conflicting national aspirations find substantial expression and qualify both peoples to take their places as independent nations in the international community and in the United Nations.

5. The partition solution provides that finality which is a most urgent need in the solution. Every other proposed solution would tend to induce the two parties to seek modification in their favour by means of persistent pressure. The grant of independence to both States, however, would

remove the basis for such efforts.

6. Partition is based on a realistic appraisal of the actual Arab-Jewish relations in Palestine. Full political co-operation would be indispensable to the effective functioning of any single-State scheme, such as the federal-State proposal, except in those cases which frankly envisage either an Arab- or a Jewish-dominated State.

7. Partition is the only means available by which political and economic responsibility can be placed squarely on both Arabs and Jews, with the prospective result that, confronted with responsibility for bearing fully the consequences of their own actions, a new and important element of political amelioration would be introduced. In the proposed federal-State solution, this factor would be lacking.

8. Jewish immigration is the central issue in Palestine today and is the one factor, above all others, that rules out the necessary co-operation between the Arab and Jewish communities in a single State. The creation of a Jewish State under a partition scheme is the only hope of removing this issue from the arena of conflict.

9. It is recognized that partition has been strongly opposed by Arabs, but it is felt that that opposition would be lessened by a solution which definitively fixes the extent of territory to be allotted to the Jews with its implicit limitation on immigration. The fact that the solution carries the sanction of the United Nations involves a finality which should allay Arab fears of further expansion of the Jewish State.

10. In view of the limited area and resources of Palestine, it is essential that, to the extent feasible, and consistent with the creation of two independent States, the economic unity of the country should be preserved. . . .

Achieving Independence

The primary objectives sought in the foregoing scheme are, in short, political division and economic unity: to confer upon each group, Arab and Jew, in its own territory, the power to make its own laws, while preserving to both, throughout Palestine, a single integrated economy, admittedly essential to the well-being of each, and the same territorial freedom of movement to individuals as is enjoyed today. The former necessitates a territorial partition; the latter, the maintenance of unrestricted commercial relations between the States, together with a common administration of functions in which the interests of both are in fact inextricably bound together.

The territorial division with the investment of full political power in each State achieves, in turn, the desire of each for statehood and, at the same time, creates a self-operating control of immigration. Although free passage between the States for all residents is provided, each State retains exclusive authority over the acquisition of residence and this, with its control over land, will enable it to preserve the integrity of its social organization. . . .

The Arab State will organize the substantial majority of Arabs in Palestine into a political body containing an insignificant minority of Jews; but in the Jewish State there will be a considerable minority of Arabs. That is the demerit of the scheme. But such a minority is inevitable in any feasible plan which does not place the whole of Palestine under the present majority of the Arabs. One cannot disregard the specific purpose of the Mandate and its implications nor the existing conditions, and the safeguarding of political, civil and cultural rights provided by the scheme are as ample as can be devised.

But in the larger view, here are the sole remaining representatives of the Semitic race. They are in the land in which that race was cradled. There are no fundamental incompatibilities between them. The scheme satisfies the deepest aspiration of both: independence. There is a considerable body of opinion in both groups which seeks the course of co-operation. Despite, then, the drawback of the Arab minority, the setting is one from which, with good will and a spirit of co-operation, may arise a rebirth, in historical surroundings, of the genius of each people. The massive contribution made by them throughout the centuries in religious and ethical conceptions, in philosophy, and in the entire intellectual sphere, should excite among the leaders a mutual respect and a pride in their common origin.

The Jews bring to the land the social dynamism and scientific method of the West; the Arabs confront them with individualism and intuitive understanding of life. Here then, in this close association, through the natural emulation of each other, can be evolved a synthesis of the two civilizations, preserving, at the same time, their fundamental characteristics. In each State, the native genius will have a scope and opportunity to evolve into its highest cultural forms and to attain its greatest reaches of mind and spirit. In the case of the Jews, that is really the condition of survival. Palestine will remain one land in which Semitic ideals may pass into realization.

At the same time there is secured, through the constitutional position of Jerusalem and the Holy Places, the preservation of the scenes of events in which the sentiments of Christendom also centre. There will thus be imposed over the whole land an unobjectionable interest of the adherents of all three religions throughout the world; and so secured, this unique and historical land may at last cease to be the arena of human strife.

Whether, however, these are vain speculations must await the future. If they are never realized, it will not, it is believed, be because of defects in the machinery of government that is proposed.

2

The Jews Must Govern Themselves

David Ben-Gurion

David Ben-Gurion was the first prime minister of the state of Israel. In the following selection, he responds to the report of the United Nations Special Committee on Palestine. The committee had recommended either partitioning Palestine into two states—a Jewish and an Arab state—or creating one federal state for both Jews and Arabs. Ben-Gurion argues strongly against the one-state option, arguing that such a policy would place Arabs in control of Jewish interests. He insists that the Jews are willing and able to govern themselves and must be granted independence.

N ow final judgement is passed by the United Nations and the Mandatory. The Mandate is to end. That is the common denominator . . . dispelling the friction between the Council of the United Nations and the British Government. No one can predict how things will go in the General Assembly. It may not decide at all, but one thing is certain: the Mandate is doomed, not just the British Mandate, but the principle. There is neither prospect nor proposal that Britain be replaced as Mandatory by another Power or an international body—in either event pledged to Zionism and the principles and aims which shaped the British Mandate a quarter of a century ago.

Whether we like it or not, there is one vivid conclusion we must draw—if governance has to be in Palestine, for the sake of the immigration and settlement which are unthink-

David Ben-Gurion, statement to the Assembly of Palestine Jewry, October 2, 1947.

able in a void, it will be our very own, or not at all. That, for good or ill, is the significance of recent political developments, external, world-wide, mightier than any will or influence of ours.

The UN Recommendations

Specifically, now, as to the recommendations of the United Nations investigators.

There were eleven unanimous recommendations, of which only the first four need concern us here, for their carrying out—and the British Government has said it accepts them—entails our taking new and difficult steps, which we would not take so long as we thought that others might manage Palestine for our benefit.

The findings are these:

—Termination of the Mandate at the earliest practicable date;

—The soonest feasible grant of independence in Palestine, on the ground that the Arabs and the Jews, after a tutelage of over twenty-five years, wish to translate their national aspirations into fact, and assuredly no arrangement will be accepted by either with the slightest willingness which does not imply swift independence;

—A brief interregnum to create the prerequisites of full sovereignty;

—The transitional administration to be responsible to the United Nations, a link representing the indispensable element of compulsion where any scheme is bound to be unpopular with Jew and Arab alike.

If governance has to be in Palestine, . . . it will be our very own, or not at all.

We may dismiss the idea of a successor Mandatory. After not more than three years, Palestine is to be independent. The British Secretary of State for the Colonies announced that his Government would prepare a speedy evacuation of the army and Administration. Should there be, in the end, an unagreed adjustment, it would suggest that someone else give effect to it. In other words, British control would cease immediately a new entrepreneur came forward.

There are two proposals before the United Nations—the majority proposal to set up two States, the minority to set up a federal, or, in Zionist jargon, a 'bi-national' State.

A Pro-Arab Plan

The minority proposal indulges in sonorous theory concerning the assurance of equality between the two nations and their historical link with a common Homeland, but warrants no solid inference. Behind it, instead, is denial of our age-long connection with Palestine. For equality between Arabs and ourselves it substitutes Arab precedence in all things, even in immigration, and, in short, produces an Arab State in the false feathers of bi-nationalism.

Behind [the federal plan] is denial of our age-long connection with Palestine.

The federal State embraces a Jewish district to which the name of 'Jewish State' is given. As to its area, to my regret I did not see the map that ought to have been annexed, but it looks to be about that of the Jewish province under the Morrison-Grady plan [a 1946 federalization plan proposed by Herbert Morrison and Henry Grady], though I would not vouch for it.

There will be two Chambers: one elected proportionately and therefore ruled by the Arab majority, the other based on equal representation. To pass into law a measure must get a majority of votes in each Chamber; if not, an arbitral committee of three Arabs and two Jews would decide and the decision become law. The President of the State would be elected by the Arab majority of both Chambers in joint session.

Over and above this, a Supreme Court with wide jurisdiction was invented, to interpret the Constitution, and we know what interpretation can lead to. It would adjudicate whether a federal or 'State' law was compatible with the Constitution, and pronounce in cases of conflict between local and federal laws. Its judgement would be unappealable. It would, under the Constitution, have an assured Arab majority of at least four to three. This majority could interpret and veto Jewish 'State' laws as it pleased. The federal Government, with an Arab majority, would wield full authority in national defence, foreign affairs, currency, federal taxes, waterways, communications transport and immigration.

We are willing, fit and ready to gather up the reins of government instantaneously.

At any moment, therefore, Jewish immigration might come under ban. Only in the three transitional years would it be guaranteed, and then into the Jewish district alone, in numbers not exceeding its economic capacity and not necessarily to the full absorptive extent; the rights of the citizens of the Jewish district would have to be considered, and the rate of natural increase. And all as determined by a committee of nine, three Jews, three Arabs, and three of the United Nations representatives.

Liability for the immigrants during the triennium would fall on the Yishuv. The Jewish Agency disappears. Thereafter, immigration is in the hands of the federal Government, as I have explained, and that is as much as to say in the hands of an Arab majority. The Arabs have lost no time in declaring that not another Jew will be let in. . . .

Jews Will Gather the Reins

The status quo cannot go on: it has been condemned on all hands. It is hard to guess when the British will actually leave—three months, three years, or thirty, there is no telling. We know of 'provisional' occupations that lasted sixty. So let us be neither over-sanguine nor cast down. We are vitally concerned that Britain should not, under any pretence whatever, keep on implementing the policy of the White Paper [the 1939 British policy statement that limited Jewish immigration]. What we want is mass immigration. The majority proposal provides for 6,250 persons monthly to enter during the transition period beginning on 1 September 1947. There is an account to settle with Britain for shutting out thousands of Jews since the White Paper appeared, and we may let history make that settlement. But a new chapter is opening—the instant chapter of what is to befall in immigration now: this month, this year, next year. For us, now, there is no countenancing the White Paper's policy one moment after the Assembly of the United Nations ends, for is it not shorn of all international sanction, constitutionally and morally indefensible?

Moreover, we must at all costs prevent chaos and anarchy ensuing.

To sum up, it is all a question of effectuation, for both the United Nations and ourselves. . . . Britain assures us she will not carry out any United Nations' decision, but neither will she resist any, so be it she is rid of the concomitant task. We, therefore, tell the world that we will ourselves discharge it, that we are willing, fit and ready to gather up the reins of government instantaneously.

We are twain—the elect of the Jewish people and the elect of the Yishuv. Alone, neither can perform the task. The Yishuv, indeed, is also a part of the people, but is so nearly concerned that it must here be a vanguard as well, as it was before in reconstructing Israel and vindicating Zionism. But this is no personal issue of us who live in Palestine. The majority on the Committee sees it as a problem of world Jewry, and so, we think, does public opinion generally.

The majority framed its conclusions under the impact of two compelling revelations. First, it found here not just one more Kehillah, but the nucleus of a Jewish nation, a Jewish State in embryo. Second, words exchanged with an unknown Jew in an unnamed camp in Europe, words that should be broadcast in every spoken tongue, a simple story of past sufferings, and of why he wants to come here and nowhere else. Thus the Committee learned that Aliyah [literally "going up"; Jewish immigration] is not shallow submission to Zionist propaganda, but a deep compulsion, elemental, mocking death. This the members saw again with their own eyes in ships that bore to Palestine the exiled and the slain, in camps that shelter those who ran the gauntlet.

This is our native land; it is not as birds of passage that we return to it.

There was, however, a *tertium quid*—and careful study of the report brings it out: the existence of an international commitment to the Jewish people, the flickering still of a spark of conscience in the world, the widespread recognition that the commitment must be honoured, even if only in part, even if only a helpless, homeless, stateless folk was its object.

All of Jewry was that object, not the Yishuv alone, all of

Jewry broke into the Land, all of Jewry seeks independence. So, too, let all of Jewry demand that an interim Jewish Government be set up to execute an interim policy under United Nations supervision and with aid thence, and primarily an interim policy of large-scale immigration and rescindment of the White Paper. If a final policy we could accept were propounded meanwhile, we should start on that likewise.

No more protests and clamour, not another day of a vacuum in theory, jurisdiction and ethics. We shall bear the grave responsibility ourselves, untried though we have been in the arts and burdens of sovereignty for the last eighteen hundred years. The strain will be terrific. There is a local pretender to the throne, backed by millions of common creed and speech. But between acquiescing in the White Paper, with its locked gates and racial discrimination, and the assumption of sovereign power, there can, in truth, only be one choice. Perhaps we are unready, immature—but events will not wait on us. The international calendar will not synchronise itself to ours. We are set the problem and must solve it. I have told you how: supervised by the United Nations, helped by the United Nations, but in our own name, answerable to ourselves, with our own resources. . . .

Relations with Arabs

This is our native land; it is not as birds of passage that we return to it. But it is situated in an area engulfed by Arabic-speaking peoples, mainly followers of Islam. Now, if ever, we must do more than make peace with them; we must achieve collaboration and alliance on equal terms. Remembering what Arab delegations from Palestine and its neighbours say in the General Assembly and in other places, talk of Arab-Jewish amity sounds fantastic, for the Arabs do not wish it, they will not sit at the same table with us, they want to treat us as they do the Jews of Baghdad, Cairo and Damascus.

That is the attitude officially proclaimed, and it is not to be scoffed at; considerable forces in the Arab realm, and beyond, are behind it. Neither should we overrate it, or be panicked by it. As Jews, and more so as Zionists, we must forego facile optimism and barren despondency. Basic facts are our allies and no concatenation of events can shake or alter them: the tragedy of the Jews, the desolation of the Land, our unbreakable bond with it, our creativity—they have brought us thus far, whether other things helped or hindered.

There are basic facts in the Arab realm also, not only transient ones, and understanding of them should blow away our pessimism. They are the historical needs of the Arabs and of their States. A people's needs are not always articulate, its spokesmen may not always be concerned for them, but they cannot be stifled for long, eventually they force their swelling way out into expression and satisfaction. . . .

A final fact. From our work in Palestine, from the society we are constructing, our economy and science, our culture and humanity, our social and fiscal order, and from no other source, must enlightenment come to our neighbours, for if they do not learn from us and labour with us, it is with strangers, potent and tyrannous, that they will find themselves partnered.

They in turn have much to give us, they are blessed with what we lack. Great territories, ample for themselves and their children's children, even if they are far more prolific than they are today. We do not covet their expanses nor will we penetrate them—for we shall fight to end Diaspora in Arab lands as fiercely as we fought to end it in Europe, we want to be assembled wholly in our own Land. But if this region is to expand to the full, there must be reciprocity, there can be mutual aid—economic, political and cultural—between Jew and Arab. That is the necessity which will prevail, and the daily fulminations of their leaders should not alarm us unduly—they do not echo the real interests of the Arab peoples.

Come what may, we will not surrender our right to free Aliyah, to rebuild our shattered Homeland, to claim statehood. If we are attacked, we will fight back. But we will do everything in our power to maintain peace, and establish a Cupertino gainful to both. It is now, here and now, from Jerusalem itself, that a call must go out to the Arab nations to join forces with Jewry and the destined Jewish State and work shoulder to shoulder for our common good, for the peace and progress of sovereign equals.

3

Declaration of the Establishment of the State of Israel

Jewish People's Council

On May 14, 1948, the day that the British Mandate for Palestine formally expired, the council of the Jews that had been the community's political authority during the mandatory period met at the Tel Aviv Museum and approved the following proclamation of independence for the state of Israel. The acknowledged leader of the council, David Ben-Gurion, became the head of state with the expectation that democratic elections would be held when the coming war was over.

EretzIsrael (the Land of Israel) was the birthplace of the Jewish people. Here their spiritual, religious and political identity was shaped. Here they first attained to statehood, created cultural values of national and universal significance and gave to the world the eternal Book of Books.

After being forcibly exiled from their land, the people kept faith with it throughout their Dispersion and never ceased to pray and hope for their return to it and for the restoration in it of their political freedom.

Impelled by this historic and traditional attachment, Jews strove in every successive generation to reestablish themselves in their ancient homeland. In recent decades they returned in their masses. Pioneers, ma'pilim (immigrants coming to EretzIsrael in defiance of restrictive legislation) and defenders, they made deserts bloom, revived the

Jewish People's Council, "The Declaration of the Establishment of the State of Israel," www.mfa.gov.il, May 14, 1948.

Hebrew language, built villages and towns, and created a thriving community controlling its own economy and culture, loving peace but knowing how to defend itself, bringing the blessings of progress to all the country's inhabitants, and aspiring towards independent nationhood.

In the year 5657 (1897), at the summons of the spiritual father of the Jewish State, Theodore Herzl, the First Zionist Congress convened and proclaimed the right of the Jewish people to national rebirth in its own country.

We . . . hereby declare the establishment of a Jewish state in EretzIsrael, to be known as the State of Israel.

This right was recognized in the Balfour Declaration of the 2nd November, 1917, and reaffirmed in the Mandate of the League of Nations which, in particular, gave international sanction to the historic connection between the Jewish people and EretzIsrael and to the right of the Jewish people to rebuild its National Home.

The catastrophe which recently befell the Jewish people—the massacre of millions of Jews in Europe—was another clear demonstration of the urgency of solving the problem of its homelessness by reestablishing in EretzIsrael the Jewish State, which would open the gates of the homeland wide to every Jew and confer upon the Jewish people the status of a fully privileged member of the community of nations.

Survivors of the Nazi holocaust in Europe, as well as Jews from other parts of the world, continued to migrate to EretzIsrael, undaunted by difficulties, restrictions and dangers, and never ceased to assert their right to a life of dignity, freedom and honest toil in their national homeland.

In the Second World War, the Jewish community of this country contributed its full share to the struggle of the freedom and peaceloving nations against the forces of Nazi wickedness and, by the blood of its soldiers and its war effort, gained the right to be reckoned among the peoples who founded the United Nations.

On the 29th November, 1947, the United Nations General Assembly passed a resolution calling for the establishment of a Jewish State in EretzIsrael; the General Assembly required the inhabitants of EretzIsrael to take such steps as were necessary on their part for the implementation of that resolution. This recognition by the United Nations of the right of the Jewish people to establish their State is irrevocable.

This right is the natural right of the Jewish people to be masters of their own fate, like all other nations, in their own sovereign State.

Accordingly we, members of the People's Council, representatives of the Jewish community of EretzIsrael and of the Zionist movement, are here assembled on the day of the termination of the British mandate over ErctzIsrael and, by virtue of our natural and historic right and on the strength of the Resolution of the United Nations General Assembly, hereby declare the establishment of a Jewish state in EretzIsrael, to be known as the State of Israel.

WE DECLARE that, with effect from the moment of the termination of the Mandate being tonight, the eve of Sabbath, the 6th Iyar, 5708 (15th May, 1948), until the establishment of the elected, regular authorities of the State in accordance with the Constitution which shall be adopted by the Elected Constituent Assembly not later than the 1st October 1948, the People's Council shall act as a Provisional Council of State, and its executive organ, the People's Administration, shall be the Provisional Government of the Jewish State, to be called "Israel."

We appeal . . . to the Arab inhabitants of the State of Israel to preserve peace and participate in the upbuilding of the State.

THE STATE OF ISRAEL will be open for Jewish immigration and for the Ingathering of the Exiles; it will foster the development of the country for the benefit of all its inhabitants; it will be based on freedom, justice and peace as envisaged by the prophets of Israel; it will ensure complete equality of social and political rights to all its inhabitants irrespective of religion, race or sex; it will guarantee freedom of religion, conscience, language, education and culture; it will safeguard the Holy Places of all religions; and it will be faithful to the principles of the Charter of the United Nations.

THE STATE OF ISRAEL is prepared to cooperate with the agencies and representatives of the United Nations in implementing the resolution of the General Assembly of the 29th November, 1947, and will take steps to bring about the economic union of the whole of EretzIsrael.

WE APPEAL to the United Nations to assist the Jewish people in the buildingup of its State and to receive the State of Israel into the comity of nations.

WE APPEAL in the very midst of the onslaught launched against us now for months to the Arab inhabitants of the State of Israel to preserve peace and participate in the upbuilding of the State on the basis of full and equal citizenship and due representation in all its provisional and permanent institutions.

WE EXTEND our hand to all neighbouring states and their peoples in an offer of peace and good neighbourliness, and appeal to them to establish bonds of cooperation and mutual help with the sovereign Jewish people settled in its own land. The State of Israel is prepared to do its share in a common effort for the advancement of the entire Middle East.

WE APPEAL to the Jewish people throughout the Diaspora to rally round the Jews of EretzIsrael in the tasks of immigration and upbuilding and to stand by them in the great struggle for the realization of the ageold dream the redemption of Israel.

Placing our trust in the Almighty, we affix our signatures to this proclamation at this session of the provisional council of state, on the soil of the homeland, in the city of Telaviv, on this Sabbath eve, the 5th day of Iyar, 5708 (14th May, 1948).

David BenGurion
Rabbi Kalman Kahana
Aharon Zisling
Yitzchak Ben Zvi
Saadia Kobashi
Daniel Auster
Rachel Cohen
David Zvi Pinkas
Mordekhai Bentov
Moshe Kolodny
Eliyahu Berligne
Rabbi Yitzchak Meir Levin
Eliezer Kaplan

Fritz Bernstein
Abraham Katznelson
Rabbi Wolf Gold
Meir David Loewenstein
Felix Rosenblueth
Meir Grabovsky
David Remez
Yitzchak Gruenbaum
Zvi Luria
Berl Repetur
Dr. Abraham Granovsky
Golda Myerson
Mordekhai Shattner
Nachum Nir
Ben Zion Sternberg
Eliyahu Dobkin
Zvi Segal
Bekhor Shitreet
Meir WilnerKovner
Rabbi Yehuda Leib Hacohen Fishman
Moshe Shapira
Zerach Wahrhaftig
Moshe Shertok
Herzl Vardi

4

The Arab League's War Against Israel Is Justified

Arab League

When the British brought the question of Palestine to the United Nations, the Arabs made no secret of the fact that they opposed any solution that did not result in the creation of an Arab state in all of Palestine. When the UN voted to partition Palestine and create an Arab and a Jewish state, the Arabs made clear they would oppose the implementation of the resolution by force. Almost immediately after the UN vote, Arab attacks on Jews began. When the British decided to withdraw their forces once and for all from Palestine, the Jews announced they would declare their independence on May 14, 1948. That night the armies of Jordan, Egypt, Syria, and Lebanon invaded Palestine with the intention of destroying the newly declared state of Israel. The umbrella political organization to which all the Arab states belonged, the Arab League, issued the following statement on May 15, as their forces were advancing, outlining their reasons for using military force to prevent the establishment of a Jewish state.

1. Palestine was part of the former Ottoman Empire subject to its law and represented in its parliament. The overwhelming majority of the population of Palestine were Arabs. There was in it a small minority of Jews that enjoyed the same rights and bore the same responsibilities as the [other] inhabitants, and did not suffer any ill-treatment on account of its religious beliefs. The holy places were inviolable and the freedom of access to them was guaranteed.

Arab League, "Arab League Declaration on the Invasion of Palestine," www.mfa. gov.il, May 15, 1948.

2. The Arabs have always asked for their freedom and independence. On the outbreak of the First World War, and when the Allies declared that they were fighting for the liberation of peoples, the Arabs joined them and fought on their side with a view to realising their national aspirations and obtaining their independence. England pledged herself to recognise the independence of the Arab countries in Asia, including Palestine. The Arabs played a remarkable part in the achievement of final victory and the Allies have admitted this.

3. In 1917 England issued a declaration in which she expressed her sympathy with the establishment of a National Home for the Jews in Palestine. When the Arabs knew of this they protested against it, but England reassured them by affirming to them that this would not prejudice the right of their countries to freedom and independence or affect the political status of the Arabs in Palestine. Notwithstanding the legally void character of this declaration, it was interpreted by England to aim at no more than the establishment of a spiritual centre for the Jews in Palestine, and to conceal no ulterior political aims, such as the establishment of a Jewish State. The same thing was declared by the Jewish leaders.

Britain Reneges

4. When the war came to an end England did not keep her promise. Indeed, the Allies placed Palestine under the Mandate system and entrusted England with [the task of carrying it out], in accordance with a document providing for the administration of the country, in the interests of its inhabitants and its preparation for the independence which the Covenant of the League of Nations recognised that Palestine was qualified to have.

5. England administered Palestine in a manner which enabled the Jews to flood it with immigrants and helped them to settle in the country. [This was so] notwithstanding the fact that it was proved that the density of the population in Palestine had exceeded the economic capacity of the country to absorb additional immigrants. England did not pay regard to the interests or rights of the Arab inhabitants, the lawful owners of the country. Although they used to express, by various means, their concern and indignation on account of this state of affairs which was harmful to their be-

ing and their future, they [invariably] were met by indifference, imprisonment and oppression.

6. As Palestine is an Arab country, situated in the heart of the Arab countries and attached to the Arab world by various ties—spiritual, historical, and strategic—the Arab countries, and even the Eastern ones, governments as well as peoples, have concerned themselves with the problem of Palestine and have raised it to the international level; [they have also raised the problem] with England, asking for its solution in accordance with the pledges made and with democratic principles. The Round Table Conference was held in London in 1939 in order to discuss the Palestine question and to arrive at the just solution thereof. The Governments of the Arab States participated in [this conference] and asked for the preservation of the Arab character of Palestine and the proclamation of its independence. This conference ended with the issue of a White Paper in which England defined her policy towards Palestine, recognised its independence, and undertook to set up the institutions that would lead to its exercise of the characteristics of [this independence]. She [also] declared that her obligations concerning the establishment of a Jewish national home had been fulfilled, since that home had actually been established. But the policy defined in that [White] Paper was not carried out. This, therefore, led to the deterioration of the situation and the aggravation of matters contrary to the interests of the Arabs.

England administered Palestine in a manner which enabled the Jews to flood it with immigrants.

---

7. While the Second World War was still in progress, the Governments of the Arab States began to hold consultations regarding the reinforcement of their co-operation and the increasing of the means of their collaboration and their solidarity, with a view to safeguarding their present and their future and to participating in the erection of the edifice of the new world on firm foundations. Palestine had its [worthy] share of consideration and attention in these conversations. These conversations led to the establishment of the League of Arab States as an instrument for the co-operation of the

Arab States for their security, peace and well-being.

The Pact of the League of Arab States declared that Palestine has been an independent country since its separation from the Ottoman Empire, but the manifestations of this independence have been suppressed due to reasons which were out of the control of its inhabitants. The establishment of the United Nations shortly afterwards was an event about which the Arabs had the greatest hopes. Their belief in the ideals on which that organisation was based made them participate in its establishment and membership.

The events which have taken place in Palestine have unmasked the aggressive intentions . . . of the Zionists.

---

8. Since then the Arab League and its [member] Governments have not spared any effort to pursue any course, whether with the Mandatory Power or with the United Nations, in order to bring about a just solution of the Palestine problem: [a solution] based upon true democratic principles and compatible with the provisions of the Covenant of the League of Nations and the [Charter] of the United Nations, and which would [at the same time] be lasting, guarantee peace and security in the country and prepare it for progress and prosperity. But Zionist claims were always an obstacle to finding such a solution, [as the Zionists], having prepared themselves with armed forces, strongholds and fortifications to face by force anyone standing in their way, publicly declared [their intention] to establish a Jewish State.

Unjust Partition

9. When the General Assembly of the United Nations issued, on 29 November 1947, its recommendation concerning the solution of the Palestine problem, on the basis of the establishment of an Arab State and of another Jewish [State] in [Palestine] together with placing the City of Jerusalem under the trusteeship of the United Nations, the Arab States drew attention to the injustice implied in this solution [affecting] the right of the people of Palestine to immediate independence, as well as democratic principles and the provisions of the Covenant of the League of Nations and [the Charter] of the United Nations. [These States also] de-

clared the Arabs' rejection of [that solution] and that it would not be possible to carry it out by peaceful means, and that its forcible imposition would constitute a threat to peace and security in this area.

The warnings and expectations of the Arab States have, indeed, proved to be true, as disturbances were soon widespread throughout Palestine. The Arabs clashed with the Jews, and the two [parties] proceeded to fight each other and shed each other's blood. Whereupon the United Nations began to realise the danger of recommending the partition [of Palestine] and is still looking for a way out of this state of affairs.

10. Now that the British mandate over Palestine has come to an end, without there being a legitimate constitutional authority in the country, which would safeguard the maintenance of security and respect for law and which would protect the lives and properties of the inhabitants, the Governments of the Arab States declare the following:

First: That the rule of Palestine should revert to its inhabitants, in accordance with the provisions of the Covenant of the League of Nations and [the Charter] of the United Nations and that [the Palestinians] should alone have the right to determine their future.

The Governments of the Arab States have found themselves compelled to intervene in Palestine.

Second: Security and order in Palestine have become disrupted. The Zionist aggression resulted in the exodus of more than a quarter of a million of its Arab inhabitants from their homes and in their taking refuge in the neighbouring Arab countries.

The events which have taken place in Palestine have unmasked the aggressive intentions and the imperialistic designs of the Zionists, including the atrocities committed by them against the peace-loving Arab inhabitants, especially in Dayr Yasin, Tiberias and others. Nor have they respected the inviolability of consuls, as they have attacked the consulates of the Arab States in Jerusalem. After the termination of the British mandate over Palestine the British authorities are no longer responsible for security in the country, except to the degree affecting their withdrawing forces, and [only] in the areas in which these forces happen to be at the time of withdrawal as announced by [these authorities]. This state of affairs would render Palestine without any governmental machinery capable of restoring order and the rule of law to the country, and of protecting the lives and properties of the inhabitants.

Third: This state of affairs is threatening to spread to the neighbouring Arab countries, where feeling is running high because of the events in Palestine. The Governments of the Member States of the Arab League and of the United Nations are exceedingly worried and deeply concerned about this state of affairs.

The only solution of the Palestine problem is the establishment of a unitary Palestinian State.

Fourth: These Governments had hoped that the United Nations would have succeeded in finding a peaceful and just solution of the problem of Palestine, in accordance with democratic principles and the provisions of the Covenant of the League of Nations and [the Charter] of the United Nations, so that peace, security and prosperity would prevail in this part of the world.

Fifth: The Governments of the Arab States, as members of the Arab League, a regional organisation within the meaning of the provisions of Chapter VIII of the Charter of the United Nations, are responsible for maintaining peace and security in their area. These Governments view the events taking place in Palestine as a threat to peace and security in the area as a whole and [also] in each of them taken separately.

Sixth: Therefore, as security in Palestine is a sacred trust in the hands of the Arab States, and in order to put an end to this state of affairs and to prevent it from becoming aggravated or from turning into [a state of] chaos, the extent of which no one can foretell; in order to stop the spreading of disturbances and disorder in Palestine to the neighbouring Arab countries; in order to fill the gap brought about in the governmental machinery in Palestine as a result of the termination of the mandate and the non-establishment of a lawful successor authority, the Governments of the Arab States have found themselves compelled to intervene in

Palestine solely in order to help its inhabitants restore peace and security and the rule of justice and law to their country, and in order to prevent bloodshed.

Imposing Peace

Seventh: The Governments of the Arab States recognise that the independence of Palestine, which has so far been suppressed by the British Mandate, has become an accomplished fact for the lawful inhabitants of Palestine. They alone, by virtue of their absolute sovereignty, have the right to provide their country with laws and governmental institutions. They alone should exercise the attributes of their independence, through their own means and without any kind of foreign interference, immediately after peace, security, and the rule of law have been restored to the country.

At that time the intervention of the Arab states will cease, and the independent State of Palestine will co-operate with the [other member] States of the Arab League in order to bring peace, security and prosperity to this part of the world.

The Governments of the Arab States emphasise, on this occasion, what they have already declared before the London Conference and the United Nations, that the only solution of the Palestine problem is the establishment of a unitary Palestinian State, in accordance with democratic principles, whereby its inhabitants will enjoy complete equality before the law, [and whereby] minorities will be assured of all the guarantees recognised in democratic constitutional countries, and [whereby] the holy places will be preserved and the right of access thereto guaranteed.

Eighth: The Arab States most emphatically declare that [their] intervention in Palestine was due only to these considerations and objectives, and that they aim at nothing more than to put an end to the prevailing conditions in [Palestine]. For this reason, they have great confidence that their action will have the support of the United Nations; [that it will be] considered as an action aiming at the realisation of its aims and at promoting its principles, as provided for in its Charter.

Chapter 3

Looking Back at the Creation of Israel

1

The Creation of Israel Was a Miracle

Paul Johnson

In the following excerpt, Paul Johnson maintains that Israel came about partly as the unlikely result of the defining events of the twentieth century—particularly the two world wars. By eliminating the Turkish Empire, World War I transformed the notion of a Jewish home in Palestine from a theoretical idea into an actual possibility. World War II created a political climate in which the Soviet Union and the United States both considered support of Israel to be in their best interest. These circumstances—combined with the Jewish people's fierce determination not to be exterminated—allowed the state of Israel to come into existence. Johnson is the British author of *A History of the Jews*.

The state of Israel is the product of more than 4,000 years of Jewish history. "If you want to understand our country, read this!" said David Ben-Gurion on the first occasion I met him, in 1957. And he slapped the Bible. But the creation and survival of Israel are also very much a 20th-century phenomenon, one that could not have happened without the violence and cruelty, the agonies, confusions, and cross-currents of our tragic age. It could even be argued that Israel is the most characteristic single product, and its creation the quintessential event, of the twentieth century.

Certainly, you cannot study Israel without traveling the historical highroads and many of the byroads of the times, beginning with the outbreak of World War I in 1914. That great watershed between an age of peace and moderation and one of violence and extremism set the pattern for all that followed, and marked a turning point as well in the fortunes of Zionism. . . .

The Effects of World War I

World War I had a double effect on Zionism, transforming its program from a theoretical into a real possibility but also ensuring that the creation of the Jewish state would be bloody. Until 1914, the men who ran the British empire, though sympathetic to Zionism, were inclined to fob off Jewish leaders with schemes for developing a slice of Africa. Turkey was a traditional British ally, and keeping its ramshackle possessions together was a prime object of British policy. What put an end to all that was the fateful decision of the Turks to join the side of Germany in the war. In a dramatic speech in November 1914, the British Prime Minister, H.H. Asquith, announced: "The Turkish empire has committed suicide."

The creation and survival of Israel . . . could not have happened without the violence and cruelty, the agonies, confusions, and cross-currents of our tragic age.

Immediately, a Palestinian Zion became conceivable, and what would be known as the Balfour Declaration was in train. But the British decision to end the Turkish empire in the Middle East also presupposed the existence of new Arab states as well, and inevitably brought into being Arab nationalism. It is here that [nineteenth-century Zionist thinker Theodor] Herzl's initiative and dynamism proved to be so crucial. Timing is all-important in history. No doubt a Zionist political movement would in due course have come into existence without Herzl. By launching it in the 1890's, Herzl gave the Jews, in effect, a twenty-year headstart over the Arabs. Even before the war began, Zionist leaders had been in touch with leading British policymakers, and they exploited the possibilities produced by the war with great energy and sophistication.

It is amazing, in retrospect, that the Zionists were able

to secure the Balfour Declaration—ensuring the "best endeavors" of the British government to achieve "the establishment in Palestine of a national home for the Jewish people"—in 1917, while the war was still undecided, thus preempting the postwar negotiations and settlements of national claims. By the time the Arabs got themselves organized as an international pressure group, at the Versailles Peace Conference, it was too late. They did win their Arab states, but the Jews had already gained their national home and were settling it with all deliberate speed.

But World War I also introduced unprecedented degrees of violence and extremism into the world, and these too held consequences for the future of Israel. Gone was any possibility that the Jewish national home might integrate itself peacefully with its Arab neighbors, paying for its presence in their midst by teaching them the modern arts of agriculture and commerce. The so-called Arab Revolt that began in 1936 and that was encouraged and rewarded by the British mandatory power confirmed local Arab leaders in the view that their most promising option against the Zionists was force. What had driven out the Turks and created the new Arab states could also be employed, in due course, to extirpate the Jews. This became a fixed Arab notion, so that in time, both within Palestine and across the Middle East as a whole, Arab leaders, faced with the choice of negotiation or war would invariably choose war—and invariably lose.

> *The violence bred by the searing years 1914–18 . . . decisively changed the moral climate of Europe, . . . with fateful results for the future Jewish state.*

The violence bred by the searing years 1914–18 also decisively changed the moral climate of Europe, again with fateful results for the future Jewish state. In the wake of the war, extremist regimes seized power and ruled by force and terror—first in Russia, then in Italy, and finally in Germany. The transformation of Germany from the best-educated society in Europe into a totalitarian race-state was, of course, determinative. Although the anti-Semites of Central Europe had always treated Jews with varying degrees of cruelty and injustice, up to and including murderous pogroms and expulsion, it was only with Hitler that actual extermination became a possible program. The outbreak of World War II provided the covering darkness to make it not just possible but practical.

> *The Holocaust destroyed by far the greater proportion of European Jews. . . . But it also united much of the rest of world Jewry behind the Zionist project.*

The Holocaust destroyed by far the greater proportion of European Jews, the pool from which Zionism had drawn both recruits and moral fervor. But it also united much of the rest of world Jewry behind the Zionist project, and brought into existence the American Jewish lobby, the prototype of all the great lobbies of the later 20th century. In the perspective of the Holocaust, moreover, it became clear that Zion had to be not merely a "national home" but a refuge, and a fortress. Finally, the Holocaust spurred the Palestinian Jews (and the refugees who joined them) to create the military means to defend the citadel. If World War I created the new Zion, it was World War II that made possible the Israeli army.

In the last half-century, over 100 completely new independent states have come into existence. Israel is the only one whose creation can fairly be called a miracle.

Heroic Fighting

I observed the drama of 1948–49 from the security of an ancient Oxford college, where I was an undergraduate. Academic opinion was then, on balance, favorable to the new Zion: many dons had been brought up in the philo-Semitic tradition of *Daniel Deronda* (1876), George Eliot's novel about a young man who discovers his identity as a Jew and dedicates himself to the Zionist cause, and they welcomed Israel as an intellectual and moral artifact. But opinion was also virtually unanimous that the state would be crushed. That was assuredly the view of most governments and military staffs: the notion of the Jew as a soldier had not yet captured the Western imagination.

In 1948, the Haganah, Israel's defense force, had 21,000 men, as against a professional Arab invading army of 10,000 Egyptians, 4,500 in Jordan's Arab Legion, 7,000 Syrians, 3,000 Iraqis, and 3,000 Lebanese—plus the "Arab Liberation Army" of Palestinians. In equipment, including armor and air power, the odds were similarly heavy against Israel. Revisionist historians (including Israeli ones) now portray the War of Independence as a deliberate Zionist land grab, involving the use of terrorism to panic Arabs into quitting their farms and homes. They ignore the central fact that the Zionist leaders did not want war but rather feared it as a risk to be taken only if there was absolutely no alternative. That is why in 1947 the Zionist leadership had accepted the United Nations partition scheme, which would have given the nascent state only 5,500 square miles, chiefly in the Negev desert, and would have created an impossible entity of 538,000 Jews and 397,000 Arabs. Arab rejection of this scheme was an act of supreme folly.

In the last half-century, over 100 completely new independent states have come into existence. Israel is the only one whose creation can fairly be called a miracle.

Of course the Jews fought heroically, and performed prodigies of improvisation: they had to—it was either that or extermination. No doubt they fought savagely, too, on occasion, and committed acts that might appear to lend some coloring to the revisionist case. But as a whole that case is historically false. It was the Arab leadership, by its obduracy and its ready resort to force, that was responsible for the somewhat enlarged Israel that emerged after the 1949 armistice, and the same mind-set would create the more greatly enlarged Israel that emerged after the Six-Day War of 1967. In another of the paradoxes of history, the frontiers of the state, as they exist today, were as much the doing of the Arabs as of the Jews. If it had been left to the UN, tiny Zion probably could not have survived.

Soviet and American Help

Another paradoxical aspect of the Zionist miracle, which we certainly did not grasp at the time and which is insufficiently understood even now, is that among the founding fathers of Israel was Joseph Stalin. Stalin had no love for Jews; quite the contrary, he murdered them whenever it suited his purposes. In his last phase, indeed, he was becoming increasingly paranoid; had he lived, he might well have carried out an extermination program rivaling Hitler's. Moreover, like Lenin before him, Stalin had always opposed Zionism. He did so not only as a Great Russian imperialist but as a Marxist, and he was consistent on the matter up to the end of World War II and again from 1950 to his death in 1953. But during the crucial years 1947–48, he was guided by temporary considerations of Realpolitik, and specifically by what he saw as the threat of British imperialism.

Stalin ignorantly supposed that the way to undermine Britain's position in the Middle East was to support the Jews, not the Arabs, and he backed Zionism in order to break the "British stranglehold." Not only did he extend diplomatic recognition to Israel but, in order to intensify the fighting and the consequent chaos, he instructed the Czech government to sell it arms. The Czechs turned over an entire military airfield to shuttle weaponry to Tel Aviv; the Messerschmitt aircraft they supplied were of particular importance. Then, in mid-August 1948, Stalin decided he had made a huge error in judgment, and the obedient Czech government ordered a halt to the airlift within 48 hours. But by then the war had effectively been won.

Stalin ignorantly supposed that the way to undermine Britain's position in the Middle East was to support the Jews, not the Arabs.

The fledgling Israeli state was equally fortunate when it came to America, benefiting from a phase of benevolence that once again might not have lasted. President Truman was pro-Zionist, and he needed the Jewish vote in the 1948 election. It was his decision to push the partition scheme through the UN in November 1947 and to recognize the new Israeli state (de facto, not de jure) when it was declared in May 1948. But the contrary pressure he had to face, both from the State Department under George C. Marshall and from his Defense Secretary, James V. Forrestal, was immense. If the crisis had come a year later, after the cold war started to dominate the thinking of the West to the exclusion of almost everything else, it is likely that the anti-Zionist forces would have proved too strong for Truman. As it was, American backing for Israel in 1947–48 was the last idealistic luxury the Americans permitted themselves before the realities of global confrontation descended.

Thus, in terms both of Soviet and of American policy, Israel slipped into existence through a window that briefly opened, and just as suddenly closed. Once again, timing—or, if one likes, providence—was of the essence.

2

The Creation of Israel Was a Heroic Response to Genocide

Ben Kamin

In the following selection, Ben Kamin insists that Israel came about primarily as a response to the genocidal politics of Adolf Hitler. Those who are attempting to destroy Israel threaten to undo a heroic and redemptive accomplishment. Kamin, the senior rabbi of Congregation Beth Israel in San Diego, California, recalls his early childhood in Israel at the time of its birth in order to stress his view that peaceful coexistence between Jews and Arabs is possible.

I was born in Israel just a few years after its inception in 1948. My father and mother were there, however, as the British withdrew on May 14 of that year, lowering the Union Jack over the port of Haifa, and raising the stakes considerably for the 600,000 Jews in mandatory Palestine now left to confront a host of Arab nations planning to invade and destroy the nascent Jewish state.

I remember living in that idyllic place as a child. It was long before suicide bombings, murderous plots laid out by dictators who trade oil for blood, and before dreadful skyjackings in Europe and America that somehow had something to do with the sweet osprey birds that flew about the desert of our little homeland.

Many of my classmates in the dusty village of Kfar-Saba were the children of Holocaust survivors who had been res-

Ben Kamin, "On Israel's Birthday: Today, What Does Its Life Mean?" *San Diego Union-Tribune*, May 14, 2002. Copyright © 2002 by Union-Tribune Publishing Company. Reproduced by permission of the author.

cued by Haganah soldiers like my own father, smuggled into Palestine from Cyprus and other places in the wake of the Nazi insanity. The names in my fourth grade classroom hailed from Russia, Brazil, South Africa, Germany, Poland and Yemen. We all planted onions and sunflowers in the reddish earth around the schoolyard and we sang songs in the free language of Hebrew.

The Meaning of Israel's Birth

There was a time when you could easily recite the meaning of Israel's birth, and it's worth remembering now. Israel only came into being because Europe had slaughtered the Jews and then because the United Nations had a stunning vote in its Security Council: By a tally of 33 to 13, the United Nations partitioned Palestine into two states, one Jewish and one Arab.

Israel's birth in 1948 was a heroic and healing response to the politics of murder.

The Jewish Agency, still heaving from the genocide and desperate to create a sanctuary for the exiles, agreed. The independent Arab nations, manifold times larger than Israel, declared their intention to finish what the Nazis had started. These are the facts; even as the ensuing Arab invasion of the Jewish territories served to displace the parallel victims of this blunder—the Palestinian people.

Whether or not Palestinian leaders still want that separate state or not, or even if they indeed covet the full region and would still plan to consume the sovereign state of Israel, the Palestinian people themselves still need to feel they belong somewhere—just as we Jewish children of the remnant felt we belonged somewhere back in the days following Israel's birth.

Learning from the Past

But before either one of us, Arab or Jew, can plan the future, we must learn the past. We were both always there in that land, even as the wind brought the Romans, the Crusaders, the Ottomans, the British, and so many others to help set us against each other.

My childhood memories include the thick citrus smell

of orange groves that lay between Kfar-Saba and the minarets of the neighboring Arab village of Qalqilya. We actually lived in peace; there was no fear in the air—'til the distant Egyptians and Syrians decided to exterminate the Jewish state in 1967 and suddenly every orange tree, every brook of water, every synagogue and every mosque would become a flash point.

Israel's birth in 1948 was a heroic and healing response to the politics of murder.

The death of Israel, now actively sought by hatemongers from Argentina to France to Egypt to Iran, would disavow every good instinct that was found in humankind after Auschwitz and Hiroshima.

Israel's emergence was supposed to have been accompanied with the emergence of a free Palestine in the first place; who can blame those of us in the Jewish community who truly care about the children of both Kfar-Saba and Qalqilya enough to require Israel's continuity just as much as we seek a just solution?

The parents who would send their children to blow themselves up in Jewish pizza parlors and at Passover gatherings, the men and women who would applaud the inferno of Sept. 11, 2001, and who would suggest that the Jews that made the desert green again are some kind of Nazi incarnation are people who never breathed in the fragrance of oranges across a warm valley of conciliation. They certainly never read a book that tells the true story of a people who survived and just want to live.

Chronology

1882–1903
The First Aliyah (large-scale immigration of Jews to Israel), mainly from Russia, occurs.

1896
Theodor Herzl publishes *The Jewish State*.

1897
The First Jewish Zionist Congress is convened by Herzl in Basel, Switzerland; the Zionist Organization is founded.

1904–1914
The Second Aliyah, mainly from Russia and Poland, occurs.

1909
The first kibbutz, Degania, is founded.

1914–1918
World War I occurs.

1916
The Arab revolt against Ottoman Turkish rule begins.

1917
Four hundred years of Ottoman rule is ended by the British conquest; the Balfour Declaration favors a Jewish Palestinian state.

1919–1923
The Third Aliyah, mainly from Russia, occurs.

1922
Great Britain receives Palestine as a mandate from the League of Nations.

1923
Britain divides Palestine into two districts; the eastern three-fourths of territory comprises Transjordan; the remaining territory is set aside for the Jewish National homeland.

1924–1932
The Fourth Aliyah, mainly from Poland, occurs.

1933–1939
The Fifth Aliyah, mainly from Germany, occurs.

1936–1939
Anti-Jewish riots are instigated by Arab militants.

1939
Jewish immigration is severely limited by the British white paper.

1939–1945
World War II occurs.

1945
The League of Arab States is formed in Cairo.

1947
The United Nations proposes the establishment of Arab and Jewish states in the Holy Land.

1948
May 14: The Declaration of Independence of the State of Israel is established; the British mandate ends.
May 15: Israel is invaded by five Arab states.

May 1948–July 1949
The War of Independence occurs.

1948–1952

A mass immigration to Israel from Europe and Arab countries occurs.

1949

Israel signs armistice agreements with Egypt, Jordan, Syria, and Lebanon; Jerusalem is divided under Israeli and Jordanian rule; first Knesset (parliament) is elected.

For Further Research

Yigal Allon, *The Making of Israel's Army*. New York: Universe Books, 1970.

———, *My Father's House*. New York: W.W. Norton, 1976.

George Antonius, *Arab Awakening: The Story of the Arab National Movement*. New York: Capricorn, 1965.

Moshe Aumann, *Land Ownership in Palestine 1880–1948*. Jerusalem: Academic Committee on the Middle East, 1976.

Shlomo Avineri, *The Making of Modern Zionism: Intellectual Origins of the Jewish State*. New York: BasicBooks, 1981.

Aryeh Avneri, *The Claim of Dispossession*. New Brunswick, NJ: Transaction Books, 1984.

Mitchell Bard, *The Complete Idiot's Guide to Middle East Conflict*. New York: Macmillan, 1999.

———, *Myths and Facts: A Guide to the Arab-Israeli Conflict*. Chevy Chase, MD: Arab-Israeli Cooperative Enterprise, 2001.

———, *The Water's Edge and Beyond*. New Brunswick, NJ: Transaction Publishers, 1991.

Menachem Begin, *The Revolt*. New York: E.P. Dutton, 1978.

Yitshaq Ben-Ami, *Years of Wrath, Days of Glory: Memoirs from the Irgun*. New York: Shengold, 1996.

David Ben-Gurion, *Israel: A Personal History*. New York: Funk & Wagnalls, 1971.

———, *Israel: Years of Challenge*. New York: Holt, Rinehart, and Winston, 1963.

———, *The Jews in Their Land*. New York: Doubleday, 1974.

———, *Letters to Paula*. Pittsburgh: University of Pittsburgh Press, 1972.

———, *My Talks with Arab Leaders*. New York: Third Press, 1973.

————, *Rebirth and Destiny of Israel*. New York: Philosophical Library, 1954.

Folke Bernadotte, *To Jerusalem*. London: Hodder and Stoughton, 1951.

Aharon Cohen, *Israel and the Arab World*. New York: Funk & Wagnalls, 1970.

Larry Collins and Dominique Lapierre, *O Jerusalem!* New York: Simon & Schuster, 1972.

Abba Eban, *Abba Eban*. New York: Random House, 1977.

————, *My Country: The Story of Modern Israel*. New York: Random House, 1972.

Foreign Relations of the United States 1947. Washington, DC: Government Printing Office, 1948.

Martin Gilbert, *The Arab-Israeli Conflict: Its History in Maps*. New York: Weidenfeld & Nicolson, 1993.

————, *Exile and Return: The Struggle for a Jewish Homeland*. Philadelphia: Lippincott, 1978.

————, *Israel: A History*. New York: William Morrow, 1998.

Ben Halpern, *The Idea of a Jewish State*. Cambridge, MA: Harvard University Press, 1969.

Arthur Hertzberg, *The Zionist Idea*. Philadelphia: Jewish Publication Society, 1997.

Theodor Herzl, *The Diaries of Theodor Herzl*. New York: Peter Smith, 1987.

————, *The Jewish State*. London: Central Office of the Zionist Organisation, 1934.

Chaim Herzog, *The Arab-Israeli Wars*. New York: Random House, 1984.

David Horowitz, *State in the Making*. Westport, CT: Greenwood, 1981.

Z'ev Jabotinsky, *The War and the Jew*. New York: Altalena Press, 1987.

Samuel Katz, *Battleground: Fact and Fantasy in Palestine*. New York: Bantam, 1973.

Jon Kimche, *The Second Arab Awakening*. New York: Henry Holt, 1973.

———, *There Could Have Been Peace: The Untold Story of Why We Failed with Palestine and Again with Israel*. New York: E.P. Dutton, 1973.

Dan Kurzman, *Genesis 1948: The First Arab-Israeli War*. New York: World Publishing, 1970.

Walter Laqueur. *A History of Zionism*. New York: Shocken, 1976.

———, *The Road to War*. London: Weidenfeld & Nicolson, 1968.

Walter Lacqueur and Barry Rubin, *The Israel-Arab Reader*. New York: Penguin, 2001.

Netanel Lorch, *One Long War*. New York: Herzl Press, 1976.

Richard Meinertzhagen, *Middle East Diary 1917–1956*. London: Cresset Press, 1959.

Golda Meir, *My Life*. New York: Dell, 1975.

Uri Milstein, *History of Israel's War of Independence*. 4 vols. Lanham, MD: University Press of America, 1996–1999.

Benny Morris, *Righteous Victims: The Birth of the Palestinian Refugee Problem, 1947–1949*. Cambridge, England: Cambridge University Press, 1989.

Conner Cruise O'Brien, *The Siege: The Saga of Israel and Zionism*. New York: Touchstone Books, 1986.

Daniel Pipes, *The Long Shadow: Culture and Politics in the Middle East*. New Brunswick, NJ: Transaction Publishers, 1990.

Yehoshua Porath, *The Emergence of the Palestinian-Arab National Movement, 1918–1929*. London: Frank Cass, 1996.

———, *Palestinian Arab National Movement: From Riots to Rebellion: 1929–1939*. Vol. 2. London: Frank Cass, 1977.

Yitzhak Rabin, *The Rabin Memoirs*. Berkeley and Los Angeles: University of California Press, 1996.

Howard Sachar, *A History of Israel: From the Rise of Zionism to Our Time*. New York: Alfred A. Knopf, 1998.

Nadav Safran, *Israel: The Embattled Ally*. Cambridge, MA: Harvard University Press, 1981.

Tom Segev, *1949: The First Israelis*. New York: Henry Holt, 1988.

Robert Silverberg, *If I Forget Thee O Jerusalem: American Jews and the State of Israel*. New York: William Morrow, 1970.

Christopher Sykes, *Crossroads to Israel: 1917–1948*. Cleveland: World Publishing, 1965.

Shabtai Teveth, *Ben-Gurion and the Palestinian Arabs: From Peace to War*. London: Oxford University Press, 1985.

———, *Ben-Gurion: The Burning Ground 1886–1948*. New York: Houghton Mifflin, 1987.

Chaim Weizmann, *Trial and Error*. New York: Greenwood Press, 1972.

Index

About the Editor

Mitchell Bard is the executive director of the nonprofit American-Israeli Cooperative Enterprise (AICE) and a foreign policy analyst who lectures frequently on U.S.-Middle East policy. Dr. Bard is also the webmaster for the Jewish Virtual Library (www.JewishVirtualLibrary.org), the world's most comprehensive online encyclopedia of Jewish history and culture.

Bard holds a Ph.D. in political science from UCLA and a master's degree in public policy from Berkeley. He received his B.A. in economics from the University of California, Santa Barbara. He lives in Maryland with his wife, Marcela, and sons, Ariel and Daniel.

Policymaking
in
American
Public Education

a framework for analysis

John Thomas Thompson
North Texas State University

Prentice-Hall, Inc., Englewood Cliffs, New Jersey

Library of Congress Cataloging in Publication Data

THOMPSON, JOHN T
    Policymaking in American public education.

    (Prentice-Hall educational administration series)
    Bibliography: p.
    Includes index.
    1. School management and organization—United
States. I. Title.
LB2805.T5   379'.151'0973   75-5841
ISBN 0–13–685370–6

Prentice-Hall Educational Administration Series
    William Ammentorp, *Consulting Editor*

Educational System Planning
    Roger A. Kaufman
Development of Information Systems for Education
    Khateeb M. Hussain
Understanding Communities
    James A. Conway, Robert E. Jennings, and Mike M. Milstein
Educational and Organizational Leadership in Elementary Schools
    Thomas J. Sergiovanni and David L. Elliott
Policymaking in American Public Education
    John Thomas Thompson

Printed in the United States of America

10 9 8 7 6 5 4 3 2 1

Prentice-Hall International, Inc., *London*
Prentice-Hall of Australia, Pty. Ltd., *Sydney*
Prentice-Hall of Canada, Ltd., *Toronto*
Prentice-Hall of India Private Limited, *New Delhi*
Prentice-Hall of Japan, Inc., *Tokyo*
Prentice-Hall of Southeast Asia (Pte.) Ltd., *Singapore*

Contents

Preface

This book is an outgrowth of several years' effort to develop a course in policymaking in American public education that would meet two objectives: (1) enable students to understand the forces, processes, and conditions that interact to shape the direction of public education; and (2) acquaint students with several conceptual models that might possibly assist in explaining educational policymaking. Although there are a number of studies on various aspects of policymaking on the market, no text was found to provide the conceptual framework of the entire policy system.

This study attempts to develop a conceptual framework that can be used to visually explain the parties, processes, and interactions in the policy process. Through the use of an Eastonian model an inquiry has been made for each level of government as to the following: (1) Who are the parties interacting in the policy system? (2) What do they bring with them to the system as to (a) their role expectations, (b) their perception of the world, and (c) their sources of influences and power? (3) What environmental factors affect the system, and how do the various parties perceive the environment differently? (4) How do the various social systems interact with the broader environment, and what access do they have to decision-making centers? And, finally, (5) What are the policymaking processes?

In each section a visual model shows the interrelationships of the various subsystems and how they affect policy formation. The models in each succeeding section relate back to earlier sections so that one may sense the dynamics and interrelationships of all of the factors involved in educational policymaking. These models, developed as teaching aids, were found to be most useful for providing a conceptual overview of how the multitude of factors and processes intermesh.

Many of my colleagues and students have encouraged and assisted me in this undertaking, and it is impossible to acknowledge all by name. I am

especially grateful to the students, graduate and undergraduate, whose discussion in seminars helped stimulate this book and to my colleagues in both the College of Education and the Political Science Department who encouraged me to this effort. I wish to express a special thanks to Professors Myron Basom and Maurice Wear of the University of Wyoming for their advice and assistance and to Alfred Evans for his editorial help. Finally, I am grateful to my beloved wife and children who have, as always, supported me in this endeavor.

John Thomas Thompson

Politics
and Education

Traditionally, American educators have denied that education is political. The conventional wisdom has been that politics and education are entirely separate and that educators should work to keep politics out of education. The reasons for this fear of politics vary, but they reflect in part the revulsion against the spoils or patronage politics that characterized the last part of the nineteenth century as well as the fear of conflict that is so much a part of politics.

Despite the credo that schools are apart from politics, education is and always has been intimately interrelated with politics. Education makes a significant contribution to the stabilization and transformation of political systems. Schools are the agencies that propagate the historical lore of the people—the myths, the beliefs, and the faiths—and thereby aid in the process of political indoctrination or socialization, an essential function in every political system. We have only to remember that when political systems have undergone radical transformations, as, for example, after the French, the Russian, or the more recent Chinese or Cuban revolutions, the efforts of the new rulers were immediately directed toward revamping the whole educational system. The structure, personnel, curricula, and even the clientele of the educational institutions underwent serious modifications, comparable in intensity and scope to the alterations and transformations introduced into the strictly political agencies of government, such as the police, military establishment, and civil service. New rulers have typically sensed that the success of their regimes is intertwined with the ideas and patterns of behavior transmitted through the educational system.[1]

In the modern industrial state, educational programs also are designed to staff the manpower needs of the industrial complex and to supply per-

[1]David Easton, "The Function of Formal Education in a Political System," *School Review*, Autumn 1957, pp. 309–10.

sonnel at the managerial levels to administer the economic system. Schools
are the apparatus through which economic and social stratification is either
preserved or overcome. We have long recognized this function of education, and it has been an integral part of the American dream to use public
education as the means for upward social and economic mobility for those
disadvantaged by social background or birth.[2]

Because of these vital functions, education is one of the most potent
political institutions in the American setting. As an institution it is instrumental in developing and preserving the political and social orders. In
turn, politics is intimately involved in education. Every aspect of the operation of the educational system is affected by politics. Establishment and
organization are under the authority of the state; what will be taught, who
will attend school, and who will do the teaching, as well as all other
aspects of education, are determined by laws made in the political arena.
Groups and individuals who possess the resources of power and influence
exert, or will exert when they believe it advisable, tremendous efforts to
shape and mold the system to their way of thinking and to tailor the curriculum to meet their special needs. In addition, schools must enter the
competitive arena of politics with demands for money and other resources
necessary for their operation. If we are to understand the educational system, we must also understand the political system in which it operates.[3]

Approaches to the Study of Politics

The relationships of politics to education are difficult to understand, in
part because of the elusive nature of politics. Philosophers since Plato
have debated the nature of politics with little agreement. Understanding
politics is even more difficult for the average citizen because the concept
of politics conjures up various images. Politics is often conceived of
simply as partisan politics; that is, who wins elections and gets into office.
In this light, politics is often thought of as "dirty," as having to do with
political corruption and patronage. Despite our profession of a devotion to
democracy, a system based upon political decisions being made by the
people, the average citizen frequently denigrates the politicians who make
the system possible. We differentiate between politicians and statesmen, with
the connotation that the politician is base while the statesman is noble.

---

[2]Nicholas A. Masters, "The Politics of Public Education," in *Perspectives on
Educational Administration and the Behavioral Sciences* (Eugene: University of
Oregon, 1965), p. 111.

[3]Thomas H. Eliot, "Toward an Understanding of Public School Politics," *American Political Science Review*, December 1959, pp. 1032–1050; *cf.* Jesse M. Unruh,
"The Politics of Education," *Proceedings of the National Conference of State Legislators* (December 4–6, 1966), pp. 17–21.

Another commonly held view connects politics with policies of government—the outputs of the system. Laws, ordinances, decisions, and administrative actions are evidence of politics, and politics is simply thought of as what is done by the political system.

Still another view of politics conceives of politics as process, as how the political system works. This systems approach is a more complex conception of politics and requires an understanding of how governmental processes work and how human behavior affects those processes. It is this type of understanding about politics that is needed to comprehend the relationships between politics and education.

Unfortunately, there is no precise explanation for the way the American system operates. Countless theories have been advanced which claim to account for the institutional arrangements and procedures we devise to conduct our political affairs. They range all the way from the normative natural rights theory at the heart of our Bill of Rights to the most recent behaviorism which would make a "science" out of politics. Each in a way has contributed to an understanding of the political system, but no single theory fully explains the American political process. The remainder of this chapter elaborates on various approaches found useful for understanding how the political system works.

Politics as Conflict Regulation. An underlying premise of all efforts to understand political processes is that politics arises out of the human situation. Man's physical needs and social wants constantly press against the scarcity of resources. Individuals have different wants and needs; and in the interaction with other people, the preferences of some individuals inevitably conflict with the preferences of others. Tensions frequently arise between men of differing preferences, particularly when insufficient resources exist to satisfy the wishes of everyone. Choices have to be made between competing demands. This is the source of social conflict—the seedbed of politics.[4]

Politics, the struggle over the allocation of social values and resources, is a process of conflict regulation. It involves making choices, or decision making as to how the power of government will be used, which in turn determines the distribution of advantages among people. Harold Lasswell, the political scientist, suggested this definition of politics when he described politics as *"Who gets what, when, and where?"* In this sense politics connotes the idea of people using influence and power to effect policies agreeable with their preferences.[5]

---

[4]Lewis A. Froman, Jr., *People and Politics: An Analysis of the American Political System* (Englewood Cliffs, N.J.: Prentice-Hall, Inc., 1962), pp. 1–15.
[5]Robert A. Dahl, *Modern Political Analysis* (Englewood Cliffs, N.J.: Prentice-Hall, Inc., 1963), pp. 14–22.

Education is one of the most intimate functions of government—it deals with people's most prized possession, their children. There are numerous educational matters that inevitably seem to produce conflict. Much of this conflict arises over what will be taught, as is readily apparent if one examines the educational controversies in recent years. Different groups propose different things: basic courses versus "frills," national patriotism versus the UN, college curriculum versus vocational education, old-fashioned health courses versus sex education, first grade versus kindergarten and prekindergarten, and so forth.[6]

Conflict also arises over how a school will be conducted. Selection of teachers and books has been the center of much controversy throughout our history. Similarly, where children will be taught has been a major dispute. The issue of segregation and where children will be taught has plagued us since the Civil War, and today the violent dispute over busing and de facto segregation in our cities stems from the different preferences of black and white parents. Who should control education also frequently divides communities. The question here is, What role should the educational profession have in educational policymaking? The public at large? Minorities in our large cities have most recently raised this question with their demands for decentralized boards of education.[7]

Money is involved in many of the educational disputes. How much tax money should be spent on education, who is to pay the taxes, and how educational funds are to be spent are issues constantly requiring decisions. Education also has to compete with other governmental functions for funds in the political process; the competition is often between schools and sewers or some other governmental program. At times the competition is between various levels of education, that is, elementary and secondary versus higher education.[8]

In addition to these disputes, much local politics revolves around schools because schools are the largest builders (or one of the largest builders) and purchasers of supplies in the community. The questions of where schools should be built, by what contractor, who is to furnish supplies to the schools, and so forth, involve a large number of people in

[6]John H. Bunzel, "Pressure Groups in Politics and Education," *National Elementary Principal*, January 1964, pp. 12–16.

[7]Jason Epstein, "The Politics of School Desegregation," in *Politics of Urban Education*, ed. Marilyn Gittell and Alan G. Hevesi (New York: Frederick A. Praeger, Inc., 1969), pp. 288–303; *cf.* Mario Fantini, "Community Participation," in *ibid.*, pp. 323–37; and Mario Fantini, Marilyn Gittell, and Richard Magat, *Community Control and the Urban School* (New York: Praeger Publishers, 1970).

[8]Unruh, "Politics of Education," pp. 17–21; *cf.* Michael D. Usdan, David Minar, and Emanuel Hurwitz, Jr., *Education and State Politics: The Developing Relationship between Elementary-Secondary and Higher Education* (New York: Columbia University Press, 1969), pp 1–11.

school decisions. Also, the economic and status rewards within the educational establishment are competed for by various members of the educational profession.[9]

Group Theory of Politics. Although politics arises out of the nature of the human situation, the study of politics is more than looking at individuals acting alone. Political processes operate from a group basis. To achieve a desired objective in public policy, an individual must join with others who have similar preferences. He will usually find it more expedient and fruitful to join forces with like-minded persons in a pressure or interest group. Since individuals normally have a number of different wants or demands to place upon the political system, they may belong to many interest groups, not all of which have like views toward all questions of public policy.[10]

It is a part of American political tradition to curse the "special interest" for producing conditions that citizens find undesirable in the community. Pressure groups, however, are a vital part of representative government. Any voluntary organization attempting to influence public policy is an interest or pressure group. Such a group may arise on an *ad hoc* basis to obtain a particular goal, such as children's transportation to and from school. On the other hand, interest groups may have permanent staffs like the National Educational Association and may attempt to influence public policy generally at all levels of government on a broad range of topics. Pressure groups are a major means whereby wants can be expressed or demands of the citizenry made on the political system.

Those who have studied pressure groups generally share the view that organized groups begin in response to changes in the relationships between individuals when existing institutions are inadequate to provide a means for meeting new demands made on the system. Groups come into being as collective efforts to cope with a variety of social disturbances. They seek governmental decisions that correspond to the hopes and aspirations of their members.

Nowhere is the politics of pluralism more manifest than in education. In many communities throughout the country, schools are on the receiv-

---

[9]John Gallagher, *School Board Politics in Los Angeles County* (Los Angeles: University of California, 1962).

[10]Charles Hagan, "The Group in a Political Science," in *Approaches to the Study of Politics*, ed. Roland Young (Evanston, Ill.: Northwestern University Press, 1958), pp. 38–51; David B. Truman, "The Group Concept," in *Introductory Readings on Political Behavior*, ed. S. Sidney Ulmer (Chicago: Rand McNally & Co., 1961), pp. 191–98; and Earl Latham, "The Group Basis of Politics: Notes for a Theory," in *Readings in Political Parties and Pressure Groups*, ed. Frank Munger and Douglas Price (New York: Thomas Y. Crowell Company, 1964), pp. 32–57.

ing end of turbulent pressures from groups on every side.[11] Consider some of the demands on school boards. In farming communities, farm groups press for courses that will benefit rural children. Trade unions want consumer economics and more occupation-oriented courses. Other groups argue strongly for general education courses at the expense of vocational courses. Some churches press for released-time programs; other more fundamental sects insist that every member of the school board endorse Bible reading and prayers in the classroom despite the Supreme Court decisions. Taxpayer groups want to cut educational costs to the bone, while parent groups call for increased expenditures and propose bond issues for school expansion. Minority groups also pressure schools to meet their preferences. Any chronicle of the blacks' protest of the last three decades would be incomplete without a recount of such pressures groups as the NAACP, SCC, Urban League, CORE, and SNICK. Similarly, the demands of teachers for better salaries and more of a voice in educational decision making have resulted in such organizations as the NEA and AFT, which act as pressure groups on their behalf. These are just a few of the groups that attempt to influence educational policies.

The rise of an organized interest group begets other groups of people who disagree with the preference of the first group. When blacks organize, whites with competing preferences form other groups such as the White Citizens' councils, neighborhood organizations, and so forth. Taxpayer groups mobilize when teachers organize and lobby for higher salaries. We have as a result a growing pluralism of interest competing in the public policymaking arenas.

Interest or pressure groups perform a number of essential functions in our government.[12] To begin with, the interest group provides a rallying point for the individual. It becomes a vehicle whereby individuals of like circumstances or convictions can collectively develop a position on an important issue and then bring influence to bear upon governmental policymaking. Interest groups can marshal individual opinions, organize them, and present them in a skillful way to the proper governmental official.

---

[11]John H. Fisher, "Our Schools: Battleground of Conflicting Interests," *Saturday Review*, March 21, 1964, p. 66; *cf.* Neal Gross, *Who Runs Our Schools?* (New York: John Wiley & Sons, Inc., 1958), pp. 45–48; Patricia Cato Sexton, *The American School: A Sociological Analysis* (Englewood Cliffs, N.J.: Prentice-Hall, Inc., 1967), pp. 21–25; John Bunzel, "Pressure Groups in Politics and Education," *National Elementary Principal*, January 1964, pp. 12–16; and Charles H. Wilson, "Local Pressures in Education," *National Elementary Principal*, January 1964, pp. 32–35. Several studies, however, suggest the lack of influence of interest groups on school politics. See: Eugene R. Smoley, *Community Participation in Urban School Government* (Washington, D.C.: U.S.O.E. Comparative Research Project A–029, 1965; and David Rogers, *110 Livingston Street: Politics and Bureaucracy in the New York City School System* (New York: Random House, Inc., 1968).

[12]David B. Truman, *The Governmental Process* (New York: Alfred A. Knopf, Inc., 1948).

A second function performed by interest groups has to do with delineation of issues. Opposing sides of issues are clarified by groups. For an understanding of a particular program, legislators and citizens alike often depend on the clash of opinion between those who are in favor and those who are opposed. Groups help shape attitudes and opinions of the group, and of citizens at large.

Interest groups also provide information relevant to a proposed program. To be sure, this information is often biased or selective in terms of the group's own position. At the same time, every interest group knows that distorted information may in the end be self-defeating. For instance, the proponents of a state aid program for schools realize that their own statistical data will be carefully scrutinized by the opponents of the measure. Nothing would please the opponents more than to show that the proponents had been careless in their collection of statistics. The fact that interest groups on both sides of a proposal gather information and check the information that others present gives legislators or school boards considerable confidence that they have a rather reliable base upon which to operate. The information function of interest groups is an important one.

Perhaps the most important aspect of the participation of interest groups in America is the function they perform in the process of compromise and consensus. In a pluralistic society, almost any proposal will have advocates and opponents. Out of this conflicting opinion, compromises must be made—and this is public policy. *Public policy* is defined by group theorists as the end result of the interaction of the various interested pressure groups upon one another. The role of politician (whether he be legislator or school board member) is that of decision broker. He seeks to reach some kind of compromise and, insofar as possible, consensus; agreement must be created for some kind of compromise.

A model of this process is shown in Figure 1–1. *A* and *B* in this model represent policy positions, perhaps a proposal for reorganization, or an increase in educational expenditure, or any other of countless issues.

Figure 1–1   Public Policymaking Model

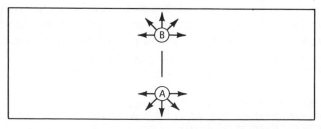

Illustration of decision-making model from Ralph B. Kimbrough, Political Power and Educational Decision-Making (*Chicago: Rand McNally & Co., 1964*), p. 16.

Various groups have different views about what should be the policy and are pulling in different ways. The policy that will be adopted will be the sum of the vector forces where each vector represents the total force and direction of each group, as determined by its age, respectability, status, size of membership, intensity of interest, and other pertinent factors.

Political Parties and Group Theory.   Political parties are still another type of voluntary organization. Whereas pressure groups normally only attempt to influence public decisions and do not attempt to elect the officials of government, political parties direct their main energies toward winning the public offices. This does not mean that pressure groups do not attempt to influence electoral politics; they do, frequently, but typically do not offer slates of candidates for election. Political parties then are a special type of organization, very much influenced by interest groups, but if a party is to win it must make its appeal to a broad spectrum of the public and cannot be as narrow on issues as an interest group.[13]

Despite the long-standing profession that education is nonpolitical and should not be involved in party politics, party politics vitally influences American education. Even in nonpartisan local elections for school board members, the functions of recruiting candidates and presenting their candidacy to the public are essential. This may be done by a group of individuals, an organized group that is in effect a quasi-political party.

Education is also dependent on political parties for the introduction of its demands into the political system. Education groups, therefore, attempt to influence the platforms of both state and national parties. Party officials are sought out, and whatever influence the groups may have on these officials is used. Furthermore, in some few cases, educational groups take positions in elections. Despite the growing recognition by many educators of the need for party support in the policymaking arena, educators are still handicapped at the state and national levels by their long-standing aloofness from party politics.

Community Influentials and Policymaking.   The function of a political system in any society is to make choices from among competing demands made by individuals and groups and to maintain the social system based upon these choices. We have long recognized the importance of who makes the public decisions, and it is part of the American democratic commitment that government, including school government, is to be government of the people. This belief has been institutionalized in a number

[13]V. O. Key, Jr., *Politics, Parties, and Pressure Groups* (New York: Thomas Y. Crowell Company, 1955), pp. 215–41; *cf.* Neil A. McDonald, *The Study of Political Parties* (New York: Random House, Inc., 1963), pp. 1–35.

of ways, such as by having periodic elections of public officials and by requiring referenda on such issues as bonding and finance. Widespread participation in government is the ideal to which democratic government aspires.

Although we have sought government by the people, not all people participate in governmental activities equally. Lack of popular participation or even apathy is all too often the normal reaction of the citizenry to governmental matters, and particularly to school government matters. Most people are relatively inactive in politics and in the community, from talking over the back fence with a neighbor about community problems to voting in elections. A few people, however, devote much time, energy, and thought to political affairs. Studies of the characteristic distribution of people on a general participation scale show that most people play little or no role in community political action. While there is some variation, approximately 55 to 60 percent of adult residents fall in the lowest quartile of participation, and 25 to 30 percent in the next quartile. Thus about 85 percent are below the midpoint on scale of participation, and only 15 percent are above the midpoint.[14]

Studies also show that when degree of participation is related to such factors as education, occupation, and age, participation tends to rise continuously and rather sharply with a rise in the level of formal education and income. It was found that those with some college experience had average participation scores 60 percent higher than the high school group, and two and one-half times as high as those whose education did not go beyond the ninth grade. Similarly, those with an income of $10,000 a year or more had average scores one-third higher than those with incomes from $4,000 to $10,000, and twice that of those with incomes below $4,000. When these two factors are combined, the differences are even more marked. Thus, those with incomes of $10,000 or more and college experience had scores five times as high as those with incomes below $4,000 and education below the tenth grade.[15]

This marked difference in participation among various community segments raises the inference of a "class bias" in the policymaking process. If the upper socioeconomic segments are overrepresented in community affairs, one would expect that their attitudes and values would tend to dominate. In school government this could affect decisions regarding curriculum, discipline, athletic programs, and expenditure of school funds; and it might result in the addition of budgeted funds for courses designed

[14]*Educational Administration in a Changing Community*, Thirty-seventh Yearbook, 1959, American Association of School Administrators, p. 58.

[15]*Ibid.*, p. 59; *cf.* John Foskett, "Social Structure and Social Participation, *American Sociological Review*, August 1955, pp. 431–38.

for college-bound students at the expense of vocational or other courses designed for terminal students.

Pursuing this line of reasoning, beginning with the classic study of George S. Counts, a number of studies have examined the recruitment process for school board members and have found that school boards throughout the nation are primarily composed of persons from the business and professional occupations. School board members and formal decision makers generally tend to be drawn disproportionately from the higher age categories and classes, and ethnic groups of higher status.[16] The conclusion that this recruitment pattern causes a "class bias" in policymaking, however, has been questioned. For example, to demonstrate that a school board composed of business and professional persons is bound to show a class bias, it is necessary first to demonstrate that different classes in the community hold different opinions on community issues. Is there a class position on education policy? It is debatable whether for many issues there are clear and consistent differences among class groups, ethnic groups, age groups, and so on, which could manifest themselves in different decisions depending on what kind of decision maker holds office. Also, it has been argued that to look to social backgrounds and personal characteristics as the major explanations of a person's behavior in a decision-making role is to deny that a given individual may act differently in different roles. Each office involves its incumbents in a set of structural relationships to others, and the actions of an officeholder are in part determined by these role expectations. Furthermore, the formal decision maker is subject to pressures from partisans of one or another policy alternative. Attempts are made to persuade, influence, or coerce him to support particular policies. Undoubtedly the actions of partisans play some part over and above predisposition and role in the outcome of some issues.[17]

Beginning in 1953 with the publication of Floyd Hunter's *Community Power Structure*, social scientists turned their attention from formal deci-

---

[16]George S. Counts, *The Social Composition of Boards of Education: A Study in the Social Control of Public Education* (Chicago: The University of Chicago, 1927); *cf.* W. W. Charters, Jr., "Social Class Analysis and the Control of Public Education," *Harvard Educational Review*, Fall 1953; and Edward L. Dejnozka, "School Board Members: Their Opinions, Status, and Financial Willingness," *Journal of Educational Sociology*, January 1963, pp. 193–98.

[17]Charles M. Bonjean and David M. Olson, "Community Leadership: Direction of Research," *Administrative Science Quarterly*, December 1964, pp. 278–300; *cf.* Peter Rossi, "Community Decision Making," *Administrative Science Quarterly*, March 1957, pp. 415–43. For an examination of the differences between the expectations of an educational system by upper middle class and working class and lower middle class, see Lillian B. Rubin, *Busing and Backlash: White against White in an Urban School District* (Berkeley: University of California Press, 1972).

sion makers to informal decision makers. Prior to Hunter's classic study, the question "Who governs?" was answered in much the same manner by both the social scientists and the lay public. Those persons occupying important offices—elected officials, high civil servants, business executives, officials of voluntary organizations, heads of religious groups, leaders of unions, and others—were assumed to be those making key decisions affecting directly or indirectly the lives of most other community residents. Hunter's study of Atlanta challenged the assumed relationship between office holding and decision making at the community level. His study indicated that while institutions and formal associations played a vital role in the execution of determined policy, the formulation of policy often takes place outside these formalized groups by a relatively small group of community influentials. Hunter concluded that Atlanta (and possibly other communities) was governed by a covert ruling elite.[18]

From Hunter's study and the writings of the late C. Wright Mills emerged a theory of community power structure.[19] Essentially, the theory is that there develops within a community an oligarchy or a ruling elite that has power to get things done and to affect all community decisions. The members of the ruling elite or top community influentials are the individuals who make decisions of importance in all those arenas of the community that impinge upon them or their group or affect in any way the operational sphere of their control.

Hunter's thesis stimulated numerous studies of various aspects of community power; many sought to identify community leaders, others examined the nature of influence and power, and still others sought to discover the bases of influence and power. Attempts were made to sharpen Hunter's system for identifying community leaders. The reputational technique used by Hunter for identifying individuals who made up the power structures essentially was to ask informants to name and rank leaders in their community, and from these answers individuals were ranked according to the number of times they were mentioned. Other researchers sought to develop entirely different techniques for studying community leadership and decision making.[20]

Robert Dahl, the Yale political scientist, challenged both Mills's thesis and his techniques. He disputed the idea that any one man or group of

[18]Floyd A. Hunter, *Community Power Structure* (Chapel Hill: University of North Carolina Press, 1953).

[19]Robert E. Agger, Daniel Goldrick, and Bert E. Swanson, *The Ruler and the Ruled: Political Power and Impotence in American Communities* (New York: John Wiley & Sons, Inc., 1964).

[20]Peter H. Rossi, "Theory, Research and Practice in Community Organization," in *Social Science and Community Action*, ed. Charles R. Adrian (East Lansing: Michigan State University, 1960), pp. 9–24.

men is so powerful as to be able to exert influence in all community
matters, and he argued that the reputational technique for identifying the
so-called power elite measured only reputed or potential power, not actual
power. Using an event analysis technique that attempted to reconstruct
how specific community decisions were made and to trace actions of
leaders in regard to decision making, Dahl found that rather than a single
group of community influentials, numerous different groups influence various decisions in the community. According to Dahl and his followers,
there is not a monolithic elite, instead there is a pluralism of individuals
who affect the different kinds of decisions that are made in a community.[21]

Later research on community power structure demonstrated that the
political influence structure varies in different communities depending on
the cultural environment. Agger and his associates created a typology of
four community power structures, namely, monopolistic, multigroup noncompetitive, competitive elite, and pluralistic, and the differences in community structures were explained by two factors: (a) the convergence or
divergence of the political leadership in ideology and (b) the distribution
of political power (that is, broad or narrow) among the citizens.[22]

Despite the unresolved issues about the nature of community leadership patterns, these studies produced a number of new insights about community political processes. A new appreciation of the power phenomena
at the local level emerged, and the nature of power and influence was
more sharply defined. In all of these studies it was found that some people
influence other people; some people have power to alter the actions and
conduct of others from what they would be otherwise; and some individuals employ their resources to sway the outcome of community decisions toward their preference.

All people do not have equal influence or power. Recognition of this
fact led to an examination of the bases or attributes of influence and
power, attributes that people cultivate and use to influence decisions affecting them. The bases of social and political power were found to include
such factors as the following: (1) control over wealth and other resources
or institutions that can be used as sanctions (e.g., banks, credit, land,
jobs); (2) control over information and communications, including the
control of information by administrators and experts, as well as control
over the mass communication media; (3) control over solidarity groups

[21]Robert A. Dahl, "The Analysis of Influence in Local Communities," in *Social
Science and Community Action*, ed. Charles R. Adrian (East Lansing: Michigan
State University, 1960), pp. 25–42; and Wendell Bell, Richard J. Hill, and Charles
R. Wright, *Public Leadership* (San Francisco: Chandler Publishing Co., 1961), pp.
99–118.

[22]Frank Lutz, "Power Structure Theory and School Board Decision Making
Process," *Educational Theory*, January 1965, pp. 19–25.

such as unions, and racial and religious groups; (4) control over status and prestige in the community; (5) personal popularity, esteem, or charisma; (6) powers of office, legality, and constitutionality; and (7) the right to vote.[23]

Additional insights as to how influence and power affect policy decisions were also obtained from the studies of community power structures. Decision making was found to evolve in a web of social relationships of both formal and informal decision makers. Community influentials interact with each other in a host of social occasions. From these contacts they come to know and understand one another's attitudes and positions on various issues; a political consensus is established, and in many instances trust and friendship develop among them. Much of the activity in the policymaking process was found to be carried out in these informal social contacts. Formal governmental agencies, such as school boards, are likely to be guided in accordance with much of this social interaction.[24]

Recognition of the importance of social interaction between formal and informal community leaders has led to still other studies of how groups and individuals relate to each other. Communications which are vital to decision making occur only if individuals and groups come into contact with each other. Interaction between groups often occurs because of common membership in two or more groups. These points of tangency provide a communication linkage between the two groups, and in any community there will be a network of such linkages. Similarly, groups must have access to formal decision makers in order to successfully influence decisions. Access to political decision makers is attained not only through friendship but through exchange relationships such as where political support is exchanged for favorable consideration on an issue.[25]

As a result of the evolution of these ideas, policymaking is viewed as the processes that turn political inputs into outputs. This transformation presupposes a degree of political consensus that provides legitimacy and enables the authoritative individuals in the system to resolve conflicts and exercise power in the allocation of resources. Within this consensus, individuals with various perceptions of their self-interest and external environment operate in fairly specialized roles according to the accepted rules of the political game. Both the style of role playing and the degree of adherence to the rules vary with the perception of the individual operating within them. However, the roles and the rules do limit the range of be-

[23]*Ibid.*

[24]Larry W. Hughes, "Know Your 'Power' Structure," *School Board Journal,* May 1967, pp. 33–35.

[25]Laurence Iannaccone and Frank Lutz, *Politics, Power and Policy: The Governing of Local School Districts* (Columbus, Ohio: Charles E. Merrill Books, Inc., 1970), pp. 26–28.

havior of these individuals, and by so doing maintain stability in the political system. These roles and rules are manifestations of the political consensus within society.

Schoolmen were quick to appreciate the importance of the concepts developed from the community power and policymaking studies. At every turn, in the professional literature, in university and college classes, as well as from sources within their own districts, superintendents were admonished to know the community power structures. Teachers too were influenced by the new ideas of power and began to seek power and influence through organization. Furthermore, as the profession has begun to reject the belief that education is not political, it has sought to develop linkages with community leaders and access to political decision makers. The following chapters will discuss the forms of linkages and access education has with community and political decision makers and the problems it faces in this regard.

Systems Theory of Politics.   The most comprehensive approach to the study of politics is the systems approach, which provides a conceptual overview of how the political system operates. As developed and used by David Easton, Gabriel Almond, and others, the analytical construct of a political system provides a means of examining the interrelationships among political actors and institutions, and of understanding the complex processes by which public policy is made. This approach assumes that the political system, that is, those human activities predominantly oriented toward the allocation of values by a society, can be separated for study. Economic, religious, and other social forces obviously influence the political system, and the interrelationships of the social forces investigated can be studied separately.[26]

Easton's model of the political system shown in Figure 1–2 provides a conceptual framework for understanding political processes. The political system as part of the broader social system receives inputs from the environment in the form of demands and supports which are converted through a series of conversion processes into outputs, or authoritative rules and actions. In turn, the outputs of the system affect the environment and as feedback may result in another demand or input on the system.

The usefulness of the macroscopic approach in describing the relationships between the cultural environment and the political processes can readily be seen when applied to educational policymaking. For example, the Russian success with Sputnik a few years ago drastically disturbed the status quo in American education. This blow to national pride was trau-

---

[26]Russell T. Gregg, "Political Dimensions of Educational Administration," *Teachers College Record*, November 1965, pp. 118–28.

Figure 1–2   A Simplified Model of a Political System

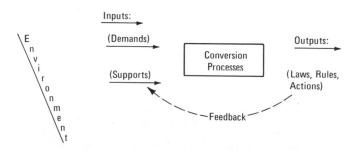

Source: David Easton, A Framework for Political Analysis *(Englewood Cliffs, N.J.: Prentice-Hall, Inc., 1965), p. 112.*

matic, and immediately there was a hue and cry that something had to be done. The question of curriculum was pushed into the center of public debate. Numerous groups were created to alter and improve our schools. New demands were put on schools for a more rigorous scientific and mathematical curriculum. The demands were in turn converted into public policy—legislatures appropriated more money, new curriculum requirements were enacted by administrative agencies, new courses were designed, new textbooks were written and adopted, summer programs for training teachers were enacted, and so forth, and as a result the output was the new math and the greater emphasis on science in our schools. In turn, these programs affected the environment, and the feedback from these actions has led to still other demands on the system, such as demands for additional vocational-technical education.[27]

The relationships between the cultural environment and the political processes are shown in a policymaking flowchart in Figure 1–3.

Other recent developments in educational politics can also be studied from the systems perspective. In addition to putting new and competing demands on the educational system, environmental changes such as the scientific and technological revolution, increasing U.S. military requirements, population growth, and urbanization and metropolitanization have made educational policies more important in the solution of national problems. Educational policies today as never before vitally affect the nation's

[27]For a discussion of the systems approach, see David Easton, *A Systems Analysis of Political Life* (New York: John Wiley & Sons, Inc., 1965); Anatol Rapoport, "Some System Approaches to Political Theory," in *Varieties of Political Theory*, ed. David Easton (Englewood Cliffs, N.J.: Prentice-Hall, Inc., 1966), pp. 129–41; and Jay D. Scribner, "A Functional-Systems Framework for Analyzing School Board Action," *Educational Administration Quarterly*, Autumn 1966, pp. 204–14.

Figure 1-3   Flowchart on Policy Formation in Education

I Basic Forces (Environmental Factors)	II Antecedent Movements and Responses (Inputs)	III Political Action (Inputs)	IV Formal Enactment (Conversion Processes and Output)	V New Demands as Result of Action (Feedback)
Social, economic, political and technological forces, usually national and worldwide in scope	Group formation Study groups Committee Studies: President's Commission Governor's Studies	By organizations usually inter- related at local, state, and national levels such as U. S. Chamber of Commerce, AFL-CIO and NEA	May be at local, state, and national levels; and through legislative, judicial executive agencies	New needs perceived which in turn cause groups to study and organize to push new programs

Adapted from Roald F. Campbell, Luvern L. Cunningham, Roderick F. McPhee, and Raphael O. Nystrand, The Organization and Control of American Public Schools, *2d edition, (Columbus, Ohio: C. E. Merrill Publishing Co., 1970), p. 39.*

goal of full employment, the national security, and the domestic peace and order. Education has become a major public issue. Public decisions about schools, like other public decisions, are being debated more and more in the national political arena. Increasingly, the political system is being required to make choices concerning educational policy from among the different courses of action that are available.

As previously stated, there is no precise explanation of how the American system works. All of these ideas contribute to an understanding of our political system. The following chapters will attempt to examine the policymaking process in American public education by drawing from all of these approaches and conceptual schemes.

Policymaking Theory:
A Framework for Analysis

Every society has to make certain fundamental choices about education. Major policies must be made regarding who will attend school, what will be taught and who will teach, how the educational system will be governed and administered, and how education will be financed. How these questions are answered depends on the interaction of a host of economic, social, psychological, cultural, and political variables. The purpose of this study is to develop a heuristic model to permit a macroscopic analysis of educational policymaking in the United States. Simply put, how can we identify the multitude of actors and factors influencing policies, and understand the social dynamics of the policy process? This chapter explains the conceptual scheme that will serve as a road map to guide our research.

Traditional View
of Educational Policymaking

Most of the older studies are of little help in understanding the dynamics of educational policymaking. In the past we viewed policymaking simply from a legal perspective; the law said that it was the responsibility of the elected representatives (the school board) to make educational policy. Furthermore, the legal concept was supported by traditional organizational theory. Traditional organizational theory, as it had evolved from Max Weber's ideas, conceived of organizations as hierarchical arrangements of workers for carrying out policies made by the legally constituted powers. According to this theory, as applied to schools, the people elect representatives to the school boards and thus give them the legal power to make school policies. The board in turn hires a superintendent or an administrator and delegates to him the authority to administer board policies. The superintendent, with the authority from the board, organizes the work

of the school and directs teachers and staff to teach and perform the duties he assigns them. Figure 2–1 illustrates the traditional organizational arrangement.

Policymaking according to this view was entirely separate from administration. The board made all policy, and there was a clear division between policymaking and administration. The superintendent was in no way a policymaker; he was only to administer the policy. Teachers were not considered as part of the policymaking process either. They were considered as being similar to workers in a factory and were to accept orders and do the work of the school organization. Of course, students were not considered in the policymaking process at all; they were the "clients" or "things" to be acted upon. In a sense, the old adage was to be applied: Students were to be seen but not heard.

The traditional organizational view is obviously inadequate today, since it does not serve as a tool to help guide the actions of educational leaders. It does not describe the dynamic processes of policymaking or consider the host of environmental variables that interact to shape policies. It does not permit us to use the new knowledge about community leadership patterns and the nature of informal power and influence. The dichotomy between policy and administration is simply not valid, as every superintendent and school board member knows. The understandings about the nature of authority cannot be explained in the framework of traditional organizational theory. Authority does not just go down the hierarchy; teachers have power to influence policy, and the authority of the superintendent to a degree depends on their acceptance of his authority. Similarly, students are not just "things" to be acted upon; they have certain powers and have a voice in policymaking, and at least they

Figure 2–1   Traditional View of Educational Policymaking

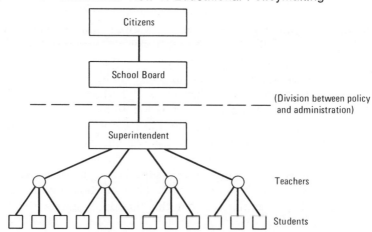

set limits on the types of policies that can be made. One has only to consider the influence that students have on dress and hair codes to realize that they do influence policy.

The need for new conceptual tools to understand policy processes is also seen in our inability to use the older theories to explain the growing intergovernmental relationships. There were a number of older models of federalism, but they are of little help in explaining the intergovernmental aspects of policymaking. One perspective of federalism saw the system as consisting of two rival governments competing for power. This "states' rights," or "dual federalism," view held that if one level of government grew, it did so at the expense of the other. There was, therefore, a continuous struggle to keep one government from encroaching on the other. Figure 2–2 illustrates this concept.

Related to the states' rights concept of federalism was the idea that the functions of government could be neatly divided among the three levels of government. It was believed there were distinct federal functions, state functions, and local functions of government. Morton Grodzins compared this view of federalism to a three-layer cake, with each layer being separated by thick icing. But as Grodzins clearly pointed out, there are no purely local functions, or purely state functions, or purely federal functions in our system of government. All levels of government in the United States share in the responsibility for all functions. Grodzins suggested that instead of a three-layer cake to explain our system, the analogy of a "marble cake"—where there are no clear-cut layers but the chocolate runs all through the cake—better explained governmental functions in this country. He and his colleague Daniel Elazar demonstrated that ours is indeed a system where all functions, including education, are shared by all levels of government.[1]

Figure 2–2 "States' Rights" Concept of Federalism

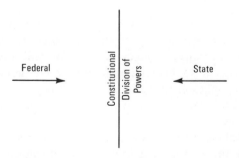

[1]Morton Grodzins, *The American System: A New View of Government in the United States*, ed. Daniel J. Elazar (Chicago: Rand McNally & Co., 1966), Part II; *cf.* Morton Grodzins, "The Federal System," in *Goals for America* (The American Assembly, Columbia University, 1960).

Grodzins's and Elazar's ideas are useful for interpreting the sharing of functions in our federal system, but they do not provide a conceptual tool for explaining the dynamics of policymaking in our federal system. Obviously, a conceptualization of educational policymaking in the United States should overcome these inadequacies and should be able to describe the dynamics of the policy processes in our federal system.

Systems Approach
to Educational Policymaking

Here we propose to view the school as a social system and to develop a model that will show the interaction of all variables influencing educational policy. The first step is to identify the variables. An attempt to enumerate factors that influence a society's policies about major educational questions readily demonstrates the complexity of educational policymaking. Decisions on major questions, such as who will attend school, depend on a host of economic, cultural, social, psychological, political, and legal factors. In Table 2–1 an attempt has been made to categorize the various factors that influence major educational policies.

Differences in societal conditions or changes in one or more of the variables shown in Table 2–1 will result in differential educational policies. For instance, a developing society with a large, dense, and young population, an economy heavily dependent on agriculture or on industry with a low level of technology, a caste system based on religious beliefs, and a political system dominated by a small oligarchy will answer the key educational questions differently from another society with a stable or declining population, an economy dependent on highly developed technology, and cultural beliefs of equality and individualism. With so many variables interacting to affect policymaking, one can conceive of an almost infinite number of societal differences that may affect policies on education.

The complexity of an educational system is further magnified when one considers that changes in any of the variables in turn affect educational policies. For instance, changes in the economic system such as an increasing technological sophistication in the above-described developing society will cause changes in educational policies regarding who will attend school, what will be taught, how it will be taught, and who will teach, as well as in other policies.

Educational policies in turn affect all of the other social systems. How a society answers the major questions about education affects the economic, social, cultural, and political conditions of a society. In essence, the social system interacts with numerous other social systems in the total

Table 2–1   Variables Influencing Major Educational Policies: Who Will
Attend School

A. Economic Factors
  1. Demographic factors—population: number and density, urban-rural ratio,
      age and sex mix; geographic location of people, housing patterns
  2. Resource base—wealth available, cost of expanding program, tax system,
      competing demands for available resources, per capita wealth; transportation
      system available, communication system
  3. State of technology—society's need for workers (e.g., rural society and sum-
      mer vacation, early industrial needs for child labor, youth and adult educa-
      tional needs); rate of change in society; educational technology available:
      teachers available, textbooks, etc.
  4. Cost of education—to society; to individual

B. Social and Cultural Factors
  1. Racial beliefs—e.g., slavery, caste system, power of dominant group, the
      minority
  2. Religious beliefs—position of male-female; view of work (Protestant ethic),
      view of change
  3. Society's status system—cultural beliefs about importance of education, role
      of education (American view of education as solution to social, economic,
      and political problems); status of educational programs; status and influence
      of educational professionals
  4. Individual motivation for education—socialization process of importance of
      education (e.g., women don't need as much education as men)
  5. Cultural beliefs about children; how to rear children
  6. Beliefs about the role of government—the nature of men and their develop-
      ment; who should be educated
  7. Nationalism—patriotism; needs of military

C. Political and Legal Factors
  1. Political ideology—nature of man, and government, role of government;
      needs to politically socialize youth; degree of freedom and openness of society
  2. Political-administrative structure—legal and constitutional requirements and
      conditions, tax system
  3. Influence and power structure—strength of groups in political process; di-
      versity of groups in society; linkages between groups
  4. Degree of stability of governmental system
  5. Military and economic needs—war or peace; needs of soldiers, needs for
      military production workers (e.g., Rosie the Riveter in World War II)
  6. Political and administrative organization of schools; organizational theory;
      concept of authority; role of teachers, administrators, students; traditional
      and legal aspects of education

D. Social-Psychological Factors
  1. Attitudes, beliefs, and values of teachers and administrators
  2. Educational backgrounds of educational personnel
  3. Roles of educational personnel and role perceptions
  4. Group affiliations and group strength of educational professionals
  5. Individual motivations, and intellectual abilities

This list is not intended to be comprehensive.

environment. It is affected by the other social systems and in turn it affects the other social systems.[2]

In addition, internal factors within the school system such as the recruitment patterns for educational personnel, social-psychological factors such as the attitudes and beliefs of teachers and administrators, organizational arrangements of schools, as well as the type of students in the student body, are major factors in educational policymaking and may at times be more influential than other external factors. In summary, the school system is a complex system comprised of an aggregation of subsystems and suprasystems interacting with numerous other social systems in the total environment.

Distinctive Features
of the American Educational System

To understand the social dynamics of educational policymaking in the United States, it is necessary first to consider those factors that give American education its distinctive features. Decentralization is the most distinctive aspect of the educational system in the United States. Under our federal system of government, educational policy is influenced by the federal government, the fifty states, and the fifteen thousand or so local school districts, most of which are entirely separate from other local governmental units. The decentralized educational control obliges school governments to adjust to the concerns of the individual school, the local community, and the separate state. Also, the educational system has had to accommodate to modern social forces, particularly to the concerns that are national in scope and are defined by federal agencies and private national bodies.

Unlike educational systems found in countries with a unitary form of government, the American public school system is a complex partnership with responsibilities distributed among the three levels of government— the local school district, the state, and the federal government. Our federal system of government lacks hierarchical controls between the various levels of government, and therefore its operation depends entirely upon a complex set of intergovernmental relations. Cooperative arrangements replace the use of authority, and the evidence of power and influence is much more subtle than under a unitary form of government.

[2]R. L. Johns, "The Economics and Financing of Education," *Emerging Designs for Education* (Conference Report, Designing Education for the Future, Denver, Colo., May 1968), pp. 193–94; *cf.* Charles Bidwell, "The School as a Formal Organization," in *Handbook of Organizations*, ed. James G. March (Chicago: Rand McNally & Co., 1965), pp. 972–81.

The local school district has fundamental responsibility for operating public elementary and secondary schools. Teachers must be employed and given specific teaching assignments; buildings must be erected and maintained; students must be assigned to appropriate classrooms; instructional supplies and equipment must be provided; policies governing the operation of America's largest business, public education, must be developed and enforced.

Each of the fifteen thousand or so school districts in this country operates under the direction of a local school board whose members, in most cases, have been elected by the people of the school district. With this network of local units overseeing education, the public schools seem to be a stronghold of local control in this country.

Localism has been the keynote of American education. During the nation's expansionist period, the reliance upon the states and the local governments for developing and supporting their own systems of education proved to be an effective means for serving general requirements for diversity in approach to the solution of educational programs. Localism, in fact, dominated the American ideology so completely that although, in legal theory, the state was responsible for education, local districts were left with almost full responsibility for providing the leadership and finances for supporting schools. The local schools developed their own political systems to support and sustain them. Clientele groups of professional educators and their "friends of education" were developed to support them in local and state political arenas.[3]

The great diversity in our country has resulted in differences in local educational systems and has supported local control of education. Even though our society has become more homogeneous because of modern economic and social forces, the United States is still one of the most heterogeneous nations in the world. Economically and culturally, various regions of our country differ greatly, and local communities differ even more. It is impossible to describe a typical community. American communities vary greatly in size and character, ranging from rural hamlets or small one-industry towns to giant industrial cities in metropolitan areas. Their socioeconomic bases vary as widely, and these differences are reflected in the life-styles of the citizenry. There are great differences in community political systems, with some communities being dominated by individual families or cliques of influential individuals and others having a much more pluralistic type of system. All of these factors have a direct influence on schools, on the type of school policies that are passed, and on the policymaking processes themselves.

[3]Roald F. Campbell, "The Folklore of Local School Control," *School Review*, Spring 1959, pp. 1–11.

Sectionalism or multistate regionalism is another factor affecting American politics. Some of the sharpest differences in public affairs grow out of regional differences. Regional peculiarities in politics and public policies—peculiarities that reflect a number of social, economic, and political processes that have similar effects upon neighboring states—also affect local and state educational systems.[4]

Differences in cultural values in the various regions vitally affect local and state educational systems. Although the United States, as a whole, shares a general political culture, every state has certain dominant traditions about what constitutes proper governmental action, and differences in state and local responses within the federal system appear to be stimulated by differences in political cultures among the states and even within the states. Daniel Elazar has suggested that the national political culture is a synthesis of three political subcultures—individualistic, moralistic, and traditionalistic—which jointly inhabit the country, existing side by side or even overlapping one another. These three political subcultures influence the operation of state and local political systems.[5] Figure 2–3 shows the distribution of the political subcultures in the United States.

In the different political subcultures, according to Elazar, people view differently what politics is and what can be expected from government. The cultural values also influence the kinds of people who become active in government and politics, and the way in which the art of government is practiced. School governments, as well as other units of government, are affected by the different values in the three political subcultures.

In the *individualistic* political culture, government is viewed simply as a utilitarian institution created to handle those functions that cannot be managed by individuals. Government need not have any direct concern with questions of the "good society" or the "general welfare." The democratic order is viewed as a marketplace. Emphasis is upon private concerns, and a premium is placed on limiting community intervention into private activities. Government is only to "give the public what it wants," and public officials are normally not willing to initiate new programs or open new areas of governmental activity on their own initiative. Politics and political participation are seen as just another method by which individuals may improve themselves socially and economically. Politicians are interested in office as a means of controlling the distribution of the favors or rewards of government rather than as a means of exercising govern-

[4]Ira Sharkansky, *Regionalism in American Politics*, (New York: The Bobbs-Merrill Co., Inc., 1970), pp. 3–4.
[5]Daniel Elazar, *American Federalism: A View from the States*, second edition, (New York: Thomas Y. Crowell Company, 1972), pp. 93–103; *cf.* Ira Sharkansky, "The Utility of Elazar's Political Culture: A Research Note," *Polity*, Fall 1969, pp. 66–83.

mental power for programmatic ends. As a result, the public tends to believe politics is dirty and no place for amateurs to play an active role.[6]

The *moralistic* political culture emphasizes the commonwealth concept of politics. Politics is part of man's search for the "good society," and only through the good society can he live the "good life." Individualism is tempered, in this culture, by a general commitment to utilize communal power to intervene in spheres of private activities when it is considered necessary to do so for the public good and well-being. Participation in community affairs is seen as a civic duty for every citizen, and public officials are viewed as having a moral obligation to promote the general welfare even at the expense of individual loyalties and political friendships.[7] President Kennedy, in his famous inaugural address, conveyed the essence of the moralistic view when he said, "Ask not what your country can do for you; ask what you can do for your country."

The *traditionalistic* political culture views the main role of government as the maintenance of the existing social order. Like its moralistic counterpart, the traditionalistic political culture accepts government as a positive factor in the affairs of the community, but only to the extent that it maintains and encourages the traditional values and patterns of life. Social and family ties are paramount in this cultural environment, and real political power is confined to a relatively small and self-perpetuating group drawn from an established elite of the "good old families." Others who do not have a definite role to play in politics are not expected to be even minimally active as citizens. In many cases, they are not even expected to vote.[8]

These three political subcultures, according to Elazar, have been distributed throughout the country by the continuous movements of people in our society, or what he terms the continuous frontiers in America. At first the westward movement or rural land frontier tended to move the three different cultures due west across the country. Later the urban-industrial frontier moved people from rural to urban areas, largely within states, although some of the movement was between cultural regions. The third frontier, the metropolitan-technological frontier, has shifted people not only from rural to urban areas but from various regions of the country to the large metropolitan areas and has resulted in a clashing of the different cultural values.[9]

School governments are obviously influenced by the political culture in which they exist. Local school systems, like local governments, gen-

[6]*Ibid.*, pp. 94–96.
[7]*Ibid.*, pp. 96–99.
[8]*Ibid.*, pp. 99–102.
[9]*Ibid.*, pp. 104–19.

Figure 2-3   The Distribution of Political Cultures within the States

Daniel Elazar, American Federalism: A View from the States, *2nd edition, pp. 106–7. Copyright © 1972 by Thomas Y. Crowell Company, Inc., with permission of Thomas Y. Crowell Company, Inc., publisher.*

M: Moralistic
I: Individualistic
T: Traditionalistic

Note: Two letters juxtaposed indicates either a synthesis of two subcultures, or the existence of two separate subcultural communities in the same area, with the first dominant and the second secondary.

erally tend to reflect regional and local values, and policy decisions are made in keeping with regional and local norms. Regional norms are important to school officials; these norms, in turn, are reinforced by the consulting patterns of contemporary officials, who know their counterparts in nearby localities and states and feel that their neighbors face problems similar to their own. Thus they are most likely to consult with regional partners before making decisions on new policies. Furthermore, school officials are more apt to share ideas in regional meetings and conferences than in national meetings. Regional norms, therefore, continue to be a major influence in educational policymaking.[10]

These three uniquely American conditions—federalism, localism, and regionalism—make for a highly decentralized educational system and give American education its most distinctive features. But the dramatic change in American society since World War II has seriously challenged the nation's decentralized educational system. The population explosion following World War II greatly increased enrollments and placed a great strain on schools. New technology, while holding out the promise of a time when most menial tasks will be performed by machines, threatens also to create a new class of paupers whose unskilled labor continues to lose its value. The national manpower needs to meet the demands of a rapidly changing technology have created problems never before faced by our educational system. The American black, suddenly militant after one hundred years of comparative docility, demands freedom now from economic and social servitude and from second-class citizenship. Our cities, for decades ignored by rural-dominated state legislatures, threaten to become factory towns, ringed by suburban gardens that try to fence in city problems along with the city poor. These forces have had a major impact on the structure and operation of the American educational system. Increasingly, the old patterns of educational policymaking have been challenged as inadequate to develop the needed national perspective to meet the rising national and international problems. American education has been plagued by conflict between national goals and local traditions to such a degree that this too might be considered as a distinctive aspect of our educational system.

The recent conflict between national and local demands has occurred concomitantly with the growing disparity between local revenue needs and local tax sources, increasing pressures on the state and federal governments to finance education. Out of these conditions have evolved new patterns of intergovernmental relations which have modified educational policymaking in this country. Any explanation of the working of the American educational system must consider the conflict between the various levels of government as well as the evolving patterns of cooperation.

[10]Sharkansky, *Regionalism in American Politics*, pp. 10–11.

Developing a Model

Two major ideas have occupied our attention to this point: (1) educational policymaking can be examined through a systems approach, and (2) the educational system in the United States is a complex system. If we are to provide the intellectual framework for studying and analyzing educational policies, we next need to develop a model to represent the organizational structure and social interactions of the educational system.

A model is a theory describing the structure and interrelationships of a system. Everyone uses models. A written description is a model that represents one aspect of reality. A mental image used in thinking is a model. A diagram used by a professor to explain a point is a model. A system model differs in its attempt to be logically complete and to permit a simulation of various actions in social life. By use of a system model the dynamic process can be studied, and each of the subsystems can be isolated for the purpose of analyzing the numerous factors influencing activities of the system. We are attempting to develop such a model of the American educational system in order to study the social dynamics of educational policymaking.

To model the policymaking system of American education, it must first be described. Boundaries must be established within which the interactions that give the system its characteristic behavior take place. The boundary is chosen to include those interacting components necessary to generate the modes of behavior of interest. To identify boundaries of the educational system and to construct a model, we asked the following series of questions about the educational system at each level of government: (1) Who are the parties interacting in the social system? (2) What do they bring with them to the system as to (a) their role expectations, (b) their perception of the world, and (c) their sources of influence and power, and what access do they have to decision-making centers? (3) What environmental factors affect the system, and how do the various parties perceive the environment differently? (4) How do the various social systems interact with the broader environment, and how do the various subsystems affect and influence other parts of the educational system? And, finally (5) What are the decision-making processes?

Answers to these five questions provided us with information about the structure of the educational system, which we have attempted to depict in a visual model illustrated in Figure 2–4. Four policy arenas are shown in the model—local, state, federal, and regional or interstate. These are arranged in a multiple-structure universe in order to represent the host of socioeconomic-cultural factors influencing policymaking processes and to signify the dynamic interactions in the policy process. With the model an

Figure 2–4   Model of the Policymaking System of American Education

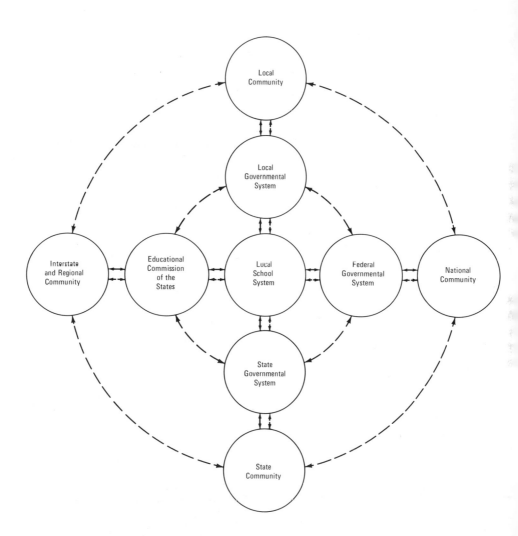

attempt is made to identify all participants and all factors in the educational system, including individuals, groups, and organizations; to examine the basis and nature of the social interactions of participants and the linkages between participants and others outside the system; and to identify the subsystems of the educational system and the numerous factors influencing their activities. Since the model is presented as a multiple-structure universe, it is possible also to study the host of interrelationships at

various levels of government and to examine the social dynamics of the policy process at all levels of government. Each segment of the model will be examined in detail in subsequent chapters.

Policymaking Processes

Modern scholarship has demonstrated that the policymaking process is more complex than the legally oriented traditional theory. Policymaking is seen as a sum of the processes in which all the parties in, and related to, a social system shape the goals of the system. These processes include those that link the various parties together and facilitate their adjustments to each other and to the environmental forces affecting them. To study these processes, materials for each governmental level are arranged here in a systems framework and are considered as a part of an input-conversion-output process. Each section includes a discussion on (a) the environment that both stimulates participants in the educational system and receives the product of the system, (b) the inputs that carry stimuli from the environment to the participants, (c) the outputs of the system that affect the environment, (d) the conversion processes that transform (convert) inputs into outputs, and (e) feedback that transmits the output of one period back to the conversion process as the input of a later time.

The conversion process is viewed as the interaction of various cultural, structural, and situational factors. Figure 2–5, which is basically an adaptation of the systems schema, represents a community policymaking model. As can be seen from this diagram, decisions and policies of community governments, including schools, depend on the interplay of structural, cultural, and situational factors.[11]

Structural factors in Figure 2–5 include both long-term "situations" and relatively unchanging elements of the community. School governments are affected by such factors as basic socioeconomic-political conditions in the community, that is, by such factors as the distribution of population by class, age, and other characteristics, the land-use patterns, the nature of the economy, the degree of political consensus or conflict in the community, the number and type of established organizations that play potential political roles, and the legal structure and powers of government.[12]

Cultural factors are the value commitments of citizens in the community at large. We have already pointed out the effects upon schools of

[11]Robert R. Alford, "The Comparative Study of Urban Politics," in *Urban Research and Policy Planning*, ed. Lee F. Schnore and Henry Fagen, Urban Affairs Annual Reviews (Beverly Hills, Calif.: Sage Publications, Inc., 1967), Vol. I, pp. 261–302.

[12]*Ibid.*, p. 264.

Figure 2–5   Community Policymaking Model

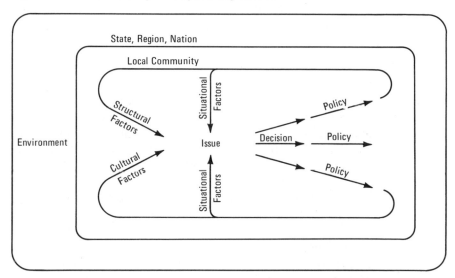

Adapted from Robert R. Alford, "The Comparative Study of Urban Politics," in Urban
Research and Policy Planning, *ed. Lee F. Schnore and Henry Fagen, Urban Affairs
Annual Reviews, Vol. 1 (Beverly Hills, Calif.: Sage Publications, Inc., 1967), p. 267.*
Reprinted by permission of the Publisher, Sage Publications, Inc.

citizens' beliefs about the proper role of schools, the legitimacy of the
demands of various groups, and the norms attached to political participation, as well as other cultural beliefs.[13]

Situational factors are short-term factors that affect decisions and policies. At any particular time, "issues" will arise in a community. Their
content and form will depend on the particular combination of all the
other factors affecting the course of political, economic, and social development of the community. Which issues are dealt with by public action
will vary at different times depending on such situational conditions as
the incumbents in public office and their political values, the membership
of the community leadership in that period, the relative strength of various
groups, or the political access such groups may have at that moment. Decisions and policies of schools depend on the interplay of all of these
factors, and for each level of government we shall attempt to identify
these factors and to explain how they interrelate.[14]

An examination of how schools adapt to these forces and how policies
are made reveals four adaptive processes, namely, identification, bargaining, legal-bureaucratic mechanisms, and coercive mechanisms. For each

[13]*Ibid.*, p. 265.
[14]*Ibid.*, p. 264.

level of government, we shall examine how these processes are used in educational policymaking.[15]

Identification grows out of a feeling of oneness with another person or group. It is what causes you to give your children, parents, spouse, or friends what they want from you and causes you to accept their outputs. You do so because you "identify" with them in the sense of seeing and feeling them as extensions of yourself, so that to have them indicate their needs to you is tantamount to your desire to satisfy them. This process of adapting to an environment is often used by school systems. Behavior of parents and students is influenced by encouraging them to identify with "our school," and this sense of common identity enables parent-teacher associations and local schools to contain conflicts over the schools. Professional identification influences the behavior of all educators. Educators have attempted to use this process to their advantage by identifying education in the public mind with the dominant goals of society. Schools are represented to be the "melting pot" for Americanization of immigrants, the vehicle for upward social and economic mobility, and the ultimate solution to many community problems. But as society becomes more urban and heterogeneous, it is more difficult to develop the sense of identity or oneness between parents and schools or between teachers, administrators, and school boards. Also conflicting community goals lessen the chance of schools' benefiting by favoring one societal goal or another. Therefore, it is more difficult to use this process of adaptation.[16]

The second adaptive process, *bargaining*, is a system of exchange; it consists of trying to get something from someone by convincing him that it is to his advantage to give it to you. Successful bargaining depends upon one's bargaining power, and that power depends on the number of alternatives one has as compared with the number one's opponent has. One has more bargaining power than another to the degree that he has more alternative sources of what he wants than the other has of what he wants. This is readily recognized in the economic sphere, but bargaining is a widely used process in all government, including school government. The legislative process is basically a form of bargaining, and it is this process that is used by school boards when conflicting views necessitate a compromise decision. Obtaining public funds for schools, as in bond elections or in a federal grant, involves bargaining; in a sense the school board bargains to provide certain services or facilities in return for the resources the public or federal government controls. Decisions about teacher salaries and working conditions are made through bargaining procedures either on a

---

[15]John E. Bebout and Harry C. Bredemeier, "American Cities as Social Systems," *American Institute of Planners Journal*, 29, No. 2 (1963), pp. 64–76.

[16]*Ibid.*, p. 66.

one-to-one basis between teacher and administrator or on a group basis involving teacher associations or unions and administrators.[17]

Legal-bureaucratic mechanisms are the third means of adaptation. Schools rely heavily upon legal authority to justify their actions. Schools also are large bureaucratic organizations, and how they respond to demands upon them depends on administrative processes. Legal and bureaucratic methods can be used only so long as the legal or bureaucratic authority is considered legitimate and is accepted by the parties involved. In recent years the legitimacy of schools' legal and bureaucratic authority has been challenged repeatedly by students, parents, and teachers.[18]

Coercive mechanisms are the final means of adaptation. Through coercive mechanisms one gets what he wants from another by so narrowing the alternatives that the latter has virtually no choice but to comply. For example, a robber who demands, "Your money or your life," coerces you because he leaves you with no acceptable alternative. Schools, like all governments, at times use coercion. In dealing with student disciplinary cases, or with parents regarding compulsory attendance laws, or in collection of taxes, a form of coercion is used. Furthermore, coercive tactics are used by teachers when they apply professional sanctions or strike; similarly, when school boards or administrators take disciplinary action against teachers they are using coercion. Racial groups and irate parents frequently use demonstrations to force schools to meet their demands, and schools often react by relying upon injunctions to coerce the parties from demonstrations.[19]

Which of these adaptive processes will be used in the policy process depends on (1) the policymakers' perception of the environmental challenges or problems they are called to act on and (2) the nature of social interaction between policymakers and various segments of the community.

Federalism and Educational Policymaking. Policymaking in our federal system is further complicated, since all levels of government share responsibility for governmental policies. To a degree all levels of government participate in the making of all governmental policies.[20] For education this means that the local, state, and federal governments all influence

---

[17]*Ibid.*, p. 65.

[18]*Ibid.*, p. 66.

[19]*Ibid.*, pp. 64–65.

[20]Michael D. Reagan, *The New Federalism* (New York: Oxford University Press, Inc., 1972); M. J. C. Vile, *The Structure of American Federalism* (New York: Oxford University Press, Inc., 1961); and Edward W. Weidner, "Decision-Making in A Federal System," in *Cooperation and Conflict: Readings in American Federalism*, edited by Daniel J. Elazar, R. Bruce Carroll, E. Lester Levine, and Douglas St. Angelo (Itasca, Ill.: F. E. Peacock Publishers, Inc., 1969), pp. 278–91.

the key educational policies of who will attend school, what will be taught, how schools will be administered, and how they will be financed. The policy output of one level of government acts as an input on the other levels of government. For example, policies of local school districts pertaining to financing of education directly affect the types of demands made on the state and federal governments. If local districts cannot or will not adequately meet demands for education, those groups pressuring for additional school finances turn to the state or the federal government with their demands. Similarly, actions of the state and federal governments influence demands made on local school districts.

Federalism results in a governmental "system within systems," with each level of government being separate but interdependent on the others. Because of the differences in the structural, cultural, and situational factors of the various levels of government, different groups and interests may have more influence in the policy process at one level than at another, and therefore policies of the various levels may and do conflict. The differences in the structural, cultural, and situational factors will be pointed out for each level of government.

By approaching educational policymaking in a systematic manner, we are able to study the relevance of the individual components of the system—how they interact in the policymaking process, and the type of policymaking processes instrumental in making educational policy. For each level of government we shall collect information about items that seem to function as conversion components, inputs, outputs, and feedback mechanisms. Then we shall consider how these factors interact to produce the policy outputs of the system.

Political System
of Local Education

To a large degree the key questions of who will attend school, what will be taught, how schools will be governed and administered, and how they will be financed depend on the policies of the fifteen thousand or so local schools. The purpose of this chapter is to describe the structure of the political system of local education, to examine how it functions, and to determine how the political system of local education affects educational policies.

The political system of local education is set off from the rest of the educational policymaking model in Figure 3–1. The three main areas of interaction—the local school system, the local community, and the local governmental system—are represented by accentuated circles. The solid-line arrows connecting these three circles are used to represent the political, legal, and administrative relationships between the three segments of the system, and the broken-line arrows represent other types of communications between the segments. The local system is part of the larger environment, as is evident from the entire model.

At the very center of the educational policymaking model is the circle representing the local school system or district. Its location signifies the importance of local school districts in educational policymaking. The circle representing the local school district is subdivided to show the parties interacting in the local school system, that is, students, teachers, administrators, and school board; or using systems' terminology, the client system, the technical system, the managerial system, and the institutional system.[1] From this perspective the school organization appears as a system

[1]Use of the systems approach to describe operations of schools is also found in the following: R. L. Johns, "The Economics and Financing of Education," *Emerging Designs for Education* (Conference Report, Designing Education for the Future, Denver, Colo., May 1968), pp. 193–94; *cf.* Charles Bidwell, "The School as a Formal Organization," in *Handbook of Organizations*, ed. James G. March (Chicago: Rand

Figure 3–1 Model Representing the Political System of Local Education

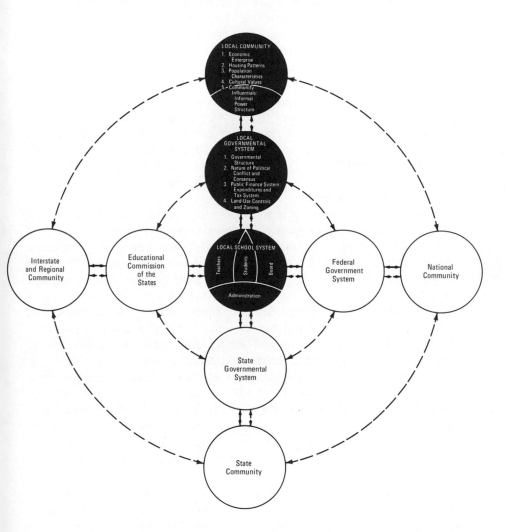

of exchange rather than as a hierarchical arrangement of authority relationships.[2] Here the superintendent and other administrators do not appear

---

McNally & Co., 1965), pp. 972–81; and Jay D. Scribner, "A Functional-Systems Framework for Analyzing School Board Action," *Educational Administrative Quarterly*, Autumn 1966, pp. 204–14.

[2]For a discussion of organizations as instruments of exchange, see Talcott Parsons and Edward A. Shils, *Toward a General Theory of Action* (Cambridge, Mass.:

as being above teachers and students, as in the traditional organization chart, but rather as a link between three different groups—teachers, students, and board. Instead of stressing the authority relationships and the traditional concepts of policymaking, this perspective suggests that the policymaking processes are shared by all parties in the school organization.

The local community, another major factor in the system, is represented by a second accentuated circle. From the local community come demands for educational programs and supports in the form of political acts and resources to carry out the school's programs. The community's socioeconomic conditions determine the nature of the school's student body as well as the degree of affluence of the district. The community's power structure and the style of politics influence the nature of the school's politics. These factors are denoted in the circle representing the local community and its environment.

The third accentuated circle represents the local governmental system. Schools are special district local governments created by state statutes and are a part of the community political system. As units of local government they are inextricably linked to the local governmental system. They are affected in numerous ways by the actions of other governmental units, and they are dependent on the local property tax along with other units of local government. Frequently, there is competition for local tax resources, sometimes of a latent nature; but at times the competition becomes so intense that the city or county and school district behave as antagonists even though they all claim to serve the interest of the same public.[3]

In fiscally dependent school districts where municipal officials participate in budget determinations for the schools and may have legal authority to determine the total amount of money for the schools, the interrelations are quite obvious. Such districts comprise only about 5 percent of the districts in the United States, but this includes many of the larger city systems. In these districts the city officials, particularly the mayors, have an important voice in school budget decisions. But even in the fiscally independent districts, mayors frequently play an important role in making the financial decisions affecting schools, particularly where pressures from organized teacher groups are for more monies than the school may raise under tax limitations. In a number of such cases the mayor has become a key factor in obtaining additional funds from the state or federal gov-

---

Harvard University Press, 1951); and Edward C. Devereux, Jr., "Parsons' Sociological Theory," in *The Social Theories of Talcott Parsons: A Critical Examination*, ed. Max Black (Englewood Cliffs, N.J.: Prentice-Hall, Inc., 1961), p. 27; *cf.* Charles A. Joiner, *Organizational Analysis: Political, Sociological, and Administrative Process in Local Government* (East Lansing: Michigan State University, 1964), pp. 5–8.

[3]Frederick H. Kerr, "Politics and Schools," *National Civic Review*, April 1966, pp. 193–98.

ernments, and in resolving certain kinds of community conflicts that are beyond the ability of the school board to resolve.[4]

Within Puts

Educational policies are shaped by both the inputs from the environment of the school system and the within puts that originate in the school organizations themselves. Inputs include demands of citizens and of members of the executive, legislative, and judicial branches of other governments. Within puts are demands arising within the organization which are shaped by such factors as the structural organization, the formal rules of the school system, the personal and professional needs of school personnel, and the attitudes, values, and role expectations of the parties in the school system.

School policies are greatly influenced by the parties within the school organization, so much so that many decisions are made entirely by professional educators. As Rosenthal stated, "School matters are and probably will continue to be the special preserve of the education expert. Their pleas of impotence notwithstanding, the educators run America's schools."[5]

There are several reasons why the educational bureaucracy has so much influence in school policies. For one thing, education is so highly valued in our society that schools and schoolmen are generally supported. Furthermore, educators have skills and expertise essential to the operation of the schools. Parents look to the professionals for leadership. In turn, schoolmen emphasize the uniqueness of their professional competencies for dealing with the complexities of education—their special education, experience, and ability. Large segments of the educated middle class have accepted the ideological concepts of educators and are so committed to professionalism that they vigorously reject community control by questioning their own qualifications to participate in school decision making. The educational bureaucracy also has a monopoly on information about the school which in turn helps to reinforce the idea that they alone have the expertise to make educational decisions. As a result, many decisions

[4]H. Thomas James, James A. Kelly, and Walter I. Garms, *Determinants of Educational Expenditures in Large Cities of the United States*, U.S. Department of Health, Education, and Welfare, pp. 68–69; Bernard Mackler and Nancy Bord, "The Role of the Urban Mayor in Education," *The Record*, March 1968, pp. 531–39; Wallace Sayre and Herbert Kaufman, *Governing New York City* (New York: Russell Sage Foundation, 1960), p. 424; and Marilyn Gittell, *Participants and Participation: A Study of School Policy in New York City* (New York: Frederick A. Praeger, Inc., 1969), pp. 155–77.

[5]Roscoe C. Martin, *Government and the Suburban School* (Syracuse, N.Y.: Syracuse University Press, 1962), pp. 61 and 97–101.

about education, particularly those pertaining to internal school-centered matters, are left almost entirely to professional educators and only rarely does an average citizen have the audacity to question the decision or the prerogative of the professionals.[6] The remainder of this chapter examines the within puts, that is, those aspects of the local school organization that affect educational policymaking.

Attitudes, Values, and Role Expectations. Each of the four parties of subsystems in the school organization brings with it attitudes, values, and role expectations that have been developed or learned from groups and associations outside the school systems, and these differing expectations may at times conflict. Students, for example, bring with them the expectations of their parents. Parents today have increasing expectations of education. Schools are expected not only to teach traditional subjects but also to develop and equip the student so that he can adjust to life. Figure 3–2 attempts to represent the interactions between various parties in the school organization and factors that influence them by connecting the various subsystems of the school organization with circles representing the sources of these attitudes, values, and role expectations.

Students, also, bring with them their own personal and psychological needs and desires for social activity, and much of the school program— sports, band, pep club, and other extracurricular or cocurricular activities —is developed toward meeting these needs. It is interesting to note that research supports educators' widely held belief that parents are more likely to lodge complaints over changes in extracurricular activities than about curricular matters. A parent is much more apt to be upset about his child's not participating in a pep squad than he is about what is taught or not taught in the social studies class.[7]

The fact that students reflect their parents' expectations and that parents are concerned with the happiness and "popularity" of their children gives students a degree of influence and power in the educational policymaking process. Before any school policy affecting students is made, the reaction of the student body and the parents must be considered. Similarly, the actions of teachers are affected by the possibility that parents may become upset and raise complaints about their performance. In a sense, parents are viewed as potential threats by teachers and administrators.[8] School personnel recognize the potential power of students and

---

[6]Alan Rosenthal, "Pedagogues and Power," in *Governing Education: A Reader on Politics, Power, and Public School Policy,* ed. Alan Rosenthal (Garden City, N.Y.: Anchor Books, 1969), pp. 291–313.

[7]M. Kent Jennings, "Parental Grievances and School Politics," *Public Opinion Quarterly,* Fall 1968, p. 364.

[8]Bidwell, "School as a Formal Organization," pp. 1003–1004.

Figure 3–2   Factors Influencing Attitudes, Values, and Role Expectations
of Parties within the Local School System

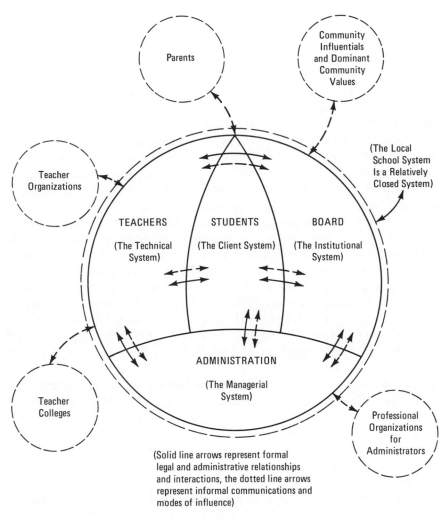

(Solid line arrows represent formal
legal and administrative relationships
and interactions, the dotted line arrows
represent informal communications and
modes of influence)

their parents and respond differently to students from different socioeconomic backgrounds.

Students may also bring pressure upon the school to change policies
that are not acceptable to them. Note how schools have been forced to
retreat from strict dress codes in the face of student opposition. Interactions of various subsystems within the school organization are shown
in Figure 3–2. The solid-line arrows represent formal legal and administrative relationships and interactions, and the broken-line arrows represent
informal communications and modes of influence.

Teachers, in addition to their personal needs, bring with them role expectations and perceptions of the world learned in their own educational experiences and professional training. In the past, teachers and administrators both were socialized by teachers colleges and held similar views of how schools were to be run. The same professors who taught superintendents about school administration taught teachers to respect and to cooperate with their administrators. Educational organizations perceived the goals of education in the same way and thus supported a similarity between teachers and administrators. In recent years teachers' views have changed. More men have entered the teaching profession, and they are— or at least they formerly were—more apt to challenge the administrators' authority than were women teachers. Teachers are learning new role expectations from the increasingly militant teacher organizations and unions.

Teachers' professional organizations often have goals that disagree with local school practices, and the more professionally oriented teachers seek to follow the professional standards rather than the bureaucratic standards of the local system.[9] Increasingly, professional associations of teachers and administrators differ in their interpretation of their respective roles in the educational process. The fact that administrators feel that they are being forced out of state teachers associations is evidence of the growing schism between these professional educators. Furthermore, teachers generally tend to perceive themselves as poorly treated by society, and many are angry about the rewards and status given them by society.[10] As a result they are organizing and applying group sanctions in an effort to influence school policies.[11]

The attitude of teachers and administrators toward educational programs also influences policies of what will be taught. Most professional educators are college graduates and have learned to value a "college education," and they therefore favor courses that lead to college attendance. Vocational or technical courses, on the other hand, do not have the status appeal to teachers or parents and thus have been given much less emphasis than the college-bound curriculum.

School board members, in addition to the personal and social factors

[9]Ronald G. Corwin, *A Sociology of Education: Emerging Patterns of Class, Status, and Power in the Public Schools* (Prentice-Hall, Inc., 1965), pp. 217–64; *cf.* Dean M. Laux, "A New Role for Teachers?" *Phi Delta Kappan*, February 1965, pp. 265–69.

[10]Harmon Zeigler, *The Political Life of American Teachers* (Englewood Cliffs, N.J.: Prentice-Hall, Inc., 1967), pp. 19–21; *cf.* "Teachers Warn Boards: You Haven't Seen Anything Yet," *American School Board Journal*, October 1968, p. 31; and Ronald G. Corwin, *Militant Professionalism: A Study of Organizational Conflict in High School* (New York: Naiburg Publishing Corporation, 1970), pp. 175–91.

[11]Alan Rosenthal, *Pedagogues and Power: Teacher Groups in School Politics* (Syracuse, N.Y.: Syracuse University Press, 1969), pp. 154–85.

that motivate them to run, bring with them the dominant values of the local community. They are the primary instrument for linking the school system to the community. As previously mentioned, school boards are predominantly composed of individuals from business and professional occupations. They are usually part of the community's informal power structure, or they interact socially with the power structure. Board positions are not typically regarded as political stepping-stones, and consequently the role of school board member is one of the last opportunities for "gentlemen in public office." Board members tend to see the world from the perspective of the dominant local values, particularly in the area of public finance.[12] The board's values frequently conflict with those of the teachers on matters of revenues and expenditures, as well as on the matter of the teachers' role in policymaking.

The main base of power for school boards, in addition to their social standing in the community, is their official position. In principle, the school board has been established as the representative of the community to exercise, within statutory limits, power over the school system, presumably for effecting the public will and protecting the public interest in the governance of the schools. The fact that school boards hold legally designated positions gives them power in policymaking.

The board, however, has serious limitations as to the degree to which it can exercise this power. First, board members are part-time officials, while other parties in the school system devote full time to school matters. They are not privy to much of the communications in the system and are thus dependent on others, particularly the superintendent, for information. The growing technical complexity in the operation of the schools has resulted in the school board's increased dependence upon the professional knowledge, experience, and expertise of professional educators. School board members may come to their jobs with the intention of developing a particular program or of achieving certain goals, only to discover that the conditions under which they can operate are circumscribed by the prior knowledge and experience of the professional educators and by the circumstances under which programs of a similar nature have been found deficient in the past.[13]

A second major weakness of school boards stems from their not representing visible constituencies that support their candidacy, ensure their election, and watch the behavior of their representatives after election. Furthermore, there is no institutionalized way, such as the existence of

[12]Martin, *Government and the Suburban School*, pp. 41–51.

[13]Norman Kerr, "The School Board as an Agency of Legitimation," *Sociology of Education*, Fall 1964, pp. 34–59; *cf*. Bidwell, "School as a Formal Organization," pp. 1003–1004.

competing parties, for them to receive continuously demands and supports from community groups. Because of the lack of a permanent tie to the community, school board members tend to become socialized with the values of professional educators. Many acts of board members are to validate acts or programs proposed by educational professionals rather than to meet demands made by citizens. There is, therefore, confusion over the degree to which the school board members are truly representative of the public within the school organization or—the reverse—are the representatives of the school organization to the public.[14]

The increasing heterogeneity of interests in American communities, coupled with the patterns of representation on school boards which weigh in favor of dominant middle-class values, raises other questions about the representativeness of the board. Serious conflicts in interests and goals as well as in concerns about the basic patterns of governance and about the orientation of programs within the schools exist among various groups within the community. When hundreds of thousands of black residents of most major cities are functionally outside of the dominant policy and social system, it is folly to claim that a white-middle-class school board represents their interests. No longer can school boards assume that the interests they represent are the interests of the entire community. These weaknesses of the board make it increasingly dependent on the superintendent.[15]

Superintendents and teachers in the past perceived education in much the same way, and generally they had similar personal and professional goals and aspirations. They attended the same teachers colleges and belonged to the same professional associations. But conflicting and different perceptions about education have developed in recent years as professional organizations of teachers and administrators have developed different goals. Conflicting interests between the two groups have been recognized, and teachers have even started to exclude administrators from their professional organizations. The traditional organizational view of administration is apparently still quite strong in the beliefs and attitudes of many superintendents, and as a result they often react as if perplexed or hurt by the

[14]For a discussion as to the nature of school districts and the role of school board members see: L. Harmon Zeigler and M. Kent Jennings, *Governing American Schools: Political Interaction in Local School Districts*, (North Scituate, Massachusetts: Duxbury Press, 1974).

[15]Harold W. Pfautz, "The Black Community, the Community School, and the Socialization Process," in *Community Control of Schools*, ed. Henry M. Levine (Washington, D.C.: The Brookings Institution, 1972), pp. 20–30; Alan A. Altshuler, *Community Control: The Black Demand for Participation in Large American Cities* (New York: Pegasus, 1970); and Leonard I. Fein, *The Ecology of the Public Schools: An Inquiry into Community Control* (New York: Pegasus, 1971).

increasing teacher militancy for more of a voice in educational policy-making.[16]

Superintendents' power comes largely from their professional expertise and the nature of the position they hold. School boards and citizens alike look to the superintendent for answers to educational questions. The status that the superintendent has both locally and nationally, as well as in professional circles, buttresses his strategic position. Since the superintendent devotes full time to school matters and all information about the schools passes through his office, he has greater power than either the board or the teachers. By withholding or disclosing information at appropriate times, he can greatly influence school policies. The increased state and federal activity in education has also strengthened the superintendent's power, since the superintendent and his staff are normally the only ones with the required knowledge about state and federal programs and the expertise for submitting grant proposals.[17]

A number of developments in recent years, however, have weakened the superintendent's position. Bureaucratization of educational administration in the larger systems is one factor that has lessened the superintendent's influence in policymaking. In many of the larger educational systems, large staffs of main office administrators are able to develop their own bases of influence either because of their expertise or because of tenure provisions. They become key participants in every decision-making area of the school and in many instances are the major determiners of school policy.[18] Similarly, the development of teacher organizations and collective negotiations has also tended to lessen the superintendent's influence in school policies.[19] Finally, the increasing community conflict over schools caused by the civil rights movement and the increasing pluralism of school districts have opened the system to a host of new groups and have tended to lessen the superintendent's influence in policymaking.[20]

[16]For example, see Thomas G. Pullen, "Superintendents' Authority Underminded?" *American School Board Journal*, November 1966, pp. 12–15; and Robert Freeborn, "Local School Boards and Superintendents," *Phi Delta Kappan*, February 1968, pp. 346–48.

[17]Roald F. Campbell, "Federal Impact on Board's Decisions," *School Board Journal*, March 1967, pp. 38–43; *cf.* Zeigler and Jennings, *Governing American Schools*, pp. 150–55.

[18]Marilyn Gittell, "Professionalism and Public Participation in Educational Policy-Making: New York City, a Case Study," *Public Administration Review*, September 1967, pp. 245–46.

[19]Rosenthal, *Pedagogues and Power: Teacher Groups in School Politics*, pp. 19–20.

[20]Gittell, *"Professionalism and Public Participation,"* p. 250; *cf.* Robert L. Carin, *The Politics of Desegregation* (Garden City, N.Y.: Anchor Books, 1969), pp. 21–23.

Ideologies of Educational Professionals.   Still another within put that influences the character of educational policymaking is the system of beliefs held by professional educators about politics and education. Educators have been notably successful in developing and conveying to others a set of ideological doctrines indicating that education is a unique governmental service that must be "kept out of politics." These beliefs have given them considerable autonomy and insulation from public pressures. As a result, the policymaking processes in a school district differ from the policymaking processes in other local governmental units. Governments of school systems are relatively closed to many of the demands of the community. In Figure 3–2 this is represented by a broken line around the school district circle, which appears as a buffer to demands from outside the system.

The set of ideological doctrines that has so influenced the structure and functioning of school governments includes a number of related beliefs. The principle of localism has been one of the fundamental tenets of educators. Since public education had its roots in local political action, a folklore was created that idealized local school districts as the last stronghold of direct democracy in American public affairs. This belief has been sustained in part by the idea that the local school district "belongs" to the citizens, ignoring the fact that the district is legally an agency of the state.[21]

A corollary of this idealized view of the local school district is that the district is composed atomistically of individual citizens endowed with equal political power, each acting on his own. Elections of school board members, according to this view, are examples of equalitarian democracy. Thus nonpartisan elections are justified, since there is no need for political parties in school government. Similarly, at-large elections rather than elections from wards or precincts are defended for school board members in many areas, since the community is viewed as an organic whole.

According to the same rationale, there is a denial of interest group activity in school governments. In fact, for the purpose of the school program, there is even a denial of the existence of conflict between major socioeconomic sectors in the community. That is, regardless of ethnic, racial, religious, economic, or political differences and group conflicts in other areas of life, education need not, and should not if it could, recognize or legitimize those differences by differentiating its educational program for various sections and classes.[22]

[21]Roald F. Campbell, "The Folklore of Local School Control," *School Review*, Spring 1959, pp. 1–11; *cf.* Martin, *Government and the Suburban School*; and Philip Meranto, *School Politics in the Metropolis* (Columbus, Ohio: Charles E. Merrill, Books, Inc., 1970), pp. 35–38.
[22]Robert H. Salisbury, "School and Politics in the Big City," *Harvard Educational Review*, Summer 1967, pp. 410–12.

In part, these beliefs grew out of the primary quest of schoolmen to keep politics out of schools, that is, away from the influence of nonschool officials. The political arena was seen as patently corrupt and marked by conflicts of a myriad of "special interests," so they emphasized that education was different from other governmental activities and should be separate from other units of local government. Supporting arguments of the uniqueness of education were developed around the theme that the growth and development of our youth was too important a function to have to compete with other less important local governmental services. Furthermore, development and education of children was more complicated and required special professional skills by teachers of high moral character; the average person, the "layman," was not competent to make judgments on the technical aspects of education.[23]

The net result of these beliefs, which educators sponsored and which the public has largely accepted, was the evolution of a special constitutional arrangement for American schools. The governance of education is conducted by special independent school districts in 95 percent of the school districts in the nation, and the politics of education, especially at the local district level, has been greatly affected by these special provisions.[24] Perhaps the most visible effect of the special school governmental system was the almost complete elimination of overt political party activity in school districts' affairs and the great influence of the professional on educational policymaking. School district politics, therefore, remains relatively closed to many community demands and tends to be a politics of insiders.[25]

Organizational Structure and Formal Rules of School Systems. The organizational structure and formal rules of school systems are still other internal factors that influence educational policymaking. With little variation, school districts follow a consistent organizational pattern for the allocation of responsibility and the flow of authority. The school board, elected or appointed, is viewed as the legal policymaking body for the school district, which is an agent of the state. The superintendent as chief school officer is seen as responsible to the board from which his authority flows. He acts as the sole formal organizational link between the board

[23]In 1937 Charles Beard presented the historical and philosophical reasons for the independence of school districts in what may still be the finest brief on support of public education. See Educational Politics Commission, *The Unique Function of Education in American Democracy* (1937).

[24]Morrel Hall, *Provisions Governing Membership on Local Boards of Education,* U.S. Department of Health, Education, and Welfare, Office of Education Bulletin 13, 1957, p. 66; *cf.* Alpheus L. White, *Local School Boards: Organization and Practice,* U.S. Department of Health, Education, and Welfare, 1962.

[25]Meranto, *School Politics in the Metropolis,* pp. 4–12; Zeigler and Jennings, *Governing American Schools,* pp. 242–54.

and the rest of the school organization. In the administrative structure beneath the superintendent, there are usually a number of building principals who are responsible to the superintendent for the operation of their buildings. The principal is usually the sole link between the central office and his building, despite the functional pattern of organization that often complements the geographic pattern in many of the larger schools. The functional pattern may be seen in organizational divisions, such as directors or coordinators of elementary schools, vocational and technical programs, personnel, and buildings. While both types of organizational structures will be present in large school districts, the presence of the functional structure seldom changes the basic pattern of unit control. At the bottom of the hierarchical structure, the teacher exerts the same type of control over his classroom.[26]

The organizational arrangements of the school system influence educational policymaking in a number of ways. For one thing, the policy dialogue within the school organization takes place among parties who are unequal in rank and consequently unequal in authority over final decisions. The fact that authority in school is hierarchically structured is important in shaping the nature of school policies. Students obviously have little power to influence school decisions, whereas the politically elected or appointed school board has considerable power in the policymaking process. Other parties in the school recognize the legitimacy of the board to exercise power in policymaking. Furthermore, because the board is the symbol of public control, there is a strong tendency for professional school personnel to tailor their recommendations to fit what are believed to be board members' views on many policy issues.

Although the board is recognized as being influential in the policymaking process, the superintendent is normally more powerful. The board has legitmacy and formal authority, but the superintendent has tools of decision making and organizational control, as well as knowledge, information, professional stature, time, duration in office, staff assistance, and unity. The superintendent is therefore more like a leader rather than a servant of the school board. He is not merely the "hired hand" to carry out the board's policies, but, on the contrary, he is at least as much a policymaker as he is a manager, and on some issues he has an almost irresistible voice in school affairs.[27]

The superintendent's influence reflects not only the strength of his position but also the weakness of other parties in the school organization.

[26]Frank W. Lutz and Laurence Iannaccone, *Understanding Educational Organizations: A Field Study Approach* (Columbus, Ohio: Charles E. Merrill Books, Inc., 1969), pp. 29–30; Zeigler and Jennings, *Governing American Schools*, pp. 14–15.
[27]Kerr, "School Board as an Agency of Legitimation," pp. 34–59.

The school board, as has been seen, lacks a visible constituency to support it and tie it to the community. This lack of constant input from the community tends to cause a feeling of alienation from the public, which leads to attempts to conceal policy issues from the public. Thus cut off from the community, school board members grow dependent on the superintendent and tend to become adapted to the professional viewpoint. Under these conditions school boards chiefly perform the function of legitimizing the policies of the professionals to the community, rather than representing the various segments of the community to the school administration. This is particularly true with regard to policies affecting educational programs or school-centered issues.[28]

Teachers and teacher organizations also have serious weaknesses. Until recently teachers were considered to be impotent in regard to educational policymaking and had little say in the formulation of school policy. Identification of teachers with professional values held by administrators and the stress of teacher organizations upon professionalism rather than upon group power left teachers largely dependent on the superintendent and the board. Even though teachers and teacher organizations have become more militant in the past decade and teachers have gained more influence in such areas of policymaking as salaries and personnel, teachers still have little influence on most school policies.[29]

Recognition of this lack of power in school policymaking is shown in the answers given by leaders of teacher organizations in five major American cities—New York, Boston, Chicago, San Francisco, and Atlanta. Table 3–1 shows the perceptions of power held by the leaders of these teacher groups: In most areas of policymaking—policy in general, school organization, personnel policy, and curriculum and instruction—administrators, that is, the superintendent and the headquarters bureaucracy along with the board, are seen as having the most influence. Teachers are seen as having little influence in any of the areas of policymaking except salary and personnel, and in several cities they are seen as having little influence even in these areas.[30]

The organizational structure also affects formal communications within the organizations and influences the types of demands that originate in the system. The school structure results in a "pinching" of communications links, with the persons at the points of linkage acting as filters to commu-

[28]Rosenthal, "Pedagogues and Power," *Urban Affairs Quarterly*, September 1966, pp. 83–102, reprinted in *Governing Education: A Reader on Politics, Power and Public School Policy*, pp. 291–313.

[29]Warner Bloomberg, Jr., and Morris Sunshine, *Suburban Power Structures and Public Education: A Study of Values, Influence, and Tax Effort* (Syracuse, N.Y.: Syracuse University Press, 1963), pp. 137–42.

[30]Rosenthal, *Pedagogues and Power: Teacher Groups in School Politics*, p. 52.

Table 3–1 The Distribution of Power: Rank Orders and Power Categories*

Policy Domain and Participant	New York		Boston		Chicago		San Francisco		Atlanta	
	RO	CY	RO	CY	RO	CY	RO	CY	RO	CY
Policy in General										
Superintendent	1	H	2	M	1	H	1.5	H	1	H
Board of Education	2	H	1	H	2	M	1.5	H	2	H
HQ's Bureaucracy	3	M	3	M	3	M	3	M	3	M
Mayor and Officials	4	M	4	M	4	M	4	M	6	L
School Principals	5	L	5	L	6	L	5	L	4.5	L
Teacher Organizations	6	L	6	L	5	L	6	L	4.5	L
Salary Policy										
Superintendent	4	M	3	M	1	H	2	M	1	H
Board of Education	3	M	2	H	2	M	1	H	2	H
HQ's Bureaucracy	5	L	4	M	4	L	5	L	4	M
Mayor and Officials	1	H	1	H	3	M	3	L	6	L
School Principals	6	L	6	L	6	L	6	L	5	L
Teacher Organizations	2	M	5	M	5	L	4	L	3	M
School Organization										
Superintendent	1	H	2	H	1	H	1	H	1	H
Board of Education	2	H	1	H	2	M	2	H	2	H
HQ's Bureaucracy	3	M	3	M	3	M	3	M	3	M
Mayor and Officials	4	L	4.5	L	4	L	5	L	6	L
School Principals	5.5	L	4.5	L	5	L	4	L	4	L
Teacher Organizations	5.5	L	6	L	6	L	6	L	5	L
Personnel Policy										
Superintendent	1	H	1	H	1	H	1	H	1	H
Board of Education	2.5	M	2	H	3	M	2.5	M	2	M
HQ's Bureaucracy	2.5	M	3	H	2	M	2.5	M	3	M
Mayor and Officials	6	L	5.5	L	4.5	L	5	L	6	L
School Principals	5	L	4	L	6	L	4	M	4	L
Teacher Organizations	4	L	5.5	L	4.5	L	6	L	5	L
Curriculum & Instruction										
Superintendent	1.5	H	1	H	1	H	1	H	1	H
Board of Education	3.5	M	3	M	3	M	3	M	3	M
HQ's Bureaucracy	1.5	H	2	H	2	H	2	M	2	M
Mayor and Officials	5	L	6	L	5.5	L	6	L	6	L
School Principals	3.5	M	4	M	4	M	4	M	4	M
Teacher Organizations	6	L	5	L	5.5	L	5	L	5	L

*Column headings RO and CY are abbreviations for rank order and category. Categories are: high (H), medium (M), and low (L), which are based on the "power assessments" of teacher leaders in each city.

nications. Lutz and Iannaccone have pictured this as shown in Figure 3–3.

Communications between teachers or principals and the school board are discouraged except where they are channeled through the administration. It is an atypical district where teachers and principals attend school board meetings and are invited to make statements on matters affecting

Figure 3–3 Chart of Organization Showing Filter Power

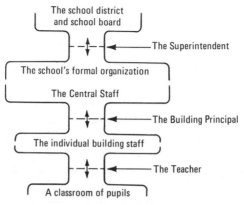

Source: Frank W. Lutz and Laurence Iannaccone, Understanding Educational Organizations: A Field Study Approach *(Columbus, Ohio: Charles E. Merrill Books, Inc., 1969), p. 31.*

school policies. The more usual pattern is the "channel-conscious district" where care is taken not to short-cut the superintendent and only the superintendent represents the school bureaucracy before the board. Teacher organizations, however, are now frequently challenging the right to communicate directly with boards about salaries and personnel matters,[31] and in many communities teachers are becoming politically active and are seeking to influence elections of school board members thought to be in favor of their positions.[32]

The formal communications pattern in turn affects the informal communications, as the organizational arrangement tends to isolate teachers from interaction with other educational personnel except those within their own school, and they are even to a degree isolated within the school because of work assignments and rules. Informal interactions and communications with others in the educational system are hindered by the organizational structure and administrative rules of the school system.[33]

This pattern of communications affects the types of internal demands, how they are presented, and where decisions are made in the organization. Basically, there seem to be three kinds of demands that originate within the system: representation of personal needs from employees of the school organization, proposals for changes in organizational arrangements and

[31]Joseph M. Crowen, "The Politics of School Board Elections," *Phi Delta Kappan,* June 1965, pp. 505–8; *cf.* Arthur F. Corey, "Educational Power and the Teaching Profession," *Phi Delta Kappan,* February 1968, pp. 331–34.

[32]Lutz and Iannaccone, *Understanding Educational Organizations,* pp. 30–32.

[33]David Minar, "Educational Decision-Making in Suburban Communities" U.S. Office of Education Cooperative Research Project No. 2440 (Evanston, Ill.: Northwestern University, 1966), p. 42.

institutional decision making, and proposals for changes in technical aspects of the educational programs.[34] These internal demands, with the exception of the demands of employees which are more and more being presented by teacher organizations, are dominated by the superintendent. The superintendent is the major controller of what demands will be presented about changes in organizational structure or in the educational programs. As the sole formal link between the school organization and the board, the superintendent and his central headquarters staff become the key decision center in the school system. The superintendent and the central headquarters staff because of their strategic position in the administration structure and the control over administrative information hold much of the power to make decisions in such areas as planning and development, budgeting, personnel selection, salary increases, and racial integration. Customary procedures such as established financial formulas and personnel policies help shape these decisions, as do inputs from the community, but other parties in the school bureaucracy normally have little influence in these decisions. Few teachers participate in school decisions other than what happens in their classrooms. Even in curriculum development, the most obvious area in which their expertise would be helpful, the central headquarters' curriculum agency seldom involves teachers in its programs of curriculum development, with the exception of a few high school specialists. The actual implementation of curriculum is dependent on the action of principals and classroom teachers, and how the curriculum is implemented may vary considerably from school to school. But this is often the only involvement of teachers or principals in curriculum decisions.[35]

Demands pertaining to personal needs of employees also are influenced to a large degree by the superintendent through the bureaucratic reward system. Public school personnel practices, including such aspects as salary increases and promotion procedures, are means by which superintendents manage the demands of personnel. However, as has already been mentioned, employees have become more militant in presenting demands, and more and more these demands are being made by group representation of teacher organizations or unions. Negotiated salary schedules have largely replaced the system of personal negotiations between the teachers and the superintendent. In this respect, the growing power of teacher organizations has modified the policy process in many school districts.

School rules and procedures as well as the attitudes of professional school personnel also influence who will attend school. Teachers and prin-

[34]Gittell, "Professionalism and Public Participation," pp. 237–51.
[35]*Ibid.*

cipals who are responsible for the control and discipline of students may give grades or apply sanctions in such ways as to discourage some students from attending school. The principal, particularly, with his authority to suspend students or even to recommend permanent expulsion, plus the responsibility for enforcing compulsory attendance laws for students in his school area, may carry out these duties in such a way as to effectively keep students from attending school. It is frequently charged that many of the so-called dropouts are actually driven out of the school by teachers and principals who are unsympathetic toward students from lower socioeconomic classes or racial groups.[36]

Other demands on the school arise out of conditions in the local community, and we shall next examine these community inputs.

[36]Bidwell, "The School as a Formal Organization," pp. 988–92; *cf.* David Spencer, "The Anatomy of Conflict: Claims of the Parties at Interest," *The Struggle for Power in the Public Schools: Proceedings of the Sixth Annual Conference*, National Committee for Support of the Public Schools, Washington, D.C., March 17–19, 1968, pp. 25–28.

chapter four

Community Inputs on Local Education

Many demands on the school system come from the community at large. These inputs on the educational system come to the schools from actors in the environment. The actors include parents and other clients of the schools, interest groups, governmental officials in the legislative, executive, and judicial branches, administrators in other administrative agencies, the mass media, and interested citizens. The inputs these actors provide to the school system include demands for educational programs and services, political support or opposition, and the resources of tax funds, legal authority, and citizens' willingness to accept employment in the school organization. The nature of the inputs depends on the dynamic interaction of such environmental factors as the political and cultural values, the socioeconomic characteristics of the community, and the governmental system.

Figure 4–1 attempts to portray visually the community inputs on the local educational system. Inputs from parents and interest groups are represented by the use of circles growing out of the community circle. The broken lines between these and the school organization represent the interaction of these groups. This figure also shows the linkage between the school board and the informal power structure of the community. As we have seen, board members are normally recruited from the ranks of the professional and business groups and tend to hold the dominant community values. They are either members of the community leadership structure or at least they socially interact with it and, therefore, reflect dominant community views. They, in turn, represent demands of the dominant community.

Parental Inputs

Except for students, parents are the most directly affected clientele group making demands on schools. Individually and collectively they make de-

Figure 4–1   Inputs on the Local Educational System

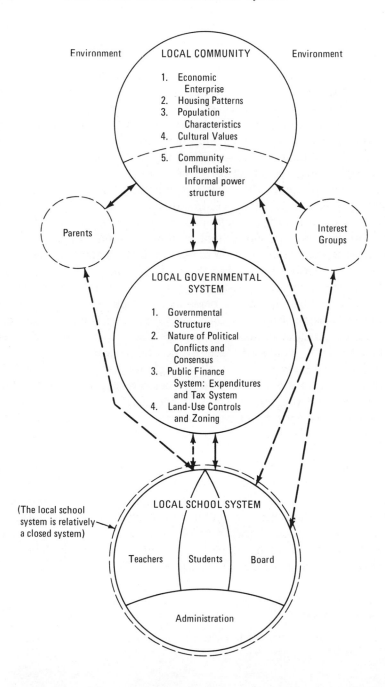

mands on the school system when they or their children feel that they have in some sense been wronged or deprived of their rights. Grievance-inspired efforts to change (and in some cases to protect) the status quo are made in such areas as racial desegregation, pedagogical innovations, student discipline, and school district units and boundaries, as well as in other areas of school administration. A perennial source of grievance is the handling of "controversial issues" in the classroom. Such demands and the fear of parental wrath apparently act as a strong behavioral constraint on school boards, administrators, and teachers.[1]

Parents have two courses of possible action when they are dissatisfied with school procedures or when they have complaints about the school. They may deal directly with their offspring and attempt to undercut or mediate what transpired at school. This method is used most frequently by parents who disagree with what is being taught in classes but do not feel that the issues at stake are vital or that they can effectively challenge the school without negative sanctions or reprisals. An alternative mode of attack is to deal directly with school personnel. Unilaterally, parents may seek redress of their grievances by presenting their demands to teachers or administrators, or even to the school board. This approach for presenting demands is much more frequently used by better-educated parents who feel secure in dealing with school personnel. Parents from the lower socio-economic groups, regardless of their grievances and their aspirations for their children, are not as apt to challenge the assigned authority represented by the better-educated teachers and administrators.[2]

Finally, if a parent feels strongly enough about a matter he may take corporate action, that is, join with other persons or groups and challenge the actions before the board, before the courts, or in school elections. Most parental demands never reach this stage, and an exceedingly small fraction of such demands wind their way to the corporate or public stage of the political process.[3]

Although most parental demands do not reach the corporate or public stage, evidence indicates that there is increasing disagreement between school administrators and parents as to the part parents should play in school policy. Perhaps the most publicized instances of such conflict were the recent confrontations between administrators of New York City public schools and parents whose children attend these schools. The IS 201 (intermediate school) struggle in Harlem revolved around the issue of

[1]Charles Bidwell, "The School as a Formal Organization," in *Handbook of Organizations*, ed. James G. March (Chicago: Rand McNally & Co., 1965), pp. 972–81.
[2]M. Kent Jennings, "Parental Grievances and School Politics," *Public Opinion Quarterly*, Fall 1968, p. 364.
[3]*Ibid.*

whether or not a locally elected board of parents and interested citizens could or could not govern this junior high school and several feeder (elementary) schools. IS 201 parents formed a negotiating committee, elected a board, and locked horns with the official New York City Board of Education and the educational professionals who were threatened by the actions of these parents.[4] The increasing tension between parents and school administrators is further documented in a recent study of a community on the West Coast—San Mateo County, California. This study showed that two-thirds of the parents and one-half of the teachers, but only one-third of the administrators, wanted parents to be more involved than they already are with what is happening to their children in school. Most administrators in San Mateo, as well as in other school districts in the United States, take the position that only they know what is best pedagogically, that school decisions are professional decisions, and that parents should play a supportive role. As they see it, parents should just make sure that the child gets to school on time—well fed and neatly dressed—and then wait for the school's periodic reports to show how well things are going, or wait for an invitation to attend the school on the prepared visiting day during "Education Week" to be told about the important role of the public schools.[5]

The extent to which the school is a closed system withdrawn from certain community demands is also evidenced by the nature of the interaction of parents and parties in the school organization. Even well-educated, middle-class parents who seek to engage in significant school decisions are deterred by either the inertial mass of the school or the aura of professional exclusivity. The atmosphere in school buildings discourages parental presence (visiting days only one or two times a year are prime evidence), and most parents visit the school mainly in response to trouble. Furthermore, carefully drawn boundaries limit what parents or parent organizations may ask of the professionals. PTA members may complain to a school board that does not offer a foreign language or a science in elementary school, but they will rarely ask for research results (or for

[4]Cynthia Parsons, "Schools, Parents at Odds: Harlem's Embattled School," *Christian Science Monitor*, July 10, 1968; cf. Maurice R. Berube and Marilyn Gittell, eds., *Confrontation at Ocean-Hill–Brownsville: The New York School Strikes of 1968* (New York: Frederick A. Praeger, Inc., 1969); and Naomi Levine and Richard Cohen, *Ocean-Hill–Brownsville: A Case History of Schools in Crisis* (New York: Popular Library, 1969).

[5]Parsons, "School, Parents at Odds"; *cf.* Mario Fantini, Marilyn Gittell, and Richard Magot, *Community Control and the Urban School* (New York: Frederick A. Praeger, Inc., 1970); Marilyn Gittell, "Community Control of Education," *Urban Riots: Violence and Social Change*, ed. Robert H. Connery (New York: Random House, Inc., 1969); Zeigler and Jennings, *Governing American Schools*, pp. 120–23; and "Parents vs. Educators: Split Widens Over Schools," *U. S. News & World Report*, January 27, 1975, p. 30.

research to be initiated) on the effectiveness of the school's program. It is tacitly understood that parents are not to ask for such information concerning the school system's criteria for teacher selection or for evidence of aggressiveness or imagination in recruitment of teachers. When such questions are asked, it is considered an encroachment on professional prerogatives, and the information is often safeguarded as being in the professional domain alone. School systems because of these professional attitudes and their widespread acceptance by the public are relatively closed to certain kinds of community demands.[6]

Parents also provide supports for schools. Parent-teacher associations are frequently used by administrators as support groups to help obtain financial and legal resources for the schools. Not only do they raise funds for their individual schools through such projects as school carnivals, they assist the administration in selling bond issues and at times even lobby the legislature in support of school legislation. PTAs and similar groups are typically middle-class organizations and to a large degree are dominated by professional educators, particularly by the school principal. However, they serve a number of other useful functions. For one thing they help mediate community conflict about education and provide a communications link between school administrators and the community. They also serve as a pool of talent from which to recruit future school board members who are interested in education and are acceptable to the professional educators.[7]

Interest Groups

Numerous interest groups in the local community make demands on schools and attempt to influence educational policies. The type and num-

[6]Mario D. Fantini, "Community Control and Quality Education in Urban School Systems," in *Community Control of Schools*, ed. *Henry M. Levin* (Washington, D.C.: The Brookings Institution, 1970), pp. 49–50. Recent HEW regulations growing out of the Poor People's Campaign require the involvement of the poor in programs of the Elementary and Secondary Education Act serving their children. One of these regulations requires local school districts to establish advisory committees to assist in the "planning, operation, and appraisal of a comprehensive compensatory education program: with at least half of the members of the Committee composed of parents of disadvantaged children attending schools receiving programs funded by Title I, ESEA." The purpose of these regulations is to help open the educational system to community demands long ignored and left out. See *Parental Involvement in Title I, ESEA*, U.S. Department of Health, Education, and Welfare, No. OE 72–109, 1972.

[7]See W. W. Wood, "What's *Right* with PTA?" and Alan A. Small, "What's *Wrong* with PTA?" *Phi Delta Kappan*, June 1964, pp. 456–57.

ber of such groups pressuring schools depends on the character of the community, with the more pluralistic communities having a greater variety of groups participating in the policy process. Generally, interest groups placing demands on schools include economic groups such as taxpayers associations and chambers of commerce, as well as other business groups hoping to profit from selling or contracting with the schools; religious and other ideologically oriented groups wanting to use the schools to transmit their particular beliefs; corporate, business, and professional groups interested in having a particular economic or social creed taught; and labor organizations attempting to spread their own gospel as well as to extend educational opportunities to the working classes. Local teacher organizations make demands on schools for more money and more power in educational policymaking. Local universities and philanthropic foundations also at times place demands on local school systems to perform programs in which they have an interest.[8] As has already been seen, there are various types of interest groups, some with well-organized staffs such as taxpayer groups that work the year round on various issues while other groups such as those proposing or opposing certain programs episodically spring up and disappear as soon as interest in the issue subsides. Similarly, there is great fluidity of groups, with some groups arising to counter claims of other groups.

Success of any group in getting its demands met depends on the resources it has at its command, the degree of concurrence between its proposals and the social and political climate of the community, and the status position of the group. Another factor affecting the strength of a group is the internal cohesiveness of the group. Each pressure group consists of a set of interests striving to define as well as achieve organizational goals. Individual group members are not always in harmony with stated goals of the parent organization. The more agreement between individual members' goals and organizational goals, the more cohesive is the group and the more effective it can be in pursuing its goals. The reverse is also true. Groups with little cohesion, no matter how large they may be, are ineffective in the governmental process. PTA groups, for example, have little cohesion, and as a result they are usually ineffective in influencing governmental policy.[9] Taxpayer groups, on the other hand, are usually much more cohesive, and even though they may have fewer members they are more influential in decisions about the expenditures of public funds.

[8]Patricia Cayo, *The American School: A Sociological Analysis* (Englewood Cliffs, N.J.: Prentice-Hall, Inc., 1967), pp. 21–36.
[9]James D. Koerner, *Who Controls American Education?: A Guide for Laymen* (Boston: Beacon Press, 1968), pp. 146–54.

Socioeconomic Inputs
from the Local Community

Numerous other inputs from the local community affect the school system. The number and type of demands and supports for schools depends
on conditions within the community. The interaction of socioeconomic-
political factors, which gives a community its unique character, determines
the types of inputs on the school system, and, in turn, the outputs of the
school help to shape these components of the community.

In a sense, a community is a dynamic system, an ecological complex
consisting of functional relationships among human groups and institutions
that share a common living space. The mix of socioeconomic factors—
basically reflected in the community's industry, housing, and population—
is constantly changing. Communities, like people, are forced to adapt to
the environment and are subject to an aging process. Each of these three
socioeconomic factors, according to Forrester, is subject to constant
change, as Figure 4–2 attempts to show.[10] The internal system of enterprise, for example, changes through several stages. At the upper left of the
figure, new-enterprise units are created. The rate at which they are created
depends on a number of variables, and schools are one of the major
causal factors. Principally as a result of time and aging, the new enterprise
shifts to the category of mature business. After the further passage of
years, mature businesses age into the category of declining industry and
still later are demolished and disappear. The flow from one category of
business activity to the next depends not only on time but on conditions in
the entire community system.[11]

The middle subsystem of Figure 4–2 represents the construction,
aging, and demolition of housing. Premium housing, associated with the
managerial-professional population, is constructed on the left. After an aging
time and depending on the need for premium housing, the premium housing declines into the worker-housing category. In addition, worker housing
is constructed directly without passing through the premium-housing category. Worker housing ages and declines into the underemployed-housing
category. The rate of obsolescence of housing again depends on a number
of interrelated factors in the community, but the quality of neighborhood
schools is one of the key factors.[12]

The third subsystem in Figure 4–2 represents three categories of popu-

[10]Jay W. Forrester, *Urban Dynamics* (Cambridge, Mass.: The M.I.T. Press,
1969), pp. 14–17.
[11]*Ibid.*, p. 19.
[12]*Ibid.*, pp. 14–17.

lation—managerial-professional, labor, and underemployed. Each category has an internal birthrate and there is also an upward as well as a downward mobility of people, and the rate of such changes is dependent on a number of factors in the community—and again schools are a vital factor in the rate of such changes and in the development of human resources.[13]

Although Figure 4–2 does not show the possible interactions of the three socioeconomic subsystems, it is obvious that there is a close interrelationship and that the change in any one area affects the others. The relative attractiveness of a community is dependent on all of these factors. The types and number of people and enterprises that move into or away from a community depends on its relative attractiveness. Schools are vitally affected by the community, that is, the demands and supports they receive from the community are dependent on these types of changes.[14] Schools, in turn, help determine to a large degree the relative attractiveness of the community. For instance, a community's ability to use some of its land for middle- or upper-income family housing or to attract new enterprises depends on a number of things, but especially on the quality of the schools that serve the community.

The dynamic nature of American communities is readily evident. Forces of urbanization since almost the beginning of our nation and especially since the Civil War have caused a continuous shift of population from rural to urban places. Since World War II the major population and economic trends associated with urbanization have changed significantly, with the dominant flow of people, jobs, and economic activities gravitating toward suburban communities rather than toward the central cities.

These population and economic changes have had a major impact on schools. Suburban schools have been seriously affected by the rapid growth of a body of persons who are largely homogeneous in socioeconomic characteristics and whose life-style is the child-oriented family. Schools become the key public service of local government for suburbanites, and much of the interest in community affairs in suburban communities centers on schools. As a result, a much larger percentage of total local expenditures goes for education in suburban communities than in other types of communities, and the schools often become the subject of bitter community conflict.[15]

Schools in the central city have faced still different problems because of recent community changes. Central cities have attracted the many-childrened, low-income families from rural areas, many of whom belong

[13]*Ibid.*
[14]*Ibid.*, p. 18.
[15]Philip Meranto, *School Politics in the Metropolis* (Columbus, Ohio: Charles E. Merrill Books, Inc., 1970), pp. 37–38.

Figure 4–2   Model of the Dynamic Structure of a Community

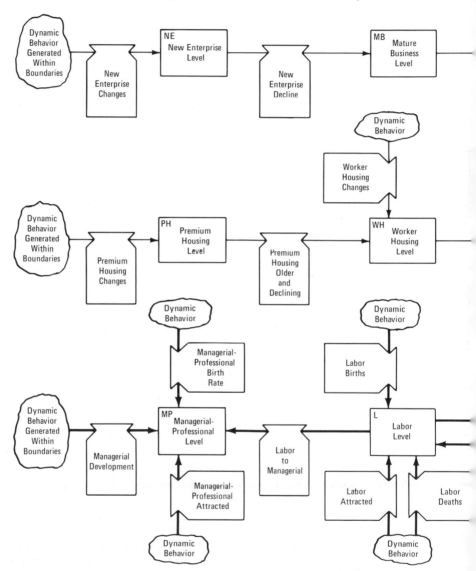

*The major levels (rectangles) and rates (value symbols) for the model of a community.

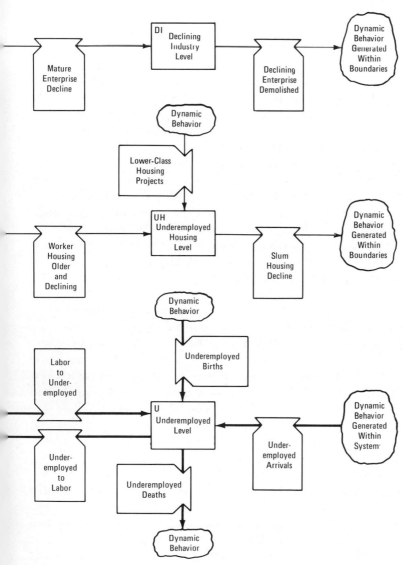

Source: Jay W. Forrester, Urban Dynamics *(Cambridge, Mass.: The M.I.T. Press, 1969), p. 16.*

to racial and ethnic minority groups—blacks, Latin-Americans, Indians, and Puerto Ricans. As they have moved into the city, many of the white middle- and upper-income families have left the city. The flight of the whites to the suburbs has resulted in an increasing proportion of blacks and other minority groups in the schools and has not only complicated the problems of integration but filled these schools with educationally disadvantaged students, thus lowering the quality of the schools. In turn, the relative attractiveness of cities has plummeted, and the exodus of white middle and upper classes has been accelerated. City schools have experienced a declining tax base as the whites have fled the city, and their financial plight has been aggravated by minority students' needs for expensive compensatory educational programs.[16]

Rural districts have also experienced dislocation as a result of the dynamics of our society. Their problems, unlike those of the cities and suburbs, however, have centered around the steadily declining population and economic base. School consolidation has been forced upon these communities as a means of justifying an educational program. In all American communities, the changing socioeconomic conditions have continuously placed new demands on schools and have radically modified the type of supports available to them.

Community Values as Inputs. The community, however, is more than just an ecological system; it is also a social order. Members of a human community not only reside and act together, they feel and think together. Communities have a social-psychological dimension that is expressed in terms of a common identity, or "we-feeling," and this consensus results in the self-conscious and willed social action of individuals and organizations of persons in the social system. The common values, beliefs, and traditions, that is, the local political culture, are an essential part of the community and act as an input on all local subsystems, including the schools.[17]

The values, beliefs, and traditions of the local citizenry determine what school governments can do and how they will do it. As has already been seen from Elazar's typology of the various political subcultures in the United States, localities in different political cultures view politics and what is expected of government differently. Schools, particularly because of the decentralized nature of our educational system and the prevalence of the ideology of local control, are greatly influenced by the values, beliefs, and prejudices of the dominant local community.

[16]*Ibid.*, pp. 59–69.
[17]Harold W. Pfautz, "The Black Community, the Community School, and the Socialization Process," in *Community Control of Schools,* ed. Henry M. Levine (Washington, D.C.: The Brookings Institution, 1972), pp. 16–17.

The school board is linked to the informal power structure of the community. In fact, the socioeconomic character of a community as well as the political culture greatly determines who are community influentials. But the dominant values and beliefs of a community are not only transmitted through community influentials, they permeate the local society and are expressed in local newspapers as well as in all communications of the citizenry. School personnel are forced to be sensitive to these dominant community views, and school personnel actually become so socialized in the dominant local values that they seldom question them.

The influence of the local political culture on schools is evident in a number of ways. Local schools, as a myriad of research has documented, reflect the dominant local prejudices of the community. Local views on integrated housing, for example, affect such school policies as how to draw school attendance zones and where to locate new schools. Despite the law of the land, many schools because of local attitudes still provide separate and unequal education as a means of keeping down many groups who try for higher places. Resistance to the inputs from the black community as to what should be taught, who should teach, and how the schools should be run is obvious in many central cities, even though cities have changed and in many instances have become predominantly black communities with different educational needs and values. Also, dominant economic values and activities in local communities are favored by local schools, as is illustrated by interdistrict expenditures on various schools and the fact that courses designed to aid a particular sector of the economy may be continued long after they are required to meet the vocational needs of most youth. The numerous vocational agricultural courses still being offered in many districts despite the drastic decline in the need for farmers are one example of local support for certain economic values.

Schools not only reflect the dominant values, beliefs, and prejudices of the community, they are in part instrumental in preserving, defining, and transmitting these views to new generations. Local schools help create the cultural and political values and beliefs of the community, and educational attitudes influence the response to various kinds of community demands.

Community demands for technical and vocational programs have generally been resisted by professional educators and much of the middle-class community because these type of programs do not have the status appeal of the college preparatory courses. As a result, most students regardless of their academic talents and interests are forced to follow a curriculum mainly developed for those planning to go to college. Public schools have also resisted expansion of certain programs beyond the traditional K to 12 (kindergarten to senior high). Head Start programs for culturally disadvantaged children in the three-year-old and four-year-old category, for

example, have had to be sponsored in many communities by agencies other than the public schools. The same type of professional resistance has confronted certain adult educational programs and programs for out-of-school youth. Public educators almost universally wanted to have nothing to do with the program to salvage the "dropouts," and the federal government therefore had to contract with private companies to conduct the Job Corps educational centers.[18]

Conflict between Parochial and Cosmopolitan Values

The parochial or local views of schools have been under continuous attack because of the dramatic changes in American society since World War II. The postwar societal changes have radically challenged the premise of the past that the school's main task is that of training a youngster to live as an adult in the local community of his birth. Localism has increasingly been challenged as not being able to develop the necessary national perspective to meet the rising national and international problems. As a result there has been a mounting conflict between the local schools and their supporters and the other levels of government representing different groups and more cosmopolitan values.

Evidence of this change, in part, is that states have more and more been called upon to provide resources and leadership for education. As states have provided more of the funds for education, the role of the state in educational policymaking has been enhanced and has resulted in increasing conflict with local districts. Consolidation of districts is one obvious area where local and state goals frequently collide. A local rural community's desire to keep the school in spite of declining enrollments conflicts with the state's broader goal of offering quality education to all youth in the most economically feasible way. Thus there is frequently intense conflict between the local citizenry and the state officials responsible for enforcing consolidation policies. This conflict itself and the way the community adapts to it is an input to the policymaking processes. There are numerous other areas where the inputs of the state force local districts to change local practices and eventually lead to conflict.

The most dramatic change in the governance of education in recent years has been the vigorous entrance by the federal government into educational policymaking. As the federal policies have attempted to carry out national goals and ideals, they have frequently conflicted with the parochial views of local communities. The most heated conflict between the

[18]*Ibid.*, pp. 20–25.

local schools and the federal government has occurred over the racial integration of schools, and this conflict has obviously affected local educational policies. Also, the host of educational programs that Congress enacted in the mid-1960s reflected mainly the interest of urban-oriented groups which previously had been largely unsuccessful on the state and local levels. Major emphasis of the federal programs was given to urban problems of poverty, civil rights, vocational education—problems of national concern which affected the urban areas most acutely. These programs in many respects have challenged the dominant views held in many local school communities and have resulted in various degrees of conflict between the two levels of government.

Inputs from Local Governments

Still other inputs into the school system come from local governments. Despite the insulation of public schools from much of the local partisan politics, they are special district governments created by state statutes and a part of the local political system. Many actions of other units of government, as well as the general political climate of the community, vitally affect schools, and in turn, the actions of school districts influence the other units of local government. Many of the conflicts in school politics spill over into the community and vice versa.

In the past the various units of local government could go much their own way. Schools educated children, counties had basic functions, such as providing welfare, cities furnished the traditional housekeeping services, such as cleaning streets, keeping sewers, providing water, and so forth, and the interrelationships among these governments were not readily apparent in the community. Any one level of local government made few demands on any other level. Seldom did officials from these different units get together to discuss common problems. Today, as a result of the increasing complexity of our urban society, the focus of local government has shifted toward the substantive problems of people, such as poverty, inadequate housing, health, unequal employment opportunities, racial conflict, and community development. Local governments are called upon not only to function in the traditional areas, but to meet these new and more urgent problems. As a result, the present responsibilities of the various local governments are not so clear cut.

In metropolitan areas, particularly, fundamental changes are under way, and schools are being compelled to expand their roles to help meet the complex urban needs. It is increasingly recognized that mitigation or amelioration of the multifaceted problems of racial segregation, discrimination, poverty, inadequate housing, and unequal employment opportunities

requires new modes of institutional cooperation and innovative responses on the part of schools as well as other societal agencies.[19] Schools are being pressured to become one of the frontline soldiers in the War on Poverty. As a result of the increase in the volume of state and federal aid, schools have been pressed to undertake many of the antipoverty programs, such as Head Start, Upward Bound, and Work Study, and programs for feeding hungry children.[20]

Similarly, schools are being pressed to become a source of health and welfare services for the neighborhood. The number of schoolchildren requiring health services has grown tremendously. Advocates for schools' assuming a greater role in solving these problems argue that this is a logical development because when a child comes into the school disabled, partially sighted, mentally disturbed, or mentally retarded, the educators must have some orderly way in which to diagnose and help that student. For this reason a number of psychiatrists, psychologists, social workers, and others with specialized training have already been drawn into the service of many public school systems. It is argued that the public school is uniquely adapted to perform these health and welfare functions. Located in the neighborhood in which its students live, the public school can be utilized for almost any form of service that extends to the children who are a part of the school, and also to the families from which they come. It is proposed, therefore, that schools or school complexes be built that will house these other social, health, and welfare services for the neighborhood.[21]

Schools are also being called upon to lessen the hostility of race relations. Planning of schools was formerly of concern only to school people, but today these school policies influence how land in a community is developed and used and may complicate the problems of segregation. Thus, location of new schools affects the peace of the city and determines the level of racial isolation and tension; and even the stability of the central city is affected by the location of schools, since the inward or outward migration of people is affected by the placement of schools.[22]

---

[19]James D. Kelly and Michael D. Usdan, "Urban Politics and the Public Schools: Myth, Reality, and Response," *Proceedings: New York Teacher's College Conference* (1968), pp. 18–32.

[20]*Ibid.*, p. 18.

[21]James Alsen, "Challenge of the Poor to the Schools," *Phi Delta Kappan,* October 1965, pp. 79–84; *cf.* "Problems of Urban Education," *Phi Delta Kappan,* March 1967, entire issue.

[22]Homer C. Wadsworth, "A Basis for Cooperation between School Districts and Municipal Governments in Metropolitan Areas," *Proceedings: First Annual Seminar on Intergovernmental Relations* (Lawrence: University of Kansas, 1966), pp. 43–47; *cf.* Luvern L. Cunningham, "A School District and City Government," *American School Board Journal*, December 1960, pp. 9–11.

Much of the controversy engulfing urban school systems throughout the nation arises out of the philosophical argument about what the role of the school can and should be. Many educational leaders question whether the schools should be in the business of social reform as well as in the business of teaching children to read and write. Educators generally do not favor the former. Until some kind of consensus is reached, many public school educators and their disadvantaged urban clients will remain at loggerheads, and the tensions between schoolmen and urban-federal administrators will continue.[23]

Even in the performance of the traditional functions of local governments, there are increasing demands that schools assume greater responsibility for general community problems. Numerous different local governments—cities, counties, and various types of special district governments—have overlapping jurisdiction and serve the same geographic area with different governmental services. Failure of these governments to communicate and coordinate their plans with other units may create serious community problems. For instance, cities zone new areas for residential developments, thereby forcing the school districts to construct new buildings or expand their transportation system. Street construction and changed traffic patterns can conflict with school locations, with resulting safety hazards for schoolchildren. On the other hand, school districts locate new buildings on sites not served by public facilities, thereby forcing cities to construct sewers, waterlines, streets, and bridges. New schools can also stimulate rapid residential development in neighborhoods where municipal services are inadequate.[24]

Today an entire metropolitan area is affected by decisions made by schools, and more and more pressures are being placed upon school districts to join with other units of local governments in attacking these problems. Despite the obvious interdependence of local governments, there is still relatively little communication between schools and other local agencies. Federal grants to schools in metropolitan areas do not have to be approved as being in conformance with metropolitan plans as do grants to all other units of local government in these areas. Thus there has been little planning of regional needs for schools in metropolitan areas; metropolitan councils of governments (COGs) and regional planning agencies have little influence in the planning or location of new schools in the

[23]Kelly and Usdan, "Urban Politics" pp. 18–19, *cf.* Thomas R. Dye, "Urban School Segregation: A Comparative Analysis," in *The Politics of Urban Education,* ed. Marilyn Gittell and Alan G. Hevesi (New York: Frederick A. Praeger, Inc., 1969), pp. 90–92; and Robert J. Haveghurst, *Education in Metropolitan Areas* (Boston: Allyn & Bacon, Inc., 1966), Chap. 3.

[24]Frederick H. Kerr, "Politics and Schools," *National Civic Review,* April 1966, pp. 193–98.

region regardless of the impact of school site selection upon the urban region. In fact, state-created local school districts have provided a convenient means of walling black and poor families into central cities while the more affluent white families have escaped to suburban communities.[25] Instead of joining with other units of government to solve regional problems, schools in some thirty-six states have established regional service centers or media centers to help meet changing educational problems on a regional basis.[26]

Much of the pressure on schools to expand their roles has come from outside groups, especially from governmental officials and administrators at the city and federal levels who are struggling with these problems and who perceive the needs to solve the urban problems differently from school officials. These differences in perception between schoolmen and city and federal officials often create tension and conflict between the various administrative levels.

Conflict over Financing of Schools. Financial pressures on local governments also cause a growing interdependence of governments, as well as increasing the complexity of intergovernmental relations. The property tax is still a major tax of all units of local government, but the revenue base is fractionated and limited in part as a result of organizational separatism in government. The relative ability of localities to deal with their public service needs varies greatly, and there is little correlation between needs and revenues.[27]

Competition for local tax resources has increased in recent years as demands for local services have outpaced the financial abilities of communities. Timing of bond elections by schools and other local governments is often competitively motivated and based on consideration of when other units are to present their issues. Bond issues by any of the overlapping units of local governments may raise the cost of all other local borrowing. Tax peaks caused by simultaneous capital improvements by various local

[25]In January 1972 a federal court in Richmond, Virginia, concluded that the maintenance of such tight little islands for segregated school districts violated the state's obligation to eliminate racially identifiable dual school systems. Bradley v. School Board of the City of Richmond, C.A. No. 3353 (E.D., Va., Jan. 5, 1972), 40 USLW 2446 (Jan. 18, 1972).

[26]*Regional Educational Service Prototypes, Operational Statutory Arrangements and Suggestions for Implementation* (Washington, D.C.: National Education Association, 1967); *cf.* Joseph Green, "The Media Centers Reviewed," *Clearing House*, January 1970, pp. 319–20; and Ira Singer, "A Regional Complex of Supplementary Educational Centers," *Phi Delta Kappan*, November 1965, pp. 142–46.

[27]L. Laszlo Ecker-Racz, "Federal State Fiscal Imbalance: The Dilemma," *Congressional Record*, 89th Cong., 1st sess., August 5, 1968; Vol. III, No. 143; *cf.* Will S. Myers, Jr., "Fiscal Balance in the American Federal System," *State Government*, Winter 1968, pp. 57–64.

governmental units frequently produce taxpayers' revolts against all bond issues or property tax increases. Simply put, the property tax today is inadequate to finance a satisfactory level of governmental service. Because of the fiscal gap between citizens' demands for services and revenues available, local governments have been forced to seek new revenues either in the form of authorization to levy nonproperty taxes or as increases in aid from both the state and federal governments.[28]

The traditional patterns for financing local education particularly are under fire from different directions. One issue is the current fiscal crisis of many school districts, and especially the large city public school systems.[29] Another is the present method of financing schools, which is under widespread attack as providing an inequality of education and thus being in violation of the equal protection clause of the Fourteenth Amendment.[30]

The nature of state and federal demands on local districts will be dealt with in detail in later chapters. This chapter and the preceeding one have attempted to describe the nature of the political system of local education and the types of demands made upon it. We next need to see how the system converts these demands—inputs and within puts—into outputs, that is, policies and actions by the school system.

[28]Alan K. Campbell and Philip Meranto, "The Metropolitan Educational Dilemma: Matching Resources to Needs," *Urban Affairs Quarterly*, September 1966; *cf.* H. Thomas James, "Interdependence in School Finance: The City, the State, and the Nation," *Proceedings: National Conference on School Finance* (Dallas, 1968).

[29]"Crisis in Finance and Governance," *Phi Delta Kappan*, September 1971, entire issue; W. Mondord Barr *et al.*, *Financing Public Elementary and Secondary School Facilities in the United States*, National Education Finance Project, Special Study (Bloomington: Indiana University, 1970), p. 370; Charles U. Daly, ed., *The Quality of Inequality: Urban and Suburban Schools* (Chicago: University of Chicago Center for Policy Study, 1968), p. 160; *Financial Status of the Public Schools* (Washington, D.C.: Committee on Educational Finance, National Education Association, 1970), p. 54.

[30]For an account of the legal attack, see John E. Coons, William H. Clune III, and Stephen D. Sugarman, "Educational Opportunity: A Workable Constitutional Test for State Financial Structures," *California Law Review*, April 1969, p. 307; Paul R. Dimond, "Reform of the Government of Education: A Resolution of the Conflict between 'Integration' and 'Community Control,' " *Wayne Law Review*, Summer 1970, p. 1005; John Silard and Sharon White, "Interstate Inequalities in Public Education: The Case for Judicial Relief under the Equal Protection Clause," *Wisconsin Law Review*, 1 (1970), p. 7; and Philip B. Kurland, "Equal Educational Opportunity: The Limits of Constitutional Jurisprudence Undefined," *University of Chicago Law Review*, Summer 1968, p. 583.

Policymaking
In Local
School Governments

Schools like all systems must adapt to their environment. To get the supports that are essential to their continued existence, systems must meet the demands placed upon them. They must convert inputs into outputs. To this point we have examined the local structural, cultural, and institutional factors affecting educational policymaking. We now turn to the conversion processes, how local schools make decisions and policies.

We shall also examine the policy output of local education to see how it affects the key questions about education—who will attend school, what will be taught, how the educational system will be governed and administered, and how education will be financed. Finally, we shall consider other consequences of local school outputs on the community and nation, as well as on all parties in the system.

Community Politics and the School Board

Popular elections of school board members, the most formal part of the process of articulating demands and expressing popular choices, link the school organization to the community. School elections, however, differ from other elections. The no-politics ideology characteristic of educators has almost completely eliminated any overt political party activity in school district affairs, and the essential functions normally performed by political parties are accomplished in other ways.

Nomination of Board Members. Nomination of school board members is one example of the differences in school elections. School systems have various methods for selecting the slate of candidates to stand for election, many of which have developed as extralegal processes. About 67 percent of school board candidates are nominated either by individual

announcements or by popular petition, while only about 13 percent are nominated by some type of formalized group process such as primary elections, caucuses, or school conventions. Table 5–1 shows the statistical breakdown of school district nominating procedures by regions of the United States.

The ease with which a person can get his name on the ballot would appear to open the door to candidacy for almost any qualified person who might desire to make the race. In practice, however, the guarantees of access often turn out to be illusory. Roscoe Martin's study of suburban school districts showed that local imperatives frequently add requirements concerning class, status, color—and political affiliation—which are unknown to the law. According to Martin, the nominations for election to the school board in Indianapolis (a city of almost half a million) were controlled for thirty years by a self-appointed citizens' committee of fewer than two hundred members. And in a suburban city in upstate New York, metropolitan area nominations were controlled for a like period by the single major industry that dominated the economic life of the community. In both instances the slates normally ran unopposed, and never during the thirty-year period was there a serious challenge to the ruling clique in either city.[1]

Table 5–1   Percentage Distribution of Elected Boards, by Methods Used to Nominate Candidates for Election, by Region

	Total		Nominating Methods					
	Number	Percent	Petition of Qualified Voters	Individual Announcement	Primary Election	Caucus	Convention and Annual School Meeting	Combination of Methods
Total school systems reporting	3,433	100.0	44.1	22.7	8.7	3.1	1.4	20.1
Region:								
Northeast	827	100.0	46.3	4.7	14.1	8.5	1.7	24.7
Northcentral	1,059	100.0	63.4	12.5	1.9	2.5	2.2	17.7
South	649	100.0	33.7	29.0	21.4	.5	1.1	14.3
West	898	100.0	26.8	46.7	2.4	.8	.4	22.3

Taken from Alpheus L. White, Local School Boards: Organization and Practice *(U.S. Department of Health, Education, and Welfare, 1962), p. 10.*

[1]Roscoe C. Martin, *Government and the Suburban School* (Syracuse, N.Y.: Syracuse University Press, 1962), p. 46.

Perhaps the most unique feature of the nominating process for school board members, however, is the role played by the superintendent and the members of the board. In many districts the superintendent plays a major role in the selection of candidates for the school board and may actually "pick" potential community leaders to run for the board. Even when he tries to remain aloof from the mechanics of recruitment and selection, the superintendent's influence is rarely insignificant. Either subtly or by direct exhortation, the superintendent may urge board members in whom he has confidence and whom he respects to stay on the board even when they wish to retire, while by omission he may contribute to the shorter tenure of board members who seem to him less useful to his ends or to those of the school system. He frequently participates formally as a discussant with occasional "veto power" in board meetings about interim appointments, and informally about potential candidates whom board members and other individuals may want to encourage. Tenure of board members to a large degree depends on the superintendent, since any scandal or controversy surrounding his work may reverberate in such a way as to jeopardize the chance of reelection of some or all of the incumbent board members. Thus the superintendent is an actor of substantial importance in the recruitment of board members. The incumbent school board members themselves often exert considerable influence over the nominating process, so much so that in periods of stable school-community relations, the school board may virtually be a self-perpetuating group.[2]

School Board Elections. School electoral politics also are different. For one thing the nonpartisan school elections are held separately from other elections, which tends to reduce community participation in school politics. Turnout for school elections is normally low, and those who vote are mostly citizens immediately and directly interested in the schools—that is, parents with children in the public schools. The lack of citizen involvement in elections is evident from one study of forty-eight suburban communities over a period of five years which found that only 9 percent of the eligible voters voted in school board elections.[3]

The lack of party organizations in school elections affects the nature of electoral politics. Electoral politics for schools tends to be the politics of factions, of pressure groups, of splinter organizations, and of temporary

[2]Joseph M. Cronin, "The Politics of School Board Elections," *Phi Delta Kappan,* June 1965, p. 508; *cf.* Keith Goldhammer, "Community Power Structure and School Board Membership," *School Board Journal,* March 1955, pp. 23–25. Zeigler and Jennings found that board members are a major source of encouragement for new members to run for the office. See L. Harmon Zeigler and M. Kent Jennings, *Governing American Schools: Political Interaction in Local School Districts* (North Scituate, Mass.: Duxbury Press, 1974), pp. 34–35.

[3]David W. Minar, "Community Politics and the School Board," *School Board Journal,* March 1967, pp. 37–38; *cf.* Zeigler and Jennings, *Governing American Schools,* pp. 55–63.

small coalitions of individuals. Low voter turnout permits minority control of most school districts and increases the chances that a relatively small well organized faction in the school district will exercise major influence over its policy. Most often control of school government is in the hands of the educational professionals and their supporters, particularly administrators operating through PTA and other groups. However, school governments are constantly exposed to capture by a more tightly knit factional group, and factional struggles frequently characterize school district elections. School elections as a result often become ideological struggles between competing groups. Schools frequently take on an air of crisis when there is the possibility of a competitive election or an open debate about education.[4]

School Referendum Elections. Referenda are another method whereby the public is directly involved in policymaking on school matters. State constitutional and statutory provisions frequently require that certain kinds of issues, especially financial and bonding issues, be presented for approval by the electorate. In recent years referendum elections have become major problems for school governments, and an increasing number of bonding and financial issues have been rejected by the citizenry.[5]

School governments have little ability to persuade the electorate to support referendum issues. The lack of active participation by the electorate in school matters weakens the school's attempts to seek public support, so schools lack what in urban politics is sometimes called "clout." They may sometimes get the teachers, parents, and children to ring doorbells, or they may rely upon the predominantly middle-class PTA and the leading civic organizations on Main Street to help sell the school program, but such efforts are ineffectual compared to the canvassing a strong party organization might do. Schools normally cannot appeal to local politicians and parties to assist them in a school matter such as a referendum election. Local politicians, because of the separation of schools from other units of local government, are relieved of the responsibility for education, and since there is usually little to be gained politically and much to be risked by entering the sensitive area of education, most politicians avoid school issues.[6]

---

[4]*Ibid.*, p. 38; *cf.* Keith Goldhammer, *The School Board* (New York: Center for Applied Research in Education, Inc., 1964); Edward Tuttle, *School Board Leadership in America* (Danville, Ill.: Interstate Printers and Publishers, 1958); and Lillian B. Rubin, *Busing and Backlash: White against White in an Urban School District* (Berkeley: University of California Press, 1972).

[5]Lucia Monat, "U.S. Schools Fight Fiscal Pinch," *Christian Science Monitor*, Chicago edition, January 4, 1969; and Alan K. Campbell, "Inequities of School Finance," *Education Review*, January 11, 1969, pp. 44–48.

[6]Robert H. Salisbury, "Schools and Politics in the Big City," *Harvard Educational Review*, Summer 1967, pp. 422–23; *cf.* Martin, *Government and the Suburban Schools*, pp. 55–63.

Passage of school referenda in recent years has become more difficult because of the growing pluralism of interests in our society and because school leaders have little social interaction with many sectors of the public and almost no means of mobilizing them into support groups. Furthermore, many of the demands on schools are now being made by the blacks, the poor, the middle-class intellectuals, and the teachers, which presents additional problems. The business community and the working and lower middle classes are less sympathetic toward these demands and are more apt to vote no on such issues. The widespread antagonistic climate toward new school demands plus the fact that approval of school bond issues invariably and immediately costs the taxpayers money makes it increasingly difficult to pass referenda.[7]

Proposals for a referendum therefore create a crisis atmosphere among school officials, requiring a carefully planned strategy for timing the issue and selling it to the public. Usually, low-gear campaigns are planned to keep referendum issues from becoming the center of controversy and stimulating a large turnout, since large turnouts seem to occur only when the community is upset and that normally means defeat for proposals.

Participation on School Issues.   Widespread popular participation in school matters presents a dilemma for schoolmen. Like the American system of government generally, school districts profess the democratic commitment. School governments are predicated on the belief that popular control over the instruments of governance is the primary guarantee against the usurpation and abuse of power; furthermore, school governments should be receptive to demands from the constituency and will benefit from popular participation in the governmental process. A look at the behavior of people in the school political process raises some rather discomforting questions about the viability of this ideal. For one thing, there is a high positive relationship between participation and dissent on both referenda and board elections. Large turnouts on school issues often bring out the "politically alienated" in the community. In those districts in which participation is high, dissent is also likely to be high, and many people will vote against the school. Thus it might be said that high participation indicates a depression of the level of community consensus on school affairs. Similarly, in school districts where there is a high rate of demand-presentation before the board, there is less consensus about the operation of the schools. Under these conditions the board and administrators operate under more stress and with much more internal conflict.

[7]Christopher Jencks, "Who Should Control Education," *Dissent*, March–April 1966, pp. 150–55; *cf.* Monat, "U.S. Schools Fight Fiscal Pinch"; and Rubin, *Busing and Backlash*, pp. 3–10.

Schools respond to these types of inputs, but whether this is beneficial or not is debatable.[8]

Schoolmen have therefore sought to develop community support only of certain groups through the process of identification. PTA booster clubs and other such groups of "friends" of education have been cultivated rather than widespread participation in school matters. Public debate is discouraged, and little information about school issues is made available to the public in an attempt to keep a low political visibility for the schools.

In part, educators have kept school issues out of public debate by "sanctifying" the position of the educational professionals, that is, by contending that some school matters can only be understood by those especially prepared as educators. "Laymen" should not concern themselves with these technical educational issues.[9] The fact that two-fifths of the voters think that educational policy is too complicated for them to understand demonstrates the success of the sanctification process.[10]

Generally, the net result of discouraging public debate and participation on school issues is a very low participation rate by the public. Studies of citizen participation in school politics show that few participate. Less than one-third of the voters participate in any kind of school matters, while less than one-tenth participate actively. There is also a widespread feeling of ineffectualness. One-third of the voters believe that they have little to say about what schools do; almost one-half believe that the only voice voters have is the act of voting; and one-fourth believe that public school officials do not care what the average voter thinks.[11] Certainly this picture of school politics is a far cry from the romanticized idea of direct democracy in school elections.

Community Conflict and the Schools

As mentioned earlier, social scientists believe that social conflict is inherently a part of man's life, growing out of competing preferences of individuals. A primary function of governments, therefore, is the regulation of conflict between competing groups and individuals; governments, in-

[8]Minar, "Community Politics," pp. 37–38; cf. Richard F. Carter and William G. Savard, *Influence of Voter Turnout on School Bond and Tax Election* (U.S. Department of Health, Education, and Welfare, 1961). Zeigler and Jennings argue the case for more political competition in their recent study, *Governing American Schools*, pp. 246–52.

[9]Laurence Iannaccone and Frank Lutz, *Politics, Power, and Policy: The Governing of Local School Districts* (Columbus, Ohio: Charles E. Merrill Books, Inc., 1970), pp. 54–55; cf. Martin, *Government and the Suburban School*, p. 98.

[10]Richard F. Carter, "Voters and Their Schools," *Phi Delta Kappan*, March 1961, pp. 245–49.

[11]*Ibid.*, p. 249.

cluding school governments, have to make choices or compromises between the competing preferences of individuals and groups.

Schoolmen have traditionally denied that conflict is inherent in school governments and have attempted to develop a system of consensus politics in the governance of schools. But a large number of public policies of widespread interest must be determined in school districts. What are the major purposes and goals of the school? What is the nature of the curriculum? Should intellectual or social development of pupils receive priority? What type of teacher personnel should be attracted and retained? How much tax money should be allotted for the operation of the schools? Where should new school buildings be located, and should an expansion program be undertaken? The decisions relating to these questions are political in that conflicting views of what the public policy should be in these matters are held by different individuals and groups in the community.[12]

School Board and Group Conflict. The conflicting views of different groups and individuals are at times presented before the school board and comprise the most visible aspect of educational politics. The common bargaining processes of legislative politics are evident in these instances. Basically, two types of issues come before the board: school-centered issues, which normally have a narrow audience appeal; and public issues, which are of interest to a larger part of the citizenry.[13]

Complaints to the school board about such school-centered issues as curriculum, textbooks, and "controversial issues" in the classroom arise infrequently and episodically under unusual conditions, and normally they shortly subside. Some of these issues emerge from grievances of parents who feel they have in some sense been wronged or deprived of their rights. Schools attempt to suppress or resolve this type of conflict on a unilateral basis or through the identification process in groups such as PTAs or other semiformal social organizations outside the schools. Occasionally, boards are forced to deal with such issues and to seek compromises through the bargaining process. This is difficult because such issues are frequently ideologically oriented, and the bargaining process does not work well in these instances. As a result an attempt is made to avoid controversial issues and suppress differences about such internal school decisions as curriculum, textbooks, and school organization. Citizen demands or suggestions about these matters are often seen as attacks on education to be ignored or counterattacked.

The issues that excite citizen concern the most about school government are the public-type decisions that mainly involve economic matters.

[12]Martin, *Government and the Suburban School*, pp. 54–56; *cf.* Alan Rosenthal, "Community Leadership and Public School Politics: Two Case Studies" (Ph.D. dissertation, Princeton University, 1960).
[13]Martin, *Government and the Suburban School*, p. 61.

The school tax rate, school building and expansion programs, bond issues to support such programs, the school budget, and teachers' salaries are perennially before the board. Chambers of commerce and taxpayer groups are the agencies through which citizens typically express their concern on these issues. The influence of economy-oriented taxpayers can be substantial, and taxpayer groups in some larger cities even develop their own professional research staffs to present their views at budget hearings.[14] Local real estate interests are also vitally concerned with the schools' decisions regarding location of new schools and real property taxes and frequently voice their views to the board.

Although this type of issue is dealt with as a normal part of the bargaining process in other units of government, schools frequently attempt to mediate the public-type issues outside of the school. It is not uncommon for one or two members from the board of education or the superintendent to communicate quietly with the local chamber of commerce leaders to reach agreement about what the school property tax rate ought to be for the following year. Similarly, real estate interests may be consulted about decisions before an issue arises in a school board meeting.[15]

Public debate at school board meetings is avoided if possible. Superintendents attempt to avoid having board members openly disagree about school policies at school board meetings. If there is not unanimity on an issue among the members of the board, a superintendent will rarely permit the issue to get on the agenda for discussion.[16] In effect, a unanimous vote conceals the arguments against a decision. Compromise between the various groups and positions in the community, an essential aspect of policymaking, is therefore difficult to detect in school politics.

Schools are not always able to avoid public debate about community issues. Some issues, such as integration of schools, are rooted so firmly in genuine conflicts of interests in the community that schools cannot escape the conflict that revolves around them. Regardless of the ideological preferences of schoolmen, such issues often bring competitive group politics to the schools.

School desegregation is widely feared by school administrators and school board members as a dangerously disruptive issue. Conflict over desegregation often serves to mobilize persons who otherwise take no interest in the schools, and to antagonize elements of the community who normally support school bond and tax referenda. Once conflict has arisen over school desegregation, the civic elite which normally influences com-

[14]Iannaccone and Lutz, *Politics, Power, and Policy*, pp. 18–23.

[15]H. Thomas James, James A. Kelly, and Walter I. Garms, *Determinants of Educational Expenditures in Large Cities of the United States* (U.S. Department of Health, Education, and Welfare), pp. 68–69.

[16]Norman D. Kerr, "The School Board as an Agency of Legitimation," *Sociology of Education*, Fall 1964, pp. 42–43.

munity decisions either does not or cannot exert much influence.[17] More radical elements assume leadership roles as the conflict intensifies. Withdrawal of traditional support groups, coupled with opposition from elements about which the schools need not normally be concerned, often deprives the local school system of a power base sufficient for dealing with the issue of school desegregation.

Schools have little or no political resources for dealing with the conflict arising from desegregation. Reliance on traditional sources of support— the superintendent's expertise, educational well-wishers, and knowledgeable outsiders—is of little use in this type of community conflict. Schools do not have the network of interactions and communication linkages needed to muster public support from the minority groups. Separation from the rest of the community political system makes it impossible for schoolmen to retreat into positions of mutual support among city officials with many programs and agencies and clientele groups. Unable to trade off one group against another, schools stand exposed to the protest of groups angry not only over school segregation but over all of the racial ills of our society.[18]

In large part the conflict over school desegregation is an ideological fight, motivated not only by the desire to place as many black students as possible in integrated schools but also by the desire to persuade or force the school board to make the strongest commitment to the concept of racial equality. The fact that the civil rights movement is more symbol oriented than welfare oriented reduces any influence the superintendent might have been able to exert to lessen the conflict by making concessions on such things as compensatory educational programs. The school board consequently faces the full impact of the community conflict and is forced to set the tone of the integration decision.[19]

Because of their highly autonomous position, school boards are poorly equipped to deal with ideological conflict. Unlike city officials, a mayor or a city councilman who must make decisions on a whole range of issues, school boards participate in a narrow range of decisions and have more to lose from social conflict over school desegregation. The mayor or the councilman can balance his voting record on the numerous controversial issues that come before the council so as to maximize his chances for reelection and further the goals he has for the city. And city officials' dependence on partisan groups normally deters any all-out war over a

[17]James S. Coleman, *Community Conflict* (Glencoe, Ill.: The Free Press, 1957), pp. 11–13; *cf.* Robert L. Crain, *The Politics of School Desegregation* (Garden City, N.Y.: Anchor Books, 1969), pp. 379–80; and Rubin, *Busing and Backlash*, pp. 90–107.

[18]Crain, *Politics of School Desegregation*, pp. 371–74; *cf.* Rubin, *Busing and Backlash*, pp. 77–89.

[19]Crain, *Politics of School Desegregation*, p. 377.

racial issue because the subsequent loss of the black vote may endanger reelection. On the other hand, the school board is likely to have only one issue—school integration—that is of public importance. If it loses the white vote on this issue, it cannot regain it by making a decision in some other area which will please this group. If a school board member is politically ambitious, school integration may be turned into an attention-getting device. School boards are therefore not well suited for mediating the controversial desegregation issue.[20]

Most public decisions on controversial issues are made through a complex bargaining arrangement, the result of elaborate negotiations involving pressures and counterpressures by the competing parties. School desegregation decisions, however, do not appear to be results of such bargaining. In a study of the politics of school desegregation in both northern and southern cities, Robert Crain and his associates found that school desegregation decisions are not made in this way. Instead, the board members largely respond to the issue according to their predispositions about civil rights—liberal boards tend to integrate, conservative boards do not. Civil rights groups are able to bargain for only minor additional concessions. Often the only alternative these groups have is to escalate the conflict into an all-out battle, but even this may fail to change the overall tone of the board's behavior.[21]

When deadlock results from the inability of school boards to compromise on such hotly debated community issues as desegregation or teachers' salaries, an attempt is made to use more coercive methods. Legal injunctions may be sought; sanctions of various kinds may be threatened or applied. But if the school is still unable to adapt to the conditions, the issue tends to be pushed to other levels of government. City, state, and federal officials—particularly mayors, governors, and the courts—may be drawn into the controversy. The history of desegregation is replete with examples of this happening. Similarly, deadlocks over teachers' salaries in recent years have been broken only by intervention of mayors or various state officials who have more political resources and skills for compromising controversial issues as well as greater ability for raising additional monies.[22]

Laymen versus Professionals. Most conflicts over education are not, however, conflicts among lay interests but between one or another lay

[20]*Ibid.*, p. 371.
[21]*Ibid.*, pp. 377–78.
[22]Gary Orfield, *The Reconstruction of Southern Education: The Schools and the 1964 Civil Rights Act* (New York: John Wiley & Sons, Inc., 1969), pp. 349–61; George La Noue, "Political Questions on the Next Decade of Urban Education," *The Record*, March 1968, pp. 517–30; and Robert Wallace, "The Battle for Urban Schools," *Saturday Review*, November 16, 1968, pp. 5–7.

group and the professionals. The classic example of this pattern is the perennial struggle over educational finances in which the educators ask for more money. Typically there is a "liberal" group which takes its cue from the professionals and supports the increase, and a "conservative" group which opposes the dominant professional opinion and is against further public expenditures. In recent years the conflict over salaries has intensified as teachers have organized and have begun to apply sanctions to force school authorities to yield to their demands. Another recurring source of conflict is the handling of "controversial issues" in the classroom or, as it is usually called by the professionals, the struggle for "academic freedom." Traditionally, schools have adapted to these matters by identifying with dominant community values. But conflict periodically does arise over teachers' economic, political, or theological views as expressed in lectures or reading lists, and again the pattern is one in which the "liberals" support professional autonomy to decide what and how to teach while the "conservatives" argue for the layman's right to decide what goes on in the school.[23]

Schools have adapted to conflict between professionals and lay groups by endeavoring to get laymen to identify with the schools or by defining certain decisions as being in the professional sphere and thus to be made only in the bureaucratic system. These techniques have largely enabled educators to control both their own concerns and those of their students. The increasing attacks upon professional control, however, indicate that these methods of adaptation are no longer effective. Expansion of teachers' power in educational policymaking as a result of collective action will probably lead to more clashes between professionals and lay interests. The growing conflict between teacher organizations and racial groups over decentralization of schools is perhaps an omen of future conflict between the teachers and the community. Similarly, the increasing demands on schools to be accountable reflects the growing alienation between professional and lay interests.

Pattern of Influence in Economic Matters. ·The claim that only professionals can make competent judgments about many areas of education has generally been accepted, and effective influence in these areas is restricted to an inside core of professionals, particularly to the superintendent and his fellow administrators. But in some areas, such as in decisions about finances, there are lateral pressures by officials and citizens from outside the school organization. Table 3–1 shows that the mayor who is

[23]Marilyn Gittell, "Teacher Power and Its Implications for Urban Education," *Educational Digest*, November 1965, pp. 25–27; cf. David Spencer, "The Anatomy of Conflict: Claims of the Parties at Interest," *The Struggle for Power in the Public Schools: Proceedings of the Sixth Annual Conference, National Committee for Support of the Public Schools* (Washington, D.C., March 17–19, 1968), pp. 25–28.

not within th school organization is viewed as influential in some school policies, particularly in determination of teachers' salaries. This apparently reflects the mayor's potentially critical role in fiscal matters, especially in cities with fiscally dependent school districts but to some degree in all cities.

As already mentioned, school decisions involving economic matters, such as the school tax rate, school building and expansion programs, bond issues to support such programs, the school budget, and teachers' salaries, are generally much more influenced by the attitudes of citizens than are decisions pertaining to purely educational matters. Even when there is no direct pressure by economy-oriented taxpayers, citizens' attitudes about public expenditures as perceived by the board and superintendent affect the decision-making process. Such decisions are also much more likely to be made through a bargaining process than are purely school-centered decisions.[24]

The distribution and exercise of power in financial decisions is somewhat different from decisions about school-centered issues where the superintendent is dominant and his professional expertise is seldom challenged. Participation in financial decisions is still limited largely to the members within the school system. The superintendent and the board together play the active roles in determining needs, assembling facts, establishing goals, adopting policies, and controlling expenditures. Only rarely and incidentally do other participants such as teachers or teacher organizations, mayors, and citizens' committees participate in these decisions. The relative power of the board, superintendent, and administrative bureaucracy in budgeting and other financial decisions, however, varies from district to district. The board is apt to take a more active role in these decisions than in educational issues. Since board members often perceive their role as that of financial conservator for the school and pride themselves on their business acumen, they are more likely to question the superintendent's proposals in these areas. But even in making fiscal decisions, the board has to rely so much upon the administrative staff to collect, organize, and present data that it is still dependent on the superintendent. The superintendent and the administration therefore have considerable authority in these decisions and can even be the dominant influence.

Courts and School Policies

Many individuals and groups who are unable otherwise to affect school policies because of the closed nature of school politics turn to the courts

[24]James, Kelly, and Garms, *Determinants of Educational Expenditures*, p. 68; *cf.* Keith Goldhammer, "The School Board and Administration in the American Perspective of Government," *School Board Journal*, December 1954, pp. 29–31.

for judicial review of school policy. The courts become a means of political expression, a way of shaping school policy.[25] The right of groups to pursue their goals through the courts was upheld by the United States Supreme Court in 1963 in the case of *NAACP* v. *Button*, which struck down state legislative restrictions on such group litigation by Virginia and other southern states. As Justice Brennan said for the Supreme Court:

> . . . In the context of NAACP objectives, litigation is not a technique of resolving private differences; it is a means for achieving the lawful objectives of equality of treatment by all government, federal, state and local, for the members of the Negro community in this country. It is thus a form of political expression. Groups which find themselves unable to achieve their objectives through the ballot frequently turn to the courts. Just as it was true of the opponents of New Deal legislation during the 1930's, for example, no less is it true of the Negro minority today. And under the conditions of modern government, litigation may well be the sole practicable avenue open to a minority to petition for redress of grievances.[26]

First Amendment Cases.   The impact of litigation on educational policy has been substantial, as any review of recent court history shows. Numerous state and local laws, policies, and administrative regulations have been challenged on the ground that they violate the constitutional guarantees found in both the state and federal Bill of Rights and the common-law rights of parents over their children.

The most crucial issues in recent years have involved religion and race. The First Amendment provision that "Congress shall make no law respecting the establishment of religion or prohibiting the free exercise thereof" has also been interpreted as limiting states and local governments in these areas. This has been the basis for a number of cases challenging such school policies as requiring pupils to salute the flag of the United States and to repeat the Oath of Allegiance, permitting children to be released from school to attend religious classes, requiring the saying of prayers and the reading from the Bible at the beginning of the school day, spending school funds to provide textbooks for parochial pupils, transporting children to parochial schools at public expense, and arranging for

[25]Of the many organizations that resort to litigation as a means of obtaining their preferences in school policies, the most active include the following: National Association for the Advancement of Colored People, American Civil Liberties Union, Commission on Law and Social Action of the American Jewish Congress, American Committee for Protection of the Foreign Born, Watchtower Bible and Tract Society (Jehovah's Witnesses), Congress of Racial Equality, and Protestants and Other Americans United for the Separation of Church and State. In addition to these more permanent organizations, *ad hoc* groups frequently arise to challenge school policies that offend them in some way.

[26]*NAACP* v. *Button*, 83 S.Ct. 328, 336 (1963); *cf. NAACP* v. *Alabama ex. rel. Flowers*, 12 L.Ed. 2d. 325 (1963).

shared-time programs whereby nonpublic schools send their children to public schools for instruction in one or more subjects during a regular school day.[27]

Schools and the Equal Protection Clause. Perhaps the most far-reaching cases, in terms of their impact on educational policies since 1954, have been those arising from the equal protection clause of the Fourteenth Amendment, namely, the segregation and the school finance cases. The issue posed by the ending of segregated education has affected almost every school and school board in the South, as well as almost every state and large city in the North. Although two decades have passed since the epic decision of *Brown* v. *Board of Education* declared separate educational facilities to be inherently unequal, many complex problems of school desegregation still plague us, as the recent problems of busing to obtain racial balance indicate.[28]

Since 1968 the traditional financial system for supporting local school districts has also been under attack in the courts as being in violation of the equal protection clause.[29] Although, constitutionally, education is the responsibility of state government, states have relied heavily upon local school districts to finance education, permitting them to levy property taxes under state statutory provisions to support education. In addition, states provide state funds to support education according to state aid formula. In the average school district, local government pays slightly more than 50 percent of the cost and the state about 40 percent, with the remainder coming from federal funds.[30]

[27]Clement E. Vose, "Interest Groups, Judicial Review, and Local Government," *Western Political Science Quarterly*, March 1966, pp. 85–100.

[28]*Ibid.*

[29]The initial legal scrimmages in the constitutional struggle involving school finance arose in Illinois in the case of *McInnis* v. *Shapiro*. This suit filed by a number of high school and elementary students attending school in four different school districts of Cook County, Illinois, challenged the constitutionality of state laws dealing with the financing of the public school system. It alleged that the state laws created a finance system that resulted in disparities in educational programs, facilities, services, and the level of educational attainment. It asked that the Illinois laws authorizing distribution of public school funds "not based upon the educational need of children" and resulting in unequal per-pupil expenditures be declared unconstitutional. The *McInnis* complaint was dismissed by a three-judge court, and the method of financing schools in Illinois was held to be neither arbitrary nor invidiously discriminatory. Later the United States Supreme Court upheld this ruling without hearing of arguments or without a written opinion. Despite this decision, by 1971 more than a dozen cases had been filed in federal courts challenging the traditional financial structure for education.

[30]Advisory Commission on Intergovernmental Affairs, *Who Should Pay for Public Schools* (Washington, D.C.: Government Printing Office, 1971), p. 2; and *AASA Convention Reporter*, highlights of 1972 Annual Convention, prepared by the editors of Education U.S.A. (February 12–16, 1972), pp. 2–3.

Under the typical state financial structure there are no provisions for equalization of district tax bases, and thus local and regional differentials in aggregate property values available for taxation are perpetuated in the district's ability to finance education. There are rich districts and poor districts, and the differences in the total assessed valuations vary considerably. Measured in terms of assessed property values per pupil, the magnitude of the differences of school districts in their ability to finance education at equivalent tax rates is typically on the order of fifty to one, or even greater. For instance, in Michigan the range in per-pupil district property valuation ranges from a high of $53,156 to a low of $1,319; in California the range is from $306,077 to $3,698; in New York the range is from over $200,000 to less than $5,000; in Texas the range is from over $100,000 to less than $10,000.[31]

Although most states provide direct "flat grants" and "foundation plans" to supplement local school districts, these supplements do little to lessen the underlying malapportionment. State "flat grants," providing a uniform per-student sum to every district without regard to its tax capabilities, do not lessen interdistrict dollar differences at all. And while most states provide a per-pupil "equalizing foundation plan" to supplement school districts, the formula for these does not equalize educational expenditures per pupil in the districts.[32]

The traditional method of financing education was successfully challenged in California, Texas, and Minnesota in 1971. In the California case, *Serrano* v. *Priest*, the California Supreme Court held that the state's system of financing education "individually discriminates against the poor because it makes the quality of a child's education a function of the wealth of his parents and neighbors" and therefore violates the equal protection clause.[33] A federal district court a few months later declared the Texas and Minnesota systems of financing schools unconstitutional on similar grounds.[34]

---

[31]John Silard and Sharon White, "Interstate Inequalities in Public Education: The Case for Judicial Relief under the Equal Protection Clause," *Wisconsin Law Review*, 1 (1970), 7; *cf.* Joel Berke, "The Current Crisis in School Finance: Inadequacy and Inequity," *Phi Delta Kappan*, September 1971.

[32]John E. Coons, William H. Clune III, Stephen D. Sugarman, "Educational Opportunity: A Workable Constitutional Test for State Financial Structures, *California Law Review*, April 1969, pp. 305–420; Harold W. Horowitz and Diana L. Neitring, "Equal Protection Aspects of Inequalities in Public Education and Public Assistance Programs from Place to Place within a State," *UCLA Law Review*, April 1968, pp. 787–816; and Neil Jon Bloomfield, "Equality of Educational Opportunity: Judicial Supervision of Public Education," *So. Cal. Law Review*, 43 (1970), 275–306.

[33]96 Cal. Rept. 601; 487 P.2d 1241 (1970).

[34]Rodriguez v. San Antonio Independent School District, C.A., No. 68-175-SA (W. D., Tex., Dec. 1971); Van Dusartz v. Hatfield, No. 3-71 Civ. 243 (D. Minn., Oct. 12, 1971).

A rash of litigation followed and threatened the financial structure of schools throughout the United States. National and state political leaders were forced to seek new methods for financing schools, as the cartoon in Figure 5–1 shows. The challenge to the governance of education was accentuated by federal court rulings in Richmond, Virginia, and in Detroit, Michigan, which held that the state's authority to draw school district lines cannot be done in such a way as to violate the state's obligation to eliminate racially identifiable dual school systems.

The United States Supreme Court backed away from the making of a revolution in educational finance in the *San Antonio Independent School District* v. *Rodriguez* case. The Court partially removed the pressures for reform of the states' educational finance system by overruling the federal district court's decision that the system of financing schools in Texas violated the equal protection clause of the Fourteenth Amendment. To many it appeared that the Supreme Court had reversed a forty-year-long commitment to equal educational opportunity for all in this five to four decision. Certainly this dramatic change in direction reflects the political controversy that has raged around the Court for the past several decades and shows the major role the Court plays in educational policymaking.

Other Legal Attacks on School Policies

A host of other less publicized school laws and policies have also been challenged in the courts by groups or individuals. State compulsory school attendance laws, smallpox examination requirements, regulations prescribing not only curricula but pupils' dress and personal appearance as well as conduct on and off school grounds, restrictions on membership in fraternities, to mention just a few, are laws and policies that have frequently been litigated as violating the due process of law as guaranteed under the state and federal constitutions. Similarly, there has been considerable controversy over who can teach, as is evident from the many cases pertaining to teacher loyalty oaths. The courts are also called upon to help devise numerous policies affecting personnel, such as the right of teachers' groups to organize, bargain, and strike against the schools.[35]

Taxpayer Suits. Public education is an important budget item for a community, and frequently taxpayers' suits are brought impeaching the collection or expenditure of school funds. Since such lawsuits may be

[35]Newton Edwards, The Courts and the Public Schools (Chicago: University of Chicago Press, 1955), pp. 564–98.

Figure 5-1   Potpourri

Bruce Shanks, Buffalo Evening News, September 10, 1972. Reprinted by permission.

brought by any taxpayer in the community, they enable a large body of the citizenry to challenge governmental action that would otherwise go unchallenged in the courts because of the technical requirement of legal standing. They afford a means of mobilizing the self-interest of individuals in the community to challenge actions of the schools. There are numerous examples of such lawsuits. An article in the *Yale Review* states that the objectives sought by plaintiff-taxpayers have varied widely and lists them in the following order: (1) challenges to the use of the eminent domain power in connection with the construction of new school facilities, (2) attacks on the constitutionality of various methods of bond financing, (3) efforts to withhold salary payments to civil servants who hold office in violation of statutory standards, (4) challenges to sales or donations of public domain to private parties, (5) cases to achieve civil liberties objectives such as the prevention of expenditures for illegal expenditures which would violate the separation of church and state, and (6) suits to reapportion school districts for elections.[36]

[36]Clement E. Vose, "Taxpayers' Suits: A Survey and Summary," *Yale Law Review*, April 1960, p. 895.

Taxpayers' suits even when unsuccessful may delay and obstruct the completion of public projects. These suits may harass the school government, but by providing the discontented minority with a means for influencing school policy, such suits tend to force school governments to be more open to the demands of the minority interests.[37]

Outputs of
the Local School System

The output of public policies that emanates from the local school districts helps to shape not only American education but the American character generally. To a large degree the key questions of who will attend school, what will be taught, how schools will be governed and conducted, and how they will be financed depend on the policy outputs of the fifteen thousand or so local schools. What schools do—the output of the system —directly affects students and their parents; teachers, administrators, and school boards; and especially the local community.

But the impact of local school policies is not only on the local community. Education, in a sense, is an essential national function; youth must be taught to become American citizens. The function of political socialization of youth is important to all nations. Children are taught to be citizens, to be Frenchmen, Irishmen, Americans, or whatever nationality. They must be politically socialized in the common traditions, beliefs, attitudes, interests, and values that make a person loyal to a particular nation. This function is essential to national integration and unity. Public schools, although not alone in this important task, are one of the most important and effective instruments of political socialization. The process of political socialization in our nation is complicated by the fact that we are a nation of immigrants, a nation of heterogeneous ethnic, racial, and religious groups.[38] Our educational system has the added responsibility of helping to integrate our society, to create a sense of national unity and identity among highly diverse people.

Education also performs important economic roles. Local school policies affect the economy not only by allocating economic resources in the local community through contracts for materials, services, and construction and by equipping youth to work in the local economy, they also help provide a trained manpower for the national labor force, and the national economy reflects how well or how poorly they perform this function.

[37]*Ibid.*, p. 913.
[38]For a review of the literature, see Herbert Hyman, *Political Socialization* (New York: The Free Press, 1959), Chap. 4; Richard E. Dawson and Kenneth Prewitt, *Political Socialization* (Boston: Little, Brown and Company, 1968), Chap. 7; *cf.* Gladys A. Wiggin, *Education and Nationalism: An Historical Interpretation of American Education* (New York: McGraw-Hill Book Company, 1962), pp. 30–40.

National economic growth and prosperity to a large degree depends on the output of the local school districts.[39]

The outputs of local schools—both actions and inactions—function as inputs to other units of government. Because of our highly integrated national economy and the mobility of our people, there is a "spillover" effect of local educational policies throughout the nation. The child who is educated in a local district in Mississippi may reside as an adult in New York, in California, or in any one of the thousand or more places in the United States. These communities will either gain or lose depending on the quality of education received in the home school district. The nation is affected similarly, and the national interest suffers if the young adult is unfit for military service because of insufficient education, or is unable to obtain employment, or has to rely on public welfare for support, or becomes involved in criminal activity as a result of his inability to adjust to modern society. This spillover effect of education places new demands on other local school districts, cities, states, and the federal government; that is, the outputs of local school governments act as inputs on other administrative agencies and governmental entities. The intergovernmental transfer of monies from one level of government to another is one way we have recognized the interrelatedness of the various levels of governmental services.

Provision of Educational Opportunities. How well do local school governments perform their administrative function? That is, how well do they provide educational opportunities for American youth? This question has been the subject of much debate in recent years. Those who praise the quality of educational outputs generally point to the successes of the educational system—the many children we educate, our being the "melting pot" for wave after wave of immigrant children, the economic prosperity of our nation, and the schools' role in preparing students for the world of work and the fact that local schools have helped preserve freedom in the nation. The decentralized structure of education is hailed as a stroke of the Founding Fathers' political genius. Local control of education is

[39]See Thomas P. Lantos, "The Economic Value of Education," *California Teachers' Association*, May 1965, pp. 10–14; Charles Benson, *Education Is Good Business* (Washington, D.C.: American Association of School Administrators and National Boards Association, 1966), Chap. 3; Nicholas Dewitt, "Investment in Education and Economic Development," *Phi Delta Kappan*, December 1965, pp. 197–99; Theodore Schultz, "Education and Economic Growth," *Social Forces Influencing American Education*, Sixtieth Yearbook, National Society for the Study of Education (Chicago: University of Chicago Press, 1961), Chap. 3; and R. L. Johns, "The Economics and Financing of Education," *Emerging Designs for Education: Program, Organization, Operation and Design* (Denver, Colo.: Designing Education for the Future, 1968), pp. 198–208.

seen as the cause for the extension of educational opportunity. It is argued that today, as in the past, schools are symbols of local pride and hope, and communities recognize this and endeavor to improve the type of education offered by their schools. The result of the decentralized system is an ever-improving quality of education for American youth.[40]

Despite these professions of faith in localism, we have as yet no accurate measure to determine how well local schools are serving all youth or what quality of education is being offered. Proposals for a system of national assessment of the quality of education have caused a long and heated public debate, and opponents have viewed the proposal as a threat to local control. A very limited system of national assessment is now being undertaken by the Educational Compact of the States.[41]

Although we do not have a measure of overall effectiveness or educational quality, we do know that one of the results of the decentralized system of education leads to great inequality between districts. The disparities in educational opportunity cause, as Conant has stated, "totally different kinds of public schools that serve the city slums and the wealthy suburbs." Despite the democratic credo of the equality of educational op-

[40]Charles S. Benson, "The Bright Side and the Dark in American Education," *Phi Delta Kappan*, September 1965, pp. 47–48.

[41]See Ralph W. Tyler, "A Program of National Assessment," *National Education Assessment: Pro and Con* (Washington, D.C.: American Association of School Administrators, 1966), Chap. 10; Harold C. Hand, "National Assessment Viewed as the Camel's Nose," *Phi Delta Kappan*, September 1965, pp. 8–12; Ralph W. Tyler, "Assessing the Progress of Education," *Phi Delta Kappan*, September 1965, pp. 13–16; "The Assessment Debate at the White House Conference," *Phi Delta Kappan*, September 1965, pp. 17–18; Robert F. McMorris, "National Assessment: Coming in 1968–69?" *Phi Delta Kappan*, June 1968, pp. 599–600; and "Accountability through National Assessment," *Compact*, October 1970, pp. 4–13.

A 1967 survey found that only seventeen states used tests to evaluate instruction and only thirteen used tests to measure student progress. The trend toward objective assessment has spread to the point where every state either has or is planning an assessment program (Educational Testing Service, *State Educational Assessment Programs*, Princeton, New Jersey, 1971, p. ix). Title III of the Elementary and Secondary Act of 1965, mandating a needs assessment, has been a major impetus for this development.

In 1968 the USOE initiated independent educational audits to verify the measurement of student achievements in Title VII and Title VIII programs. The auditor also assesses the appropriateness of the measurement procedures (J. Wayne Wrightstone, Thomas P. Hogan, and Muriel M. Abbott, *Test Service Notebook 33: Accountability in Education and Associated Measurement Problems* [New York: Harcourt Brace Jovanovich, Inc., 1968]). In the same year officials of the USOE and the Council of Chief State School Officers agreed to develop a comprehensive evaluation system to consolidate required state reporting of federally funded programs. The results of their efforts to date include twenty-seven states in the Belmont Project (so named because the initial meeting took place in the Belmont House, Elkridge, Maryland). The purpose is to furnish information on elementary and secondary programs resulting from federally assisted programs, and it is planned that all states will eventually join (Educational Testing Service, p. xi).

portunity, the quality of education a student receives depends on the school district where he happens to reside. If he resides in a school district with a high tax base, he is likely to receive a "better" educational opportunity than the student who resides in a district with a lower tax base. As we have seen, this pattern for providing education is under attack in the courts at the present time.

Critics of the educational outputs emanating from local schools focus on the failure to provide quality education to all youth. The educational outputs they point to are the statistics of students "dropping out," the racial discrimination in schools and the continued resistance of local school boards to the law of the land, the inability of schools to prepare students for working in our highly technical society, and the failure to engender a love of democratic values or even a knowledge of how the American governmental system works. They blame the low salaries and status of public school teachers on local control and allege that a political domination of localism acts as a quiet intimidation of teachers day by day, which inhibits their freedom to think freely and intelligently with their students on the large issues before us. The typical American teacher works and lives in almost daily contact with the individuals who control his tenure, his salary, his school's curriculum, and even his classroom methods. Political domination of localism openly manifests itself in the dismissal or in the failure to renew contracts of teachers offending local views and prejudices. The result, critics contend, is that as a group, public school teachers must be characterized as retiring, timid, sometimes even frightened, when it comes to controversial social questions. They do not symbolize, generally speaking, the kind of intellectual intrepidity we usually associate with intelligent and educated people.[42] The "perverse parochialism" of local systems supports local prejudices over national ideals or even national laws and thus acts as a divisive rather than a unifying force in our society.

Critics also contend that the perpetuation of our present highly decentralized system hinders the improvement of the quality of education, since any attempt to improve basic recruitment to the field of education runs afoul of the hiring, promotion, and salary policies of our many thousands of school districts, policies that districts themselves are helpless to change because of local attitudes. Local districts are peculiarly ill fitted to finance and administer the retraining of teachers toward the end that we arrive at a stage of education in which teachers as well as students are consciously engaged in a continuous process of learning.

Finally, critics of the outputs of local schools point to the ill effect

[42]For an example of such criticism, see Van Cleve Morris, "Grassroots-ism and the Public School," *School and Society*, June 1957, pp. 217–19; *cf.* Julius S. Brown, "Risk Propensity in Decision Making: A Comparison of Business and Public School Administrators," *Administrative Science Quarterly*, December 1970, pp. 473–81.

localism has upon the urban community—the continued fragmentation of the governmental system which encourages the flight of the whites in an attempt to wall out the poor and the blacks. Localism in effect is a divisive rather than a unifying force in our society.[43]

The lack of concurrence as to the quality and effect of the output of local schools illustrates the ideological nature of school politics. The question as to the quality of education or as to its effect upon youth and our society becomes a debate on fundamental principles or goals of school government—on the validity of the underlying assumptions which makes education a prerequisite not just for democracy but, in modern dress, for the reform of society itself. Educational politics, as Robert Wood has suggested, takes on the character of a constitutional convention that is constantly in session, always discussing the fundamentals of its political order. It operates, moreover, in the open atmosphere that prevailed in France after the Revolution rather than in the closeted, protected circumstances under which the American Constitution was prepared. The participants are asked to dig up their first premises by the roots and examine them anew, while constantly under public scrutiny.[44] There is little wonder, therefore, why the debate over local school outputs often becomes so violent or why educational professionals attempt to avoid open discussion about educational outputs.

Regulation of Conflict. As we have already seen, a key function of all governments is the regulation of conflict; it involves the making of choices or of decisions as to how the power of government will be used, which in turn determines the distribution of advantages and disadvantages among people. In earlier years local schools performed this function relatively well, and there were seldom open conflicts over decisions made by school governments. In recent years, however, our schools have become battlegrounds of conflicting interests, and local school governments have not been able to contain or regulate these conflicts. Increasingly, other governmental entities and levels of government have had to assume this role for the schools.

Many educational conflicts seem to be beyond the capability of local school governments to resolve. Perhaps the most conspicuous of these is the struggle over school integration. Local school governments have generally been unable to cope with this issue. Similarly, they have been unable to deal with conflicts over school finance, as is evident from the taxpayers'

---

[43]Basil G. Zimmer and Amos H. Hawley, "Factors Associated with Resistance to the Organization of Metropolitan Area Schools," *Sociology of Education*, Fall 1967, pp. 334–47.

[44]Robert C. Wood, *Suburbia* (New York: Houghton Mifflin Company, 1958), pp. 190–93.

revolts over increased property taxes and the litigation over the inequality of school districts' tax bases. The growing militancy of teacher organizations and unions has accentuated the financial inadequacies of local schools, as well as demonstrating their inability to resolve economic and political conflicts. Finally, school governments have attempted to retreat from the growing debate over the role of education and who should govern schools in the hope that the conflict will subside. Unfortunately, the crescendo of debate on these issues continues.

The failure of local schools to effectively regulate educational conflicts and to cope with the demands placed on them has resulted in increasing pressure on other levels of government to assume these roles and responsibilities for the local schools. We shall now examine the political systems of the state and federal governments to see how they are affected by these inputs and, in turn, how they adapt to them.

chapter six

Political System
of State Education

Public education in the United States operates within a legal and constitutional framework largely set by the states. The constitutions of the individual states provide with varying degrees of specificity for the establishment and upkeep of public school systems. Thus states have the fundamental legal responsibility for education, and the state political system is a major arena for making educational policies. This chapter examines the political system of state education and adds to the heuristic model we began in Chapter 3.

Educational responsibilities exercised by the states are numerous, and although the activities and methods for performing them vary, there is a commonality in the political system of American states. This, as well as the differences in state operations and structures, can be examined through the systems approach. The structure of the political system of state education is represented by the model shown in Figure 6–1. In this chapter and in the next we will identify the parties involved in state educational politics and the demands—both inputs and within puts—placed upon the system.

Politics of state education is affected by environmental factors within the state, inputs from local political subsystems, and demands from the broader environment of the nation. Figure 6–1 attempts to show the interaction of these factors. The circle at the bottom of the diagram represents the state community, that is, the cultural and socioeconomic factors affecting state politics. The circle directly above represents the state political and governmental system and the concomitant political variables. The upper three circles represent the political system of local school districts. Local schools are an integral part of the state political system of education. What they do affects the state, and vice versa. That is, the outputs of local schools act as inputs into the state political arena, and in turn the state's actions are inputs on the local system. In Figure 6–1 the formal legal and

Figure 6–1   Model Representing the Political System of State Education

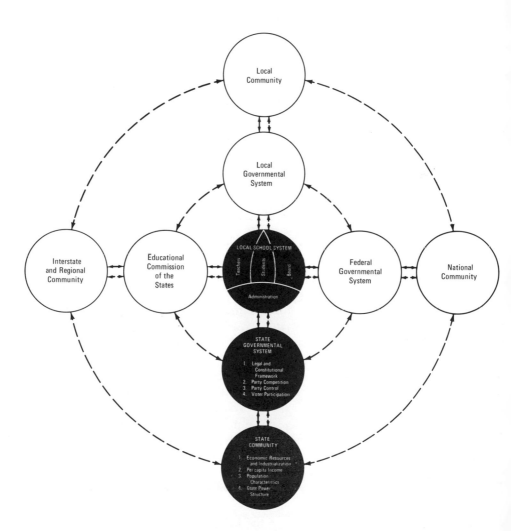

administrative relationships between the various parts of the state system are represented by solid-line arrows connecting the various parts of the model, and the informal interactions and communications are depicted by broken-line arrows.

Common Factors
Shaping State Educational Politics

American states vary culturally, socially, economically, and politically, and these factors affect the character of state politics and the politics of

public education. The outputs of state political systems and the effects of interstate differences on state educational policies will be examined in a subsequent section. But first, if we are to understand the operation of educational politics, it is necessary to consider the common characteristics of state politics. There are a number of similarities in state and local political environments.

Legal and Functional Factors. One basic difference between state and local districts is their constitutional and legal powers. States as constitutional units in the federal system have plenary powers over local governments except where restricted by state or federal constitutional provisions. A school district, on the other hand, is legally an agent of the state and as such is responsible for the state function of public education within a geographical area. As a result, a school district is legally subject to the control of the state. While it has many characteristics of incorporated local governmental bodies such as cities, the district's powers are more restricted. School boards have and can exercise only those powers that are granted explicitly or those that are implied or necessarily incidental to the powers expressly granted by the state legislature.

Educational responsibilities exercised by the state, in contrast to those assigned to local schools, are more numerous and varied. In general, each state legislature has created a school district system and has defined the powers and duties of local school boards, including the power to levy a property tax within prescribed limits. Funds for school districts are also provided from state tax sources. State regulatory provisions apply to numerous aspects of education, including such matters as compulsory attendance laws, minimum standards for the operation of schools, certification of teachers, curriculum requirements, and selection of textbooks. Regulatory provisions often apply both to public and to private schools in the state, and state departments of education are responsible for their enforcement. Teacher-training institutions, teacher retirement systems, and state schools for the deaf and blind are usually operated by the state. Because of these types of activities, state actions affect more people in more different ways than do the actions of local school districts. In fact, the state is so involved in education that seldom does a state legislative session conclude without passing legislation affecting public elementary and secondary education.

Political Factors. Education at the state level operates in a more partisan environment than at the local level, even in one-party states where competing factions replace parties. States are more pluralistic, encompassing as they do all local systems and affecting a greater variety of individuals and groups in more ways. State officials obtain office through partisan politics, and the issues they have to resolve are more political, since there is greater competition and more conflict between groups in the state political arena. Political bargaining is more frequently the process used in

resolving state issues. Success in the state political arena, therefore, depends on such political factors as the access and influence groups and individuals have with the partisan state officials, and the ability of groups and individuals to marshal the resources of political power.

Only recently has education been forced to openly enter the state political competition. In the past, educators attempted to gain their ends at the state level in much the same way they did at the local level, through a form of consensus politics.[1]

Characteristically, during the consensus period a small group of competent and politically resourceful superintendents of the larger and more prestigious school districts could influence if not dominate a consortium of educational interest groups. This educational leadership worked directly with the key state officials, particularly with rural or small-town legislators who held important legislative committee chairmanships. Educators' demands were normally presented in low-key fashion, and educators relied heavily upon professional expertise to persuade state officials. State politics of education was basically a consensus politics dominated by professionals.[2]

The political environment of education has been changed drastically in recent years, and state politics of education is experiencing a shift from the consensus politics of the professional priesthood to the conflict politics of the public governing-place. Several factors have effected this change: (1) the legislative reapportionment decisions by the Supreme Court in the mid-1960s caused a realignment of state power—no longer are the rural and small-town legislators the power brokers they were in the past; (2) there is a growing pluralism among groups speaking for education or placing demands on the educational system, and at the same time a continuing dissolution of the once almost monolithic structure of professional educators—no longer can administrators speak for all educators; (3) growing militancy of teachers' groups and the separation of the educational establishment into different and even competitive associations have fragmented the united front presented by professional educators; (4) the unanimity of citizen support has dissolved, and an increasing number of citizens, including minority groups are pressuring for their own preferences in education; (5) the growing interests of private business in education have brought still another group into the making of educational policy, and today, instead of one voice speaking for "education," the babel of competing tongues is heard, and often in strident and militant tones; and (6) the transformation of state educational politics has been influenced by the inability of local districts to resolve many of the difficult governmental

[1]B. Dean Bowles, "The Power Structure in State Politics," *Phi Delta Kappan*, February 1968, p. 337.
[2]*Ibid.*, p. 338.

problems, such as the financial and racial problems, and by the schools'
unwillingness to assume the new roles they are being called upon to assume
in our urbanized society. These contentious issues have therefore been
pushed into the state political arena. State educational politics as a result
of the changes has become more akin to the typical competitive state
politics, and there has been a significant shift in power affecting the control
and support of schools to the state level.[3]

Fiscal Factors. Still another major difference in state and local political environments is the state's much larger tax base and plenary powers
to levy taxes. With the exception of self-imposed constitutional limitations
on the state's power of taxation and the federal restrictions on taxation of
interstate commerce, the state may levy taxes as it sees fit. Local governments such as school districts, on the other hand, are legally creatures of
the state and are dependent on the state for their power to tax. As we have
seen, the tax power of school districts is severely restricted and has normally been limited to the property tax since colonial days. But local governments are not only limited by the legal restrictions on their powers, they
are also restricted by the economies of their size. Because they have no
jurisdiction beyond their boundaries, if they increase taxes too much people
and industry will move to avoid the taxes. Competition between communities for industry acts as a major constraint on local property taxes. Requirements for public referenda also make it difficult to raise local taxes,
since voters often exhibit an irrational aversion to increased taxes on their
property.[4]

State tax structures generally rely most heavily upon consumption
taxes, that is, upon general and special sales taxes. This tax base has several
advantages. Perhaps most important, it gives the state a larger and more
elastic tax source than that available to local governments. Tax revenues
automatically increase as the state grows and prospers or as inflation
increases; in this sense, state taxes are elastic. There is a continuing
increase in state revenues without boosting rates, whereas for local districts
growth or inflation first increases expenditures and only later do the increases in property values result in additional revenues. State consumption
taxes draw less complaint from the public than property taxes. Sales taxes
get "more feathers with less squawk," since the public does not mind paying
taxes a penny at a time as much as it does coming up with one large yearly

[3]*Ibid.*, pp. 338–40; *cf.* Michael D. Usdan, David W. Minar, and Emanuel Hurwitz, Jr., *Education and State Politics* (New York: Columbia University Press, 1969),
pp. 163–74.
[4]*Fiscal Balance in American Federal System* (Washington, D.C.: Advisory
Commission on Intergovernmental Relations, 1967), I, 107–13; *cf.* A. James Reichley,
"The States Hold the Key to the Cities," *Fortune,* June 1969, p. 134.

sum to pay property taxes. Also, normally there are no referendum requirements for states to increase sales taxes as there are to increase local
property taxes.[5]

In recent years local schools have been forced to seek additional funds
from the states. As enrollments swelled and demands for educational
services increased in the post–World War II period, the cost of educational
services outran the financial ability of many local districts. State systems of
financing education were expanded, and the state proportion of total public
school expenditures grew continuously; it increased from only 17 percent
in 1900 to approximately 50 percent at present. Table 8–1 shows the
percentage of financial support for the various states throughout the nation.

Impetus for even greater state support of education has resulted from
the score of recent cases following the precedent established in the *Serrano*
and *Rodriguez* cases challenging the commonly used method of financing
public schools as violating the equal protection clause of the Fourteenth
Amendment. Pressures on states to develop new methods to support
education continue even though the U.S. Supreme Court in a five to four
decision ruled that state financial systems did not violate the Fourteenth
Amendment.[6]

As the states' share of the cost of education has increased and pressures
for still additional state expenditures have continued to grow, education
has become more politicized, since perhaps no other issues are as heatedly
contested as taxing and spending of public monies. Raising state expenditures for education draws many groups into the political fray who would
not otherwise be involved in educational politics. New political alignments
have arisen to support or oppose educational demands, and the political
conflict over education has been intensified.

Inputs into the Political System
of State Education

As education has been drawn more into the state political arena, groups
seeking to influence educational policies have been forced to develop
political power and influence. In this section we will attempt to identify the
parties seeking to influence state educational policies and the sources of
their political strength, and we will try to answer the following questions:
What groups and individuals initiate action? Who presents demands? Who
contacts, cajoles, pleads with, and persuades persons in authority and in-

---

[5]L. Laszlo Ecker-Racz, "Federal-State Fiscal Imbalance: The Dilemma," *Congressional Record*, 89th Cong., 1st sess., August 5, 1965, Vol. III, No. 143.

[6]Charles W. Rudiger and Ruben Pollack, "Full State Funding: An Idea Whose
Time Has Come," *School Management*, November 1971, pp. 18–20; and K. Forbus
Jordan, "A Workable Plan for Full State Funding of Public Education," *American
School Board Journal*, March 1971, pp. 66–68.

fluence? What types of access do educational groups have to formal policy-makers? Who arouses and mobilizes citizens at the grass roots? And which pressure groups are the most influential?

As in most policy areas, relatively few policy proposals pertaining to education result from general public pressures or a wave of public protest. Instead, those groups that are most directly affected by state policies initiate and push for their enactment. In education this is also true, and the real laborers working to shape educational policies are the educational professionals. Teachers, superintendents, and principals are most directly affected by state school policies, and thus they organize on a statewide basis in an attempt to influence state policies. Figure 6–2 shows the various educational groups placing demands on the local schools—teachers, administrators, school boards, and students-parents have statewide organizations to push for policies favorable to them.

State Teachers' Associations and Unions. Teachers, like all individuals and professionals with common interests, are impelled to form associations to work for favorable state policies. State educational policies affect teachers most directly. State laws pertaining to such matters as minimum salaries, teacher retirement plans, tenure or dismissal provisions, and other conditions of employment vitally affect teachers. As a result there are many associations representing teachers and other educational professionals. The largest of these, the National Education Association, has affiliates in every state. In recent years a rival organization, the American Federation of Teachers, has developed and has sought to become the spokesman for teachers. The AFT is a much smaller organization and is more union orientated than the NEA.[7]

State education associations affiliated with the NEA are found in every state and all have professional staffs that include at least an executive director working to influence state policies. They perform, as do all private interest groups, a variety of functions. They mobilize consent within their own organization and determine legislative programs at annual or periodically held state conventions. They publicize their proposals to the membership in monthly journals and newsletters, seeking a common political front. Also, they attempt to inform and convince the public of the rightness of their positions. Throughout the year they work to develop favorable relationships with key political leaders, and they lobby, cajole, and attempt to persuade legislators and governors, as well as candidates. In some states they even support individual teachers who run for the state legislature. Finally, they seek coalitions and alliances with other groups in an attempt to build a strong political base.[8]

[7]Alan Rosenthal, *Pedagogues and Power: Teacher Groups in School Politics* (Syracuse, N.Y.: Syracuse University Press, 1969), pp. 22–28.
[8]Stephen K. Bailey *et al., Schoolmen and Politics: A Study of State Aid to Education in the Northeast* (Syracuse, N.Y.: Syracuse University Press, 1962), pp. 57–102.

Figure 6–2 Inputs on the State Educational System

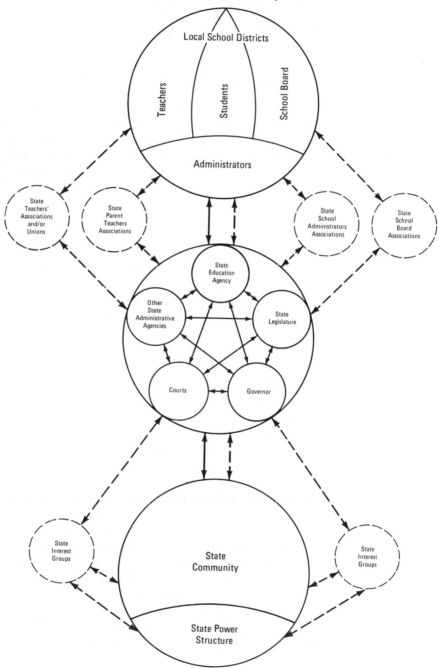

The effectiveness of education associations varies from state to state. In some states, education associations are very influential. In the northeastern states, for instance, Bailey and his associates found that educational interests (chiefly the NEA affiliates) in the early 1960s were quite powerful.[9] Another study reported that state education associations in three midwestern states, Illinois, Michigan, and Missouri, were considered by legislators as being among the most powerful interest groups in their states.[10] The same conclusion has been reached in a number of other single-state studies, and it is generally agreed that state education associations are the main source of educational demands made upon states.[11]

State education associations, however, suffer from some inherent weaknesses which increasingly limit their effectiveness in today's political environment. For one thing, state NEA affiliates are not very cohesive groups. Membership of both teachers and administrators, as well as other educational professionals such as teacher college professors, dilutes the degree of agreement about common goals. Increasingly, the old alliance between these professional groups is strained, and differences in their outlooks weaken the associations. Perhaps an even more serious limitation is the "no politics in education" ideology, which professional associations have continually espoused. Teachers continue to be apathetic about politics in general and quite naive about state politics. A large percentage of the membership in state education associations perceive their primary role to be the disseminating of intellectual and professional information rather than acting as a lobby organization for teachers. The high rate of turnover in membership of state education associations, which corresponds to the rate at which teachers leave their profession, seriously hinders state NEA affiliates. Many teachers join the state education association only because of a sense of professional obligation or because of subtle, and sometimes not so subtle, pressures by their principals and this also weakens the organization in its political roles.[12]

State education associations, therefore, have little political currency with which to operate in the political market. Although they have relatively

[9]*Ibid.*

[10]Nicholas A. Masters *et al., State Politics and the Public Schools: An Exploratory Analysis* (New York: Alfred A. Knopf, Inc., 1964), pp. 1–319.

[11]Dean Bowles, "Educational Pressure Groups and the Legislative Process in California, 1945–66" (Ph.D. dissertation, Claremont Graduate School, 1966); and A. E. Starkey, "State-Level Educational Decision-Making" (Ph.D. dissertation, University of Texas, 1966). State legislators in a nationwide survey in 1963 named the state teachers' association as one of the most powerful pressure groups in their respective states. Wayne L. Frances, *Legislative Issues in the Fifty States: A Comparative Analysis* (Chicago: Rand McNally & Co., 1967), pp. 40–42.

[12]James D. Koerner, *Who Controls American Education?: A Guide for Laymen* (Boston: Beacon Press, 1968), pp. 96–99. Administrative pressure to join NEA has diminished as NEA has become increasingly militant in its demands.

large memberships, they can deliver few votes. In fact, they seldom openly support the candidacy of anyone. Instead, they formally maintain a non-partisan position, and at the most quote positions of all candidates in their journals.[13] Since they normally do not enter the political ring to advocate or support candidates or party positions, they have little with which to bargain in dealing with state politicians. In turn, they have little access to the key state policymakers, the politicians.

Most state educational associations are poorly prepared to do "political battle" when they are forced to fight for what they consider their vital concerns. In some of their attempts to direct statewide political actions, such as the teacher strike in Florida in 1966, the results have been disastrous.[14] State education associations normally avoid political conflicts and prefer to maintain their traditional roles as professional advisors and to rely upon older forms of adaptation found to be successful at state and local levels.

Another factor weakening state education associations is that as representatives of teachers, they are always seeking more money from the state and tend to equate higher teacher salaries automatically with quality education. At the same time, they are hesitant to openly support tax increase proposals or back those politicians who have to endure public protest over tax increases.

Since proposals to increase taxes generate more conflict than almost any other issue, the dominant economic groups in the state often mobilize against them. Counterpressures to educators' requests for more monies are often exerted by conservative interests and politicians to keep taxes from being increased. For instance, demands are more and more being made that educators be held "accountable for public funds" and the outputs of schools such as gains in students' knowledge and the effects upon their behavior be demonstrated to justify additional monies for education.[15]

[13]The policy of noninvolvement in party politics appears to be changing. The National Education Association, it is reported, is considering setting up a national unit to endorse and support political candidates. Although a few of its state-level affiliates operate such groups, this would be the first time that the national organization has actively backed specific politicians. *Phi Delta Kappan*, March 1972, p. 455.

[14]Gayle Norton, "The Florida Story," *Phi Delta Kappan*, June 1968, pp. 555–59; *cf.* Parke B. Loren and Ira A. England, "Florida Education: Running a Political Obstacle Course," *Phi Delta Kappan*, September 1968, pp. 27–32.

[15]"Accountability '70," *Compact*, October 1970, entire issue.

Teachers generally have been suspicious of the accountability movement, and particularly of a system that linked their salaries to achievement measured by examinations. At its August 1970 convention the American Federation of Teachers formally opposed performance contracting and resolved to wage a national campaign against its use. It denounced performance contracting as "educational gimmickry" and suggested that it amounts to business exploitation of children. The National Education Association at its July 1970 convention adopted a resolution that urged its state and local affiliates to "resist school evaluations by non-professional personnel, such as those being conducted under contract between the Department of H.E.W. and private, profit-making firms." Thomas Fitzgibbon, *The Use of Standardized Instruments with*

All educational organizations, including state NEA affiliates, have been forced to become more politically oriented because of recent changes in state political environments. The rise of the American Federation of Teachers with its more militant orientation has given teachers an alternative organization which is more willing to use group power to obtain its ends. The local successes of the AFT and the increasing competition for membership has forced state education associations, as well as the National Education Association, to become more militant.[16]

The AFT, however, suffers from perhaps even more serious weaknesses as an interest group attempting to influence state policy. For one thing, it has a much smaller membership and can actually speak for only a minority of educators. Although it is a more cohesive group, the union affiliation and the big-city image—except in the highly urbanized states with large union presence in state politics—incurs all of the antiunion and anti-big-city bias prevalent in the politics of many states. The AFT, as a result, has even less access to the real centers of state power than do state education associations. Furthermore, AFT tactics are more suitable to the local level than they are to the state level, and with few exceptions, AFT has had relatively little success in influencing educational policies at the state level.

State organizations of teachers, whether NEA affiliates or AFT, are major sources of educational demands on the state. By making such demands they perform an important role in the state policymaking process.

State Administrators' Associations. In the past, state education associations had an all-inclusive membership, and they were open to all who worked in education. It was widely believed that all educators held common goals for education. Administrators in this period were looked upon as particularly competent teachers who had been chosen to serve as leaders of teachers. Therefore administrators not only were members of state education associations but normally held the key positions in the associations. There was no need for administrators to have their own organization, since they could advance their positions through the state education association. In the California Teacher Association, for instance, Bowles recalls:

> The leaders and council of CTA were administrators. There wasn't a need at that time for a militant administrators organization. They were all in CTA.

Urban and Minority-Group Pupils (New York: Harcourt Brace Jovanovich, 1971), pp. 86–87; *cf.* "How Education Groups View Contracting," *Nation's Schools,* October 1970, pp. 86–87.

[16]Alan Rosenthal, "Pedagogues and Power," *Urban Affairs Quarterly,* September 1966, pp. 83–102; *cf.* Rosenthal, *Pedagogues and Power,* pp. 22–48.

> Historically CTA was the organization through which the superintendents ran their organization. It was our [the administrators'] vehicle.
>
> CTA! There was no problem. We were CTA, CTA was controlled by superintendents of schools, local schools.
>
> Administrators within CTA gave teachers the classroom teachers association as a temporary sop to give them something to do but not to have control of CTA.[17]

With the development of teacher militancy during the past decade, the policy of lumping all educators into the same organization has become increasingly difficult to maintain. Teachers' demands for collective negotiations placed administrators in an entirely new role. No longer could they claim to be just teachers leading teachers. Administrators were forced to assume a management role in the labor-management context, a role for which many administrators were neither professionally prepared nor psychologically suited. But as the only professional employee selected by the board, the superintendent was forced to act as the executive officer representing the board in these proceedings.[18] As these new relationships developed, the all-inclusive membership of state education associations gradually broke down. In state after state, administrators had to create separate organizations to speak for their interests. This was also true at the national level. The prestigious American Association of School Administrators had a difficult time maintaining its relationships with the NEA and not offending important elements among the aggressive classroom teacher units.

Today there are separate state associations of school administrators in a number of states. In comparison with teacher organizations these groups are relatively small, but their influence exceeds their numerical size. The position of the school administrator, particularly the local superintendent, gives him much more status, and his professional views are sought out and listened to more than the views of teachers. Most superintendents are more politically astute than teachers and have various types of communication linkages with local and state political elites. In fact, administrators of large cities often have on their staffs governmental relations officers to work with state and federal political and administrative personnel. Furthermore, they appear to state leaders to be more conservative, since they, unlike teachers,

---

[17]Bowles, "Power Structure in State Politics," p. 337.

[18]Ronald G. Corwin, *Militant Professionalism: A Study of Organizational Conflict in High School* (New York: Appleton-Century-Crofts, 1970), pp. 52–53; *cf.* Neal Gross and Robert E. Herriott, *Staff Leadership in Public Schools: A Sociological Inquiry* (New York: John Wiley & Sons, Inc., 1965); and Fred M. Heddinger, "Superintendent and Board-Staff Relations: Changing Dimensions of Education Roles," *School Boards Chart a New Course: Proceedings of the 1966 Convention of the National School Boards Association*, pp. 247–54.

are not continuously and solely requesting additional monies for salary increases.

Despite these strengths, administrators' organizations have some serious weaknesses. Administrators are the men in the middle. On the one hand, they have the school board to pacify; and on the other, the increasingly militant teachers—and these two groups often push for entirely different policies. Administrators are forced to try to conciliate both groups without offending their boards, to whom ultimately they owe their positions. The role of conciliator is always difficult and sometimes precarious. Nevertheless, administrators, particularly superintendents, still play an important and perhaps the key role in both local and state educational policymaking.

State School Board Associations. The third group placing demands on the state regarding educational policies is the state school board association. These groups found in every state, differ from the professional education associations in a number of ways. They are much smaller, although approximately 90 percent of the local school boards in the states are represented in state school board associations. Local school board members comprise a more diverse group than the educational professionals and are performing a part-time, unpaid function. State educational policies do not affect them personally in the same way that they affect professional educators; therefore, state policies are not as vital to them individually. Nor are state school board associations as cohesive as their professional counterparts. Furthermore, since school board members usually come from the more conservative elements of the community, they are less interested in changing the status quo. Rather, their main efforts more often are against proposals for change made by other educational groups. Frequently they are pitted in the legislative halls not only against the professional education groups but also against the state board of education over such issues as local control, school district reorganization, teacher certification, and other educational measures.[19]

Despite their relatively small size and lack of cohesiveness, state school board associations have considerable influence both at the state and at the national level. Board members are often local leaders—bankers, lawyers, merchants, real estate developers, wives of the professional and managerial classes, and the like—which automatically gives them greater access to state politicians. Since they are inclined to express conservative positions, their advice is more apt to be listened to and followed because it is usually easier not to change than to change state policy.[20]

[19]Koerner, *Who Controls American Education?*, pp. 99–100.
[20]Harold V. Webb, "Role of the State and National School Board Association," *Facing Challenges to the Public Schools, Proceedings of the 1962 Convention of the National School Boards Association,* pp. 30–34.

In a speech before the 1962 National School Boards Association Convention, the executive director of that organization described the NSBA's power, and much of what he says also applies to state politics. He claimed that

> NSBA, which represents many conservative business and professional inter-
> ests, probably is given more weight by ear-to-the-ground members of Con-
> gress than the groups which represent "only" the teachers.[21]

At the state level this is equally true. Local state legislators frequently check the opinion of local school board members, leaders in their communities, before taking a position on educational measures. For these reasons, state school board associations are among the most influential interest groups affecting educational policy.

State school board associations, however, are not as influential as they might be. The associations are frequently dominated by rural elementary board members, the most numerous type on school boards. As a result the statewide organization has difficulty agreeing upon a policy that is acceptable to all school boards, especially to urban board members. Also, state school policy is not personally as important to board members as their full-time occupations and activities, which tends to keep them from serving on state or national advisory committees where many of the ideas for new policies are incubated. For instance, in 1966 Representative Edith Green of Oregon reported that an analysis of the membership of twenty-five advisory committees to the Office of Education showed that of some three thousand members appointed, only four were school board members.[22] Professional educators, on the other hand, not only have an immediate stake in getting involved in such activities but also gain in status in the educational community for participation on such committees.

Still another weakness of state school board associations is that school board members' duties are demanding more and more of their time as society grows increasingly complex and this complexity is reflected in our schools. New and unfamiliar problems require school board members to spend considerable time on school policies, which in turn makes the board members more dependent on the professionals for guidance. Because of these limitations on school board members, the potential power of state school board associations is much greater than their actual power in state educational policymaking.

Parent Organizations.   The fourth and final statewide group growing

---

[21]*Ibid.*, p. 33.

[22]Edith Green, "The Role of the School Board in Society," *School Boards: A Creative Force, Proceedings of the 1967 Convention of the National School Boards Association*, pp. 9–12.

out of local school systems consists of the various parent organizations, the Parent-Teachers Association being the most notable. The PTA is by far the largest educational organization, and it has both state and national offices. About one-half of all parents with children in public schools, it is estimated, are members of the local PTA. To the vast majority of parents, however, membership in the PTA means little more than that they paid the annual dues to help raise money for the local school. Few parents join the PTA to shape educational policies. In fact, a major weakness of the PTA is its lack of organizational goals. In a sense the PTA's only purpose is to give parents a sense of participation in school matters and to support local school administrators in the community, and consequently many parents and teachers feel that PTAs are a waste of time. Obviously, there is little cohesion in this large, amorphous, predominantly middle-class group, and seldom can it agree on a firm stand about any state or national issue. PTAs therefore rarely have any influence on state policies, although some members may dutifully visit every session of the state legislature to support positions of the educational professionals.[23]

Parent groups are at times influential in shaping educational policies. But normally it is only when an educational crisis erupts that parents play the game of politics seriously. In these instances, parents often form *ad hoc* groups to apply pressure at key points in state government. In the civil rights conflict, this has repeatedly occurred. Most recently, white parents against school busing have pressured state politicians, who at times have sought to delay decisions in an attempt to ride out the storm, knowing that ideological issues often subside as rapidly as they arise. Black parents, and parents of other disadvantaged minorities, have on various occasions also formed groups to press for their positions. Although in no cases have they matched the size, resources, and influence of the competing white-middle-class organizations,[24] they do present demands, and particularly in certain urban-industrial states where minorities represent potential swing votes, play an important role in determining state educational policy.

Other Group Inputs. A number of other groups are directly affected by state educational policies, since state actions involve taxation and regulatory activities as well as the operation of certain educational facilities. In Figure 6–2 these groups are shown growing out of the circle representing the state community.

[23]Koerner, *Who Controls American Education?*, pp. 148–49.

[24]Harmon Zeigler and Karl Johnson found that in the direct interaction process, business interests have a strong advantage in that their representatives constitute the largest single bloc of lobbyists, include a disproportionate number of ex-legislators, and receive more solicitations from legislators in response to initiated interactions than any other lobbyists. See *The Politics of Education in the States* (New York: The Bobbs-Merrill Co., Inc., 1972), pp. 157–58.

Education is one of the most expensive state functions, and there are continuous demands for still additional expenditures. Major economic interest groups, because of the impact of state tax policies upon them, are forced to be concerned with educational policies. Frequently, taxpayers' associations or research leagues are created by economic groups to undertake studies of state expenditures and taxes, and these conservative economic organizations have considerable influence on state politics. Normally these associations do not openly speak against education, since being against education is like being against motherhood. Instead they call for "fiscal responsibility," which to them means keeping state expenditures and state taxes low, particularly those taxes with a direct impact upon them.[25]

Major economic groups are obviously influential in state politics. They normally have full-time staffs working to protect their tax positions, and these offices may act as public relations experts and lobbyists for the industry. Contributions to political campaigns and parties ensure their access to state politicians and party leaders. They also attempt to elect conservative legislators and governors who agree with their positions. In turn, these officials work for frugality in state spending. In many states a conservative ethos so dominates state politics that politicians who urge increased expenditures may be risking their political careers. In Figure 6–2 the dominant economic groups and the key individuals in these groups are represented in the state community circle as being part of the state power structure.

Education is just one of a host of important services performed by the state, and frequently supporters of other state programs organize so that their preferred programs will "get a fair share" of state funds. Groups supporting highways, public health, welfare, higher education, or any one of a number of other state programs often compete with public education groups. This competition is particularly keen in many states between interest groups supporting elementary and secondary education and higher education. Alumni groups of state colleges and universities are often called forth to protect their "ole alma mater" against encroachments on state funds by public schools. Similarly, highway user groups and clientele groups of other state agencies organize and attempt to influence state policy when they feel their interests are being threatened by competition of educational interests.

Groups supporting private and parochial schools also at times enter the political arena attempting to influence state educational policies, since these institutions are affected by state actions. State regulatory provisions, for instance, may apply directly to all schools. Laws pertaining to teacher salary schedules indirectly affect nonpublic educational institutions, since any substantial advantage given to public schools in the form of higher

25Bailey *et al., Schoolmen and Politics,* pp. 46–47.

salaries for teachers may create a competitive disadvantage in attracting qualified staffs to the nonpublic schools. The increasing financial plight of parochial schools in recent years resulted in mounting pressure in a number of states for public financial aid to help support certain programs in these schools. State education politics is therefore important to these private educational groups, and they are often active in the political arena.[26]

Use of the state's regulatory powers brings still other groups into educational politics. For instance, the state's power to regulate textbooks causes publishing companies to become involved in state political processes. Other private companies are affected by state building and purchasing requirements. State regulations regarding school curricula and certification requirements for teachers affect still other interests. Many ideologically oriented groups, such as the American Legion, conservative farm and business groups, and labor unions, at times push for enactment of laws adding courses that they feel are desirable to the curriculum. Such groups also often attempt to influence state policies controlling who can teach. In recent years such issues as teacher loyalty oaths, certification requirements, and tenure provisions have been the subject of intense debates in many states, with ideologically oriented groups being in the vanguard of this conflict.

State operation of such institutions as the state schools for the blind and deaf and the teacher colleges bring still other groups into state educational politics. Demands of these institutions are supported not only by professional staffs and other employees but also by certain clientele groups which support the institution's position in the political process. Teacher colleges are especially important in state educational politics. These colleges are able to develop large support groups of alumni, and many of the proposals for state educational policies are conceived by professors of education—the "scribblers," as Bailey and his associates called them. Many of the ideas and proposals that have become the basis for state educational policies have been originated by these academics.[27]

Inputs from the Federal Government.   Federal actions such as court decisions, grants in aid and other legislative enactments by Congress, and administrative actions by the executive departments also yield important inputs affecting state educational policies. In our federal system all levels of government influence all other levels of government, and this is especially true in the vital function of education. In a later chapter we shall examine in detail the inputs from the federal government and their effects on state educational policies. In the next chapter we shall examine the effects of state government itself on shaping educational policies.

[26]"State Aid to Private Education," *Compact*, February 1970, entire issue.
[27]Bailey *et al., Schoolmen and Politics*, pp. 23–26.

chapter seven

Governmental Within Puts on State Educational Policy

State educational policies are shaped not only by the demands or inputs from the environment but also by the character of state political institutions and individuals holding political office (i.e., within puts from the state political system).[1] In Figure 6–2 various institutional offices involved in state educational policymaking are represented by small circles within a large state governmental circle. Interactions of these institutional parties (i.e., the governor, legislature, courts, educational agencies, and other state administrative agencies) are shown by arrows connecting the various circles. The influence of these institutional parties and the effect of such factors as the structural organization, the formal rules of the system, the interaction of various parts of the state organization, and the political and personal characteristics of state officials will be considered here.

Office of the Governor

One major institutional party affecting state educational policy is the governor. The governor plays a major role in educational policymaking despite the doctrine of separation of powers between the three branches of government and the decentralized nature of states' administrative structures. In recent years his influence in policymaking has been enhanced by the growth of the state government's involvement in such functional fields as education. Not only have the governor's executive functions of seeing that the laws are "faithfully executed" multiplied, but governors are increasingly being called upon to assume a leading role in legislation. Gov-

---

[1]Harmon Zeigler and Karl F. Johnson in *The Politics of Education in the States* (New York: The Bobbs-Merrill Co., Inc., 1972) use a similar theoretical framework to study how much influence legislators have in the conversion of educational demands into policy outputs.

ernors are instrumental in initiating and proposing policies, in preparing budgets to support state programs, and in shepherding their proposals through the legislature. The governor's "legislative program," or those bills initiated by the executive office and the bureaucracy, are major sources of legislative proposals.[2]

Education as a Political Liability.   Preparation of an executive budget, the budget system used in most states, gives the governor additional power in the policy process, since there is no more crucial decision than allocating state resources.[3] The budget power, however, is not without its limitations, and it frequently forces the governor into a political and fiscal dilemma. Balancing the budget carries with it the politically unpopular duty of either proposing reductions in state expenditures or raising additional taxes to meet increases in expenditures. Both alternatives are politically unpopular, but raising additional taxes to meet the constantly increasing demands of education is one of the most dangerous political shoals governors face.

The political fortune of governors often depends on how they handle educational demands. Governors are elected from a statewide constituency, and to get elected they must normally make a broader and more liberal appeal on issues than state legislators who have smaller and more homogeneous constituencies. Education in recent years has become a campaign issue difficult to avoid because it affects many people directly and intimately, and in many states it has become a highly charged issue. The biggest controversies are from the negative standpoint, such as people against busing, or sex education, or student unrest, or some other aspect of education. Normally, so long as the schools are operating in their customary way they get little attention, and almost no one makes the improvement of education the number one state priority. Few parents ever approach candidates, or write or telegram public officials, with a program to upgrade American schools. Education only becomes an issue when something threatens to change the system, such as integration.[4] To get elected, a gubernatorial candidate must be attuned to popular attitudes about educational issues, and if the educational issues cannot be avoided, he must speak and act in a manner acceptable to the dominant views.

[2]Duane Lockard, *The Politics of State and Local Government* (New York: The Macmillan Company, 1963), pp. 358–64.

[3]Joseph A. Schlesinger, "The Politics of the Executive," in *Politics in the American States.* ed. Herbert Jacob and Kenneth Vines (Boston: Little, Brown and Company, 1971), p. 230; *cf. Book of the States, 1969–70* (Lexington, Ky.: Council of State Governments, 1970), pp. 144–52.

[4]Federal Executive Order A-95 requiring review and comment on all federal grants by the governor has strengthened governors' powers over federal grant programs.

Once elected, governors often find the issue of education even more troublesome. One problem is that there is little agreement about what should be done in education. Even within the educational establishment it is difficult to define any specific mutual objectives—there are no widely agreed-upon concrete goals for education. A governor can expect little political support from educational interests, the political party, or the general public on such tough questions as school finance or desegregation. Few actively support tax increases to carry out campaign promises, and the governor is apt to be blamed for whatever action is taken on the highly sensitive issue of desegregation. The dangers inherent in educational issues are evidenced by the wrecks of numerous governors' political careers since World War II.

Recognition that there is not much political gain to be made from education without great risks acts as a damper on gubernatorial leadership on educational problems requiring an increase in state educational expenditures or action to desegregate schools or to fundamentally change the educational system. On the other hand, the highly volatile issue of school desegregation has been used as a major campaign issue in a number of southern states.

Powers to Shape Educational Policy.   In most states the executive authority is fragmented, especially in the field of education. There are boards or commissions, appointed in diverse ways, for vocational education, vocational rehabilitation, higher education, community and junior colleges, and general secondary and elementary education, as well as various individual college boards. All of this authority is spread out in so many ways that a governor, the chief executive charged with the responsibility for advancing the cause of the state, has little authority over the educational establishment. He has few if any planning tools to help him look to the future needs of education.[5] And, no matter how strongly he feels about the way the state should go, he is burdened with such a multiplicity of boards and commissions and such a diffusion of authority and responsibility that he is not really responsible or really accountable.[6]

Because of conflicting political pressures and organizational weaknesses of the office, governors are often in the unenviable position of having to act as advocate for change and increased educational programs and at the same time being forced to hold the line and not raise taxes or take measures disturbing to certain ideologically oriented groups. They attempt this difficult feat in a number of ways and use all of the formal and political powers they possess.[7] Table 7–1 shows how widely governors'

[5]Craig S. Barnes, "Who Cares about Education?" *Compact*, April 1971, pp. 3–4.
[6]Lockard, *Politics of State and Local Government*, pp. 380–89.
[7]Schlesinger, "Politics of the Executive," pp. 222–36.

Table 7-1 A Combined Index of the Formal Powers of the Governors

	Tenure potential	Appointive powers	Budget powers	Veto powers	Total index
New York	5	5	5	5	20
Illinois	5	5	5	5	20
Hawaii	5	5	5	5	20
California	5	4	5	5	19
Michigan	5	4	5	5	19
Minnesota	5	4	5	5	19
New Jersey	4	5	5	5	19
Pennsylvania	4	5	5	5	19
Maryland	4	5	5	5	19
Utah	5	3	5	5	18
Washington	5	3	5	5	18
Ohio	4	4	5	5	18
Massachusetts	5	5	5	3	18
Wyoming	5	2	5	5	17
Missouri	4	3	5	5	17
Alaska	4	3	5	5	17
Tennessee	3	5	5	5	17
Idaho	5	4	5	3	17
North Dakota	5	1	5	5	16
Kentucky	3	4	5	4	16
Virginia	3	5	5	3	16
Montana	5	3	5	3	16
Nebraska	4	3	4	5	16
Connecticut	5	4	4	3	16
Delaware	4	1	5	5	15
Oklahoma	4	1	5	5	15
Alabama	3	3	5	4	15
Wisconsin	5	2	5	3	15
Colorado	5	1	4	5	15
Louisiana	4	2	4	5	15
Georgia	3	1	5	5	14
Oregon	4	2	5	3	14
Nevada	5	2	5	2	14
Arizona	2	1	5	5	13
South Dakota	1	4	5	3	13
Maine	4	2	5	2	13
Vermont	2	4	5	2	13
Kansas	2	2	4	5	13
Arkansas	2	4	3	4	13
Iowa	2	3	5	2	12
New Hampshire	2	2	5	2	11
Rhode Island	2	3	4	2	11
New Mexico	1	1	5	3	10
North Carolina	3	2	4	1	10
Mississippi	3	1	1	5	10
Indiana	3	5	1	1	10

Florida	3	2	1	3	9
South Carolina	3	1	1	3	8
West Virginia	3	3	1	1	8
Texas	2	1	1	3	7

Source: Joseph A. Schlesinger, "The Politics of the Executive," in Herbert Jacob and Kenneth N. Vines, eds., *Politics in the American States: A Comparative Analysis,* Second Edition, p. 232. Copyright © 1971 by Little, Brown and Company (Inc.). Reprinted by permission.

formal powers vary from state to state and ranks their strength on a five-point scale in accordance with their budget, appointive, and veto powers and their tenure potential (length of terms and provisions for succeeding themselves).

In those states where the governor has power to appoint the members of state boards of education or the state superintendent, he may make such appointments as a means of influencing educational demands of the state bureaucracy. Or he may attempt to affect schools through the budget or his use of the veto, especially in those states where he has an item veto which permits the disapproval of specific items without vetoing the entire measure. Creation of a governor's commission to study educational needs is another frequently used device that can be used to delay action as well as to mobilize public support for new programs, greater expenditures, and increased taxes. To some degree the governor's visibility—his being the most widely known state official and the leader of the political party—permits him to make issues and to focus public attention on or away from certain state problems, particularly in competitive two-party states where the governor is leader of one party.[8] The governor may call special sessions of the legislature to deal with a specific issue like educational finance, and he may as chief executive inject himself into local educational issues, as a number of southern governors have so dramatically illustrated in the controversy over school desegregation. The options available to governors vary from state to state, since the formal and political powers of the office differ, but in all states the governor is influential in educational policymaking, and groups interested in education must deal with him.

The political context of the office of the governor is a major factor shaping all state policies, including educational policy. Interest groups, such as state education associations that hope to influence educational policy, must recognize the power of the governor's office, and the reality

[8]*Ibid.,* pp. 229–30; *cf.* Lockard, *Politics of State and Local Government,* pp. 373–74.

that the governor is essentially a political creature. His success depends on his ability to muster political support, and his very existence forces him to be attentive to those with political resources. Therefore, groups with political assets have access to the governor and can influence policy through him; those without do not have political access and cannot shape public policy. As we have seen, educational groups generally have few political resources that could give them access to the governor because of their insistence that education should be divorced from politics.

State Legislatures

State legislatures, which in theory are the fount of all state laws and the final authority on allocation of public funds, are another major institutional party affecting educational policymaking. All state constitutions make provisions for public schools and acknowledge state responsibility for the maintenance and support of a system of public schools.[9]

Education is a state function despite the common misconception that it is a local responsibility. Local schools may do only what they are authorized to do by law enacted by the state legislature. They are unable to expand their programs or powers without repeatedly returning to the state legislature to plead their case for additional authority and resources. State legislatures are in effect the super–school board of the state, and obviously these legal and constitutional powers are a major influence shaping educational policymaking.[10]

Weaknesses of State Legislatures. State legislatures, however, have continued to lose power and influence to the governor and state executive agencies. State executive agencies have become increasingly instrumental in policymaking. State bureaucracies have taken over functions that were traditionally discharged by legislatures. In fact, bills that affect state executive agencies by giving or taking away authority and responsibilities are often drafted by the very agencies that the legislation affects. Agency administrators are regarded as most expert in different policy areas, so their recommendations are given special consideration. Budgets in states with executive budgets are largely decided in the governors' office where the real competition between agencies takes place. Although Ways and Means

[9]Herbert Kaufman, *Politics and Policies in State and Local Governments* (Englewood Cliffs, N.J.: Prentice-Hall, Inc., 1963), pp. 30–32.

[10]Alexander Heard, *State Legislatures in American Politics* (Englewood Cliffs, N.J.: Prentice-Hall, Inc., 1966), pp. 154–57; *cf.* Wilder Crane, Jr., and Meredith W. Watts, Jr., *State Legislative Systems* (Englewood Cliffs, N.J.: Prentice-Hall, Inc., 1968), pp. 1–13.

committees remain a hurdle appropriation bills must clear, legislatures are not as influential in expenditure policies, and the state executive agencies and bureaucracies have become major decisional forces in state policy-making.[11]

American states have not all evolved in the same way, and although structurally and constitutionally they may appear quite similar, the differences between state legislatures are striking. Legislatures reflect different sets of political and social forces, traditions, and practices, and consequently they function differently. The character of political demands, the ways in which demands are made, and the kinds of bargaining and maneuvering in response to them differs in various states. Distribution of powers within state legislatures varies from state to state. The fifty legislatures are, in short, all things. Some are powerful, some are weak. Some are authoritative on questions on which others are powerless. Some are efficient and well organized for their functions, while others are nearly chaotic in their ineffectiveness. Some are dominated by disciplined and powerful parties, others are torn by dissidence and factional rivalry. These political differences to a large degree determine how legislatures meet the constitutionally mandated duties for education.[12]

Party Competition in States. The character of state legislative politics is most directly influenced by the extent of party competition within a state and within the legislative districts. There is a wide variation in the patterns of state politics. At one end of the continuum, there are eleven southern states where the Democratic party has nearly always elected the governor, and minority party representation in the legislature is negligible. At the other end of the continuum, there are ten states where neither party has had dominant legislative control, and legislative majorities and gubernatorial winners have alternated between the two parties. Between these two extremes there are varying patterns of one-party dominance and limited two-party competition. Table 7–2 classifies state legislatures according to the degree of one-party control and two-party competition.

An analysis of Table 7–2 reveals that the majority of states are one-party states or limited two-party states where one party controls one or both houses of the legislature most of the time. The noncompetitiveness of state politics is even more evident within state legislative districts. Even in those states where legislatures may shift from one party to another, the shift results from competition in a few districts rather than genuine competition in most districts of the state.[13]

[11]Lockard, *Politics of State and Local Government*, pp. 272–73.
[12]Crane and Watts, *State Legislative Systems*, pp. 39–44.
[13]*Ibid.*, pp. 96–98; *cf.* Jacob and Vines, *Politics in the American States*, p. 87.

Table 7–2   State Legislatures Classified According to Degree of One-Party Control, 1947–1966*

A. 1. One-party States: Same party controlled the governorship and both houses throughout the period, and minority representation was negligible (all Democratic states).

Alabama   *Arkansas*   *Louisiana*   *Mississippi*   *South Carolina*

2. One-party States: Same party [Democratic] controlled the governorship and both houses throughout the period, and the minority representation was negligible [but Republicans were stronger here than in the group above, and this second group had developed a greater degree of two-party competitive politics].

Florida   *Georgia*   *North Carolina*   *Tennessee*   *Texas*   *Virginia*

B. States with One Party Dominant: Same party controlled both houses throughout the period but did not always control governorship, and (except for Oklahoma) minority party occasionally had over one-fourth of the seats in at least one house.

DEMOCRATIC: *Arizona, Kentucky, Maryland, Oklahoma, West Virginia*
REPUBLICAN: *Kansas, New Hampshire, Vermont*

State Legislatures Classified According to Degree of Two-Party Competition, 1947–1966

State	Senate			House			Governorship	
	D	R	Tie	D	R	Tie	D	R

C. 1. Limited Two-party States: Same party controlled both houses throughout most of the period and the governorship at least half the time.

South Dakota	2	18	—	—	20	—	2	18
North Dakota	0	20	—	2	18	—	6	14
New Mexico	20	0	—	18	2	—	12	8
New York	2	18	—	2	18	—	4	16
Maine	2	18	—	2	18	—	6	14
Iowa	2	18	—	2	18	—	8	12
Wisconsin	0	20	—	4	16	—	6	14
Wyoming	0	20	—	4	14	2	8	12
Missouri	18	2	—	16	4	—	20	0
Illinois	4	16	—	4	16	—	10	10
Rhode Island	8	6	6	20	0	—	14	6
Idaho	6	14	—	2	18	—	6	14

2. Limited Two-party States: Same party controlled both houses throughout most of the period but usually not the governorship.

Michigan	2	18	—	2	16	2	14	6
New Jersey	0	20	—	6	14	—	12	8
Ohio	4	14	2	4	16	—	12	8

3. Limited Two-party States: Two houses controlled by different parties during most of the period.

Nevada	0	18	2	20	0	—	12	8
Connecticut	14	6	—	2	18	—	14	6

D. Two-party States: Neither party had dominant legislative control, and in most cases party control of legislature approximated control of governorship.

Pennsylvania	0	18	2	8	12	—	8	12
Indiana	4	16	—	6	14	—	10	10
Washington	12	6	2	16	4	—	10	10
Massachusetts	8	10	2	16	4	—	10	10
Delaware	14	6	—	12	8	—	10	10
Colorado	6	14	—	10	10	—	12	8
Oregon	8	10	2	8	12	—	2	18
California	8	10	2	8	12	—	10	10
Utah	10	10	—	8	10	2	4	16
Montana	10	10	—	10	10	—	4	16

Source: *The Legislative Process in the United States*, by Malcolm E. Jewell and Samuel C. Patterson, pp. 143–44. Copyright © 1966 by Random House, Inc. Reprinted by permission of the publisher.

*Alaska and Hawaii are omitted because of their brief terms as states, and Nebraska and Minnesota are omitted because they have nonpartisan legislatures. The time period is 1946–1965 for states with off-year elections: Kentucky, New Jersey, Virginia, Mississippi, and Louisiana.

Some Effects of Party System on Policymaking Processes. The state political party system is a major factor affecting policymaking processes, and all interest groups including educational groups must adapt to partisan divisions within the state. The influence of parties, in other than the purely one-party states, varies roughly according to the degree of party competition. In many states parties are important actors in the policy process, and in some states they are the most significant determinant of policy decisions. Their support is crucially necessary to the passage of any measure. Interest groups must therefore seek support of party leaders and attempt to influence party platforms.[14] Here again educational groups are disadvantaged because of their traditional "non-political" stance.

The general noncompetitiveness of state party politics also has a great impact on state policymaking. For one thing, interest groups are ordinarily more influential. Where one-party politics prevails, divisions on public policy obviously are not along party lines; instead, divisions tend to follow interest, regional, or factional lines. In this type of legislative system, interest groups originate most policy proposals, organize support for the passage of bills, and follow them through the legislative maze until they are enacted into law.[15]

Interest groups in the states at the less competitive end of the partisan continuum perform many of the usual functions of political parties. This is especially true regarding recruitment and financing of legislative candidates. In one-party states the primary election, that is, the nomination process, is more significant than the general election. Since all candidates

[14]George S. Blair, *American Legislatures: Structure and Process* (New York: Harper & Row, Publishers, 1967), pp. 292–306.
[15]Crane and Watts, *State Legislative Systems*, pp. 90–98.

in these primaries are of the same party, they cannot turn to the party for financial support to run their primary campaigns. Interest groups are the foremost source of these funds. The influence of those interest groups with financial or political means to assist candidates is enhanced, and they have a greater access to these candidates. Although candidates are not as dependent on interest groups for financing their elections in the more competitive states, interest group support, both financial and symbolic endorsement, is needed and helpful to candidates seeking office in all states.[16]

Interest groups gain access to public officials by aiding and supporting them in elections. As we have seen, one of the serious weaknesses of educational groups is that they do not have—or at least have not often used—political or financial resources to help nominate or elect candidates and therefore do not have the access to or the influence with politicians as do some other interest groups.

Low Visibility of State Legislators.   Another result of the noncompetitiveness in state party politics is that persons desiring to influence legislation must deal with each individual state legislator rather than with a responsible political party that can be held accountable in future elections. Since political parties have little control over how individual legislators vote in noncompetitive states, persons or groups attempting to influence policy must persuade individual legislators. This is difficult not only because of the number of legislators but also because of the "low visibility" of state legislators. There is little or no way the general public can know state legislators or the kind of representation they are giving their constituents. Most state legislators are not newsworthy, so the mass media carry relatively little information about state legislative matters. Stories that are publicized do not normally deal fully with the complex issues involved, and seldom do they discuss legislators' voting positions. Little can be learned about what goes on in the state legislature from official records. Few states publish anything similar to the verbatim reports in the *Congressional Record*. Most legislative records show only a relatively few roll-call votes, and then only the final vote which may not accurately reflect individual legislators' in the debates. Few keep any records of committee hearings, although these hearings are often the centers of real decision making. The net effect is that there is no way individuals, except full-time lobbyists, can be fully aware of what takes place in the state legislature.[17]

[16]David B. Walker, "State Legislatures in a Changing Federal System" (Address before the Southeastern Assembly on State Legislatures in American Politics, Atlanta, March 31, 1967); printed in *Congressional Record* 90th Cong., 1st sess., May 11, 1967, Vol. 113, No. 74.

[17]Edgar L. Morphet and David L. Jessen, eds., *Emerging State Responsibilities for Education* (Denver, Colo.: Improving State Leadership in Education, 1970), pp. 24–25.

Lack of knowledge about state legislators and legislation seriously hinders statewide interest groups with a widely scattered membership, such as education. It is especially difficult for educational groups to keep their members informed on legislative matters and to mobilize any political clout. Obviously this weakens the influence of educational groups in shaping state educational policies.

Influence of State Agencies.   Lack of competitive political parties and party leadership also permits functional bureaucracies to play a greater role in policymaking. Legislatures in one-party states are more dependent on the expertise of administrators, and administrative agencies can more easily promote legislation through their clientele groups or supporters. Thus the agriculture department can call on farmers to push policies it wants enacted, or the state highway department can mobilize a host of groups economically affected by the department, such as highway users, truckers, motel operators, restaurants, gasoline companies, and construction firms, to lobby for its legislative program and requests for appropriations.

Unfortunately, state education agencies do not have strong cohesive clientele groups to support their legislative proposals. Although education benefits almost everyone indirectly, few recognize a direct economic effect from activities of state education agencies, which consequently receive little support from clientele groups. Not even all educators identify with or support identical legislative proposals. This is due in part to the divisions in the educational establishment, and in part to the strong and pervasive tradition of localism and the view that state education agencies should exercise only essential custodial functions.[18]

Other Legislative Within Puts.   A host of other aspects of state legislative procedures—the way state legislative districts are constructed, low salaries of legislators, rapid turnover in composition of the state legislature, every-other-year sessions, and lack of professional staffs to assist legislators and legislative committees—affect state policymaking. Our point here is not to examine the weaknesses of state legislatures but to show that these political factors—the within puts—vitally affect state policymaking. All interest groups, including educational groups, must operate in the political context of the legislature if they are to be successful in obtaining their desired objectives.

[18]*Improving State Leadership in Education,* Annual Report of the Advisory Council on State Departments of Education (U.S. Department of Health, Education, and Welfare, 1966), p. 5; *cf.* Ward W. Keesecher, *State Boards of Education and Chief State School Officers* (U.S. Department of Health, Education, and Welfare, 1950), pp. 7–10.

State Education Agencies

Permanent state education agencies, a third type of institution involved in educational policymaking, are of fairly recent origin in American states. Although every constitution provides that education is a state responsibility, states traditionally have sought to develop and administer public education through units of local government. Only as local programs of education became increasingly complex, and demands for services outstripped local districts' ability to supply them, did most states establish central agencies for education.[19]

Because of the historical reliance on local control of education, American states do not have a politically centralized administrative office similar to the Ministry of Education found in many other countries. We have, instead, a highly fragmented and decentralized educational structure. State-level administration of education is carried out through a triumvirate of a state board (or several boards responsible for various aspects of education), a state superintendent of education, and a state department composed of a professional staff.[20]

The various state education agencies differ considerably, despite some basic similarities in organization pattern. In effect, we have fifty different organizational plans for administering education at the state level.[21] Figure 7–1 illustrates the structure and function of six state education agencies and shows how the methods of organizing the various components of the state educational agency differ.

Methods of Selection.   Methods by which the members of the several components of the central educational agency are selected differ widely. For instance, in the forty-eight states having a state board of education (Illinois and Wisconsin are the exceptions), members are (1) elected by the people or representatives of the people, or (2) appointed by the governor, or (3) serve ex officio by virtue of state office or position held. In some states a combination of these methods is used to select board members. As can be seen in Table 7–3, in thirty-four states the state school board members are selected by gubernatorial appointment.

[19]Robert F. Will, *State Education: Structure and Organization* (U.S. Department of Health, Education, and Welfare, 1964), pp. 7–11; *cf.* R. L. Johns, "State Organization and Responsibilities for Education," *Implications for Education of Prospective Changes in Society* (Conference Report, Designing Education for the Future, Denver, 1967), pp. 245–66.

[20]*Book of the States, 1970–71,* p. 305.

[21]Roald F. Campbell, Gerald E. Sroufe, and Donald H. Layton, eds., *Strengthening State Departments of Education* (Chicago: University of Chicago, 1967), p. 9.

Figure 7-1 State Education Structure and Function Charts

I. State of ALASKA

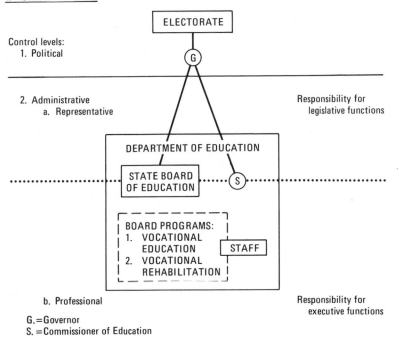

Control levels:
1. Political

2. Administrative
   a. Representative

Responsibility for legislative functions

b. Professional

Responsibility for executive functions

G. = Governor
S. = Commissioner of Education

II. State of CALIFORNIA

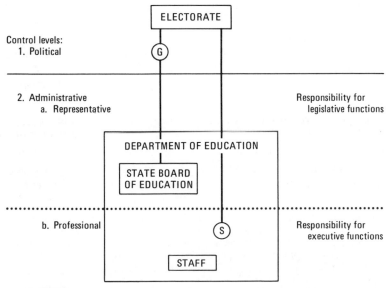

Control levels:
1. Political

2. Administrative
   a. Representative

Responsibility for legislative functions

b. Professional

Responsibility for executive functions

G. = Governor
S. = Superintendent of public instruction; ex officio director of education

III. State of LOUISIANA

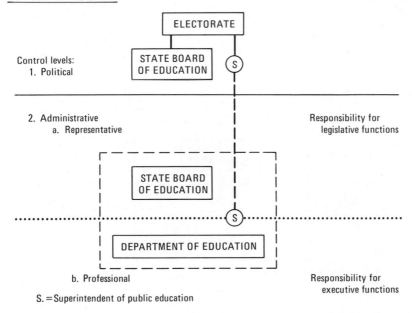

Control levels:
1. Political

2. Administrative
   a. Representative

Responsibility for
legislative functions

b. Professional

Responsibility for
executive functions

S. = Superintendent of public education

IV. State of MARYLAND

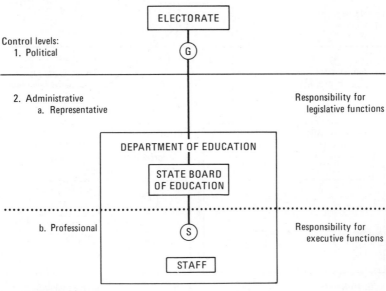

Control levels:
1. Political

2. Administrative
   a. Representative

Responsibility for
legislative functions

b. Professional

Responsibility for
executive functions

G. = Governor
S. = Superintendent of schools

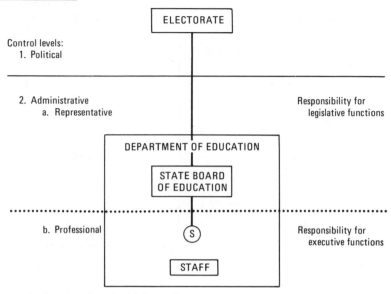

V. State of OHIO

ELECTORATE

Control levels:
1. Political

2. Administrative
   a. Representative

Responsibility for
legislative functions

DEPARTMENT OF EDUCATION

STATE BOARD
OF EDUCATION

b. Professional

(S)

STAFF

Responsibility for
executive functions

S. = Superintendent of public instruction

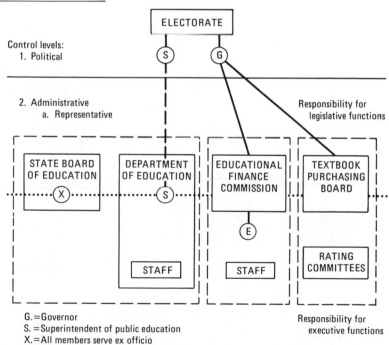

VI. State of MISSISSIPPI

ELECTORATE

Control levels:
1. Political

(S)   (G)

2. Administrative
   a. Representative

Responsibility for
legislative functions

STATE BOARD
OF EDUCATION

(X)

DEPARTMENT
OF EDUCATION

(S)

EDUCATIONAL
FINANCE
COMMISSION

TEXTBOOK
PURCHASING
BOARD

(E)

STAFF   STAFF

RATING
COMMITTEES

G. = Governor
S. = Superintendent of public education
X. = All members serve ex officio
E. = Executive secretary, educational finance commission

Responsibility for
executive functions

Source: Robert F. Will, State Education: Structure and Organization (*U.S. Department of Health, Education, and Welfare, 1964*), p. 43, 49, 77, 81, 90, 115.

126

Table 7–3   Classification of States according to Method of Selecting State Boards and Chief State School Officers, 1969

Method of Selection	States
I. State School Board Members	
A. Ex officio (majority or more of board)	Florida, Mississippi
B. Appointed by governor	Alabama, Alaska, Arizona, Arkansas, California, Connecticut, Delaware, Georgia, Idaho, Indiana, Iowa, Kentucky, Maine, Maryland, Massachusetts, Minnesota, Missouri, Montana, New Hampshire, New Jersey, North Carolina, North Dakota, Oklahoma, Oregon, Pennsylvania, Rhode Island, South Carolina, South Dakota, Tennessee, Vermont, Virginia, West Virginia, Wyoming
C. Elected by the people or representatives of the people	Colorado, Hawaii, Kansas, Louisiana, Michigan, Nebraska, Nevada, New Mexico, New York, Ohio, Texas, Utah, Washington
II. Chief State School Officer	
A. Appointed by governor	New Jersey, Pennsylvania, Tennessee, Virginia
B. Elected by popular vote	Alabama, Arizona, California, Florida, Georgia, Idaho, Illinois, Indiana, Kentucky, Louisiana, Mississippi, Montana, North Carolina, North Dakota, Oklahoma, Oregon, South Carolina, South Dakota, Washington, Wisconsin, Wyoming
C. Appointed by state board of education	Alaska, Arkansas, Colorado, Connecticut, Delaware, Hawaii, Iowa, Kansas, Maine, Maryland, Massachusetts, Minnesota, Michigan, Missouri, Nebraska, Nevada, New Hampshire, New Mexico, New York, Ohio, Rhode Island, Texas, Utah, Vermont, West Virginia

Source: Adapted from Robert F. Will, State Education: Structure and Organization (U.S. Department of Health, Education, and Welfare, 1964), pp. 16 and 20; and Book of the States, 1970–71 (Lexington, Ky.: Council of State Governments, 1970), p. 305.

Methods of choosing the state superintendent of education, commonly called the chief state school officer, also differ widely. Table 7–3 shows that in twenty-five states the state superintendent is appointed by the state board of education, in four he is appointed by the governor, and in twenty-one he is elected directly by the people. The long-term trend is toward appointment by the state board of education. (See Table 7–4.)

The third part of state education organizations, the state department of education (SDE), consists of the professional staff that performs the work essential to carry out the duties assigned to it. These agencies also differ widely, since they have been given different powers and have been

Table 7–4   Methods Used by States to Select Chief State School Officers:
Selected Years 1900–1969

Method	1900	1910	1920	1930	1940	1950	1960	1969
Appointed by state board of education	3	4	8	8	8	13	22	25
Appointed by governor	7	7	6	7	8	6	5	4
Appointed by general assembly	3	1	—	—	—	—	—	—
Popular election	31	33	34	33	32	29	23	21
Ex officio	1	1	—	—	—	—	—	—
Number of states	45	46	48	48	48	48	50	50

Source: Robert F. Will, State Education: Structure and Organization *(U.S. Department of Health, Education, and Welfare, 1964), p. 20. Information for 1969 taken from* Book of the States, 1970–71 *(Lexington, Ky.: Council of State Governments, 1970).*

shaped by different historical circumstances. In their earliest days these state educational agencies performed essentially regulatory roles of dispensing financial assistance and monitoring personnel and business accounts. Later they were assigned responsibilities for operating special schools for the handicapped, such as the blind and the deaf, and were given duties to provide a variety of technical assistance services to local school systems.[22]

Increasing Demands on SDEs. In recent years states have been forced to assume new roles in education because of social, economic, and demographic changes that have threatened to undermine the essential local character of public education. Statewide services to strengthen local school systems have been expanded, and the functions of state educational agencies have multiplied. State departments of education are increasingly being looked to for leadership.[23] Table 7–5 divides the major activities SDEs are called upon to perform into five major areas: operational, regulatory, service, developmental, and public support and cooperation.

More and more, state departments of education are being called upon to plan a statewide educational system capable of meeting the needs of a rapidly changing society and to communicate educational needs to the public and elected officials. In many instances they are given a degree of discretionary power over the expenditure of state and federal monies.

[22]*Improving State Leadership in Education,* pp. 46–48.
[23]Kenneth H. Hansen, "State Organization for Education: Some Emerging Alternatives," in Morphet and Jessen, *Emerging State Responsibilities for Education,* pp. 37–63.

SDEs are also being called upon to evaluate and hold accountable schools throughout the state. This is obviously a politically controversial function, as it offends the basic tenet of localism. Teachers and administrators see state evaluations as a threat to "professionalism" and a possible tool to be used in staff evaluation. Proponents of a stronger state agency tend to

Table 7–5 Some Major Activity Areas in State Departments of Education

1. OPERATIONAL
   A. State schools for handicapped
   B. Specific programs (e.g., vocational rehab.)
   C. Teachers colleges
   D. Miscellaneous

2. REGULATORY   (essentially arise from specifications of state constitutions and codes such as curriculum and teaching standards, school construction, school buses, civil defense and fire drills, accounting for funds)
   A. Approval   ACTIVITIES UNDER 2 and 3 ARE
   B. Classification   DIRECTED TOWARD SUBORDI-
   C. Application of sanctions   NATE UNITS
   D. Supervision
   E. Distribution of funds

3. SERVICE   (based on department's expertise)
   A. Advising and consultations
      (1) on individual projects
      (2) with groups (workshops, etc.)
   B. Publications, other aids
   C. Dissemination of research

4. DEVELOPMENTAL (IMPROVEMENT OF SERVICES)
   A. Planning   ACTIVITIES UNDER 4 ARE PRI-
   B. Research   MARILY   DIRECTED   TOWARD
   C. In-service education   THE SDE ITSELF
   D. Evaluation
   E. Recruiting and staffing
   F. Departmental supporting services (internal),
      and intra-departmental coordination

5. PUBLIC SUPPORT AND COOPERATION
   A. Public relations (general)   ACTIVITIES   UNDER   5   ARE
   B. Political activity   GEARED TO OUTSIDE PERSONS
         —with legislature   AND AGENCIES
         —with governor
   C. Interagency relations
      1. Regional labs and other federal programs
      2. Other departments of state government
      3. Higher institutions

Source: Strengthening State Departments of Education, (editors) Roald F. Campbell, Gerald E. Stroufe, and Donald H. Layton (Chicago: Midwest Administration Center, University of Chicago, 1967), p. 9.

view SDEs' roles as being comparable to those of the federal Department of Health, Education, and Welfare. They would have state education agencies provide both educational and political leadership and serve as a communication link between the educational professionals, the general public, and the political leaders, including the formal decision makers.[24]

Political Weaknesses of State Education Agencies. Unfortunately, state education agencies have generally been unable to keep pace with the growing demands for leadership and services. They have been especially weak in the public support activities, such as public relations; political activities with the legislature, governor, and other politicians; and relations with various governmental and nongovernmental agencies.[25]

Historically, public support activities have not been given a high priority by state education agencies. These endeavors were viewed as marginal to the other services that had to be performed. Even today relatively few state agencies have made a serious and continuing effort to keep citizens in general informed about emerging needs and the progress being made, or the problems encountered, in meeting them. The reports and materials prepared by state education agencies are usually professionally oriented and seldom communicate effectively to a majority of citizens whose support is essential.[26]

Communication between political leaders and educators is essential if educators are to be influential in shaping educational legislation and in obtaining adequate appropriations. But it is often difficult for educators, including state education agencies, to develop stable relationships with political officials. This weakness is due in part to the structure of state agencies and in part to the "no politics" ideology of educators. Education has historically not been treated as a regular branch of general government, but as a separate domain governed by laws peculiar to it. The separateness of education from other state governmental functions, plus the fragmented structure of state education agencies, has tended to isolate education from the main political processes. This isolation from state politics has been defended and justified by professional educators and many others as necessary to safeguard democracy, to prevent dictators and demagogues from capturing the minds of youth, and to "keep politics out

[24]Campbell, Sroufe, and Layton, *Strengthening State Departments of Education,* p. 12; *cf.* Robert A. Klamie, "A Comparison of the Desirability and Feasibility of Accountability Measures as Perceived by Public School Administrators and Teachers" (Ph.D. dissertation, North Texas State University, 1973).

[25]Hansen, "State Organization for Education," p. 59.

[26]*Ibid.,* p. 13; *cf.* Fred F. Beach, *The State and Education: The Structure and Control of Education at the State Level* (U.S. Department of Health, Education, and Welfare, 1955), pp. 3–5; and *Reinforcing the Role of States in Education,* Second Annual Report of Advisory Council on State Departments of Education (U.S. Department of Health, Education, and Welfare, 1967), p. 28.

of education." Similarly, the board structure for education has been hailed as "one of America's greatest contributions to the science of public administration." But this insistence on autonomy and on keeping politics out of education has created a barrier between educational leaders and state politicians who ultimately are responsible for educational policies.[27]

No part of the state education agency—board, superintendent, or department—has ready political access to, or regular communication linkages with, the political leaders making key decisions about education. State board members, for instance, are seldom persons of great political influence or high status and prestige in the state. Usually they are relatively unknown in political circles and have little status or influence with key political leaders. They can open few doors or persuade few politicians about the policies the state should have pertaining to education.[28]

The story is largely the same with other components of the state education agency. In some states the only exchange between the legislature and the department of education takes place once a year when the budget committee meets. Perhaps even more detrimental is the general lack of communication between the governor's office and the state superintendent. In some instances the governor views the state superintendent as a potential competitor, especially in the states where the superintendent is popularly elected. Thus educators have little input on these political officials and almost no way to influence them to undertake needed political actions.[29]

Education's fragmented structure enables elected officials to escape responsibility for educational problems. Governors and legislators can avoid making difficult political decisions about education without suffering politically. Simply by taking no position, they can leave controversial decisions to the educational agencies which are largely impotent to effect change without legislation or appropriations.[30]

In terms of the legislature, problems of state education agencies are compounded by the absence of an identifiable and visible clientele, other than local districts and educators, to do battle for them. Furthermore, SDEs often get caught up in the social and political conflicts of the states.

[27]Roald F. Campbell, "State Organization and Responsibilities for Education: Supplementary Statement," *Implications for Education of Prospective Changes in Society*, Conference Report, pp. 270–71.

[28]Harold Howe II, "Unfinished Work for the States" (Address before a panel on "Education: The Federal-State Relationship" at the Annual Convention of the National Conference of State Legislative Leaders, mimeographed (Washington, D.C., November 18, 1966).

[29]Schlesinger, "Politics of the Executive," pp. 215–16.

[30]Lockard, *Politics of State and Local Government*, pp. 295–96; *cf.* Ira Sharkansky, *Public Administration: Policy-Making in Governmental Agencies* (Chicago: Markham Publishing Co., 1970), pp. 182–89; and Hansen, "State Organization for Education," p. 27.

Rural and urban forces continue to be at odds in nearly every state. Perhaps partly because most legislatures—despite the impact of the one-man one-vote rule—are still rural-suburban dominated, the education agencies tend to be thought of as agencies primarily concerned about the smaller school systems throughout the state and as neither responsible for nor particularly concerned with many emerging statewide problems or with the urgent problems of the cities. State agencies do not even have full backing from all districts and educators.[31]

Another major political bind in which state education agencies find themselves is the long-standing three-way conflict over where ultimate responsibility for control of educational matters should reside. The educational professional, and the supporting lay groups such as school boards and parent-teacher associations, believe that education is a technical and professional matter that the legislative and executive branches of state government should support, but with which they should not interfere. But the state legislatures typically see themselves as being more responsive to the people than state educational agencies and as having the prerogative of spelling out quite specifically what the functions of education should be, and how the educational system should be operated. The governor often feels frustrated because he has virtually little to say about how this large and important segment of state government is conducted. As a result of the conflicting perspectives, it is not surprising that many state education agencies are neither well regarded nor very well supported when the annual or biennial appropriation sessions roll around.[32]

Evidence of the legislative weakness of state education agencies is found in their inability to get necessary resources to carry out their functions. As late as the mid-1960s twenty-one states employed fewer than fifty professional staff members in their departments of education. Personnel shortages were so acute that most state departments could not fully perform the administrative duties delegated to them. Consequently, state education agencies were not prepared to provide the kind of statewide leadership required for educational improvement. Although this serious shortage of personnel has been partially alleviated by federal grants aimed specifically at strengthening state education agencies, as well as by increased state funding, the lack of political influence is still quite obvious in that state departments of education continue to suffer from the chronic miserliness of state financing.[33]

[31]Hansen, "State Organization for Education," pp. 27–28.

[32]*Improving State Leadership in Education*, pp. 5–6; *cf*. Howe, "Unfinished Work for the States," pp. 6–7.

[33]Michael D. Usdan, David W. Minar, and Emanuel Hurwitz, Jr., *Education and State Politics: The Developing Relationship between Elementary-Secondary and Higher Education* (New York: Columbia University Press, 1969), pp. 1–2.

Jealousy of local school districts because of their prerogatives is another cause of the weakness of state education agencies. As the state agency has become more important in decisions pertaining to allocation of state and federal funds and school district consolidation, the competitiveness between the local districts and the state agency has increased. The shift of the decision-making locus in recent years has upset much of the traditional educational thinking and has led to political opposition by local districts and educators. Although state departments of education have grown more powerful as a result of their increasing control over state and federal funds, local districts continue to have political power with local legislators which helps counterbalance their influence.

Other State Administrative Agencies

Education is just one of many of the state governments' programs. In fact, it is just one aspect of a number of programs, such as health services, antipoverty programs, recreation, and crime prevention, affecting the intellectual development of the citizenry. State governments provide numerous other services as well as regulating many personal and corporate activities. Each of these state activities has an administrative organization, and each state organization develops internal goals and loyalties and seeks support from outside groups. Competition between agencies for authority and for the state's limited resources is, therefore, a natural part of the administrative environment, an important factor affecting the actions of state government.

In this competition, agencies turn to the groups directly affected and served by them. These groups perceive the importance of an agency's serving them and take a more direct interest in the agency's well-being. They can be mobilized to support the agency in the battle for budget and power. Some state agencies, as we have already seen, can rely upon powerful economic groups for political support before the legislature and in budget hearings. State education agencies are weakened by their not having well-identified economic groups that can be mobilized to support them.

Competition between Public and Higher Education.   Another factor that weakens education in state politics is that education is normally divided between public education, that is, elementary and secondary education, and higher education, and there is increasing conflict between the levels of education in the state arena. The division of the state's educational system into compartments separated by the break between the twelfth and the thirteenth year is the result of historical accident. There seems to be no particular natural merit in this division. Arguments based

on maturity, learning capacity, and the like are doubtful, and similar cases can be made with equal validity for a variety of other breaking points. But the division of the educational system has had a major impact on the state politics of education.[34]

Since the two levels of education developed separately, each was forced to acquire its own political support system. Each sought out its own clientele and support groups and thus had different bases of political power. Public education developed as a local institution. Control over the schools was left largely to local districts, which financed them through the property tax. Public schools were not as dependent on the state financially as were the public colleges and universities and were much less influential at the state level. Colleges and universities, on the other hand, developed as unique state institutions. Constitutional stipulations in a number of states provide for their creation. The great prestige of higher education, plus well-placed alumni, provides the basis of political power and ensures their support.[35]

The net result of the division between the two branches of education was that they developed as if they were inherently different and separate kinds of education. There were few relationships between the levels of education, and these dealt mainly with teacher education. Universities and colleges tended to dominate these relationships, as can be seen in the histories of the NEA and the teacher colleges.

Recent developments in the politics of education have seriously challenged the arbitrary division between the two educational spheres. There is a growing list of public policy problems involving both levels of education. The most obvious and competitive is the fiscal question. With public schools turning increasingly to the states for revenues and higher education's financial needs multiplying, competition between the levels of education promises to become even more intense if full state financing of public education becomes the accepted pattern.[36]

State Courts

State courts are another important institution affecting educational policy-making. Although the rough and tough aspects of state politics that determine "who gets what, when, and how" are hidden by legal orientations that permeate every phase of the states' judicial process, state courts like legislatures and executives are omnipresent features of state policymaking.

[34]*Ibid.*, pp. 170–78.
[35]*Ibid.*, pp. 6–7.
[36]*Ibid.*, pp. 6–7.

Courts seldom engage in activities that are as visibly distributive as are legislative appropriations, gubernatorial presentations of budgets, or adoptions of textbook selections by state education agencies, but courts play an important role in making state policies.

Making of Common Law. State judiciaries participate in the allocation of values, the essence of politics, in a number of ways. For one thing, they make law—the common law, which is as significant in many areas as is statutory and administrative law.

Such important areas as contracts and torts, and much of the law of domestic relations, have been developed from the precedents of earlier cases. This court-made law directly affects the policies and actions of schools. The powers and duties of teachers and their relationships to students are primarily defined by common-law principles, for instance. Similarly, the validity of contracts made by schools, and the liability or nonliability of schools for accidents or injuries caused by the negligence of schools or their employees, are determined according to principles of common law. Almost every aspect of school policy is shaped by this body of court-made law.[37]

Conflict Resolution. Courts also are called upon to interpret state statutes, and this obviously affects the policy process. The most dramatic evidence of judicial power occurs when a court holds invalid the act of a legislature. The power of judicial review permits the judiciary to declare statutes to be in violation of the constitution. Constitutional questions can be and frequently are raised in ordinary litigation.[38]

Two of the most common suits broadly affecting educational matters are those where the intent is to require a governmental body or official to carry out a function that is alleged to be a duty, and those where it is sought to halt or to prevent some action that is alleged to be unauthorized by law. The latter types of cases, as we have already seen, are frequently brought as taxpayers' suits.

Much of the litigation to require governmental officials to carry out mandated functions arises out of the question of what will or will not be taught. State legislation frequently requires that certain subjects be taught and that others be prohibited. But it is the court that rules on challenges to such statutes by parents claiming the right to direct the education of

[37]C. Gordon Post, *An Introduction to the Law* (Englewood Cliffs, N.J.: Prentice-Hall, Inc., 1963), pp. 62–78; *cf.* Newton Edwards, *The Courts and the Public Schools* (Chicago: University of Chicago Press, 1955), pp. 200–617.

[38]Walter Murphy and C. Herman Prichett, *Courts, Judges and Politics: An Introduction to the Judicial Process* (New York: Random House, Inc., 1961), pp. 433–39.

their children against the power of the state to prescribe the type of education a child should receive. Courts in deciding such cases make policy, and their decisions often set the pace of social changes possible in the schools.[39]

State courts also affect educational policies in the host of cases where the actions of schools are challenged by parents, students, and teachers. The judiciary defines the relationships between the various parties in the school and sets the limits on the authority of school officials. Courts are also frequently involved in defining the relationship between state and local educational agencies, as in cases involving district consolidation, or state department regulations and the withholding of state funds. As a result of their involvement in such cases, courts to a degree shape not only the policies schools may make but also the administrative procedures schools must follow.[40]

Attorney General Opinions.   Still another part of the state judicial system that affects educational policies is the Office of State Attorney General, the state's principal lawyer. In most states the attorney general writes opinions as to the legality of certain school policies or actions upon request of local or state school officials. These interpretations of the law are binding upon schools until they are overruled by the courts or new legislation is enacted changing the law. The power to interpret expenditure laws in effect gives the attorney general great control over how state monies are to be expended. In some states all local bonds must be submitted to the attorney general so that he can determine their legality. Thus in certain school matters the attorney general may play an important role in state policymaking.

In Chapters 6 and 7 we have attempted to describe the political system of state education and the types of demands made upon it. We shall now see how the system converts these demands—inputs and within puts —into outputs, that is, state policies and actions.

[39]Post, *Introduction to the Law*, pp. 145–48.
[40]Edwards, *Courts and the Public Schools*, pp. 23–46.

chapter eight

Educational Policymaking in State Government

Out of the maelstrom of conflicting demands and institutional claims, state policies arise. This chapter looks at the unfolding political drama of state educational politics and examines the conversion processes that turn inputs into policy outputs. Finally, state educational outputs and their effect on local and federal policies are reviewed.

Changing Educational Demands

As a result of the rapid societal changes in recent years, the educational system has been bombarded with new demands—demands that not only require new responses from state government but also modify the functioning of the entire educational system. Consequently, major changes have occurred in state educational politics. Local control, which has been the dominant feature of American education, has eroded because of the inability of local districts to meet the growing demands for education, and there has been a significant shift in the power affecting the control and support of education. Increasingly, the state has been called upon to provide resources and leadership for education. The state has become the major arena for decisions pertaining to financial education as well as for many other "hard" political decisions.

Money and Education. The increasing educational demands on state governments have revolved around three major problem areas, commonly referred to as the "crises" in public education. The first was a deficit in facilities and personnel due mainly to the deferred spending during the Great Depression and World War II and to a rapid rise in the birthrate, the so-called postwar baby boom.[1] Local resources were inadequate to meet

[1] Mario D. Fantini, "Alternatives for Urban School Reform," *Harvard Educational Review*, Winter 1968, pp. 160–175.

these demands, and states were called upon to assume an ever-expanding share of the costs of education. When states have faltered in supplying requested increases, demands for federal aid have intensified.

Increased participation of state and federal governments in financing education resulted in continued centralization and major changes in the relationships between component parts of the educational system. Traditionally, the locus of educational decision making has been in the local district. Within individual schools and school systems, administrators and boards made most of the major decisions, teachers made the minor decisions, and students and parents usually went along. In recent years decision making has become more complex, not only has there been a lateral dispersion of decision-making power to other groups, lay and professional, but the state and federal governments have become major participants in decisions as their financial role has expanded.

Growing militancy of teachers' groups is another aspect of this problem of resources. More and more state educational groups make their demands on state governments, and increases in teachers' salaries and the improvement of other personnel policies are determined largely at the state level, with state politicians holding the key to their success.

The greater reliance of teachers on the state is due, in large part, to the limits on the financial resources of local districts and the greater tax base of states. But teachers have also turned to the state to protect their position from adverse actions of local boards who may more easily apply sanctions. On a statewide basis, teachers have greater strength than they do at the local level, and hence they seek state legislation to protect them from local powers with such measures as tenure or continuing contract laws, authorization for collective negotiations, and so-called professional standards acts permitting teachers to judge charges of unprofessional conduct against teachers.

Curriculum and the School. The second "crisis," escalated to a national emergency by Sputnik, was the inadequacy of training in science and mathematics. Sputnik led to additional offerings in these fields, and in turn to changes in other areas of the curriculum as well.[2] But, equally

---

[2]*Ibid.; cf.* p. 169.

It has been suggested that educational inadequacies in preparing young people were hidden by the Depression, when jobs were scarce, and then by World War II, when the need for manpower was so great that educational deficiencies did not preclude employment. The children of the poor left school in favor of employment, thereby ignoring educational failure, and the children of the wealthy sought academic excellence in private schools. The public schools were left with a largely satisfied middle class; those not satisfied did not have an effective mechanism for airing their grievances. This state of affairs, however, was radically altered after the postwar prosperity leveled.

significant, the crisis subjected professional educators to criticism in an area where they had been almost invulnerable because of the aura of professionalism. Since Sputnik, schools have been increasingly under attack by parents and politicians. Educational professionals are frequently challenged to demonstrate the value (the policy outcome) of various programs and activities, particularly when requesting additional funds or authority.

Criticism of educational outcomes coupled with a growing resistance to demands for additional state funds has led to counterdemands for public accountability by educators. Educators have long been accustomed to being held accountable in a fiscal sense for funds spent. But today educators are also being ordered to render an accounting for educational quality and results, as well as for educational expenditures. New methods of measuring educational results, such as the so-called planning, programming, and budgeting system (PPBS), are being instituted for both local and state educational agencies. This accounting method requires that goals for the educational system be identified as behavioral objectives against which to measure pupil progress. The leadership role for defining and establishing educational goals has largely fallen on state education agencies, and thus they are more involved in the fundamental school decisions of what will be taught, who will teach, and how schools will be administered and evaluated.

Urban Crisis and the Schools.   The essence of the third and present crisis in public education is the realization that the system has failed a major segment of the population. This failure was the most intractable crisis all along, but it did not emerge prominently until the nation took official cognizance of poverty amidst affluence and until the nonwhite fourth of society's economic underclass began to assert its civil rights and demand a full share in political and economic opportunity. This crisis, although not limited to urban areas, is commonly referred to as the crisis of urban education.[3]

To a large degree the urban school crisis is a race problem. The blacks' drive for equality, plus the continuing mass migration of blacks and Latin Americans to the city followed by the whites' flight to the suburbs, has accentuated the problems of urban school systems. Schools have been

---

Populist sentiment is a strong influence upon American thought. In principle, each child should have an adequate education. Yet approximately one in four leaves school before high school graduation, and in 1965 one in four failed the mental test required for armed forces induction. Obviously, Americans would not tolerate major failure of one-fourth of their airplanes or automobiles, but that is the percentage, minimally, of students who fail academically. A basic reason for the recent emphasis upon accountability is public dissatisfaction with the performance of the public schools. Jack Sterner, "Accountability by Public Demand," *American Vocational Journal*, February 1971, pp. 33–37.

[3]*Ibid.*

bombarded with strife growing out of the civil rights movement, de facto segregation, busing, demands for decentralization of urban districts, struggles between white teachers and black students and parents, and problems of governing and financing urban education. Schools also have been engulfed in the needs of the cities and forced to assume new roles to help solve the pressing social and economic problems caused by racism and poverty.[4]

Local districts are obviously not equal to these tasks. Therefore all levels of government, but especially state governments, have been forced to become more involved in educational problems. Numerous state legislative and executive actions have been taken; some to delay, others to maintain the peace and to help local districts meet these problems. States are being forced to enlarge their role in ensuring equal opportunities to all students. The federal courts in a number of recent decisions have required states to assume the primary responsibility for desegregation and for overcoming the last vestiges of a dual school system.[5] States are being pushed into these difficult political decisions more than ever before.

The racial revolution is only one facet of the drive for equality. New demands from poorer districts for equality of educational opportunity raise equally complex questions. The demands for the "one scholar, one dollar" principle—a suggested variant of "one man, one vote"—are challenging traditional patterns of educational finance, and states are being pressed to revise the entire financial system, and perhaps even the entire governmental structure, for education. These developments promise a still larger role for state governments in education.

Conflict over Education

As a result of the rapid changes in American society and the new demands on the educational system, conflict over education has become a major aspect of state politics. New demands trigger conflict because not all people perceive the effects of change or the objectives or needs of education in the same way, nor do all people have identical values. New demands affect people in different ways; some stand to gain from state educational policies and others stand to lose. From these different perceptions, values, and expectations emerges the conflict that is the basis of educational politics.[6]

[4] Robert J. Havighurst, *Education in Metropolitan Areas* (Boston: Allyn & Bacon, Inc. 1966).
[5] One typical case was U.S. v. Texas, 321 F.Supp. 1043; 330 F.Supp. 235; aff. mod., 447 F2d. 441; stay den., 404 U.S. 1206; cert. den., 404 U.S. 1016.
[6] The ideas for this section were taken mainly from Paul H. Conn, *Conflict and Decision Making: An Introduction to Political Science* (New York: Harper & Row, Publishers, 1971).

Conflict over educational issues often reflects other conflicts in our society and arises out of, or at least is nourished by, the more lasting divisions of society. The major political cleavages, such as the divisions between rural and urban, black and white, and the haves and have-nots, intensify conflict in many educational issues—desegregation of schools, expansion of educational programs, taxation and state funding of education. The more serious the political cleavage, the more difficult it is to resolve the educational conflict.

Character of Educational Conflict. The content of educational demands and the character of conflict that ensues in state politics tend to range along two dimensions: the ideological-pragmatic dimension on the one hand, and the comprehensive-incremental on the other. Issues in the ideological-pragmatic continuum range from those challenging existing ideologies or strongly held beliefs to those relatively devoid of ideological overtones but affecting the economic, social, or political positions of various groups. The comprehensive-incremental dimension, however, is concerned with whether the resolution of conflict would require major or minor change in the political, social, or economic institutions: Does the demand require restructuring of institutions and hold entry into new areas of governmental activity or merely an incremental change in a program?[7]

Conflicts over ideological issues abound in state educational politics. School desegregation, teaching of religious beliefs (Bible reading and prayers in school), teaching of patriotism and other cultural values, loyalty oaths for teachers, and textbook selection and adoption are common examples of ideological issues. They are the source of some of the most heated and intense conflicts in state politics. One reason for the intensity of this type of conflict is that there is little or no way of compromising on ideological issues: One side wins, and the other loses—a zero-sum conflict, as political scientists call it. This type of demand attracts a great deal of public attention and emotional fervor, as is evident in the school desegregation issue. In some instances, politicians use such issues in election campaigns, and this attracts attention and more groups join the political fray. Ideological questions are usually decided in favor of the dominant cultural attitudes in the state unless legal or political norms of the national community force a different decision. School desegregation is an obvious example of an ideological conflict where outside legal and constitutional factors affect decisions that otherwise would not be made in some states.

Conflicts over more pragmatic issues also abound in state educational politics. Educational policies affect the economic and status position of people differently, with some standing to gain and others to lose. Such

[7]*Ibid.*, pp. 72–73.

issues as salary increases for teachers, changes in teacher certification and tenure laws, expansion of educational programs upward to the thirteenth and fourteenth grades or backward to the preprimary level, proposals for district consolidation, and funding to strengthen state departments of education all promise benefits to some and deprivations to others.

Proposals for increasing teachers' salaries, for example, are obviously favored by teachers, so they and their associations initiate, plan, and work for the enactment of such measures. Other groups threatened with higher taxes or the reduction of other programs that benefit them oppose such proposals just as vigorously. Political conflict ensues. But this type of conflict is normally not as intense as conflict resulting from ideological issues. For one thing, economic issues do not generate the widespread emotional involvement, since not as many people perceive these proposals as a threat and do not get involved in the political controversy. Compromise acceptable to both teachers and opponents is possible. In this sense it is not a zero-sum conflict; both sides can win or partly win in the bargaining process. There is not the bitterness involved in ideological issues, nor are groups as polarized by these matters.

The intensity of political conflict over proposals to increase expenditures for education depends in part on the state's economic condition. In a state in which the amount of resources the government can spend remains constant, that is, where the economy is stagnant or growing very slowly, increased demands for education may create a situation nearer to a zero-sum conflict because the additional educational expenditures will cause a tax increase or monies will have to be taken from other programs. In prosperous states, however, it is possible that in any given year the amount of money that the government will be able to spend on various programs will be greater than in the preceding year even without raising taxes. Under these circumstances, demands for additional monies for education do not represent as serious a threat to other state programs or to those who are subject to taxation. It is possible for taxpayers to maintain their wealth, and even expand it, and at the same time support through taxes enlarged public programs such as education. The intensity of political conflict over educational expenditures, therefore, depends on the condition of the state's economy.

Issues involving changes in social or political positions are more difficult to resolve than disputes over purely economic matters. For instance, intense and bitter conflict frequently arises over state requirements for consolidating local school districts. This type of change is a threat not only to the political position of local districts and their officers but also to the status of the local community. Such proposals as continuing contracts or tenure provisions for teachers, or authorization for collective negotiations

by educational groups, are frequently the cause of fierce political controversies because they affect the power positions of various parties in educational government. Similarly, measures to strengthen state departments of education in relationship to local districts are often resisted because they change the status and power of these agencies. Proposals effecting changes in the relationship between the federal government and the state or local levels cause even more opposition and tend to take on the aura of an ideological issue, since they influence cultural beliefs about "states' rights" and the inherent nature of our governmental system.

Considering educational demands from the comprehensive-incremental dimension, those issues requiring the most comprehensive changes cause the greatest amount of conflict and vice versa. For instance, it is much easier to make a change in a state financial formula for supporting schools than it is to originally enact such a formula or to rework the entire system of financing education. The greater the change required, the more people affected and the more intense the political conflict.

Demands and changes are essentially incremental. But many of the demands growing out of the urban school crisis call for revamping the entire system, and this in part explains the intensity of conflict over education today. The present legal and political attacks on financing schools through the property tax, if ultimately successful, will require major alterations in the states' tax system and will dramatically change the patterns of influence in the governance of education. Similarly, the school desegregation cases forced comprehensive change in the social and educational system and, as a result, generated some of the most heated conflict in the entire history of American education.

Converting Educational Demands into State Policy

Educational politics has in many ways become similar to the politics of other issues in a democratic society. In educational politics as in state politics generally, some people want something from government and build a coalition of influence to get it; other people with different preferences join each other to block or modify the designs of the first group; strategic and tactical campaigns are conducted to persuade proximate decision makers; and the constitutional wielders of power determine winners and losers by laws passed and executive and judicial actions taken. This process is continuous, and as soon as a governmental decision is made, a new dialectic begins.

The conversion process whereby inputs, demands of individuals and

groups, are enacted into outputs of public policies might be conceived of as a series of interactions between the actors in the policymaking process.[8] First, groups articulating demands for change contact and interact with constitutional decision makers. In these interactions, groups present their demands, inform and attempt to persuade the decision makers of the rightness of their cause, argue and apply influence, and make compromises in an effort to shape public policy. Second, formal decision makers, the constitutional wielders of power, interact with one another. Persuasion, pressures, and bargaining are aspects of these interactions also. Third, the implementation of state policies requires interaction between state and local officials. This section will focus on these interactions in the conversion process. Certain interactions between state and federal officials also influence state educational policies, as will be seen in a subsequent chapter.

Interaction between Educational Lobbies and Legislators. Educational interest groups' access to state political leaders and their ability to gain politicians' support, as we have already mentioned, are lessened because of their insistence that education is nonpolitical and their refusal to become involved in partisan or electoral politics. Like all lobbies, however, educational groups must match their organizational structure and political style to the political characteristics of state institutions if they are to be successful. Since the political environments of the states differ widely, the organizational style of leadership in educational associations, and the interactions with state decision makers, also differ in the various states.

Laurence Iannaccone examined differences in state educational politics and constructed a typology of four organizational patterns to classify state educational lobbies and their methods of interacting with state legislatures. Type I of these patterns, found in Vermont, New Hampshire, and Massachusetts, is called the local-based disparate system. This organizational pattern is characterized by an extreme sense of localism. Both legislators and schoolmen (but particularly schoolmen) represent their local constituency first of all, and an attitude of provincialism pervades the entire system. State educational organizations, therefore, are seldom able to reach agreement on conflicting positions within the organization and to present a unified program to the legislature. Instead, accommodation of educational legislation is normally hammered out inside the legislature, usually on the floor of each house. Legislators in this system view teachers as being controllable by their administrators and thus turn to key local superintendents for advice and information on education. The little information legislators get about educational matters from these local sources tends to

---

[8]Charles E. Lindblom, *The Policy Making Process* (Englewood Cliffs, N.J.: Prentice-Hall, Inc., 1968), pp. 28.–29.

be unscientific and personalistic. The main point of linkage between schoolmen and state legislators in this system is between local school administrators and local legislators.[9]

Type II, the most common pattern of state organizational structures linking the legislature and profession, is characterized by a statewide pattern of interaction as found in New York, Missouri, New Jersey, and Rhode Island. Schoolmen in this so-called monolithic system customarily speak to the legislature on behalf of education, according to interest lines rather than geography. All major education groups, including the state school board association, the NEA affiliate, the school administrators, some voluntary citizens' groups such as the state PTA, and the state department of education jointly work out a legislative program. Conflicting viewpoints are accommodated inside the educational monolith, and a solid front is presented to the legislature. The result is a pyramid of associations interested in educational legislation, with leaders at the apex of the pyramid acting as the chief spokesmen before the legislature.[10]

Leadership within the educational monolith is normally dominated by school administrators and ex-school administrators who are able to co-opt support of other educational groups. Also, experts and authorities in school administration and finance from academia, the so-called scribblers, are informally co-opted to help formulate a legislative program and marshal information to support the program. Friendly legislators are co-opted by the educational group and become major supporters of the group's measures. These legislators, through the interaction with educators and the information provided to them, develop reputations of being experts on educational matters among their colleagues. Lobbyists for educational groups appear before committees with other prestigious members of the profession to help build a case for the legislative program, and the educators' research division provides a great deal of information pertaining to pending legislation. A virtual monopoly of information is maintained by the educational monolith, and the legislature is conditioned to depend on it for its data. The statewide monolithic system, although preferred by pedagogues, has been criticized as being a closed system and as having a rural bias because of the way offices in state organizations are apportioned among the various educational groups.[11]

Type III of the linkage structure between legislators and professionals is called the statewide fragmented system and is found in Michigan and California. Here statewide associations of school board members, teachers

---

[9]Laurence Iannaccone, *Politics in Education* (New York: Center for Applied Research in Education, Inc., 1967), pp. 37–42.

[10]*Ibid.*, pp. 42–43.

[11]*Ibid.*

in the AFT and NEA state affiliate, school administrators, and parent groups come to the legislature disunited, often in conflict rather than consensus. They present separate and competitive proposals to the legislative process. The differences among educational groups are highly visible to the legislators, who are often forced to take sides and whose perceptions of various segments of the educational professionals tend to depend on their agreement with positions of the various groups. The open conflict over educational policies draws many who would otherwise never be involved in educational politics into the fray, and the process mobilizes social power from far-flung networks not usually participating in the legislative process.[12]

Type IV of Iannaccone's linkage structure, called the statewide syndical system, is found in Illinois. In this structure, governmental officials and representatives of most of the major interests that have a direct and tangible stake in the outcome of educational decisions jointly serve on a specially created governmental body, the Illinois School Problems Commission (SPC), which functions much like a legislative council. According to its legislative charge, the SPC is to ". . . conserve legislative time, save unnecessary expenses, improve ensuing debate, and restore legislative activity to the high place in government which it merits." As a result of this authority and the prestige it has gained over the years, its decisions are usually accepted with minimal debate on the floor or even in committee. In effect, the SPC has become the locus of educational decision making, and it is here that differences between educational groups are accommodated.[13]

Iannaccone suggests that patterns of interaction between educational associations and legislators change from one political type to another over a period of time as the state's political environment changes. The locally based disparate pattern of state educational politics graduates into the statewide monolithic type. Similarly, the statewide, but fragmented, structural pattern seems to come after the monolithic one, and in turn the syndical structure follows because of fatigue and deadlock over educational issues.[14]

Interaction between Formal Decision Makers. Although interest groups can initiate considerations of a policy, only governmental officials can formalize state policies. State policymaking requires cooperative action by a number of governmental decision makers—the governor, legislature,

---

[12]*Ibid.*, pp. 43–44.
[13]*Ibid.*, pp. 44–45.
[14]*Ibid.*, pp. 70–81.

courts, and various other officials. Figure 8–1 shows the interrelatedness of state decision makers in educational policymaking.

Each branch of state government performs a specialized policy task different from any others, but each is dependent on others in the process. To make policy, each of these decision makers must influence the others to cooperate with him. The policy process at this stage becomes a matter of how the formal decision makers interact with one another and the means by which they cooperate in policymaking.[15]

State officials adjust to one another through the same processes that all systems adjust to one another—through identification, bargaining and negotiating, rules and laws, and pressure and coercion. The process of identification plays a large role in obtaining the necessary cooperation. Shared norms by the political officials and the public at large not only help to keep disputes from arising but also help to resolve conflicts and to determine what will or will not be done by government. Identification is used frequently as a means of persuasion. Officials attempt to persuade others by appealing to common loyalties, partisanship, love of the state and its ideals and history, and ties of kinship or friendship, as well as by

Figure 8–1   Interaction Between Formal Decision Makers in State Educational Policymaking

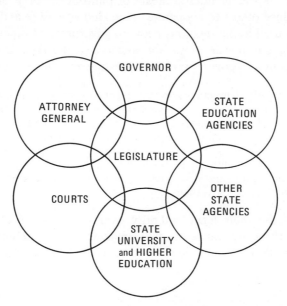

[15]Lindblom, *Policy Making Process*, pp. 30–31.

use of rational arguments. Persuasion through identification often involves finding a way to make a policy one desires serve the values of another policymaker.[16]

Bargaining between formal decision makers is also common. This involves an exchange—doing something if another will do something in turn. "Logrolling," or legislative bargaining, is where legislators in effect say, "You support my bill, and I'll support yours." Political debts also may be used in bargaining, and whenever possible without damage to their own interest, politicians do favors for other officeholders with the knowledge that at some future date they can use this obligation as a means of getting cooperation on an issue vital to them.

When persuasion fails, formal decision makers fall back on rules. Rules specify what each participant in policymaking can and cannot do, as well as what he must do, whom he must obey, and whom (if anyone) he can command. The constitution and laws, legislative and administrative rules, and judicial decisions and procedures, as well as approved and traditional ways of conducting government, make up these rules. These normally are voluntarily accepted because refusing to accept them would incapacitate a policymaker in his relations with other policymakers who play the game by the rules.[17]

But if all of these methods fail and cooperation cannot be obtained, the open use of power including threats of punishment or promises of rewards may induce others to cooperate. This kind of power and coercion is less frequently used in the relations between governmental officials than the other methods, but power plays are sometimes effective. Lockhard has written about southern governors' use of pressure as follows:

> It is fairly standard practice now for executive leaders to make a careful tabulation of legislative votes on gubernatorial programs and to tell dissenting legislators that if attitudes and votes are not changed, they will get no more jobs for constituents, no more state-aid for rural roads in their districts, no more of the favors that are the lifeblood of state legislators. This relationship is not subtle, it is direct, brutal; and it is effective. Executive politicians now can—and do—back recalcitrant legislators against the wall and read the "riot act" to them.[18]

Governors use their legal authority over expenditures and jobs not simply to intervene in legislative policymaking but to induce legislators to cooperate with them—to concede specifically an extralegal authority to the governors.

[16]*Ibid.*, pp. 32–34; also see pp. 82–83.
[17]*Ibid.*, pp. 34–37.
[18]Duane Lockard, *The Politics of State and Local Government* (New York: The Macmillan Company, 1963), p. 372.

In these interactions between formal decision makers, state education agencies, especially the state superintendent and the state board, have the vital job of persuading the governor and legislature regarding policy needs of education, and of striking bargainings wherever possible to advance these policies.[19] State education agencies may at times fall back on legal rules to protect themselves and the cause they support. At times they may even attempt to apply pressure on governors and legislatures through mobilization of interest group power or timely announcements to the public, which may embarrass these officials politically. As we have already seen, state education agencies have not unanimously accepted responsibility for these political roles and in some states have not cultivated the prerequisite political resources.

Interaction between State and Local Education Agencies. Interaction between state and local education agencies, another aspect of the conversion process, is most apparent in the implementation of state policy. State education agencies are responsible for seeing that state policies are carried out, in addition to their legislative and administrative roles in formulating policies. Implementation is a matter of influencing local schoolmen so that their actions correspond to the expectations formulated in state politics.

As a result of the tradition of localism and the decentralization of our political system, state agencies cannot rely upon bureaucratic authority, as is done in some more centralized countries. How does a state education agency induce local compliance with state policies? Here, as in the relationships between state officials, cooperation of local officials is induced through variations of the processes of identification, bargaining, rule making, and pressuring.

State agencies depend to a large degree on feelings of identification to induce cooperation. Acceptance of the legitimacy of the law is the most basic reason for compliance, and it causes local schoolmen to feel obligated to comply with state directives. The state is seen as having "the right" to command obedience, and it is "the obligation" of local. officials to obey. State officials, also, because of their professional ties are able to blur the distinction between the state and local programs and to stress the common professional program. Local schoolmen more readily comply if they conceive of state policies as "our program" rather than "their program." The state agencies' involvement in drafting legislation ensures them of a major voice in designing legislation that is enforceable. The ability of state

[19]Edgar L. Morphet and David L. Jessen, eds., *Emerging State Responsibilities for Education* (Denver, Colo.: Improving State Leadership in Education, 1970), pp. 55–57.

officials to provide information or know-how for local officials also helps create a sense of professional comradeship between local and state officials which encourages cooperation.[20]

State agencies also bargain and negotiate with local officials to get compliance with state policies. The discretionary authority of state agencies, such as the power to recommend approval or disapproval of special grant requests and the power to use resources as they see fit, permits them to bargain with local officials who desire these resources. One of the most powerful resources with which to bargain is money, since availability of funds quickly attracts the interest of local schoolmen.[21] Under most state laws, state education agencies have until recently had relatively little discretion over state funds, since they were distributed according to a detailed formula. In recent years, SDEs have been given more discretionary power over the expenditures of both state and federal aid funds, and this has increased their power over local districts. Intangible rewards available to state agencies, such as their ability to control certain prestigeful interactions in education circles or to give public praise to local districts and individuals, also may be used as a kind of exchange for cooperation.[22]

Reliance on rules is used when other means of cooperation fail. State agencies are often forced to fall back on rules in heated disputes over such matters as consolidation of districts or desegregation. In these situations state officials in effect say, "In order to qualify for state funds you must comply with state law" or "The court has so ordered and its decision must be obeyed."[23]

Pressure and coercion also may be used to force local compliance. Threats to withdraw or withhold certain benefits create anxiety in local officials and may lead to compliance. Another less drastic type of pressure is the giving of a "conditional acceptance rating" on requests for special state funds and indicating that the proposal will be acceptable to the state provided that certain alterations are made. Criticisms against schools or individuals may be another form of coercive action. Lawsuits or threat of lawsuits against the district or the individual unless state law

[20]Roald F. Campbell, Gerald E. Sroufe, and Donald H. Layton, *Strengthening State Departments of Education* (Chicago: University of Chicago, Midwest Administration Center, 1967), pp. 49–54.

[21]*Ibid.*, pp. 46–47.

[22]A search of the state laws revealed that eleven states provide, by statute, for the withholding of state school funds from school districts. Some statutes provide a "blanket policy" which in effect says that compliance with all the provisions of the state board or department of education is a prerequisite to participation in state school funds; other statutes provide for the withholding of funds only for specifically enumerated reasons. The eleven states are Alaska, California, Colorado, Massachusetts, Utah, Georgia, Illinois, Pennsylvania, New York, Washington, and Wyoming.

[23]Campbell, Sroufe, and Layton, *Strengthening State Departments of Education*, pp. 47–49.

is complied with is still another form of pressure. Most state agencies use this type of power sparingly because of the strong and lasting repercussions it causes.[24]

The states' power over local districts is by no means absolute. School districts, because of the general acceptance of local control, have considerable political power. School districts and individual educators may counteract pressures of the state agency through political support of legislators, governors, or other key political figures. Because of the political strength of local districts, state agencies generally have been given relatively little discretionary power over local districts. Most state agencies attempt to identify with local schoolmen in order to share in their political strength.

Policy Outputs and Outcomes

We have examined to this point the determinants of state educational policy and the policymaking processes. Figure 8–2 recapitulates the effects of socioeconomic and political characteristics on state policy outputs. Since the character of American education is shaped by state policies, it is important to understand how state educational policies serve the two major functions of government, that is, providing for the essential services of education and regulating social conflict.

The policy outputs of the states vary widely. Each of the fifty states enacts its own laws to organize and finance education, and these policies reflect the differences in value commitments of the people as well as the social, political, and economic conditions. As there are rich states and poor states, state and local education expenditures can range from a low expenditure of $543 per pupil in Alabama to a high of $1,468 in New York and $1,432 in Alaska. (See Table 8–1.) The tax efforts made to support education and the percentage of state and local contributions also

Figure 8–2 Model for the Analysis of Educational Policy Outputs

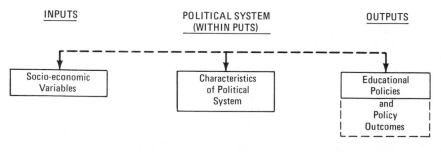

Table 8-1 Educational Expenditures for Public Elementary and Secondary Schools

Estimated current expenditures for public elementary and secondary schools per pupil in average daily attendance, 1971–72

1.	New York	$1,468	24.	Ohio	871
*2.	Alaska	1,432	25.	Louisiana	867
3.	New Jersey	1,289	26.	Washington	866
4.	Vermont	1,208	27.	Kansas	854
5.	Michigan	1,148	28.	Arizona	853
6.	Connecticut	1,130	29.	Florida	850
7.	Delaware	1,097	30.	New Hampshire	847
8.	Pennsylvania	1,073	31.	Indiana	837
9.	Maryland	1,071	32.	Missouri	812
10.	Wisconsin	1,069	33.	New Mexico	807
11.	Hawaii	1,039	34.	Maine	803
12.	Illinois	1,032	35.	Georgia	788
13.	Rhode Island	1,006	36.	South Dakota	781
14.	Oregon	979	37.	North Dakota	740
15.	Iowa	965	38.	Idaho	732
†16.	California	952	39.	⎰Nebraska	713
17.	Minnesota	941		⎱West Virginia	713
18.	Wyoming	940	41.	Texas	705
			42.	South Carolina	700
			43.	Utah	696
	UNITED STATES	929‡	44.	North Carolina	695
			45.	Tennessee	659
19.	Nevada	910	46.	Kentucky	650
20.	Massachusetts	907	47.	Mississippi	634
21.	Colorado	905	48.	Oklahoma	633
22.	Montana	904	49.	Arkansas	601
23.	Virginia	875	50.	Alabama	543

NEA. *Estimates of School Statistics, 1971–72*, p. 37.

*Reduce 30% to make purchasing power comparable to figures for other areas of the United States.

†Changed by California after publication of *Estimates*.

‡Figure for national average per pupil expenditure does not include late revision of California figure.

Current expenditures per public-school pupil in average daily attendance as percent of national average, 1971–72

1.	New York	158.0	24.	Ohio	93.8
2.	Alaska	154.1	25.	Louisiana	93.3
3.	New Jersey	138.8	26.	Washington	93.2
4.	Vermont	130.0	27.	Kansas	91.9
5.	Michigan	123.6	28.	Arizona	91.8
6.	Connecticut	121.6	29.	Florida	91.5
7.	Delaware	118.1	30.	New Hampshire	91.2
8.	Pennsylvania	115.5	31.	Indiana	90.1
9.	Maryland	115.3	32.	Missouri	87.4
10.	Wisconsin	115.1	33.	New Mexico	86.9

11.	Hawaii	111.8	34.	Maine	86.4
12.	Illinois	111.1	35.	Georgia	84.8
13.	Rhode Island	108.3	36.	South Dakota	84.1
14.	Oregon	105.4	37.	North Dakota	79.7
15.	Iowa	103.9	38.	Idaho	78.8
16.	California	102.5	39.	Nebraska	76.7
17.	Minnesota	101.3		West Virginia	76.7
18.	Wyoming	101.2	41.	Texas	75.9
			42.	South Carolina	75.3
			43.	Utah	74.9
	UNITED STATES	100.0	44.	North Carolina	74.8
			45.	Tennessee	70.9
19.	Nevada	98.0	46.	Kentucky	70.0
20.	Massachusetts	97.6	47.	Mississippi	68.2
21.	Colorado	97.4	48.	Oklahoma	68.1
22.	Montana	97.3	49.	Arkansas	64.7
23.	Virginia	94.2	50.	Alabama	58.4

NEA, *Estimates of School Statistics, 1971–72*, p. 37.

Total current expenditures for public elementary and secondary schools in 1970–71 as percent of personal income in 1970

1.	Alaska	7.7	28.	Connecticut	4.6
2.	Vermont	7.2		Pennsylvania	4.6
3.	Wyoming	6.2		Washington	4.6
4.	New Mexico	6.0			
5.	Montana	5.9			
6.	Michigan	5.7		UNITED STATES	4.6
7.	Iowa	5.5			
	Louisiana	5.5	31.	Arkansas	4.5
	Utah	5.5		Georgia	4.5
10.	Maine	5.4		Indiana	4.5
	North Dakota	5.4	34.	Florida	4.4
	South Dakota	5.4		North Carolina	4.4
13.	Arizona	5.3		Rhode Island	4.4
	Delaware	5.3		Tennessee	4.4
	Minnesota	5.3	38.	California	4.3
	Mississippi	5.3		Kansas	4.3
	Oregon	5.3		New Hampshire	4.3
	Wisconsin	5.3	41.	Kentucky	4.2
19.	Idaho	5.1		Nevada	4.2
20.	Colorado	5.0		Ohio	4.2
	New York	5.0		Texas	4.2
	South Carolina	5.0	45.	Illinois	4.1
23.	Hawaii	4.8	46.	Alabama	4.0
	Maryland	4.8		Missouri	4.0
25.	New Jersey	4.7		Oklahoma	4.0
	Virginia	4.7	49.	Nebraska	3.8
	West Virginia	4.7	50.	Massachusetts	3.7

NEA. *Estimates of School Statistics, 1971–72*, p. 36.
Survey of Current Business, August, 1971, p. 31.

Source: NEA Research Report 1972-R1, Ranking of the States, 1972 (*Washington, D.C.: National Education Association, 1972*), p. 63.

vary widely. In American education there are no uniform or national standards as there are in some unitary countries.

The outcome or the effect these differences will have on education is not fully known. In fact, until recently we have used the terms *policy outputs* and *policy outcomes* synonymously. Such groups as the NEA often employed expenditure levels as measures of policy outcomes with the implication that the more the government spends, the more the people benefit. But this assumption is now being challenged, and a distinction is being made between policy outputs and policy outcomes. Increasingly, demands are being made for a measurement of outcomes—a measurement of how well the educational goals of the state are being achieved.[25] Since the early 1960s there has been a movement calling for a national assessment program to measure the growth or decline in educational attainment that takes place over time in key learning areas. A long and bitter debate over national assessment has resulted, caused in part by the fear of the impact of state comparisons, as well as by the difficulty of defining policy goals for education. We still do not know how well state educational systems perform.[26]

Despite our inability to measure how well educational goals are being accomplished, states can boast that they have responded to educational problems. Two of the major problems of the last twenty years, the deficit in facilities and personnel and the needed changes in the science and mathematics curriculum, have largely been overcome. Furthermore, it is frequently claimed that differences in state educational systems help preserve the federal system. By socializing youth in the local culture and teaching a love for the state and parochial ways, state educational systems help preserve federalism, since federalism rests upon a desire of people to retain their separate and parochial ways, as well as to be unified in a national system.

It is parochialism of our state school system, however, that has caused much of the conflict over education in recent years. The clash of national

[25]Ronald E. Weber and William Shaffer, "The Costs and Benefits of American State-Local Government Policies" (Paper delivered at 1972 Southwestern Political Science Association, San Antonio), pp. 1–2.

[26]Morphet and Jessen, *Emerging State Responsibilities for State Education*, pp. 147–48; *cf.* James Hazlett, "Looking Forward to National Assessment Results," *School Administrator*, June 1970, p. 11; "National Assessment: Measuring American Education," *Compact*, February 1972, entire issue; James Cass, "Profit and Loss in Education," *Saturday Review*, August 1971, pp. 39–40; John Catallozzi, "Accountability and Responsibility in Education," *Journal of Education*, December 1971, pp. 21–29; Stephen M. Barro, "An Approach to Developing Accountability Measures for the Public Schools," *Phi Delta Kappan*, December 1970, pp. 196–205; and James R. Richburg, "The Movement for Accountability in Education" (Paper read before the Annual Convention, National Council for the Social Studies, Denver, November 1971).

and state values over school desegregation has led to violent conflict at times. National priorities—the scientific and technological revolution, the increasing military requirements, the problems of urbanization and metropolitanization—demand change, which has often been resisted because of parochial views. Deadlocks have frequently occurred in state legislatures over urban school problems. As a result of rural and suburban control, coupled with an antiurban bias, states have neither met the challenge of the urban educational crisis nor provided for equality of educational opportunity. The urban school crisis has not been met by the states, and much of the conflict arising out of this problem has been pushed to the federal level. Many of these issues are left to be solved by the federal courts or Congress through grants-in-aid programs. We shall discuss the federal system and its influence on educational policy in the next chapter.

chapter nine

Political System
of Federal Education

Public education has traditionally been considered a local and state function, as education is not mentioned in the Constitution of the United States. The federal government, however, is, and has been since its earliest days, deeply involved in education. The interrelated nature of American federalism results in the federal government's involvement in this as in all areas of public concern.

Federalism not only affects the structural arrangement of American government but permeates the relationships of all aspects of politics. Governments at all levels are linked into a "system of systems," which allows the whole and its constituent parts to retain their respective integrities. Politics at each level differs; each responds to political demands in its own way because of the differences in the structural, cultural, and situational factors affecting each level. But policymaking in this "system of systems" is highly interrelated. What any one level of government does, or does not do, in turn affects the other levels of government.[1]

All levels of government in a sense are involved in all policies, including educational policies. For instance, what local and state governments do—that is, the policy output—on such matters as school finance or school desegregation, directly affects the types of demands made on the federal government. If local and state governments do not, or can not, meet demands for adequately financing schools or do not remove barriers of segregation, the groups making those demands turn to the federal political arena in an attempt to shape educational policies. Similarly, what the federal government does affects both local politics and state politics, which in turn act as major determinants on federal policies.

---

[1]M. J. C. Vile, *The Structure of American Federalism* (New York: Oxford University Press, Inc., 1961), pp. 2–3; and Edward W. Weidner, "Decision-Making in a Federal System," in *Cooperation and Conflict: Readings in American Federalism* (Itasca, Ill.: F.E. Peacock Publishers, Inc., 1969), pp. 278–92.

Expanding Role of the Federal Government

The role of the federal government in the field of education is changing under the impact of modern economic, demographic, and political forces that generate national interests. Nationalization—and to a large extent internationalization—of the environment in recent years has created stresses in the educational system and has brought about an increased involvement of the federal government in American education. The most prominent change resulted from the educational legislation enacted by Congress during the 1960s.

For a number of years but especially since the decade of the 1960s, education has increasingly become a basic tool for strengthening various aspects of our society. The Department of Defense, for example, established programs in the military services to remedy the educational deficiencies of draftees. These programs were designed to not only increase the overall effectiveness of our defense establishment but also strengthen the economy by returning to civilian ranks large numbers of young men who would supposedly be better employees and citizens because of the education they had received while in uniform. The Labor Department developed manpower training programs in schools and colleges to improve the work skills of the labor force. The Office of Economic Opportunity was assigned the tasks of improving the work skills of school dropouts through the Job Corps and attacking the problems caused by cultural deprivation. Working mainly through colleges and universities, the National Science Foundation supports teacher-training programs, with the immediate aim of improving scientific instruction in the schools and the ultimate aim of guaranteeing our ability to compete in a technological age.[2] Passage of the Elementary and Secondary Education Act of 1965, a major antipoverty measure, greatly expanded the federal government's role in education, and today it would be difficult to find a single pupil, teacher, or classroom in the nation not in some way affected by the federal government's assistance.

The use of the public schools to accomplish national goals placed new responsibilities on the educational system and changed the relationship between federal, state, and local governments. This chapter examines the structure of the political system of federal education and the societal inputs that affect federal politics of education.

[2]"Change and American Schools" (Address by Harold Howe II, U.S. Commissioner of Education, HEW, before the American Association of School Administrators, Atlantic City, New Jersey, February 13, 1967).

Political System of Federal Education

The politics of federal education is affected by environmental factors in the nation, inputs from state and local political systems, and the character of federal institutions and politics—*within puts*, as we have called these influences. The model shown in Figure 9–1 attempts to portray the interaction of these factors.

Figure 9–1   Model Representing the Political System of Federal Education

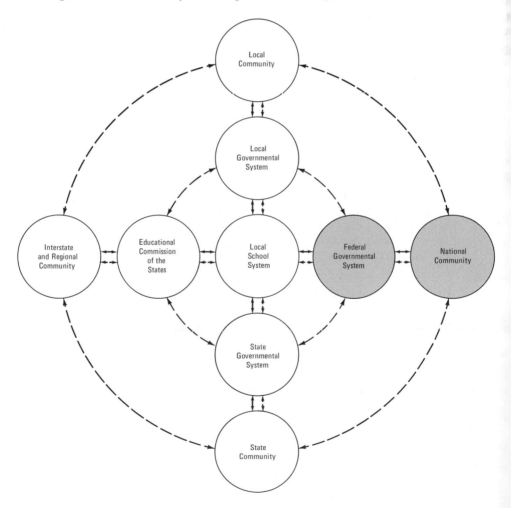

Circles representing the national community and the federal governmental system are accentuated in the model. The circle at the right of the diagram represents the national community, that is, the cultural and socioeconomic factors affecting national politics. The circle immediately to its left represents the national political and governmental system and concomitant political variables. By differentiating the national community and the political and governmental system from the state and local systems, we are attempting to show that the structural, cultural, and situational factors affecting federal policymaking differ from those of the other political arenas.

The remainder of the model represents the local and state systems, which we have already discussed. What local and state educational systems do—that is, the output of these systems—acts as an input into the federal system, and directly and vitally affects the federal government. In turn, federal actions influence state and local governments. Finally, the formal legal and administrative relationships between parts of the system are represented by the solid-line arrows connecting the various parts of the model; the informal interactions and communications, by the broken-line arrows.

Environmental Factors
Affecting Politics of Education

The national system representing the totality of the countless social, economic, and cultural differences in the United States has the most competitive political environment. There are more groups competing for a share of the policymaking pie, and because of the differences in federal politics some groups have more influence at the federal level than they do at either the state or the local level. In this more competitive political environment, education must vie for attention and resources with numerous problem areas.

Response to change. Changes in the environment in recent years have been more readily perceived at the national level. The federal government has recognized demands that were not immediately felt at other levels of government. In part this is due to the broader scope of its responsibilities and to the effect of such environmental forces as the scientific and technological revolution, population changes, continuing urbanization, racial unrest, and international crisis.

Another reason why the national government has been more responsive to societal changes is that political actors at the federal level have larger and broader-based constituencies. They are therefore forced to re-

spond to more heterogeneous groups than do the state and local politicians. They must also make broader appeals to win office and must be responsive to more diverse demands to remain in office; this is especially true of the president, the only politician with a nationwide constituency.

Dramatic societal changes in recent years have caused increasing concern over education, since such national goals as maintaining economic stability and full employment, ensuring national defense, preserving domestic tranquillity, overcoming poverty, and guaranteeing equal rights for all depend to a large degree on education. The federal government has often attempted to solve basic economic and social problems confronting our people by providing assistance to education. The commitment to education has become a matter of highest priority because many of our national goals are dependent on it, and the expanding role of the federal government in education reflects this concern.[3]

National goals often conflict with the cultural traditions and values in the states and localities, particularly such national goals as racial integration of schools, equal opportunity for minority groups and women, the war on poverty, and other urban-oriented policies. This conflict and the resistance to change by members of parochial groups is clearly reflected in the actions of politicians and pressure groups and is evidenced by the political rhetoric about federal encroachment on states' rights.[4]

Evolving Federalism.   Debate over the nature of our federal system and the role of the federal government is an ever-present aspect of the American political environment. The problem of defining federalism and the roles of the levels of government has been with us throughout our national existence. Much of our political history revolves around these issues. The fact that the Constitution was created as a pragmatic compromise between those who desired a strong central government and those who wanted practically no central government set the scene for a continuing debate between the forces of centralization and those of decentralization. Many of our great political landmarks in American history—the opposing constitutional positions of Jefferson, Hamilton, or Marshall, the Webster-Clay debates, the Civil War, the "Old Court and the New Deal," to mention just a few—pertained to the nature of the federal system. More recently in the post-World War II period, the constitutionality of federal

---

[3]"National Policy for American Education" (Address by Harold Howe II, U.S. Commissioner of Education, HEW, before the 71st Annual Convention of the National Congress of Parents and Teachers, Minneapolis, May 22, 1967).

[4]Howe, "Change and American Schools"; *cf.* Daniel J. Elazar, "Fiscal Questions and Political Answers in Intergovernmental Finance," *Public Administration Review,* September-October 1972, p. 471.

aid to education and the question of school integration have been hotly disputed issues.[5]

Since the beginning, our governmental system has continuously evolved and changed. It has never been a static system; instead, it has provided a flexibility to meet changing societal conditions. Changes in our federal system are evident in a number of areas—in legal and constitutional doctrines, in the methods of performing various governmental functions, in the division of revenues, and in the decision-making processes themselves. These changes have become particularly apparent in education in recent years.

In 1965 the groups that had worked for federal aid for over a decade were finally successful. The host of educational programs that Congress enacted in the 1960s reflected the interests of urban-oriented groups which had previously been largely ineffectual on the state and local levels because of malapportioned state legislatures. Major emphasis of the new federal programs was given to the urban problems of poverty, civil rights, and vocational education—problems that were of national concern but affected the urban areas most acutely. The increased involvement of the federal government occurred particularly because of the growing national demands and needs for more revenue to support education.[6]

Fiscal Federalism. Political decisions on how to finance education are greatly complicated by federalism. The very nature of the federal system precludes any completely clear-cut or logical division of revenues or expenditures between the levels of government. All three levels—federal, state, and local—rest upon the same revenue base, the American economy; demands for expenditures grow out of the same political environment. Both federal and state governments, within broad constitutional limits, are free to make their own decisions in the area of public finance. Local government, although more limited by state constitutional and statutory provisions, also is largely responsible for its own tax and expenditure policies. Thus a complex system of public finance has developed, with overlapping taxes, much transferring of funds from one level to an-

[5]For the most comprehensive account of American intergovernmental relations, see W. Brooke Graves, *American Intergovernmental Relations: Their Origins, Historical Development and Current Status* (New York: Charles Scribner's Sons, 1964). See also the annual reports of the Advisory Commission on Intergovernmental Relations.

[6]*Federal Role in Education* (Washington, D.C.: Congressional Quarterly Service, 1965), p. 66; *cf.* Philip Meranto, *The Politics of Federal Aid to Education in 1965: A Study in Political Innovation* (Syracuse, N.Y.: Syracuse University Press, 1967), p. 139; and Eugene Eidenberg and Roy D. Morey, *An Act of Congress: The Legislative Process and the Making of Education Policy* (New York: W. W. Norton & Company, Inc., 1969), p. 256.

other, and considerable legal sharing of responsibilities for tax and expenditure decisions, Grodzins's analogy of "marble cake" federalism is as applicable in the area of public finance as it is in the functional aspects of government.[7]

The pattern of public finance has become increasingly complex. Down to the eve of World War I the federal tax system was relatively simple, and conflict was avoided because the federal government confined itself largely to sources that the states were forbidden to tax (customs) or which they had never seen fit to widely employ (excises). The states meanwhile were raising most of their revenues from the general property tax, a field largely protected from federal encroachment by the federal Constitution, and a host of special excise taxes. Since the early years of the twentieth century, however, states have been forced to develop supplementary revenues, as has the federal government. Much overlapping state and federal taxes resulted, and conflict over revenue sources intensified. Today's complex pattern of public finance reflects the never-ending demands on all levels of government and the growing competition for revenues. The dominant tax pattern shows that the federal government relies most heavily upon the income tax for its revenues, while the states depend mainly on general sales and consumption taxes.[8]

Local governments, as creatures of the states, were forced until quite recently to rely almost solely upon the property tax—the least flexible revenue source. Since World War II, however, demands for expenditures by local governments have outrun their tax abilities and have caused two developments: (1) the growth of local nonproperty taxes (such as sales, excise, and wage taxes), and (2) the increase of intergovernmental transfers to local governments from both the state and the federal level.

Diversification of local revenue sources has resulted in even more overlapping of taxes, piling tax levies three levels deep in some instances. Also, expansion of intergovernmental transfers of funds to local governments has pushed local finance decisions more into the state and national political arenas, resulting in more sharing—and more political conflict—in the making of these decisions.[9]

---

[7]Graves, *American Intergovernmental Relations*, pp. 437–76; *cf.* Frederick C. Mosher and Orville F. Poland, *The Costs of American Governments* (New York: Dodd, Mead & Co., 1964), pp. 61–90; and *Fiscal Balance in the American Federal System* (Washington, D.C.: Advisory Commission on Intergovernmental Relations, 1967), Vol. I.

[8]*Fiscal Balance in the American Federal System* (Washington, D.C.: Advisory Commission on Intergovernmental Relations, 1967), Vol. I.

[9]*State and Local Finances: Significant Features 1967 to 1970* (Washington, D.C.: Advisory Commission on Intergovernmental Relations, 1969), p. 181; *cf. State and Local Finances and Suggested Legislation* (Washington, D.C.: Advisory Commission on Intergovernmental Relations, 1970), p. 212

Today's pattern of public finance gives the national government great advantages over the other levels of government. It has the broadest and most flexible tax source, the income tax. Revenues from personal and corporate income taxes reflect closely the gross national product. The bounties of government—tax revenues—accrue to the federal government, since growth of the economy automatically means more tax resources. The nation's broader power to borrow and control the monetary system also puts it in the best strategic position to cope with cyclical emergencies. Fiscal decisions, as a result, are not as politically difficult or dangerous to national officeholders. Local constituents do not feel the impact of decisions to tax and spend at the federal level as directly or as immediately as they feel fiscal decisions made at the state and local levels.[10]

On the other hand, the burdens of government—the expenditures— have fallen most heavily on local and state governments. Local and state governments—particularly local governments—have borne the brunt of the demands for more domestic governmental services. Progress in industrialization, in living standards, and in social consciousness means more demands on local and state governments.[11] Since 1945 local and state expenditures have increased much more rapidly than federal expenditures, and local and state debt has increased at a much faster rate than federal debt.[12]

Pressures for increasing intergovernmental transfers of funds have been created by this imbalance between the burdens and bounties of government. Local governments have sought aid from the states and the federal government because they have more flexible tax systems. Figure 9–2 attempts to show the differences in the burdens and bounties of government.

Intergovernmental transfers of funds in the form of grants-in-aid or shared taxes have been a part of our financial system since the earliest days of the Republic. However, the most rapid growth of such transfers— both from the states and from the federal government—have occurred in recent years as urban-metropolitan problems have become more severe.[13] Politics has increasingly centered on such questions as how to respond to

[10]L. Laszlo Ecker-Racz, "Federal-State Fiscal Imbalance: The Dilemma," *Congressional Record*, 89th Cong., 1st sess., August 5, 1965; Vol. III, No. 143; *cf.* Joel S. Berke, "The Current Crisis in School Finance: Inadequacy and Inequity," *Phi Delta Kappan*, September 1971, pp. 2–7.

[11]Ecker-Racz, "Federal-State Fiscal Imbalance."

[12]*State and Local Finances: Significant Features 1967 to 1970*, (Washington D.C.: Advisory Commission on Intergovernmental Relations, 1969), pp. 28–53.

[13]Graves, *American Intergovernmental Relations*, pp. 417–573; *cf.* Forrest E. Conner, *The Realities of School Finance* (Washington, D.C.: American Association of School Administrators, 1971); *Urban America and the Federal System* (Washington, D.C.: Advisory Commission on Intergovernmental Relations, 1969); and *Urban School Crisis* (Washington, D.C.: Urban Education Task Force, HEW, 1970).

Figure 9–2   Distribution of Burdens and Bounties to the Different Units of
Government

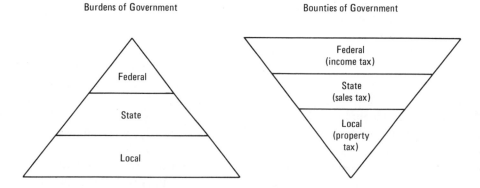

the problems caused by continuing urbanization and how to finance the growing demands of local governments. Most recently, the question being debated is how such transfers should be made and what form federal and state grants should take—categorical grants or revenue sharing.[14] Conflict over federal and state aid to education has become a permanent issue.

Federal politics of education is also affected by political, social, and economic diversities between the states, and particularly by the disparities in the states' support of education. States' ability to support education varies widely, as is evidenced by comparisons of such statistics as state expenditures per pupil, percentage of state income spent on schools, and range of teachers' salaries. Inequalities in educational expenditures have accelerated demands for additional federal aid to education.

It is argued that federal grants should reduce state-to-state inequalities and provide the same educational opportunities for all. It is also argued that as a result of the "spillover" effect of education, national goals are being threatened by the wide inequalities in state educational systems. The level of education in every state affects the well-being of all because of the unified national economy and the great mobility of our people.[15] Opponents of additional federal expenditures for education, on the other hand, see diversity between the states as a fundamental aspect of fed-

[14]*Federalism in 1971: The Crisis Continues, 13th Annual Report* (Washington, D.C.: Advisory Commission on Intergovernmental Relations, 1972); *cf.* Frank B. Withrow, "The U.S. Office of Education as a Part of the Problem" (Presentation given at the Conference on the Consolidation of Special Revenue Sharing Educational Legislation, Dallas, March 12, 1971).

[15]Leta Linzer Schwartz, *American Education: A Problem-Centered Approach* (Boston: Holbrook Press, 1970), pp. 145–56; *cf.* Sidney W. Tiedt, *The Role of the Federal Government in Education* (New York: Oxford University Press, Inc., 1966), pp. 33–70.

eralism and insist that education should remain a state responsibility.[16] The litany that "control follows the purse" is often used to buttress these arguments, as is illustrated in the political cartoon in Figure 9–3. Continuing debate over equalization of education between the states is inherent in the system because of the very nature of federalism.

Inputs Into the Political System of Federal Education

Out of the pluralistic national environment arise a multitude of groups attempting to influence federal policies pertaining to education. In the model shown in Figure 9–4, the various groups are represented by circles arising out of the national environment and making demands on the governmental system.

Many who are only indirectly concerned with education have been drawn into the policy arena because of the expansion of the federal role.

Figure 9–3   Hardly Anyone Refuses to Sign

Reg Manning in the *Laramie Daily Boomerang*, June 18, 1965. Reprinted by permission of the artist, the newspaper, and the McNaught Syndicate.

[16]Barry Goldwater, "In Place of Federal Aid," in Schwartz, *American Education*, pp. 157–62; *cf.* Tiedt, *Role of the Federal Government*, pp. 71–104.

Figure 9–4 Group Inputs on the Federal Government

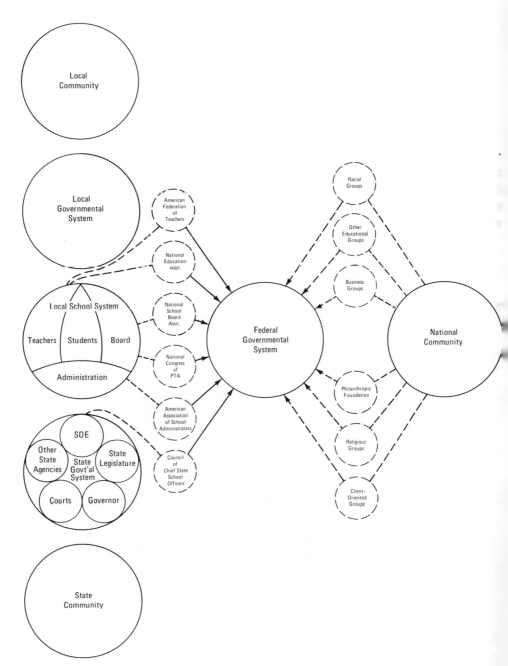

The influence of federal educational policies affects numerous aspects of life, including such matters as the individual's economic and social position, the rate of societal change, and public fiscal policies—that is, the size of public expenditures, the priority of various programs, and the form and rate of taxation. Many groups attempt to use federal educational policies to advance their primary objectives, which may not be education per se. Racial groups, for instance, hope to affect social change and civil rights through federal educational policies. Other groups, such as the insurgent poor, religious sects and parochial schools, philanthropic foundations, labor unions, and private industry, seek to advance their own primary goals through federal educational policies.[17]

Economic gain motivates some groups, such as book companies and consultant firms, which have an obvious economic stake in federal policies. Generally, business and industry want students trained specifically for them, research that can be applied, and loyalty to the free-enterprise system. Others are motivated by ideological causes; they may desire change in society or may feel threatened by societal changes. Right-wing groups want left-wing groups stamped out—and vice versa. For whatever reason, more groups are involved in educational politics at the federal level than at the other levels, and the political processes of bargaining and negotiations are more open.

Professional Education Groups.   As in state and local politics, professional groups are most vitally affected by educational policies and are the main articulators of educational demands. But at the national level, there are a greater number of educational groups. More than 500 regional and national associations of education, nearly 150 college professional

[17]Patricia Cayo Sexton, *The American School: A Sociological Analysis* (Englewood Cliffs, N.J.: Prentice-Hall, Inc., 1967), pp. 21–36. In the legislative struggle to enact federal aid to education the group alignment was as follows: The major organizations that supported federal aid for education were the National Education Association, AFL-CIO and its affiliates, American Federation of Teachers, Council of Chief State School Officers, National Congress of Parent-Teachers, American Association of University Professors, American Association of University Women, Americans for Democratic Action, National Farmers' Union, American Parents Committee, American Veterans Committee, National Association for the Advancement of Colored People, American Jewish Congress, Baptist Joint Committee on Public Affairs, Protestants and Other Americans United for Separation of Church and State, and Unitarian Fellowship for Social Justice. These groups opposed distribution of funds to private and parochial schools (Catholic groups favored aid only if assistance was provided for parochial schools).

Organizations that opposed federal aid included the U.S. Chamber of Commerce, Council of State Chambers of Commerce, National Association of Manufacturers, Southern State Industrial Council, National School Board Association, Investment Bankers Association of America, American Farm Bureau, American Legion, and Daughters of the American Revolution. Meranto, *Politics of Federal Aid*, pp. 544–55.

societies, 50 religious educational associations, and 15 international associations bring the total to nearly 1,000 groups in some way attempting to affect educational policies.[18]

Such a conglomeration of associations obviously exhibits a tremendous variety in size and intent. There is lack of agreement as to the needs of education, especially between elementary-secondary education groups and higher education groups. Although their interest in education to some extent overlaps, there is much disagreement and a great amount of friction between the two. Even within each of the major branches of the educational enterprise there is division. Senator Wayne Morse described the lack of unity among educational groups as follows:

> In the first year of President Kennedy's administration, we suffered a setback in Congress in respect to educational legislation. We passed an education bill in the Senate, but were unable to get to conference with the House.
>
> This was very disturbing to the then President of the United States, and he called me down to the White House because I was chairman of the Subcommittee on Education.
>
> The President asked me what I thought had happened. I will paraphrase what I said, but I will paraphrase it very accurately. . . . I said: "Mr. President, there is a nonunity among these educational groups in the country. The higher education people are interested only in higher education. And the elementary and secondary education people are only interested in their field of education. The same is true with vocational education, technical education, and with junior colleges.
>
> We need some unity, or we will not get any education legislation. They have a common objective, but they do not know it. There is also the public-private split. Let us face it, the split is over the religious issue."[19]

Elementary-Secondary Groups. The main groups representing elementary-secondary education are the counterparts of the state-local organizations, namely, the National Education Association, the American Association of School Administrators, the National School Boards Association, and the National Congress of Parent and Teachers Association. The American Federation of Teachers also attempts to influence national policy, and the United States Catholic Conference speaks for parochial schools.[20] Figure 9–4 shows these groups arising out of the local and state systems and placing demands on the federal government.

[18]Francis Keppel, "Education Lobbies and Federal Legislation," in *Challenge and Change in American Education*, ed. Seymour Harris and Alan Levensohn (Berkeley, Calif.: McCutchan Publishing Corp., 1965), p. 63; *cf.* Russell Thackery, "National Educational Organizations and the Changing Politics of Education," *Phi Delta Kappan*, February 1968, pp. 312–15.

[19]*Congressional Record—Senate*, December 15, 1967, p. S18953.

[20]R. Joseph Monsen, Jr., and Mark W. Cannon, *The Makers of Public Policy: American Power Groups and Their Ideologies* (New York: McGraw-Hill Book Company, 1965), pp. 150–176.

NEA, with over a million members, is the outstanding spokesman for public school teachers. With a large budget—$28.5 million in 1971— NEA maintains a sizable staff for lobbying and for the galaxy of other activities normally performed by professional associations.[21] An example of its political activities in 1971 was the mobilization of its members to send 250,000 letters and telegrams to the president in support of a cabinet post for education.[22]

Despite its membership and wealth, NEA is not rated as being a very effective lobbying group by most observers. For instance, the former U.S. Commissioner of Education, Frances Keppel, has written about NEA legislative accomplishments in Congress:

> . . . If asked what, on balance, it has accomplished during the past century on behalf of the primary and secondary schools, one would have to reply, "Not much." NEA has tried. It has been both vocal and active. It has presented many resolutions and through other channels, it has proposed appropriations by the Federal Government for both general and specific purposes. But . . . NEA's efforts bore little fruit.[23]

A number of reasons explain the limited success. For one thing, the power and position of every lobbying organization in Washington quickly becomes a known factor. Congressmen who are considering whether to vote for a given educational measure are already aware of NEA's general position. For most practical purposes its general position is a constant, as familiar to them as the economic and occupational facts about their own constituency. Similarly, the political strength or clout of every group is common knowledge.[24] NEA is not viewed by politicians as having much political clout. This is the result of several factors: the nonpolitical ideology of teachers, the rate at which teachers leave their profession, the fact that NEA is a holding company for numerous specialized interests in education and suffers from internal weakness, and the poor political record of NEA in the past.

Developing a coalition of groups, preferably of those whose support is not already taken for granted, therefore becomes a primary task of educational groups hoping to effectively influence legislation. Congressmen give much more weight to coalitions that include organizations outside of education—the U.S. Chamber of Commerce, the AFL–CIO, or other politically active groups at the local level, such as the League of Women

---

[21]Sam M. Lambert, "Report of the Executive Secretary," *Annual Conference Proceedings,* National Education Association (Washington, D.C., June 26–July 2, 1971), pp. 16–17.

[22]*Ibid.*, p. 18.

[23]Keppel, "Education Lobbies," p. 65.

[24]Elliot Richardson, "Educational Lobbies and Federal Legislation," in *Challenge and Change in American Education,* ed. Harris and Levensohn, p. 56.

Voters. Such groups are politically important back home and may affect a congressman's political future. They therefore have more influence.

The other educational groups attempting to influence national policies —the AFT, AASA, and PTA—suffer from many of the same weaknesses as NEA, and perhaps even more so. They too have been relatively ineffectual in influencing educational policies. Only through the formation of alliances with other groups can they hope to enact national legislation.

Coalitions Affecting Educational Policies. The need for broad-based coalitions to enact federal legislation is clearly seen from the history of policies that have been passed. Most of the federal government's educational policies and programs were undertaken for reasons other than a conscious concern for the network of schools and colleges. Since the legislation affected interests other than education, a wide assortment of groups was drawn into the policy process. For instance, the legislation in 1787 providing for school aid in the Northwest Territory was not motivated solely out of a concern for education but, in part, as a means of attracting settlers to the territory. Education was a good inducement to settlers, so other groups such as land companies joined in the effort to pass the measure.[25]

Similarly, the National Defense Education Act of 1958 was intended mainly to strengthen the defense establishment, and it therefore gained tacit if not open endorsement from defense-oriented groups and their supporters, such as the U.S. Chamber of Commerce, which normally opposed legislation expanding the federal role in education. The host of legislation enacted in the mid-1960s was designed primarily to improve economic conditions by increasing the skills of labor or overcoming poverty. As a result, many groups including labor unions and civil rights groups actively supported the legislation. It is easier to enact educational legislation that affects other than educational problems per se, since other groups can be pulled into a coalition with educational groups.[26]

Educational groups have become increasingly aware of the need for creating alliances. A most notable example was the coalition of all educational groups from preschool to the adult- and graduate-level institutions in the "Full Funding Campaign" of 1969. Under a steering committee of representatives of the major educational interests and their supporters— the National Education Association, National Catholic Education Association, American Council on Education, Urban Coalition, American Library Association, Impacted Areas Superintendents, Research Council

[25]Keppel, "Education Lobbies," p. 64.
[26]Meranto, *Politics of Federal Aid*, pp. 52–58; *cf.* Eidenberg and Morey, *Act of Congress*, pp. 52–68.

of the Great Cities, and American Book Publishers Council—this coalition waged a major drive to get Congress to fully fund educational programs.[27] Only a veto by President Nixon stymied the effort.[28]

The Nixon veto clearly indicates also that federal politics of education is affected not only by the inputs from various groups.[29] Within puts, that is, the structure, procedures, and personalities of federal officeholders, are a major factor in federal policymaking. We now turn to the effects of these within puts on educational politics.

[27]Stanley J. McFarland, "The Emergency Committee for Full Funding of Education Programs—What Is It?" mimeographed (Washington, D.C., n.d.).

[28]Helen P. Bain, "Report of the President," *Annual Conference Proceedings,* National Education Association (Washington, D.C., June 26–July 2, 1971), pp. 13–14; *cf. Congressional Quarterly,* Weekly Report, February 5, 1971, p. 358, and 1970 Weekly Report, p. 2992. Political lessons were learned from this experience, as is demonstrated by NEA's creation of a Task Force on the National Political Structure.

[29]*Annual Conference Proceedings,* National Education Association (Washington, D.C., June 26–July 2, 1971), pp. 384–85.

chapter ten

Governmental Within Puts on Federal Educational Policy

Federal educational policies are influenced not only by the demands of individuals and groups but also by the type of federal political institutions and individuals holding office (i.e., within puts from the federal political system). The basic features of American government—federalism and the nondisciplined and noncentralized party system, separation of powers and bicameralism, organization and procedures in the several departments of government, routinized political "interference" in administration, national supremacy and judicial review—all shape the political arena and significantly influence the federal policy process. Individuals and groups, in turn, tailor their demand strategies to meet the institutional setting within which the formal decisions are made.

In Figure 10–1 various institutional offices involved in educational policymaking are represented by small circles within a large federal governmental circle. Interactions between these institutional parties (i.e., the

Figure 10–1 Governmental Within Puts on the Federal Government

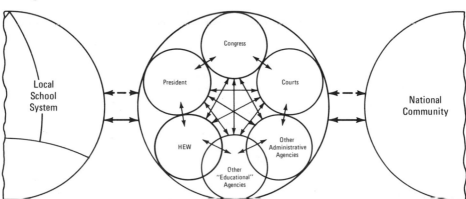

president, Congress, courts, HEW, and other federal administrative and "educational" agencies) are shown by arrows connecting the various circles. The influences of the institutional parties and the effect of such factors as the structural organization, the formal rules of the system, the interaction of various parts of the federal organization, and the political and personal characteristics of federal officials will be considered here.

Parties and Politics

The diffused governmental system of the United States is mirrored in the diffused political system. The party system, which is organized on the state level, consists of nearly autonomous political organizations in the fifty states and acts as a bulwark to ensure that those who make policy at the national level will be responsive to local interests. Federalism, by providing local centers of power and patronage independent of the federal authority, gives support to the local nature of party organization; and the separation of powers, by separating presidential politics from congressional politics, and by removing the need of a cohesive party organization in the legislature, powerfully strengthens the decentralizing tendencies in American politics.[1]

Loyalties of party politicians by necessity are to local parties, since they depend on them for reelection. All elected federal officials, including the senators, the congressmen, and even the president, depend on state parties for their election. In a sense, there are no national politicians, only state and local politicians serving at the national level. They dare not forget the parochial values of local constituents or be against vital local interests and expect to be reelected. The party system thus ensures development of federal policies that maximize noncentralized government and local control.

American national parties are only loose associations of state and local party groups. Their main purpose is to meet every four years to nominate a presidential candidate and draft a party platform for him to run on. But the platform does not bind congressmen—that is, ours is a nondisciplined party system. Members of Congress do not necessarily vote in favor of positions declared in the party platform. In fact, they are more apt to vote their constituency, to be influenced by their perception of local constituent desires rather than by the party position.

The locally based, nondisciplined nature of American political parties helps preserve the federal system but makes it difficult to provide for

[1]M. J. C. Vile, *The Structure of American Federalism* (New York: Oxford University Press, Inc., 1961), pp. 34–35.

equalization of education between the states or to enact civil rights measures. Proposals for equalization cause conflicts between the rich states and the poor states, and the local orientation of party politics militates against equalization. Although individual congressmen may occasionally support a certain financial-aid formula on principle against constituency interest, the greater number feel that their responsibility lies in serving as delegates protecting their constituents' interests. Congressmen from the richer states, therefore, are bound by local loyalties to oppose proposals to tax their constituents more in order to give to the poorer states.[2] Similarly, congressmen voting on civil rights issues take positions following the local cultural traditions rather than those of the national party.

Effect of Separation of Powers on Policymaking. The governmental and political structures ensure an evolutionary policy process. Separation of powers among the three branches of government and bicameralism in the legislative branch result in differing constituencies and length of terms for the various offices. Consequently, no single or transitory majority can gain control of all branches of government. Instead, it takes a concurrent majority of both Houses of Congress and favorable action by the president to enact major policy. But since national elections are held every two years, there is continuous change in the membership of the various branches and it is difficult to obtain or maintain a concurrent majority in all branches.[3]

There are many possible veto points in the federal policy process. Policies have to run the gauntlet of two separate houses of the legislature, the president, and perhaps even face a challenge in the courts. Then they are administered by a "politically sensitive" bureaucracy that is open to continuous political attacks. Major changes or innovations such as initiation of federal aid to education or civil rights legislation, therefore, occur infrequently, only when there is a general and widespread consensus in the country that results in concurrent majority in all branches of government.

It usually takes a crisis like the Great Depression of the 1930s or a series of such events as occurred in the mid-1960s—the assassination of President Kennedy, the election of 1964, and the widespread sympathy for the civil rights movement—to create a national consensus capable of causing major alterations in public policies. Normally, change in federal policies occurs incrementally through an evolutionary process. Thus the structure and the procedures of government provide for basic stability in governmental policy.

[2]Frank J. Munger and Richard F. Fenno, Jr., *National Politics and Federal Aid to Education* (Syracuse, N.Y.: Syracuse University Press, 1962), pp. 35–36.

[3]Eugene Eidenberg and Roy D. Morey, *An Act of Congress: The Legislative Process and the Making of Education Policy* (New York: W. W. Norton & Company, Inc., 1969), pp. 98, 158, and 175–77.

Separation of powers and the different procedures of various branches also provide multiple access points that enable groups to influence public policy. Groups may seek to influence public policy through the president, the Congress, or the administration, and if unsuccessful, turn to the courts. The desegregation and legislative apportionment suits in the 1960s, for instance, resulted in major changes in public policy. On these issues, minority and urban groups, who were unable to effect a change in other political arenas, were able to shape public policy through the federal courts. In turn, this change affected the entire policy process because the laws—the ground rules for dealing with the race problem and legislative apportionment—were altered.

Since all branches of government play a significant role in the policy process, we will now examine how each branch influences educational policy.

The Presidency

As federal involvement in education has increased, the Office of the President has become a major, if not the major, policymaking center for education. In terms of the formal Constitution, the president need only be involved in the policymaking processes through decisions to approve or disapprove legislation enacted by Congress. But as the executive department has evolved, the president of the United States has become, as it is frequently expressed, many men; he performs many roles in addition to his constitutionally designated roles as chief executive and commander in chief.[4] He is deeply concerned in the totality of the policymaking process, and executive recommendations play a major part in determining what Congress does.

President's Roles in Educational Policymaking. Growth of the president's roles and responsibilities has placed him more and more into educational policymaking. His role as "manager of the economy" with respon-

---

[4]"The President is the Chief of State, the Ceremonial head of the Nation. He is the Chief Executive, responsible for much in the formulation of policy and in the administration of government. He is the political leader of his party. He is Commander-in-Chief of the Armed Forces, head and chief spokesman for the nation in matters of foreign policy, and he is chief legislator, proposing legislation, prodding Congress to get his program enacted, and exercising (or threatening to exercise) his veto power when the legislative product is not to his liking. He acts as manager to keep the economy on an even keel with full employment. And, in addition, since the President is the only official elected by all the people, he is in a unique sense their leader. He can never stop being any of these things and still be a successful President, for his effectiveness in any one role has its bearing on his effectiveness in each of the others." W. Brooke Graves, *American Intergovernmental Relations: Their Origins, Historical Development, and Current Status* (New York: Charles Scribner's Sons, 1964), p. 170.

sibility for maintaining full employment and for keeping the economy on an even keel forces him to be concerned with education. Education is a major factor affecting the nation's economic well-being. It is frequently used to help solve economic problems, to overcome unemployment and poverty, to increase productivity of the labor force, and to retrain workers as a result of technological changes. Federal expenditures for education have recently become a major item in federal spending, which directly affects the economy. Education has become a large element in the congressional pork barrel, and the problem for the president is not so much that of inducing congressional support for education as it is that of keeping congressional support for education within fiscal and budgetary bounds. The size of the federal educational budget has become a much-debated issue in the efforts to control inflation.

Similarly, the president's role as commander in chief focuses his attention on manpower problems of the armed services. The goal of many federal educational programs is to improve the defense system. The National Defense Act of 1958, for instance, was enacted to reduce the rejection rate of draftees because of inadequate education, and the National Science Foundation was in part created to improve the schools' science programs.[5] Education in the form of veterans' benefits—the so-called GI bills—have been used as a bonus to persons who served in the services, and as a cushion to protect the labor market from the many returning veterans.

The president's constitutional responsibility for seeing that the laws are faithfully executed has pulled him into the controversial school desegregation issue. Presidents Eisenhower and Kennedy were forced to use federal troops and marshals to enforce court desegregation orders in several southern states during the late 1950s and early 1960s. Today, the anti-discrimination provision of Title VI of the Civil Rights Act of 1964, which provides that no person shall be discriminated against because of race, color, or national origin in any program or activity that receives federal assistance, puts the president in the middle of some of the hottest political issues. The intensely debated ideological issues of busing for the purpose of dismantling dual school systems, de facto segregation, and transferring students between suburbs and the central city to ensure integration have also become problems that the president has difficulty avoiding, since he is responsible for seeing that the laws are faithfully executed.[6]

[5]Stephen K. Bailey, *The Office of Education and the Education Act of 1965*, Interuniversity Case Program #100 (New York: The Bobbs-Merrill Co., Inc., 1967); *cf.* Paul E. Marsh and Ross A. Gortner, *Federal Aid to Science Education: Two Programs* (Syracuse, N.Y.: Syracuse University Press, 1963), pp. 24–29.

[6]A survey of recent history shows how difficult it is for the president to avoid the desegregation issue. See "With All Deliberate Speed: The First Ten Years," *Phi Delta Kappan*, May 1964, entire issue; and John C. Hogan, "School Desegregation—North,

Increasingly, presidents have attempted to use education to help reduce the racial conflict and to improve socioeconomic conditions in the
nation. Much of the legislation initiated by the president in the 1960s,
such as the War on Poverty, manpower training programs, Model Cities,
and a number of other federal programs affecting education, were designed
to ameliorate the urban crisis and conditions caused by poverty and
racism. The Emergency School Act of 1972 was enacted at the behest
of President Nixon for the same purpose.

Education as a Political Issue.   As the president has become more
involved in educational decisions, educational issues have become politically more important to him. Winning the presidency, the supreme goal
of both political parties, requires the building of a coalition, a combination
of interests and political forces capable of delivering a majority of the
electoral votes. Until the 1950s education was not a crucial issue that
presidential candidates had to be concerned with in building a winning
coalition, although political parties have included educational planks in
their platforms since 1872.[7] Even as recently as the election of Harry S.
Truman, education was not one of the decisive issues. President Truman
ran on a platform that endorsed federal aid to education, and he made
it a part of his Fair Deal Program presented to Congress, but it was not
an issue crucial to his election.[8] In fact, President Truman devoted only
fourteen lines to the educational question in his memoirs.[9]

South, East, West: Trends in Court Decisions, 1849–1973," *Phi Delta Kappan*, September 1973, pp. 58–63. In Adams v. Richardson, U.S. District Court Judge Pratt
delivered a stern rebuke to the Nixon administration for failure to carry out the
mandates of the court in school desegregation. 356 F.Supp. 92 (1973).

[7]Munger and Fenno, *National Politics*, pp. 96–98.

[8]Philip Meranto, *The Politics of Federal Aid to Education in 1965: A Study in
Political Innovation* (Syracuse, N.Y.: Syracuse University Press, 1967), p. 101.

[9]Although it is difficult to quantify the degree of presidential interest for a
particular issue, a suggestion of the relative importance of federal aid as indicated by
President Truman is found in the space allotted it in his two volumes of memoirs.
Measured by lines and compared with other domestic issues of the time, this retro-
spective index of attention shows the following:

Brannan Plan for Agriculture	210 lines
Civil Rights Legislation Program	226
Displaced Persons—Immigration	6
Federal Aid for Education	14
Full Employment Bill of 1945–46	170
Government Health Insurance	290
Postwar Price Controls	373
Public Housing Programs	147
Taft-Hartley Labor Act	131
Tidelands Oil Issue	302

Harry S Truman, *Memoirs* (Garden City, N.Y.: Doubleday & Company, Inc., 1956),
2 vols.

Education has become a crucial issue in presidential politics because of the desegregation cases and the increasing pressures for federal aid. Dwight D. Eisenhower was the first president to be caught up in the school desegregation conflicts, and he was compelled to send troops into Little Rock, Arkansas, to enforce the decision of the United States Supreme Court. He was also pressured into supporting an expansion of the federal role in education through the National Defense Act of 1958 after the Soviets' breakthrough in space.[10] But John F. Kennedy was the first president to make aid to education a major element in his domestic program and to give it vigorous personal support. Aid to education was a major issue in 1960, and Kennedy was forced to come out against grants to parochial schools to counter the criticisms against him as a Roman Catholic.[11]

Education has become vitally important in presidential politics since 1960. Lyndon B. Johnson, a former teacher himself, made no secret of his desire to be remembered as the "education president," and he campaigned actively in support of education measures in 1964.[12]

In the presidential campaigns of 1968 and 1972 education was an even more important campaign issue. The third-party candidacy of George Wallace in 1968, with his threat to "throw the brief cases of the HEW bureaucracies into the Potomac River," reflected the growing resentment of many people, and especially the southerners, with the intensified activities of the federal government to desegregate schools. Republican candidate Richard Nixon, who was attempting to build a winning coalition composed in part of southerners and suburbanites who had fled the cities to escape the incoming blacks—the so-called Southern Strategy—was forced to move toward a similar position on school desegregation or risk the loss of support from these groups.[13]

With the start of the 1972 campaign, school desegregation had definitely become a national issue. Court desegregation cases required an affirmative action by districts to desegregate and to bus students from segregated to integrated schools if necessary.[14] These cases affected northern as well as southern schools. Busing was an intensely bitter national issue which no presidential candidate could avoid. George Wallace again,

---

[10]Munger and Fenno, *National Politics*, pp. 103–4; *cf*. Meranto, *Politics of Federal Aid*, pp. 102–3.

[11]Meranto, *Politics of Federal Aid*, pp. 103–4.

[12]Thomas E. Cronin, "The Presidency and Education," *Phi Delta Kappan*, February 1968, p. 295; *cf*. Eidenberg and Morey, *Act of Congress*, pp. 228–31; *cf*. Meranto, *Politics of Federal Aid*, pp. 132–36.

[13]Douglas M. Fox, "Federal Urban Policies since 1945," in *The New Urban Politics: Cities and the Federal Government*, ed. Douglas M. Fox (Pacific Palisades, Calif.: Goodyear Publishing Co., Inc., 1972), pp. 97–100.

[14]Green v. County School Board of New Kent, Virginia, 88 S.Ct. 1689 (1968); Swann v. Charlotte-Mecklenburg Board of Education, 403 U.S. 912, 91 S.Ct. 1267 (1971); *cf*. James C. Harvey and Charles H. Holmes, "Busing and School Desegregation," *Phi Delta Kappan*, May 1972, pp. 540–42.

this time as a Democratic contender, made school desegregation a key issue in his campaign, and his success in a number of state presidential primary elections "sent a message" to the other aspirants for the office.

After Governor Wallace was shot and withdrew from the campaign, Republican candidate Nixon's efforts to consolidate his "new majority" were easier to accomplish. But the busing issue presented the Democratic party with a serious problem. The traditional Democratic coalition since the 1930s had been built from such diverse groups as urban, labor, and minority groups from the large industrial states plus the traditionally "Solid South." There was no way a Democratic candidate could respond to the busing issue without offending a major segment of this coalition. And considering the makeup of the Democratic National Convention in 1972, there was probably no way a potential candidate could get the nomination with a strong antibusing position. Education presented the Democrats with a classic dilemma.[15]

As can be seen from this brief history of recent presidential campaigns, education has become an important national issue that affects the outcome of presidential elections. Once elected, the problems of education continue to plague presidents, and education policy requires an increasing amount of attention from the executive department.

Involvement in Policy Formation and Execution. Policy matters requiring the president's attention have continued to multiply since the earliest days of the Republic. The presidency has always been a big job, but in recent decades it has become much too big to be handled by one individual. Today a huge executive establishment "takes care that the laws are executed." At the head of this establishment sits not a single man but a superbureaucracy, the Executive Office of the President. At the apex of the conglomeration of agencies is the president himself, whose motive power—theoretically at least—puts the government into action.[16] It is the president who has the final and awesome power of decision, or as Mr. Truman so succinctly said, "The buck stops here."

Modern presidents are expected to propose a legislative program that will deal with major problems facing the country. In a sense, the most critical phase of policy formation—planning and initiating—is increasingly centered in the White House and executive bureaucracies. The president is in fact spoken of as "the chief legislator."[17]

In the process of planning educational legislation, there is no dearth of advice about what should be done. Opinions from the most celebrated

[15]See Donna Green, "The Candidates Equivocate on Seven Education Issues," *Phi Delta Kappan*, April 1972, pp. 472–75.

[16]Graves, *American Intergovernmental Relations*, pp. 170–71.

[17]Malcolm E. Jewell and Samuel C. Patterson, *The Legislative Process in the United States* (New York: Random House, Inc., 1966), pp. 299–307.

specialists pour in along with advice from many an earnest ill-informed citizen. Counsel comes through the mail, in editorials and columns, from electronic media, from cabinet members and members of the Executive Office staff, from bureau memorandums, and from presidential advisory councils, commissioners, and consultants. The president may call upon the entire federal administration for assistance. An abundance of advice also emanates from Congress, and interest groups constantly strive to make their views known.[18]

The problem is that much of this advice is conflicting. The president's chief role, therefore, becomes one of seeking harmony among the conflicting proposals and striking an acceptable compromise upon which major interests can agree. In a sense, presidential leadership demands some of the talents of the congressional power broker.[19] An example of this type of leadership is seen in President Johnson's success in working out the compromise on federal aid to education in 1965.

The president's legislative role also involves him in the process of attempting to influence Congress. He has to prod, sell, persuade, and at times threaten to get his "legislative program" enacted.[20] He is intimately involved in the workings of Congress, and their relationship is tightly interdependent. Regular and routine meetings between the president and the legislators, as well as the establishment of an elaborate congressional liaison office in the executive branch, testify to the pervasive interaction and spirit of interdependence that characterizes the relationships between the White House and Capitol Hill.[21]

The president's place in the legislative process has aptly been described as that of a fulcrum between diverse participants and forces in the external and internal environments of Congress. But his legislative powers are circumscribed, even though he plays a key role. He can bring people together, but the hard bargaining and negotiation is the province of all the participants. Some minimal level of agreement must be achieved by the group participants and the interests within Congress, or the policy outcome is likely to be postponed or the issue avoided.[22]

[18]Cronin, "Presidency and Education," p. 295.

[19]Harold Seidman, *Politics, Position, and Power: The Dynamics of Federal Organization* (New York: Oxford University Press, Inc., 1970), p. 67.

[20]The president has a number of formal and informal powers which he may use in dealing with Congress. These include the veto and threat of a veto, the power to make legislative recommendations in his State of the Union Message, the authority to call special sessions, his unique position and ability to focus public attention on an issue, his political position as chief of the party, patronage and his ability to help or hinder reelection of members of Congress, and his greater access to information in the executive department. See Jewell and Patterson, *Legislative Process*, pp. 301–36.

[21]*Ibid.*, pp. 320–25.

[22]Eidenberg and Morey, *Act of Congress*, pp. 328–29.

The president's power over the budget involves him directly in the appropriation process, as well as providing him with a tool of executive control over administrative agencies. Requests for appropriations from all federal agencies must be submitted to the Office of Management and Budgeting, and the hearings it conducts in the process of framing the president's budget determine a ceiling on the appropriations that an agency can expect to receive from Congress. Through the budgeting process, the president is vitally involved in the setting of priorities as to how the federal government will spend its resources. All federal agencies must clear their communications with the legislature through the Office of Management and Budgeting so that the consistency of these communications with the president's policy goals can be checked.[23]

The president's powers, here too, are circumscribed. Congress enacts the appropriation bills, and only Congress can authorize expenditures. Interest or clientele groups of various agencies openly, and administrative agencies covertly, may attempt to influence Congress not to follow the president's budget recommendations and to increase appropriations.[24] Throughout the Nixon administration, educational interests, as well as the Office of Education, were at odds with the priorities set by the president's budget and sought relief through the Congress.[25]

In the event that Congress appropriates more funds for a unit than have been requested in the president's budget requests, he has another weapon: Through the Office of Management and Budgeting, the president controls the allocation of funds from the Treasury to the agencies, so he can prevent an agency from spending in excess of his earlier recommenda-

[23]Frances E. Rourke, *Bureaucracy, Politics, and Public Policy* (Boston: Little, Brown and Company, 1969), pp. 32–33; *cf.* Ira Sharkansky, *Public Administration: Policy-Making in Government Agencies* (Chicago: Markham Publishing Co., 1970), pp. 97–98; and Carl R. Sapp, "Executive Assistance in the Legislative Process," in *Public Administration and Policy*, ed. Peter Wolf (New York: Harper & Row, Publishers, 1966), pp. 178–88.

[24]Rourke, *Bureaucracy, Politics, and Public Policy*, pp. 18–19; *cf.* Aaron Wildavsky, *The Politics of the Budgeting Process* (Boston: Little, Brown and Company, 1964), pp. 32–35.

[25]At the NEA's 1971 Annual Convention, spokesmen for the association were openly critical of President Nixon's priorities. Helen P. Bain, the association's president, roasted the president as follows:
"This is the most antieducation administration that this country has had in many years. This Administration has repeatedly made statements that were calculated to reduce confidence in public education. On rare occasions, Mr. Nixon has asked educators to serve on such task forces as Urban Education, Higher Education, and Student Unrest. In each instance, he has discredited and ignored the reports. It seems that the Administration attacks the schools because that is much cheaper than financing them. Our concern for the adequate financing of education is shared by the Congress of the United States, which felt strongly enough to override the President's veto of education appropriations." NEA, *Addresses and Proceedings*, Annual Meeting (Detroit, 1971), p. 13.

tion.[26] This obviously is politically unpopular to those groups and agencies adversely affected and may cause political repercussions in Congress or in future elections. Education again is an example of such a conflict during the Nixon administration. President Nixon repeatedly refused to spend funds appropriated by Congress for certain educational programs, and these actions led to a serious political confrontation between the president and Congress and to the enactment of anti-impoundment legislation.[27]

In his role as chief administrator, the president is also involved in execution of policy. He is responsible for seeing that the work of the federal government is carried out. He has the authority to appoint the political heads of federal agencies, including the commissioner of the Office of Education. Again he shares this power with Congress, and in many instances the Senate must approve executive appointments. The Senate's power over confirmation forces a president to take into consideration the wishes of clientele groups affected by the appointments.[28] For instance, presidential appointees to the Office of Education must be acceptable to the major educational interest groups, such as NEA and ACE, or these groups may attempt to block the appointment through their congressmen.[29] Later in this chapter we will consider the Office of Education in more detail.

Congress

The Constitution vests in Congress "all legislative powers" of the federal government. Congress has the formal responsibility for enacting laws, for appropriating funds, and for overseeing the administration of government. It is in Congress, therefore, that the most critical and climactic battles are waged over public policy.

As a representative body, Congress reflects the diversity of our society and is the focus for all the demands made on government. An almost infinite number of demands from individuals, interest groups, administrative agencies, and political parties, as well as from the president and the executive branch, make Congress the vortex of the policymaking struggle. To deal with these demands—to resolve conflicts and build the required

[26]Sharkansky, *Public Administration*, p. 97.

[27]Louis Fisher, "Impoundment of Funds: Uses and Abuses," *Congressional Record*, February 4, 1974, S1162–S1175; *cf.* Marcus Raskin, *Notes on the Old System To Transform American Politics*, (N.Y.: David McKay Company, Inc., 1974), pp. 76–78.

[28]Sharkansky, *Public Administration*, pp. 74–75; *cf.* Herman M. Somers, "The President as Administrator," in *Public Administration and Policy*, ed. Peter Woll (New York: Harper & Row, Publishers, 1966), p. 120.

[29]Seidman, *Politics, Position, and Power*, pp. 104–18.

consensus necessary to enact public policy—Congress has organized itself into a system of committees and has established complex procedures and practices to direct its work.

Congressional activity proceeds in accordance with the requirements of its decision-making machinery. There is, for example, the succession of formal stages through which legislative contests must proceed—from the introduction of a bill, through committee and to the floor in each chamber, through conference committee and to the president. Well-established procedures and practices—some explicitly formulated (like those involving the Rules Committee in the House), others implicitly understood (like those circumscribing the informal processes of bargaining)—structure the entire process.[30]

Legislative organization and procedure is an apparatus of leadership. Key legislators such as committee chairmen, party leaders, or subject-matter experts, because of the structure and procedures, can force the contest to flow through them and hence subject it to their special influence. The legislative process may be used to block as well as to pass legislation. Taken together, these institutional and personal factors shape the strategies of those interest groups, executives, and congressmen who seek, in varying alliances, to produce congressional decisions favorable to them.[31]

Committee System.   The main work of Congress occurs in committees. Legislative committees not only make key decisions with regard to legislation and appropriations but also oversee the administration of policies by administrative agencies. It is in committee that all demands for legislative decisions start their legislative journey, and the infighting and action in committee often determines how they fare in the policy process. Also, committee oversight of administration forces agencies to answer for their stewardship and thus influences their operations.

Standing committees of Congress to a degree coincide with major administrative areas in the government. The power and prestige of each of these committees, in part, reflects the power of affected interest groups, as well as the significance of the policy area.[32]

Educational Committees.   The relative weakness of educational interests in national politics is evident from the lack of prestige given to the standing committees responsible for this policy area. Neither house of

30Nelson W. Polsby, *Congress and the Presidency* (Englewood Cliffs, N.J.: Prentice-Hall, Inc., 1964), pp. 62–81.

31Munger and Fenno, *National Politics,* pp. 106–7.

32Jewell and Patterson, *Legislative Process,* pp. 202–4; *cf.* Seymour Scher, "Congressional Committee Members as Independent Agency Overseers: A Case Study," *American Political Science Review,* December 1960, pp. 911–20.

Congress has a standing committee devoted exclusively to education. The House of Representatives has a Committee on Education and Labor, and the Senate combines education and a number of other policy areas in the Committee on Labor and Public Welfare. Labor normally is the chief interest of members of these committees, and party selections are influenced by the members' views on labor, not education. Education is not the primary concern in either of these committees. In fact, most members on these committees profess only minor interest in education.[33]

Membership on these committees responsible for education is not sought after, as is membership on some of the more powerful and prestigious committees. This is due to a number of reasons. These committees must deal with highly ideological issues, fraught with emotion and controversy, which often places the members in an uncomfortable sort of public visibility which may be politically dangerous to their reelection. Furthermore, since members of the committees are chosen primarily because of their stance on the labor-management issue, members come to their work with an advanced state of commitment and tend to line up according to their ideological positions. It is difficult to use normal methods and tactics to build consensus among members. Few minds are changed from the hearings, and conflict tends to dominate committee proceedings.[34]

Educational issues that in themselves often tend to divide people along ideological lines—states' rights versus federal involvement in education, church-state relations, and the race problem—are further aggravated, since they are infected with the hostility produced by the labor-management cleavage. The atmosphere of these education committees makes it even more difficult to build the essential consensus needed to enact legislation on educational matters. Furthermore, since membership on these committees is not considered to be the most desirable of committee assignments, there is a relatively rapid turnover rate which makes it difficult to develop the educational expertise necessary. In turn, members of these committees have less influence in the floor debates than some others, since they are not viewed as subject-matter experts and since individual committee members often openly oppose and attempt to sabotage the committees' recommendations.[35]

[33]Julius Menacker, "The Organizational Behavior of Congress in the Formulation of Educational Support Policy," *Phi Delta Kappan*, October 1966, p. 79.

[34]*Ibid.; cf.* Munger and Fenno, *National Politics*, pp. 109–12; and Nicholas A. Masters, "Committee Assignments in the House of Representatives," *American Political Science Review*, June 1961, pp. 345–57.

[35]Meranto, *Politics of Federal Aid*, pp. 113–17; *cf.* Munger and Fenno, *National Politics*, pp. 120–21.

Educational Bills in Other Committees. Other standing committees also have jurisdiction over some aspects of education. Congress has not developed a precise definition of education, and thus the major committees designed to handle educational bills are assigned only a portion of them. Because of jurisdictional confusion, many aspects of education are sent to other than the House Committee on Education and Labor and the Senate Committee on Labor and Public Welfare.

Educational measures that fall under the jurisdiction of committees that are not subject to the high visibility, emotional controversy, and lack of harmonious personal relationships found in the two designated education committees have tended to fare better in the legislative process. For instance, the National Science Foundation was originally under the Interstate and Foreign Commerce committees, later was placed under the Space committees of both houses, and more recently returned to the House Committee on Labor and Education and the Senate Committee on Labor and Public Welfare. Educational exchange programs of the State Department and the International Cooperation Administration are the responsibility of the Foreign Affairs Committee of the House and the Foreign Relations Committee of the Senate. Land-grant college matters are handled by the Agriculture committees, while college housing and loan programs are the responsibility of the Money and Banking committees.[36] There has not been the controversy over these programs that there has been over similar measures in the regular educational committees.

Educational measures are also dependent on other legislative committees, such as the powerful House Rules Committee and the appropriations committees of both chambers. The House Rules Committee, which has power to determine which bills will be considered by the House of Representatives, for years kept federal aid-to-education bills from reaching the floor.[37] Since appropriations committees control the money once legislation is enacted, they vitally affect educational programs. The House Appropriations Committee, which claims constitutional power to initiate all appropriations bills, is especially important. It sees itself as the guardian of the federal treasury and critically considers all budget requests, including educational budgets.[38]

As education has become a more significant national issue, Congress

[36]Menacker, "Organizational Behavior of Congress," pp. 79–80.

[37]Munger and Fenno, *National Politics*, p. 9. As an example, see Congressman Halpern's statement proposing a bill to establish a department of education, *Congressional Record*, August 1, 1968, p. H8087.

[38]Richard F. Fenno, Jr., "The House Appropriations Committee as a Political System: The Problem of Integration," *American Political Science Review*, June 1962, pp. 310–24.

has devoted an increasing amount of time to it, which is evidenced in the volume of legislation enacted. This has led to a number of proposals to give education a more prominent position in both the legislative and the executive branch of government. Proposals have been introduced to create new legislative committees to deal exclusively with educational matters. Similarly, bills to create a cabinet-level department of education have been recommended. Although educational interests have pressed for these changes, they have not had the political power necessary to achieve them.[39]

Educational Issues in Congressional Campaigns. Educational interest groups' relative lack of influence in Congress is due to a number of factors. Education is not as crucial a campaign issue for congressmen as it is for presidential candidates. Congressmen, unlike presidential candidates, do not have to worry about building a nationwide coalition to win office. They only have to concern themselves about matters vital to local constituents. Due to the widely held traditional beliefs about local control of education, constituents normally do not look to congressmen on educational issues. With the exception of some of the highly emotional issues such as desegregation and school busing, congressmen can largely avoid educational issues in most campaigns.

Usually it is "good politics" to avoid educational issues in campaigns, since there is danger of offending many groups by taking a position and little danger from saying nothing or making only general comments about educational problems. Teachers and other educational interest groups that might take exception to this omission have little political influence because of their nonpolitical ideology and lack of involvement in political campaigns. That education is not a crucial campaign issue to most congressmen tends to make educational problems appear somewhat less significant to Congress than they are to the president who increasingly is having to deal with them.[40]

Federal Administrative Agencies

The influence of the federal bureaucracy has been greatly enhanced as the roles of the federal government have expanded. Almost every aspect of education from the preschool to the postgraduate level is affected by fed-

[39]Menacker, "Organizational Behavior of Congress," p. 79.

[40]By actively campaigning for congressional candidates, college and university students have become a factor in the election of congressmen. This has forced some candidates to take a stand on educational issues that they might otherwise have ignored. Another factor that may affect congressional candidates' positions on educational issues is the eighteen-year-old vote.

eral agencies. Some thirty or more autonomous agencies whose programs involve authorization by more than half of the legislative committees in Congress administer federally financed educational programs. They provide assistance to elementary-secondary schools, to state departments of education, and to colleges and college students; support research and specialized research facilities; sponsor programs for improving the curricula and teaching methods in science and mathematics, as well as in other areas of learning; undertake a miscellany of vocational education, "other defense education assistance," and Indian education services; and make grants to public libraries, and support the Library of Congress and the Smithsonian Institution. Federal agencies also undertake far-reaching programs of manpower development and economic opportunity and training programs for the retarded and disabled; provide a lunch program for many of the schools throughout the nation; and operate various types of schools and academies related to the armed services. Furthermore, the actions of many federal agencies that have no responsibility for education often have a direct impact on schools.[41]

The Office of Education. The major administrative agency responsible for federal educational programs is the United States Office of Education (USOE). About one-third of the federal educational budget is the responsibility of USOE. The other two-thirds is handled by at least thirty or so different departments and agencies.[42] Although USOE is only a branch of the Department of Health, Education, and Welfare and administers only a fraction of federal educational expenditures, its annual budget is greater than that of five of the current cabinet departments.[43]

Development of USOE. Only in recent years has USOE grown to its present size and influence. For three-quarters of a century it maintained a low level of bureaucratic visibility in the executive branch of government. In spite of programmatic accretions in such fields as the support of land-grant colleges, vocational education, and cooperation with New Deal agencies in carrying out educationally oriented relief programs, USOE remained a relatively small and insignificant federal agency which was shunted from one department to another.[44]

[41]William G. Land, "Can Federal Education Programs Be Coordinated?" *Phi Delta Kappan*, March 1965, pp. 347–48.

[42]*Congressional Record—House*, August 1, 1968, pp. H8087–88.

[43]The authorized budget for the Office of Education for fiscal 1973 was $5.3 billion. This exceeded the amount budgeted for the Departments of Commerce, HUD, Interior, Justice, and State and was nearly as large as the budgets of the Departments of Transportation, Labor, and Agriculture. See *Budget of the United States, 1974* (Washington, D.C.: Government Printing Office, 1973), pp. 40–41.

[44]Munger and Fenno, *National Politics*, pp. 77–79.

From 1869 to 1939 USOE was virtually an autonomous agency within the Department of the Interior. Largely without administrative responsibilities, its primary mission was to engage in data collection and compilation. Its low status meant that new programs such as the vocational education programs established in 1917 by the Smith-Hughes Act were often placed in other agencies. Not until 1933 were vocational programs transferred to USOE. During this period USOE had few friends apart from the National Education Association, the American Association of School Administrators, and the Council of Chief State Officers, whose Washington staffs and constituencies found USOE's statistical and advisory services of direct value. There was at least some validity to the widely held assumption that USOE was the "kept" agency of these private associations.[45]

A reorganization in 1939 moved the Office of Education into the Federal Security Agency, to the chagrin of FSA. FSA in turn served as the basis of the Department of Health, Education, and Welfare in a later reorganization by President Eisenhower in 1953. This new conglomerate department lumped together three highly controversial areas—health, education, and welfare—over which we have fought some of our bitterest political battles. USOE, however, grew rapidly in the 1950s and emerged as a major agency in the executive structure as a result of the passage of the permanent programs of federal aid to impacted areas, the Cooperative Research Act, and the National Defense Education Act of 1958.[46]

Passage of the Elementary and Secondary Education Act of 1965 (ESEA) and the infusion of vast new funds into the educational structure that was to be administered by USOE raised the office almost overnight from poorhouse cousin to grand mogul of educational largess. Not only did its staff and budget mushroom, but also its functions were greatly expanded. Whereas before the office had performed only supportive roles for local and state educational agencies, it now assumed a much more active leadership role in the educational partnership.[47]

Expansion of Functions.   The commissioner of USOE became a key official in planning educational programs during the "Great Society" years, and Commissioner Francis Keppel set a new pattern of legislative leadership for the office. He performed a vital role in the passage of the historic Elementary and Secondary Education Act of 1965, acting as an intermediary broker of ideas, moving among various arenas: the Presidential Task Force on Education, HEW and USOE planning staffs, the White

[45]*Ibid.*, p. 79.
[46]Stephen K. Bailey and Edith K. Mosher, *ESEA: The Office of Education Administers a Law* (Syracuse, N.Y.: Syracuse University Press, 1968), pp. 17–19.
[47]William G. Land, "The Shakeout in USOE," *Phi Delta Kappan*, September 1965, pp. 31–33.

House, the Congress, the press, and the professional associations and interest groups. USOE legislative draftsmen helped hammer out the provisions that all-important interest groups could accept. The Office of Education in this period became a major shaper of educational policy.[48]

USOE was given unprecedented discretionary powers to determine the ground rules as to how the federal funds were to be spent by the legislation enacted in the 1960s. Implementing complex and controversial legislation is rarely simple. Laws are neither self-explanatory nor self-executing in any detailed sense. Regulations and guidelines have to be defined as to how provisions of the legislation are to be carried out, a process that in itself involves creative acts of discretionary judgment. USOE's power in educational policymaking has been greatly enhanced because of its authority to implement the federal laws.[49] It has the power to approve or disapprove grant applications, which has led some to note that USOE has both the "carrot" and the "stick" over local and state educational agencies.

Congress's requirements that USOE report yearly vis-à-vis the ESEA and other educational legislation gives the Office of Education additional power. To carry out the congressional mandate, USOE is required to audit and evaluate state and local educational agencies, and generally to monitor how federal funds are being spent. In turn, state and local education agencies are required to report to USOE on the operations of programs using federal monies.[50]

Reporting normally connotes an authority-subordinate relationship, and USOE's "evaluation" procedures have therefore been fraught with controversy. The so-called Coleman Survey on Equality of Educational Opportunity, the first major attempt of the Office of Education to use sophisticated social science analysis to evaluate educational performance across the nation, caused spirited attacks on both the study and the office.[51] Similarly, a study on "Assessing the Progress of Education" caused even more of a storm and raised fears that national assessment would lead to federal control and a dictated curriculum.[52]

---

[48]Bailey and Mosher, *ESEA*, pp. 40–42.

[49]*Ibid.*, pp. 98–100.

[50]*Ibid.*, pp. 124–25.

[51]The Coleman Report: Controversial Report on Education; What It Really Means," *U.S. News and World Report*, December 1968, pp. 44–45; *cf.* James K. Kent, "'The Coleman Report,' Opening Pandora's Box," *Phi Delta Kappan*, January 1968, pp. 242–44.

[52]This study was conducted under a Carnegie Corporation–Ford Foundation grant, with the encouragement of the commissioner of education. For a report of debates at the White House Conference on National Assessment, see "The Assessment Debate at the White House Conference," *Phi Delta Kappan*, September 1965, pp. 17–18; *cf.* Harold C. Hand, "National Assessment Viewed as the Camel's Nose," and Ralph W. Tyler, "Assessing the Progress of Education," *Phi Delta Kappan*, September 1965, pp. 8–16; and *Contemporary Issues in American Education* consultant's papers prepared for use at the White House Conference on Education, HEW (Washington, D.C., July 20–21, 1965).

Another development at the federal level, which has affected state and local operations, is the planning-programming-budgeting system. PPBS consists of four basic elements. The first, and most difficult part of PPBS, is the definition of program objectives in concrete terms. Every program, it is assumed, has an output; that is to say, every program has something that it is designed to accomplish within a given period of time. To make sound budgetary system decisions, it is necessary to compare output with costs. Since federal agencies, including the Office of Education and the Office of Management and Budgeting, have begun to evaluate grant programs in this fashion, this budgetary system has been forced on state and local systems.[53]

Educational research is another function of USOE that has changed and expanded dramatically in the last fifteen years. The Office of Education has always carried out a research program, although historically it consisted mainly of surveys and compilations of educational data to assist local and state educational agencies, not to change the system. Changes and reforms in education have traditionally been seen as the responsibility of local districts. In recent years, however, the Office of Education has assumed major responsibility for instituting changes and reforms in the educational system through a program of research and development.[54]

The concept of large-scale research and development as a systematic approach to bring about change and the attainment of educational goals is relatively new. Beginning in 1954 with the passage of the Cooperative Research Act, USOE began to funnel modest grants into educational research. Following the orbiting of Sputnik and the passage of the National Defense Education Act of 1958, substantial federal support was given for educational research to increase the quantity and quality of scientists, engineers, and foreign language specialists. USOE's research role was enlarged by this act, and in cooperation with the National Science Foundation, it supported curriculum revision aimed at major transformation of the defense-related aspects of the American educational system.[55] Even greater emphasis was given to research and development by the Office of Education following the passage of the Elementary and Secondary Education Act of 1965. The goals of this legislation primarily were to aid the educationally deprived and to provide for equality of education, and this

[53]Bailey and Mosher, *ESEA*, pp. 187–88.

[54]Nicholas A. Masters, "Some Political Problems Involved in Educational Planning," in *Planning and Effecting Needed Changes in Education* (Denver, Colo.: Designing Education for the Future, 1967), p. 148.

[55]Charles H. Judd, "Staff Study Number 19," *Research on the United States Office of Education* (Washington: Advisory Committee on Education, 1939), pp. 15–18, 24–43; and Francis Chase, "R & D in the Remodeling of Education," *Phi Delta Kappan*, February 1970, pp. 299–304.

raised even more complex problems to which there were no ready solutions. Research on how to change the educational system in order to accomplish these goals was accentuated.[56]

Under provisions of the ESEA, the Office of Education created a nationwide system of university-based research and development centers to engage in problem-oriented research, and a system of regional laboratories to undertake programs that would help create and disseminate improvements in education. The R and D centers were to undertake basic research, draw on interdisciplinary research in the universities, supplement and codify the research and theoretical formulations, and fit the relevant knowledge and technologies into systematic frameworks that would facilitate further development. The Educational Laboratories were to undertake more applied research aimed at changing and improving the educational system.[57]

The increasing involvement of the federal government in functions formerly considered to be exclusively local and state government functions appeared to many to be a radical departure from local control in education. Federally sponsored research and development was seen as a premeditated intervention into the very heart of the educative process which would influence all aspects of education including what is to be taught and how it is to be taught. The concern over the increasing leadership role of the federal government in education generated a great deal of political controversy and in part gave the impetus for the creation of the Educational Commission of the States.[58]

Numerous types of compensatory educational programs were initiated in the 1960s as a result of the national goals for education and the desire to change the educational system. But by 1970 the nation's mood had changed. Reflecting this change, President Nixon in his March 3, 1970, message to Congress said:

> . . . We must stop congratulating ourselves for spending nearly as much money on education as does the rest of the entire world—$65 billion a year on all levels (an estimated $90 billion for fiscal 1973)—when we are not getting as much as we should out of the dollars we spend. . . . We must

[56]Sidney L. Besvinick, "Universities and Sponsored Research Policy," *Phi Delta Kappan,* October 1966, pp. 72–74; *cf.* Bailey and Mosher, *ESEA*, pp. 138–39.

[57]Chase, "R & D in the Remodeling of Education," pp. 299–304; *cf.* Francis S. Chase, *The National Program of Educational Laboratories: An Independent Appraisal of Twenty Educational Laboratories and Nine University Research and Development Centers* (Washington, D.C.: U.S. Office of Education, Department of Health, Education, and Welfare, 1968).

[58]Francis S. Chase, "Some Effects of Current Curriculum Projects on Educational Policy and Practice," *School Review,* Spring 1962, pp. 132–47; and David U. Levine, "The States Run Scared," *Phi Delta Kappan,* November 1965, pp. 134–35.

stop letting wishes color our judgments about the educational effectiveness of many compensatory programs, when—despite some dramatic and encouraging exceptions—there is growing evidence that most of them are not yet measurably improving the success of poor children in schools.[59]

President Nixon proposed the creation of a National Institute of Education (NIE) to undertake the systematic search of the factors that affect what children learn. This agency was to bring to education the same degree of intellect, intensity, and direction that we have come to expect in health (NIH), in aerospace (NASA), and even in agriculture. All federal educational research was to be consolidated in NIE and the assortment of R and D programs conducted by the Office of Education transferred to the new agency. NIE was to be a part of HEW, but separate from the Office of Education.[60]

The Elementary-Secondary Education Act of 1972, which was signed into law on August 1, 1972, created the National Institute of Education. In addition to its responsibilities for developing its own research program, NIE has responsibility for administering those continuing projects transferred from USOE, the now defunct Research and Development Centers and Educational Laboratories.[61]

USOE and Civil Rights.   Enforcement of the Civil Rights Act of 1964 involved the Office of Education in another controversial function. This act, passed the year before the breakthrough of federal aid to education and the availability of large sums of federal monies, states in sweeping language that

> no person in the United States shall on the ground of race, color, or national origin, be excluded from participation in, be denied the benefit of, or be subjected to discrimination under any program or activity receiving federal financial assistance.

Each federal department and agency is responsible for making sure that discrimination does not exist in the programs and activities it assists, and federal funds may be cut off if programs are discriminatory.

[59]President Nixon's Message to Congress, March 3, 1970, cited in "The National Institute of Education: A Brief Outline of Its History, Status, and Tentative Plans," prepared by NIE staff (Washington, D.C., n.d.), mimeographed.

[60]Chester E. Finn, "What the NIE Can Be," *Phi Delta Kappan*, February 1972, pp. 347–51; *cf.* Richard A. Dershimer, "Will the Bureaucrats and Engineers Ruin NIE?" *Phi Delta Kappan*, December 1971, pp. 250–51; Robert E. Levien, *National Institute of Education: Preliminary Plan for the Proposed Institute* (Rand Corporation, 1971); and Thomas L. Reddick, "National Institute of Education: An Open Door to the Future," *School and Community*, November 1972, p. 84.

[61]"The National Institute of Education: A Brief Outline of Its History, Status, and Tentative Plans."

Enforcement of these provisions led to the so-called Second Reconstruction of Southern Education, as well as involving the Office of Education in the controversies of northern de facto segregation. At the time of the passage of the act, 99 percent of the black students in the eleven southern states attended segregated schools, even though ten years had elapsed since the historic *Brown* decision had declared segregated schools unconstitutional. Under provisions of the Civil Rights Act, responsibility for ensuring that federal grants were not made to those districts with segregated schools was placed upon the Office of Education. Thus USOE became a major arena for the desegregation conflict, and the office as never before became a change agent responsible for administering a social revolution.[62]

Originally, it was assumed that Title VI could be administered by the existing staff in the Office of Education, just as any other change in the legal requirements for federal grants. Responsibility for civil rights was to "pervade" the operating programs, and in the earliest period members of the Office of Education attempted to "negotiate desegregation" plans in this fashion with the exasperated southerner. Conflict arose almost immediately, and particularly after the passage of ESEA in 1965 made large amounts of federal grants available to schools. The office became deeply involved with the courts, the Justice Department (Commission on Civil Rights), the Office of Economic Opportunity, the Department of Agriculture, HUD, and the Department of the Interior (Indian Affairs) in working out desegregation orders and regulations pertaining to federal aid programs. Soon there was an almost continuous stream of congressional complaints about the office's enforcement actions. In time these criticisms led to the creation of a separate Office for Civil Rights (OCR) directly responsible to the secretary of HEW. Later congressional pressures resulted in the decentralization of the OCR and the creation of regional offices to administer this law.[63]

Reaction to USOE's Growth. Although most educational groups, and particularly NEA, have long urged the creation of a separate department of education, the burgeoning activities of the Office of Education have not been greeted with wild enthusiasm by all, particularly by school admin-

[62]Gary Orfield, *The Reconstruction of Southern Education: The Schools and the 1964 Civil Rights Act* (New York: John Wiley & Sons, Inc., 1969), pp. 102–50.

[63]*Ibid.*, pp. 264–304; *cf. Policies on Elementary and Secondary School Compliance with Title VI of the Civil Rights Act of 1964* (Washington, D.C.: U.S. Department of Health, Education, and Welfare, 1968); *HEW and Civil Rights* (Washington, D.C.: U.S. Department of Health, Education, and Welfare, n.d.); *HEW and Title VI: A Report of the Organization, Policies, and Compliances of the Department of Health, Education, and Welfare under Title VI of Civil Rights Act of 1964* (Washington, D.C.: U.S. Commission on Civil Rights, 1970).

istrators and school boards.[64] In fact, the growing power of USOE, and its attempts to carry out national goals of education and to overcome local resistance to these goals, has often been met with open hostility by the same groups that called for a department of education. Political opposition has also grown as USOE's influence in educational matters has evolved.

The major criticism of the Office of Education is related to the idea of categorical aid, that is, the granting of aid by a federal agency for only certain programs determined to be part of the national goals for education. Providing aid on a categorical basis is seen as an infringement upon local autonomy of the schools in order to achieve a broad, national objective, such as educating the children of the poor, training new scientists, or integrating the schools. Many school administrators and school boards believe that the local school system should preserve its autonomy and should make its own plans and have the overriding authority to make decisions. Hence they prefer to have federal money without any strings, to be spent as the local school board decides, and preferably without the "paper blizzard" that categorical grants create.[65] The Nixon administration's proposal for Education Special Revenue Sharing, which is discussed in the next chapter, was a political response to the growing criticisms of the USOE and categorical grant programs.

The proposal for education revenue sharing would obviously greatly reduce the power and leadership role of the USOE. Local or parochial values would influence educational policymaking more than national values or goals, and thus power would be returned to the local districts. Obviously this was a new thrust or counterthrust in the never-ending game of politics which could result in as dramatic a change in USOE as did the breakthrough of social legislation in the 1960s.[66]

[64]Munger and Fenno, *National Politics*, pp. 1–18; Helen Bain, "The Argument for a Department of Education," *Phi Delta Kappan*, September 1971, pp. 11–12.

[65]Masters, "Some Political Problems Involved in Educational Planning," pp. 146–47; Arthur H. Ricc, "Federal Guidelines Actually Control Public School Policy," *Nation's Schools*, June 1966, pp. 10–104; W. W. Wayson, "The Political Revolution in Education, 1965," *Phi Delta Kappan*, March 1966, pp. 333–39; and Nicholas A. Masters and Lawrence K. Pettit, "Some Changing Patterns in Educational Policy Making," *Educational Administrative Quarterly*, Spring 1966, pp. 84–85.

[66]"The U.S. Office of Education as Part of the Problem," Commissioner's Conference, 1971 (Speech presented at Regional Meeting in Dallas, March 1971), mimeographed. For a statement supporting federal categorical grants, see Harold Howe II, "National Policy for American Education" (Address before the 71st Annual Convention of the National Congress of Parents and Teachers, Minneapolis, May 22, 1967), mimeographed; Harold Howe II, "Change and American Schools" (Address before the American Association of School Administrators, Atlantic City, New Jersey, February 13, 1967), mimeographed; and Harold Howe II, "Objectives for Federal Funds" (Address at Morehead State University, Morehead, Kentucky, July 21, 1967); "Federal Government's Remaining Job in Education" (Conversation between Harold Howe II and Samuel Halpern, *Congressional Record*, January 15, 1969), pp. E205–56.

Similarly, the Nixon administration's proposal for merging the Office of Education into a larger Department of Human Resources reflected the hostility toward USOE. The new DHR would contain all of the present DHEW except the National Institute of Occupational Safety and Health and the Office of Education's Public Library Construction program. In addition, DHR would contain from other departments such programs as the school lunch, and the food stamps and commodity programs, from Agriculture the manpower administration and Women's Bureau from Labor; the health and migrant programs from OEO; and the college housing construction programs from Housing and Urban Development.[67] Such a department would be much larger than any in existence today, and would in effect tend to reduce the visibility of the Office of Education and perhaps reduce its power with Congress and educational clientele groups.

Education and Other Federal Agencies

As we have seen, some thirty agencies are responsible for administering various aspects of the federal education and training programs. Education is a major assignment for some agencies, such as the Departments of Labor, Defense, and Interior, the National Science Foundation, and the National Foundation on the Arts and Humanities. For others, education is only an incidental function. Actions of certain agencies, such as the Office of Economic Opportunity, the U.S. Commission on Civil Rights, and the Departments of Labor and Defense, as we shall see in the next chapter, are major forces of change on the educational system. Still other agencies, which have no official responsibility for education, such as the agencies administering economic, labor, welfare, and tax policies, have a direct impact on the nation's educational system. For example, actions of the Department of Housing and Urban Affairs in approving grants and loans for housing directly influence community schools. Enforcement of the Internal Revenue Code pertaining to charitable institutions affects school integration, since these actions stimulate or deter the growth of private schools created to avoid integration, the so-called segregation academies. In a sense, almost all federal agencies indirectly affect the nation's schools.

The Judicial System

The United States Supreme Court, as one of the constitutionally coequal branches of the federal government, occupies a unique position in our

[67]"The U.S. Office of Education as Part of the Problem"; John K. Meagher, "Why a Department of Human Resources Is Needed Now," *Phi Delta Kappan*, September 1971, pp. 8–10.

society. The American high court, as it has evolved, has become a full partner in the policymaking process. Groups dissatisfied with the outcome of the political system often turn to the courts in an attempt to affect public policy. Acts of Congress and of state legislatures are frequently challenged in the courts, as are executive and administrative actions. Court decisions, such as the school desegregation cases, frequently initiate some of our most intense conflicts in other political arenas. In fact, most of our difficult political issues—particularly those arising out of ideological conflicts—tend ultimately to be treated as legal questions and dealt with by the judiciary.[68]

The courts affect educational policies in a host of ways. For one thing, the broad decisions affecting the operation of the government influence the educational system. For example, the decisions of the 1930s upholding the national government's powers to spend for the "general welfare," as defined by Congress, permitted the proliferation of the grants-in-aid program that today plays such an important part in our educational system. Similarly, the Supreme Court's rulings on legislative apportionment during the 1960s changed state and local politics and obviously affected educational policymaking. The Court's broad interpretations of the commerce clause which served as the basis for upholding the Civil Rights Act of 1964 have also had a major impact on education.[69]

School policies have most directly been influenced by the courts' efforts to protect the citizen against government, the civil liberties cases. The constitutional guarantees found in the Bill of Rights and the Fourteenth Amendment limit federal and state authority over the individual. These restrictions on the powers of government to encroach upon the rights of individuals have particularly affected state and local educational decisions, since the impact of state and local governments upon the day-to-day life of most citizens is greater than that of the national government.

Educational policies have been the basis of a host of civil rights suits, suits challenging almost every area of educational policymaking. These have included challenges to the states' authority to compel attendance at public schools,[70] to require ROTC,[71] to compel individuals to salute the flag or to pledge allegiance to it.[72] Other suits based on the establishment clause of the First Amendment have challenged religious education in the

[68]For a discussion of courts in the policy process, see Henry J. Abraham, *The Judiciary: The Supreme Court in the Government Process* (Boston: Allyn & Bacon, Inc., 1965), pp. 89–111.

[69]Samuel Krislow, *The Supreme Court in the Political Process* (New York: The Macmillan Company, 1965), pp. 79–105.

[70]Pierce v. Society of Sisters, 268 U.S. 510 (1925).

[71]Hamilton v. Regents of the University of California, 293 U.S. 245 (1934).

[72]Minersville School District v. Gobitis, 310 U.S. 586 (1940); West Virginia State Board of Education v. Barnette, 319 U.S. 624 (1943).

schools, including prayer and Bible reading,[73] as well as the so-called release-time programs for students to attend religious exercises during school hours.[74] Expenditures of public funds for textbooks or the transportation of parochial students have also been litigated under provisions of the First Amendment.[75] School policies involving who can teach, and the right to require loyalty oaths of teachers, have frequently been before the courts.[76] The racial revolution to a large degree has been advanced by Court decisions over the past several decades.[77] More recently, Court decisions pertaining to the patterns of state organization and financing of schools have affected state school policies in these areas.[78] In fact, it is difficult to find a single area of school policies in which the Court is not in some way involved. Critics of the Court have accused the Court, as a result, as acting as the "super school board for the nation."

The Supreme Court's power to effect policy changes, however, is limited; its only genuine power is the power to persuade—the purse and sword are in other hands. Its authority arises from the sense of legitimacy of its decisions; the acceptance of decisions as being "right" or "constitutional." The integration situation in recent years has dramatically called attention to the intricacies and limitations of the Court's power to obtain compliance with unpopular decisions. The Supreme Court's decisions are often thwarted or delayed through the actions of the lower courts and state legislatures. Also, the situation has demonstrated the reliance of the Court upon federal administration and, above all, local officers for enforcement of Court decisions.[79]

In the 1960s and early 1970s public hostility against certain Court decisions led to a political counterrevolution, and open friction developed between the president and the Court over the civil libertarian decisions of the Warren Court. The 1964, and particularly the 1968, Republican presidential campaigns raised the Court's decisions as major political issues. As the election and subsequent actions of Richard M. Nixon demonstrated, the controversy penetrated more deeply than most campaign rhetoric. President Nixon, beholden to the South for his nomination and election in 1968, attempted to make good his debt by continuing to attack the Court, and he systematically set about to alter past decisions and remake

[73]Engel v. Vitale, 370 U.S. 241 (1962).

[74]Illinois ex rel. McCollum v. Board of Education, 333 U.S. 203 (1948); Zorach v. Clauson, 343 U.S. 306 (1952).

[75]Cochran v. Louisiana State Board of Education, 281 U.S. 370 (1930); Everson v. Board of Education of Ewing Tp., 330 U.S. 1 (1947).

[76]Wieman v. Updegraff, 344 U.S. 183 (1952); Adler v. Board of Education of City of New York, 342 U.S. 485 (1952).

[77]See especially Brown v. Board of Education of Topeka, Kansas, 347 U.S. 483 (1954); Cooper v. Aaron, 358 U.S. 78 (1958).

[78]San Antonio School District v. Rodriguez, 411 U.S. 1, 93 S.Ct. 1278 (1973).

[79]Abraham, *Judiciary*, pp. 115–17.

the Court. The ultimate impact of these actions by President Nixon can only be guessed at by contemporary historians; however, recent decisions by the Burger Court show that the Court is retreating on some of the more civil libertarian positions. This change of direction is certain to affect the operation of the nation's schools.[80]

To this point we have examined the structure of the federal political system and the inputs or demands for educational policies. We shall now examine the conversion process and the way that federal policies affect the educational system.

[80]Theodore L. Becker and Malcolm M. Feeley, eds., *The Impact of Supreme Court Decisions* (New York: Oxford University Press, Inc., 1973), pp. 5–6. For a discussion of how these actions are affecting the schools, see "The Ship of Integration Is Going Down," *Harper's Magazine*, June 1972, pp. 66–67.

chapter eleven

Educational Policymaking at the Federal Level

The policymaking processes are basically the same at the federal level as at the state and local levels, although the structural, cultural, and situational factors are different and the national political environment is more comprehensive and pluralistic. The processes of bargaining and identification, and the use of legal-bureaucratic and coercive mechanisms, are readily evident in federal policymaking. This chapter examines the federal responses to educational problems and the processes whereby the inputs and within puts are converted into federal policy outputs. It also considers the feedback effects of federal policies on state and local systems and the pattern of interaction between the three levels of government.

The dynamics of federal educational policymaking are studied by examining three major policy issues, namely, financing education, developing curriculum, and meeting urban educational needs. Each of these is and long has been a major political problem and has involved all three levels of American government.

Financing Public Education

How to finance education has been a persistent public problem during much of our history. Since the turn of the century, growing financial pressures have resulted in the trend toward consolidating schools into larger districts and greater state participation in financing education. As the burden of state and local taxes became heavier, demands for federal aid have grown more insistent.

The dramatic post-World War II increases in educational demands—demands caused by such factors as the "population explosion," the backlog of construction and personnel needs during the Depression and the war years, the increasing expectations from schools, and the continuing

urbanization of the nation—seriously strained traditional financial patterns. Attempts to meet these demands resulted in burgeoning state and local budgets, tax rates, and bonded indebtedness. The old pattern of financing education became increasingly inadequate, and pressures mounted for federal aid to education, the last untapped source of revenue for public school education.

The federal government was not a major participant in financing public schools before World War II, although it had long made grants for limited and specific educational purposes. The earliest aid to states for education, in the form of land grants, was made under the Articles of Confederation in 1785 and 1787. The federal government throughout our history has provided aid for certain educational programs, but federal concern has been for limited and specific purposes, such as aid for vocational education. Similarly, allocations of funds were made to local schools in the Depression days of the 1930s and during World War II to help schools meet the serious problems caused by these emergencies. Despite a number of such provisions, the amount of federal aid was very limited in comparison with the expenditures of local and state governments.[1]

Struggle for Federal Aid to Education. Since the 1870s numerous proposals have been made for a program of general federal aid to education, but the main push for federal aid to education followed World War II. Proponents of federal aid in these years argued that the national needs for education were not being met, that states and local governments could not solve the nation's educational problems, and that the federal government should help equalize educational opportunities between the wealthier and the poorer states.[2]

Proposals for federal aid to education inevitably became intertwined with a host of controversial issues which acted as barriers to their enactment. Three major obstacles were the issues of race relations, church and state relations, and federal controls or states' rights. Conflict over these continuously plagued proponents of federal aid, and no general federal aid legislation was enacted although numerous bills were introduced.[3]

Positions of some groups changed entirely during the long years of debate over federal aid to education. For instance, the South in the earliest

[1]Sidney W. Tiedt, *The Role of the Federal Government in Education* (New York: Oxford University Press, Inc., 1966), pp. 14–32.

[2]Frank J. Munger and Richard F. Fenno, Jr., *National Politics and Federal Aid to Education* (Syracuse, N.Y.: Syracuse University Press, 1962), pp. 1–18.

[3]*Ibid.*, pp. 46–75; *cf.* Philip Meranto, *The Politics of Federal Aid to Education in 1965: A Study in Political Innovation* (Syracuse, N.Y.: Syracuse University Press, 1967), pp. 52–66.

days was among the most ardent supporters. Southern states stood to benefit greatly under proposed allocation formulas which considered both the needs and the resources of the states. Southern senators from 1918 to 1954 led the Senate campaigns for federal aid to education. Then the Supreme Court in the *Brown* v. *Board of Education* decision declared segregation of schools to be unconstitutional, and as if struck by a thunderbolt, the Dixie Climate soured. From then on federal aid bills were seen as a threat to integrate southern schools, and the South became a major opponent of federal aid to education.[4]

Spokesmen for the black community—especially the NAACP—were in favor of federal aid to education but only if the desegregation process was to be speeded up. In the pre-1954 period, when the Court doctrine of "separate but equal" was the law of the land, black leaders favored federal aid to education, but only if funds to the states were to be divided equally with black schools. Southerners objected to any controls as to how the money would be spent, so even in that period the southern whites and blacks were in conflict over federal aid to education. After 1954, black groups took an adamant position against funds unless the schools were desegregated. Congressman Adam Clayton Powell, the black congressman from Harlem, added an amendment to all aid-to-education bills introduced, stating that no federal funds were to go to schools that failed to desegregate. Since such an amendment was strenuously and adamantly opposed by southern congressmen, many of whom held key committee posts, no bills were passed. The race issue appeared to be an impossible obstacle to hurdle.[5]

The religious issue was equally complex. The Roman Catholic church favored federal aid to education, but only if parochial schools shared in these funds. Like the southerners, the Roman Catholic church had changed its position over the years. Originally it absolutely opposed federal aid to education. But in the 1940s parochial schools were faced with financial pressures similar to those of the public schools, and in 1942 the church changed its position. It no longer opposed aid to education, provided that parochial schools were to share in the funding. It was emphasized, however, that it favored federal aid only if parochial schools were included.[6]

Other groups, who might be called separationists, took the position that federal aid to parochial schools would violate the separation of church and state clause of the Constitution. These groups would support a federal

---

[4]Robert Bendiner, *Obstacle Course on Capitol Hill* (New York: McGraw-Hill Book Company, 1964), pp. 42–43.

[5]*Ibid.*, pp. 44–45; *cf.* Munger and Fenno, *National Politics*, pp. 66–70.

[6]Munger and Fenno, *National Politics*, pp. 54–61; Bendiner, *Obstacle Course*, pp. 46–49; and Philip B. Kurland, "Politics and the Constitution: Federal Aid to Parochial Schools," *Land and Water Review*, University of Wyoming (1966), pp. 476–94.

aid measure only if aid were not given to parochial schools. They included various Protestant groups, such as the National Council of Churches of Christ in America and many Lutheran, Presbyterian, and Unitarian churches and the Southern Baptists, the nation's single biggest denomination, as well as many of the educational groups, such as NEA, AASA, AFT, PTA, and CSSO. These groups took the position that no federal monies should be spent for parochial schools. Here too was a deadlock preventing action on federal aid to education measures.[7]

Another issue pertained to the control of education and the question of states' rights. Many groups, such as the United States Chamber of Commerce, the National Grange, the Daughters of the American Revolution, the American Legion, the Investment Bankers of America, and other conservative organizations, were opposed to federal aid to education because they feared federal controls over education and believed that education should remain a state function. This, too, was a strong ideological roadblock to the passage of federal aid-to-education legislation.[8]

These three issues—race, religion, and reaction—acted as bars against laws giving federal aid to education. Conflict intensified between opposing groups, and positions hardened during the long years of debate until it looked as if it would be impossible ever to pass a federal aid-to-education bill.[9]

Breaking the Deadlock.   The deadlock was broken in the mid-1960s, and compromise became possible because of a number of dramatic events.[10] The assassination of President Kennedy was one of these. This tragedy created both a national sense of grief and a national sense of guilt that we had not carried out the programs urged by the young leader. Lyndon Johnson, the new president, dedicated himself to completing the Kennedy-Johnson program. As a former teacher, he was personally committed to the advancement of education. He saw educational reform as a means of solving many of America's problems; furthermore, he wanted to be remembered as the "education president." When LBJ became president his skills as a master legislative leader were a major factor in helping to overcome the roadblocks to federal aid to education.

At the same time, the civil rights movement under the leadership of Martin Luther King was near its peak. As the movement had evolved from the bus boycott in Mobile, Alabama, to the sit-in and marches of

---

[7]Munger and Fenno, *National Politics*, pp. 62–65; Bendiner, *Obstacle Course*, pp. 49–52.

[8]Munger and Fenno, *National Politics*, pp. 46–47; Bendiner, *Obstacle Course*, p. 51.

[9]Munger and Fenno, *National Politics*, pp. 184–85.

[10]Kurland, "Politics and the Constitution," pp. 480–81.

the early 1960s, an increasing percentage of American people sympathized with its cause. One event in particular stirred Americans, the vicious use of force against the blacks by the police under the command of Police Chief "Bull" O'Conner in Birmingham, Alabama. Americans watched their television sets in horror as the police used dogs and fire hoses on black marchers. They were astounded. They witnessed a kind of brutality toward American citizens that most of them had never imagined. There was an almost spontaneous national consensus that something had to be done to protect the rights of blacks. President Johnson took up the cause and pushed for the enactment of the Civil Rights Act which had been bottled up in Congress throughout the Kennedy years. In a major breakthrough, Congress enacted the Civil Rights Act of 1964.

Title VI of this act provided that

> no person in the United States shall, on the ground of race, color, or national origin be excluded from participation in, be denied benefit of, or be subjected to discrimination under any program or activity receiving federal financial assistance.

In effect this provision enacted into law the so-called Powell amendment, and it applied to every federal loan or grant program. Southerners who had long opposed federal aid to education because of the Powell amendment no longer had a reason for fighting. This meant that a major roadblock had been removed for a federal aid-to-education measure.

A third event that helped to make it possible to enact a federal aid-to-education bill was the election of 1964. Lyndon Johnson was pitted against the conservative Barry Goldwater who ran on the slogan "A choice, not an echo" and campaigned on the differences of his conservative program, including his opposition to federal aid to education. The "coattail effect" from LBJ's massive victory brought a new liberal majority into Congress. Many conservatives, the states' righters, who had formerly opposed federal aid to education and were in key positions to block legislation, were swept out of office or were overwhelmed by the new two to one Democratic majority in Congress. Still another roadblock to federal aid to education was removed, as conservatives in Congress were no longer in a position to block legislation.

The Roman Catholics alone stood in opposition, but they were now anxious to compromise, since it was obvious that they alone could not prevent enactment of a federal aid-to-education bill. The only thing that was needed was a rationale, a means of striking a compromise with those opposed to any federal aid to parochial schools.

Working Out a Compromise. The "rediscovery of poverty" provided the needed rationale. In the early 1960s, largely because of a number of

widely publicized books, such as *The Other Americans*, Americans discovered that despite our national affluence, a large percentage of our people were hopelessly trapped in a culture of poverty.[11] President Johnson accepted this as a challenge and made the War on Poverty the main focus of his administration. Overcoming poverty became the rationale for the enactment of a federal aid-to-education bill.

The compromise, worked out by President Johnson's administration, avoided many of the old fights between groups. The religious issue was avoided by providing that federal funds would be distributed to aid poor children; the formula for distributing funds would be based upon the number of children from impoverished families in each school district. Since the funds were based upon the child-benefit theory, parochial schools as well as private schools could share in them. No one—neither the Catholic groups nor the separationists—could oppose a program that focused on poor children and that put the management in the hands of public bodies. Also, by selecting children in the five-to-seventeen age group in all families with an income under two thousand dollars as the formula, the administration found a device that would favor the rural South in its distribution and at the same time do justice to urban poverty in the North. By intertwining two priorities, that of educational funding along with that of overcoming poverty and discrimination, the administration had found the basis for compromise.[12]

Passage of ESEA of 1965. In 1965, after years of intergroup conflict, negotiations, and bargaining, the historic Elementary and Secondary Education Act of 1965 was passed. Its enactment was possible because of changes both in political inputs and in political within puts. Changes in the political environment and the situational conditions (the rediscovery of poverty, the metropolitan problem, and the civil rights movement) affected demand articulators (organized interests were more receptive for a compromise, and there was widespread agreement among the American people that something had to be done about poverty and civil rights). Furthermore, within puts or the structural factors were changed (the landslide election of 1964, the changed complexion of Congress, a new pro-federal-aid chairman of the House Education Committee, and the fact

[11]Michael Harrington, *The Other Americans: Poverty in the United States* (Baltimore: Penguin Books, Inc., 1962); cf. Ben H. Bagdikian, *In the Midst of Plenty: A New Report on the Poor in America* (New York: Signet Books, 1964); Leon H. Keyserling, *Progress or Poverty: The United States at the Crossroads* (Washington, D.C.: Conference on Economic Progress, 1964); and James N. Morgan et al., *Income and Welfare in the United States* (New York: McGraw-Hill Book Company, 1962).

[12]Eugene Eidenberg and Roy Morey, *An Act of Congress: The Legislative Process and the Making of Education Policy* (New York: W.W. Norton & Company, Inc., 1969), pp. 73–95.

that conservatives could no longer block legislation in the House Rules Committee). All of these factors combined to make enactment of the federal aid-to-education bill possible.[13]

Provisions of ESEA. The Elementary and Secondary Education Act of 1965 authorized five major programs. Title I of the act sets up a three-year program designed to aid school districts with impoverished children (95 percent of the nation's counties were affected by this section). The program provided federal grants to the states (which in turn were to distribute the funds to school districts) on the basis of the number of children from low-income families times 50 percent of each state's average expenditure per school child. The school districts could spend the funds in any way approved by state and federal educational agencies, but they had to take into account the needs of children who attended nonpublic schools. Therefore, funds were to be used for such joint public-private services as shared-time teaching or educational television.[14]

Titles II–V of the act authorized a five-year program of grants to states for purchases of textbooks and other library materials under which such books could be loaned to private schools; authorized a five-year program of grants to supplement community-wide educational centers to provide services that individual schools could not provide; expanded the 1954 Cooperative Research Act to authorize a five-year program of grants for new research, training, and research centers; and authorized a five-year program of grants to strengthen state departments of education.[15]

Development of New Policy Issues. The enactment of the ESEA marked the beginning of a new stream of policy issues. Once the ESEA was enacted, two major problems emerged: (1) the funding of the programs authorized under the act and (2) administrative controls. Was ESEA to be administered as general aid for education or as categorical aid to fight poverty? Political conflict over these issues has dominated our attention since 1965.

Conflict over Funding. The funding problem developed because the appropriation process is separate from the enactment process. Congress authorizes programs and sets appropriations ceilings in the enactment of such measures as the ESEA, but funds to pay for the programs are allocated in a separate process.

As soon as ESEA was enacted, the struggle over appropriations began.

[13]Meranto, *Politics of Federal Aid*, pp. 131–36.
[14]*Federal Role in Education* (Washington, D.C.: Congressional Quarterly Service, 1965), p. 34.
[15]*Ibid.*

The 1965–66 appropriation bill permitted all school districts to spend the full amount of their first year entitlement under ESEA. But the euphoria surrounding ESEA's beginning proved to be short lived. Competing demands for federal funds, especially for the Vietnam War, made it increasingly difficult to obtain full funding of the ESEA. The Johnson budget for fiscal 1967 contained only a modest increase in Title I funding (about 10 percent), and only three-fourths of the total authorized in the original bill. By 1968–69 education as a national priority had lost its momentum. Johnson's budget proposal was for the same amounts as the year before without any increases. For fiscal 1970, outgoing President Johnson proposed only $3.8 billion for education, although the authorization under the ESEA called for $8.9 billion. When President Nixon assumed office he further reduced the budget request to $3.2 billion. The extent of the total underfunding of education reached the staggering amount of $5.7 billion. From 1966 to 1969 the amount of federal funds available per eligible child actually decreased from $213 to $161.[16]

The dilemma of the growing spread between amounts authorized and appropriated, in combination with a cut of funds for fiscal year 1969–70 and the lateness of the appropriation process in relation to the school year, created major unrest among school administrators. These problems triggered the creation of the Emergency Committee for Full Funding of Educational Programs in 1969 and the beginning of another major conflict over educational finance.[17]

On this issue all of the major educational interest groups banded together to put political pressure on Congress. This coalition was able to push through Congress, in 1969 and in 1970, appropriation bills that exceeded the president's budget request for education. In both instances the president vetoed the measures, arguing that the expenditures would fan the fires of inflation. In a radio address to the nation on January 26, 1970, President Nixon lashed out at the "spendthrift" Congress, criticized the educational programs for the disadvantaged as being ineffective, and ridiculed the program of aid for federally impacted areas as being obsolete. Despite the president's opposition, educational interest groups won a major political battle as Congress overruled the veto by the necessary two-thirds vote, one of the few times it was able to do so during the Nixon administration.[18]

The president retaliated by impounding the funds and refusing to

[16]James F. Hughes and Anne O. Hughes, *Equal Education: A New National Strategy* (Bloomington: Indiana University Press, 1972), pp. 14–31.

[17]*Ibid.*, pp. 26–29; *cf.* Stanley J. McFarland, "The Emergency Committee for Full Funding of Education Programs—What Is It?" mimeographed (Washington, D.C., n.d.).

[18]*Ibid.*, p. 28.

spend monies that exceeded his budget request. Despite the congressional enactments, the president refused to spend these funds.

Although educators fumed, threatened lawsuits, and attempted to marshal political support for their cause, they were not able to substantially increase federal expenditures for education or to overcome the lack of unity between the president and Congress. The disagreement over the priority to be given education reflects the political changes that have occurred since 1965.

Education does not hold as high a priority among Americans today as it did in 1965. The political environment and the attitudes of American people toward education have changed dramatically. Such events as the resistance of many young people to the draft and to the Vietnam War, the growing militance of blacks coupled with the riots of the late 1960s, the chaos that occurred in the universities, and the increasing public resistance to school desegregation and busing to integrate schools have created an anti-intellectual, anti-educational atmosphere in many communities.

Partisan politics reflects this change in the American mood. In the election of 1968 the old Democratic coalition made up of the minorities, the urban political machines, the labor unions, and the Solid South, which had largely controlled the federal government since the 1930s, broke down. Blacks were fighting labor unions, the "hard hats" felt threatened by the blacks, the old urban machines had largely disappeared, and the middle-class whites had fled to suburbia scared by the turmoil of rapid social change. Law and order was the appeal of the day. The Solid South no longer had any reason to stay with the Democratic party because of the race issue. As the Democratic coalitions broke apart, Republicans were busy putting together a new coalition, a coalition that reflected the fears caused by social change. The "New Majority," as President Nixon called it, consisted of a coalition made up of the southern states, rural areas, and suburbia and the small towns, along with the traditionally conservative business support. The Republican presidential coalition, as contrasted with the Democratic, was less urban, less black, and less poor.[19]

Law and order rather than education was given first priority by this new coalition. Those War on Poverty measures causing rapid social change, such as the Economic Opportunity Act, the Model Cities Act, and the Elementary and Secondary Education Act of 1965, were frowned upon. The fact that the Elementary and Secondary Act of 1965 had been drawn

[19]Douglas M. Fox, "Federal Urban Policies Since 1945," in *The New Urban Politics: Cities and the Federal Government*, ed. Douglas M. Fox (Pacific Palisades, Calif.: Goodyear Publishing Co., Inc., 1972), pp. 94–100.

in such a way as to aid the central cities, not the suburbs, made it even more objectionable to Republican supporters. Suburbia was the only group disadvantaged by the ESEA formula. Also, the OEO and other urban-oriented legislation favored the central cities and were obviously not favored by the new coalition. Much of the conflict over the funding of education grows out of the differences between these political coalitions.[20]

As can be seen, federal educational policies of the 1960s had a direct impact on state and local political systems. The reaction to these programs—the feedback process—in turn resulted in a change in national priorities and new policy demands which were reflected by the new political coalition. The new Republican coalition, despite its victories in the presidential elections of 1968 and 1972, was not successful in getting a national consensus capable of giving it the necessary concurrent majority required to change entirely the policy directions of the government. The endless policy process goes on, only now the demands are for such programs as educational revenue sharing, with fewer initiatives and controls by the federal government.

Conflict over Administration of ESEA. The second problem growing out of the passage of the Elementary and Secondary Education Act of 1965 was how to administer it so as to accomplish the somewhat contradictory objectives of overcoming poverty and of financing education. Was the act to be general aid for education, or was it to be categorical aid for fighting poverty?

Traditionally, schoolmen wanted federal aid without strings attached. It was their belief that as professionals they knew the needs of education and that with additional revenues they could solve their problems. Federal aid was in no way to change their programs or policies; therefore, they believed ESEA was to be administered as general aid.[21]

The strategy of those pushing the War on Poverty, on the other hand, was to deal with the root causes of poverty. They saw the educational system itself as being in need of change, and they distrusted the educational establishment's capacity to serve the clients of poverty. War on Poverty proponents saw ESEA as categorical aid to be given only to change the personal and institutional factors causing poverty.[22]

After the enactment of ESEA, the United States Office of Education had the responsibility for making the guidelines and regulations to determine how this act was to be administered. Such complex legislation as

[20]*Ibid.*, pp. 98–99.
[21]Hughes and Hughes, *Equal Education*, p. 11.
[22]*Ibid.*, p. 10.

the Elementary and Secondary Education Act of 1965 always requires clarification by administrative agencies. Legislative mandates only prescribe the general policy framework, and administrators through rules and regulations are called upon to resolve the difficulties that are too thorny for the legislature to solve.[23]

Making of rules and regulations for the administration of ESEA forced the Office of Education into a difficult position. USOE had long looked to professional educators as its main support group, but now it had to decide between them and the proponents of educational change. Within the agency, there was a split between the traditionalists who agreed with the professional educators' viewpoint and the advocates of the poor.[24]

Because of the dominance of the traditionalist view, the Office of Education was slow in pushing regulations requiring funds to be spent on the poor. In fact, after the first year of ESEA, Title I, the newly created National Advisory Council on the Education of Disadvantaged Children warned that the job of reaching and helping most deprived children among the poor was failing. Federal funds were being spent by districts as if they were general aid and were not being concentrated on improving the conditions of the poor children.[25]

Great changes were to occur in the Office of Education in the next few years. Advocates of using Title I funds as categorical aid to serve only the special needs of the poverty target population became dominant. Changes were made in Title I guidelines. Increasingly, USOE's rules required that federal funds be concentrated on those children in the designated poverty areas. Slowly but steadily the interpretation of Title I's "contradictory" mandate as a program to serve the poor and deprived children gained status and legitimacy. Conflict with local school administrators and boards of education increased as the Office of Education moved to this position.[26]

The conflict between USOE and local school authorities was further intensified by the fact that under the Civil Rights Act of 1964, USOE also had the responsibility for seeing that discrimination did not exist in programs receiving federal aid. The vast sums that were involved in the Elementary and Secondary Act of 1965 made this an important power. USOE now was able to rely upon legal and administrative rules and

[23]Stephen K. Bailey and Edith K. Mosher, *ESEA: The Office of Education Administers a Law* (Syracuse, N.Y.: Syracuse University Press, 1968), pp. 98–100.

[24]Hughes and Hughes, *Equal Education*, pp. 32–33, 38–40; cf. Bailey and Mosher, *ESEA*, pp. 149–50; and Gary Orfield, *The Reconstruction of Southern Education: The Schools and the 1964 Civil Rights Act* (New York: John Wiley & Sons, Inc., 1969), pp. 57–61.

[25]Hughes and Hughes, *Equal Education*, p. 14.

[26]Hughes and Hughes, *Equal Education*, pp. 109–31.

regulations to cause state and local governments to carry out national goals pertaining to school integration. Through threats of withholding federal funds, USOE was able to force more southern districts to integrate in a single year than had integrated under court orders in the entire decade since the *Brown* decision. After 1967 southern schools experienced what Woodward has called the "second reconstruction" as a result of USOE's actions.[27]

Reaction to USOE's Actions. The rapid social change and unrest of the 1960s caused a reaction against such social action programs as ESEA, and this new mood was reflected in national politics. The elections of 1968 and 1972 and the presidential victory of the Republicans, who had been out of power, reflected this change. It also demonstrates the interrelatedness of the various levels of government. Policies and actions of the federal government, in this instance the USOE, trigger a reaction—a feedback—in the local and state political systems which in turn changes the federal government.

Change in the national political mood and opposition to USOE's role in administering categorical grants was clearly evident in the Nixon administration's proposal for Education Special Revenue Sharing. Administrative spokesmen from the Office of Education in a series of regionally held "Commissioner's Conferences" in 1971 called the USOE "a part of the problem." Categorical grants were condemned as being "a nearly impenetrable maze of separate programs each wrapped in its own special brand of red tape" and an obstacle that "severely handicaps and impedes the efforts of the states to plan comprehensively and operate effective programs of education tailored to their own particular needs."[28]

In place of the present legislation, the Nixon administration proposed Education Special Revenue Sharing which would consolidate into one legislative act all education programs lending financial support to the operation and maintenance of elementary and secondary schools. Funds would be distributed according to a formula automatically and would not require the customary grant application or state plan. Although state and local governments would be required to spend funds within the broad areas of national priorities, they would have broad discretionary powers to transfer funds and spend them as they please. Provisions of Title VI of the Civil Rights Act of 1964 would be required, but assurance was given

[27]Orfield, *Reconstruction of Southern Education*, pp. 120–22; *cf.* Hughes and Hughes, *Equal Education*, pp. 127–30.
[28]Commissioner's Conference 1971, "The U.S. Office of Education as Part of the Problem," U.S. Department of Health, Education, and Welfare, Dallas, March 12, 1971; *cf.* "Federal Officials Plug Revenue Sharing, but Schoolmen Aren't So Sure," *1973 AASA Convention Reporter*, prepared by the editors of *Education, U.S.A.*, p. 6.

by the administration of a minimum of federal interference in the setting of local spending priorities. All that would remain of the old "state plan" would be a set of legal assurances of compliance with basic federal requirements. Emphasis on national goals would shift to emphasis on local goals, and USOE's authority over the granting or evaluation of how funds were spent would be greatly lessened.[29]

Proposal of the new policy, which would largely change the thrust of federal educational legislation, illustrated several things: the continuous nature of the policy process, the effect of changes in the political environment on policies, and the type of feedback process in American politics. The difficulty of changing federal policy was also evident from President Nixon's difficulty in getting support from professional educators and educational interest groups despite their general agreement with the concept of revenue sharing and local control. In part this difficulty grew out of the lack of trust in the administration and a belief that it was really attempting to reduce overall expenditures for education.[30]

Developing a Curriculum

The process of developing a curriculum demonstrates some other ways in which the federal government influences educational policymaking. Whereas in unitary political systems such as in France and England, decisions of what will be taught are made by a central educational ministry and orders are handed down to local schools hierarchically, in the United States, because of the federal system, we rely much more on indirect methods of influencing curriculum decisions, and all levels of government are involved.[31]

Curriculum policies in our earliest history were made almost exclusively by local schools. School districts, created under state laws, historically did all of the things necessary to conduct a school. They erected school buildings, hired teachers, and told them what to teach. Curriculum was largely a local matter.

As our nation developed, however, states began to play a more important role in the operations of schools, including the setting of curricula.

[29]Commissioner's Conference 1971, "U.S. Office of Education as Part of the Solution."

[30]"Federal Officials Plug Revenue Sharing," p. 7; cf. "Washington Trends," *American School Board Journal*, June 1971, p. 6.

[31]Ideas for this section are mainly from Burton R. Clark, "Interorganizational Patterns in Education," *Administrative Science Quarterly*, September 1965, pp. 225–37; cf. Ronald C. Doll, "The Multiple Forces Affecting Curriculum Change," *Phi Delta Kappan*, March 1970, pp. 382–84; and Mariel Crosby, "Who Changes the Curriculum and How?" *Phi Delta Kappan*, March 1970, pp. 385–88.

State laws were enacted requiring certain subjects—English, mathematics, science, civics—to be taught. Additional requirements were made by state departments of education as the states began to share the responsibility for financing schools. To get state funds, local districts had to meet the state department's standards, that is, they had to teach what the state ordered, and in the manner specified. Control over textbook selection also became a means for many states to influence what was taught. States today are still vitally involved in the processes of developing curriculum.

Nationalization and even internationalization of our environment has expanded the federal government's role in curriculum policies. Increasingly complex technology, urbanization, growing interrelatedness of our economy, and development of our military position in the world place greater demands on the nation's schools. Such national goals as full employment, economic stability, racial peace, and military superiority depend in part upon what is taught in the schools.[32]

Since the federal government has no formal authority over local school districts, the question is, How does it influence curriculum decisions at the grass roots level? The federal government's influence is indirect and depends largely upon persuasion. The processes by which it influences curriculum policies can be seen in the events leading to the introduction of the "new math" and "new science" to the curriculum of the nation's schools.

New Math and New Science.   The Russians' success with Sputnik, the first spaceship in orbit, shocked the American people. How could communistic Russia, whom we considered to be relatively backward in technology, surpass us? The nation's schools caught the brunt of a critical self-examination. Why did we not have as rigorous mathematics and science courses as the Russians? For years universities had criticized public schools for not properly educating high school students and for not producing "a better product." Although these criticisms reflected, in part, the status quarrels between teachers at different levels, they also pointed out the lack of a national science or mathematics curriculum and the difficulty of getting a nationwide curriculum. Each local school district to a large degree chooses its own textbooks and decides what math and science courses it will offer. How these courses are taught depends on the ability of the individual teacher. There is no nationally mandated curriculum.

With such a decentralized system for making curriculum policies, how did we get new math and new science adopted throughout the country? Soon after Sputnik the National Science Foundation, a federal agency,

---

[32]Harold Howe II, "Change and American Schools" (Address before the American Association of School Administrators, Atlantic City, New Jersey, February 13, 1967.

financed a conference of scientists (and later a conference of mathematicians), many of whom were prestigious university professors, to propose an improved curriculum. Private foundations also soon entered into the financial support of the curriculum reform group. These respected scientists and mathematicians, acting as a voluntary and private group, set out to write a course for national school use, something that no federal agency could do directly because of probable congressional and popular opposition.[33]

Book companies, which had long been a major party influencing curriculum, were at first hesitant to publish this material because there was no market for it. Teachers generally did not know the new math or science, and they are the key to what books are selected for their schools. Teachers first had to be taught to use the materials and then persuaded to adopt textbooks containing the new materials. A demand had to be created.[34]

To instruct teachers in the new science and new mathematics, the National Science Foundation initiated and supported a program of summer institutes. Grants were made available to colleges and universities so that they could offer summer courses in these subjects. There was both a monetary and a status incentive in applying for these grants, particularly for the professors who directed and staffed these institutes. Similarly, there were stipends for teachers who became students during the summer months when most public school teachers are without an income.[35]

The summer institutes did create a demand for the new textbooks. After attending these summer courses and being impressed by their professors as to the value of the new curriculum, teachers went back to their local schools critical of the old textbooks and the old ways of teaching math and science courses. School administrators and school boards were bombarded by their teachers to "keep up and to modernize," and within a relatively short time, the new science and mathematics was a part of the curriculum throughout the land.

Without any formal authority to order a change, the federal government had initiated a major overhaul in the national curriculum. Set in motion by an agency in the executive department, the flow of influence was downward through a chain of independent groups and organizations who found it to their advantage to enter the alliance or compact. A federal agency provided the funds; a private nonprofit group received the money and developed a new course; commercial organizations made the new materials available to all units of the decentralized system; universities and colleges in all regions of the country used the new materials to train teachers; local authorities adopted the new materials and allowed

[33]Clark, "Interorganizational Patterns," pp. 229–30.
[34]Ibid., pp. 230–31.
[35]Ibid., p. 231.

their teachers to reshape the local courses. All of this was done without the use of any hierarchical authority. Individuals and groups were persuaded to cooperate, and this persuasion to a large degree depended on shared views and identification with the prestigious individuals and groups making and teaching the new curriculum. The federal government through these processes was able to change the educational curriculum.[36]

Other Federal Influence on Curriculum.   The federal government has influenced curriculum policies in a host of other instances, but typically the influence has been indirect and through a process of voluntary cooperation.[37] For instance, the Morrill Act of 1862, which provided land grants to the states for the establishment of colleges specializing in agriculture and mechanical arts, indirectly influenced public school curriculum. The practical curriculum of these "A & M colleges" challenged the classical curriculum of the traditional liberal arts colleges. In time the new general curriculum was legitimized as the A & M colleges gained prestige and graduated more and more students. High school curriculum, which has tended to emulate that of the liberal arts colleges and universities, in time adopted a general curriculum comparable to that of the A & M colleges.

Many of the federal programs in educational research, particularly during the decade of the 1960s, have influenced local school curriculum. Such innovations as the voucher system, modular scheduling, career education, and performance contract grew out of federally funded research. The Head Start, Upward Bound, Job Corps, and manpower programs were also initiated and financed by the federal government in an attempt to meet the immediate problems of the poor.[38]

Through contracts with colleges and universities the federal government, especially the Department of Defense, has been able to influence what schools teach. The Department of Defense (DOD) has the largest training and educational program, and perhaps the greatest influence on the educational system of any federal agency other than the Office of

[36]*Ibid.*, pp. 231–33.

[37]For an overview of federal influences, see Franklin Parker, "Federal Influences on the Future of American Education," *School and Society*, October 27, 1967, pp. 383–87; *cf.* Howe, "Change and American Schools."

[38]For a discussion of some of the effects of OEO, see Gary English, "The Trouble with Community Action," *Public Administration Review*, May-June 1972, pp. 224–31; Thomas K. Glennan, "OEO Experiments in Education," *Compact*, February 1971, pp. 3–5; Robert C. Atchley, "Can Programs for the Poor Survive in Middle-Class Institutions?" *Phi Delta Kappan*, December 1971, pp. 243–44; Paul Street, "Compensatory Education by Community Action," *Phi Delta Kappan*, February 1970, pp. 320–22; and Richard W. Boone, "Reflections on Citizen Participation and the Economic Opportunity Act," *Public Administration Review*, September 1972, pp. 444–55.

Education. The development of contractual relationships between universities and DOD has greatly influenced the nation's institutions of higher education. DOD's power to spend enables it to direct education along certain lines, and it has acted as a catalyst in educational technology. The technologies developed by the military services, often with the assistance of industry and educators, range from the "software" end of the spectrum to the "hardware," including pedagogical techniques in between. Such DOD innovations as language labs, programmed instructional text, closed-circuit television courses, and computerized instruction are widely used by schools throughout the nation. There is also much interest today in the application of a "systems approach" to education, which has largely been advanced by the military since the early 1950s. DOD's innovation in budgeting, the so-called PPB, is also widely used in education.[39] Here, as in other instances, the federal influence is indirect and voluntary rather than through hierarchical power.

Meeting Urban Educational Needs

The most dramatic changes in educational policymaking and in the roles of the various levels of government have occurred because of the urban-metropolitan crisis. The continuing forces of urbanization have resulted in a series of population movements which have created some of our most crucial problems. Until the 1940s urbanization meant the concentration of people largely in the central city. There was a tendency for cities, towns, and suburbs to coalesce politically as their built-up areas came into contact with one another and as their economic interdependence became more pronounced. During the 1940s, however, the trend toward annexation and consolidation slowed down, especially around the older cities. The pattern of movement was in turn followed by gradual, then more rapid, increases of population in the outlying areas. When millions of blacks during and after World War II began flowing out of the rural areas, central cities were less capable of performing the assimilative function that had been successful decades ago for other ethnic groups, and the flight of the whites to the suburbs was under way.[40]

[39]John Brademan, "Education and the Military: A Diversified Partnership," *Phi Delta Kappan*, May 1967, p. 423; *cf.* Charles L. Blaschke, "The DOD: Catalyst in Educational Technology," *Phi Delta Kappan*, January 1967, pp. 208–14; Clayton Braddock, "Project 100,000," *Phi Delta Kappan*, May 1967, pp. 425–28; and Douglas M. Knight, ed., *The Federal Government and Higher Education* (Englewood Cliffs, N.J.: Prentice-Hall, Inc., 1960), pp. 76–139.

[40]Robert J. Havighurst, *Education in Metropolitan Areas* (Boston: Allyn & Bacon, Inc., 1966), pp. 52–83; *cf.*, Max Ways, "The Deeper Shame of Cities," *Fortune*, January 1966, pp. 132–35.

Failure of political institutions in metropolitan areas to follow the pattern of actual life resulted in fragmentation of the local governmental system. The central city was surrounded by a ring of suburban cities which attracted away individuals who were the most able to finance local government and to provide the leadership for dealing with urban problems, as well as part of the commercial and industrial tax base. Central cities and central city school districts were left with aging physical plants, a declining tax base, and an increasing proportion of "high cost" people, that is, poor and culturally disadvantaged persons who needed educational, social, and welfare services.

Central city schools, which had been the finest schools in the land before World War II, bore the brunt of the growing metropolitan crisis. The changing character of city schools, student bodies—the increasing number of black, Puerto Rican, and Mexican-American students and students from the lower socioeconomic and "problem families"—gave city schools the reputation of being "blackboard jungles." This reputation, in turn, gave fuel to "white flight" and even more opposition to pleas for additional local funds for education.[41]

State governments also resisted the new urban demands. Although states have played an important role in financing schools since World War II, the plight of the central city schools was largely ignored. States have generally been unable or unwilling to undertake many needed actions. For example, in the matters of adequately financing core city schools, of dealing with desegregation and particularly with de facto segregation, or of providing vocational education and educational opportunities for the poor and culturally deprived, the states have not acted and perhaps cannot act. Self-imposed constitutional limitations, citizens' unwillingness to tax themselves, and at times hostile dominant attitudes of the citizenry, coupled with malapportionment of state legislatures prior to the Supreme Court's apportionment decisions in the 1960s, prevented states from meeting the growing needs of city schools.[42] The groups representing these urban school interests were thus forced to turn to the federal government.

[41]Robert E. Mason, "Decline and Crisis in Big-City Education," *Phi Delta Kappan*, March 1967, pp. 306–10; *cf.* Clemmont E. Vontress, "Our Demoralizing Slum Schools," *Phi Delta Kappan*, November 1963, pp. 77–81.

[42]James Kelly and Michael D. Usdan, "Urban Politics and the Public Schools: Myth, Reality, and Response," *Perspectives on Education* (New York: Columbia University, Teacher's College, 1968), pp. 18–32; *cf.* Alan K. Campbell and Philip Meranto, "The Metropolitan Education Dilemma: Matching Resources to Needs," *Urban Affairs Quarterly*, September 1966, pp. 42–63; Seymour Sacks, "Central City Educational Systems: Economic and Fiscal Aspects of Their Current Dilemmas," *State School Finance Workshop*, National School Board Association (Detroit, March 28–31, 1968), pp. 17–26.

National Goals and Federal Legislation. The year 1965 marks the beginning of a new era in educational politics. In that year the groups that had worked for federal aid for over a decade were finally successful. The host of educational programs enacted by Congress, including the Elementary and Secondary Education Act, reflected the interest of the urban-oriented groups which previously had been largely unsuccessful at the state and local levels. Major emphasis of the new federal programs was given to the urban problems of poverty, civil rights, vocational education—problems of national concern, but which affected the urban areas most acutely.

The new programs continued the traditional system of categorical aids, that is, the programs were intended to serve a specific purpose rather than the broad purpose of education generally. National goals were specified in the legislation, and grants were made to accomplish these goals. Many of these grants went directly to local governments, bypassing the state entirely, and reflecting many urban groups' distrust of the state.[43]

A major shift in the locus of decision making from local and state levels to the federal level occurred because of the numerous federal programs supported by federal appropriations. The federal government no longer stays aloof from the making and implementing of educational policy for the nation. Through the use of the categorical grants and the so-called guidelines, it actively participates in shaping educational policies.[44]

Direct Federal Participation to Change Schools. Another major change in the federal role in education is the direct involvement in conducting certain types of educational programs. Numerous compensatory educational programs for the culturally disadvantaged student are financed by federal grants. In a number of the poverty and manpower programs, such as Head Start, Upward Bound, Job Corps, and manpower training, the federal government is directly undertaking or is contracting to have educational programs conducted. Direct participation by the federal government in the programs for the culturally deprived or the school dropouts, in part, was necessary because of the resistance to such programs by local

---

[43]Max Ways, "Creative Federalism and the Great Society," in *Cooperation and Conflict: Readings in American Federalism*, ed. Daniel J. Elazar *et al.* (Itasca, Ill.: F.E. Peacock Publishers, Inc., 1969), pp. 619–32; *cf.* Advisory Commission on Intergovernmental Relations, *Fiscal Balance in the American Federal System*, Vol. II.

[44]W. W. Wayson, "The Political Revolution in Education, 1965," *Phi Delta Kappan*, March 1966, pp. 333–39; Nicholas A. Masters and Lawrence K. Petit, "Some Changing Patterns in Educational Policy Making," *Educational Administrative Quarterly*, Spring 1966, pp. 81–98; and Roald F. Campbell and Donald H. Layton, "Thrust and Counterthrust in Education Policy Making," *Phi Delta Kappan*, February 1968, pp. 290–94.

and state school officials. The only way to initiate these programs was to have the federal government conduct them.[45]

The federal government has also taken a number of actions to open the educational policymaking process to a broader range of community groups. Most of the urban-oriented legislation of the 1960s, as well as administrative policy guidelines and regulations, established policies requiring citizen participation of the "target group." Under the Economic Opportunity Act of 1964, community action agencies (CAAs) were created in communities outside of, and independent of the established local governmental system to ensure "maximum feasible participation of the poor" and to place administrative authority closer to people directly affected by the federal legislation. This action, in part, reflected a general distrust of local school boards and educational professions, who were viewed as being unresponsive to the poor.[46]

Conflict between the established units of local government and the CAAs was inevitable and was soon in coming. The provisions for "maximum feasible participation" increased the demands from the poor upon the schools. Demands for citizen participation in school policies grew as the poor became increasingly politicized through the community action agencies. Controversial demands, such as demands for decentralization of urban school districts, community control of the schools, changes in the curriculum with addition of such programs as black studies relevant to those needs of the poor, and making schools accountable for the educational success of students, were the basis for much conflict. Confrontations between the poor and the school officials and employees increased; numerous lawsuits were brought against the schools, many by OEO's legal aid division. Some litigation, such as the desegregation cases, the attacks on the district's structure, and the methods of financing education as in the *Rodriguez* case, challenged the very foundations of the educational system. Schools became the vortex of the social revolution that began in the 1960s.

Such federal programs as OEO, Model Cities, and ESEA had a great impact on the schools. Some of the most obvious changes included a new awareness of the needs of the poor and culturally deprived, the addition of mandatory requirements for citizen participation in most federal

[45]Harold Howe II, "Unfinished Work for the States," Address before the annual convention of the National Conference of State Legislative Leaders, Washington, D.C., November 18, 1966; *cf.* Max Ways, "The Deeper Shame of the Cities," *Fortune Magazine*, January, 1968, pp. 132–35.

[46]Boone, "Reflections on Citizen Participation," pp. 444–45; Atchley, "Can Programs for the Poor Survive?" pp. 243–44; Hughes and Hughes, *Equal Education*, pp. 81–82; Robert A. Aleshire, "Power to the People: An Assessment of the Community Action and Model Cities Experience," *Public Administration Review*, September 1972, pp. 428–43; and Charles Billings, "Community Control of the Schools and the Quest for Power," *Phi Delta Kappan*, January 1972, pp. 277–78.

legislation, the acceptance of some new programs (most notable, the Head Start program and the use of teacher aides), and the initiation of a number of ongoing experiments such as the voucher system and performance contracting.[47]

Political Reaction to Federal Initiative. Political opposition to these changes was expected and unavoidable. Nationwide there had been a growing taxpayer revolt against schools as education became involved in social controversy. Discontent in Congress was finally expressed in the Green amendment to the Economic Opportunity Act in 1967, which gave the established local governments more control over CAAs and the states a stronger voice in the funding of programs.[48] But as we have already seen, the growing opposition and the change in the national mood toward this program was most evident in the presidential election of 1968.

The Nixon administration, which was philosophically opposed to federal initiatives such as OEO, proposed a number of changes to return policymaking discretion to the elected state and local governmental officials. General Revenue Sharing, one of President Nixon's early proposals which was enacted in 1973, changed the manner in which federal funds would be given to state and local communities. Unlike categorical grants, general revenue sharing funds are allocated to state and local governments (but only to general purpose governments) on a formula basis, and with little or no federal stipulation as to how the monies are to be spent. State and local officials determine how these funds will be expended. CAAs on the local level have to compete with other agencies and programs in the community for these funds and, therefore, become financially dependent on elected local officials.

President Nixon's proposed reorganization plan of March 25, 1971, for revamping the executive branch of government recommended that OEO be abolished and that those functions retained be transferred to a new department. Furthermore, most OEO programs were cut out of the proposed presidential budget and the administration took steps to disband the office. Although a federal judge ruled that the president had no right to circumvent programs enacted by Congress, the War on Poverty seemed to be over and the future of the Office of Economic Opportunity looked bleak. No funds have been requested in the executive budget for OEO since 1973, and the Ford administration has indicated that it will not in the future request funds for OEO.

[47]Glennan, "OEO Experiments in Education," pp. 3–5; and Street, "Compensatory Education by Community Action," pp. 320–22.

[48]James Sundquist, *Making Federalism Work: A Study of Program Coordination at the Community Level* (Washington, D.C.: The Brookings Institution, 1969), pp. 35–41.

The downfall of OEO illustrates again the interrelatedness of the political systems. Policies and actions of federal agencies that are offensive to state and local political systems cause a political backlash—a feedback—which results ultimately in changes in the federal policies, in this instance in the abolition of OEO.

Urban Schools and the Racial Revolution. Even more controversial than the War on Poverty programs have been the federal government's actions pertaining to school desegregation. In the two decades since the Supreme Court declared unconstitutional those state statutes requiring dual school systems based on race, the federal government has become involved in areas formerly deemed to be reserved for the states or to individual action at the community level. Conflict between constitutional doctrines guaranteeing equal educational opportunity and parochial values favoring segregation has increased, and the federal government has often had to rely upon litigation and coercive action to secure compliance.

In the first decade, after the *Brown* decision, the courts assumed primary responsibility for dismantling the dual school systems. The process was painfully slow, since action was taken only when an aggrieved party brought suit against a segregated school. School systems under court order were required to develop specific plans for desegregation, subject to review of the lower federal courts. These plans instituted very selective pupil transfer systems and when school boards were pushed to take further action, they invariably adopted a "freedom of choice" method of assignment of pupils to particular schools. Under this method, school officials abdicated the function of assigning students, which they had theretofore exercised on a racial basis. For all practical purposes, "freedom of choice" meant that dual school systems remained intact, since community attitudes exerted a strong influence to ensure traditional attendance patterns. After a full decade of judicial enforcement, almost 99 percent of the black students in the eleven southern states remained in segregated schools despite the numerous legal and coercive actions taken by the federal government.[49]

Although the racial revolution at first reverberated most clamorously in the rural South, in recent years city school systems have become the main battleground over integration. The continued growth of metropolitan areas and the increasing isolation of racial and economic groups between cities and suburbs has exacerbated the problem of integrating public schools. Segregation in city schools is widespread in metropolitan areas

---

[49]Legal memorandum supplied by the Department of Health, Education, and Welfare on "Free Choice in Desegregating Public Schools," *Congressional Record*, December 4, 1967, S17785; *cf.* Orfield, *Reconstruction of Southern Education*, pp. 15–20.

throughout the country. All-black and all-white schools exist in almost every large school system because of the segregated housing patterns and the reliance upon neighborhood school attendance zones. Conflict over integrating city schools has been most intense in urban centers in the South, since they are mandated by the courts to dismantle the dual school system.[50]

Outside of the South, city schools were little affected by court decisions during the 1954–64 decade, since a legal distinction was made between schools desegregated because of state laws (de jure segregation) and those segregated because of housing patterns (de facto segregation). The constitutional prohibition against segregated schools was held to apply only to dual systems resulting from state laws; as long as state action did not cause the segregated pattern of schools, city schools were under no legal mandate to integrate.[51]

A number of developments have changed and speeded up the school desegregation process since 1964. Passage of the Civil Rights Act of 1964 is perhaps most significant. Title VI, a little-noticed provision of this act, fundamentally altered the equation of power and opened the way for a far-reaching reconstruction of race relations in public schools. This law forbade the use of federal aid in segregated schools and authorized the attorney general to bring lawsuits on behalf of black children. It put the weight of the federal bureaucracy on the side of change.

After 1965, schools were under great pressures to desegregate in order to get the large sums of federal funds made available by the Elementary and Secondary Education Act. School districts had to agree to comply with standards handed down by the courts and the USOE. Affirmative action plans were required of school districts to show how they planned to proceed toward integration, and the potential of federal funds being withheld acted as leverage to force adamant schools to desegregate. The burden of desegregation had largely been moved to administrative agencies.

Great change occurred in public schools throughout the country after 1964. In the South the facade of total resistance was smashed, and integration proceeded at an increasing rate. New pressures were put on schools in northern cities to integrate, since Title VI clearly forbade the use of federal funds whenever unconstitutional segregation existed. Civil rights groups pushed for strict enforcement to desegregate city schools, and

[50]*Racial Isolation in the Public Schools* (Washington, D.C.: U.S. Commission on Civil Rights, 1967), Vol. I.

[51]The early "northern" school segregation cases were few and conflicting. See Deal v. Cincinnati Board of Education, 369 F.2d 55 (1966); cert. den., 387 U.S. 935; on remand, 419 F.2d 1387 (1970); and Downs v. Kansas City, 336 F.2d. 988 (1962); cert. den., 380 U.S. 914. The opposite conclusion was found in Taylor v. Board of Education of New Rochelle, 294 F.2d 36 (1961); cert. den., 368 U.S. 940.

southerners who had long felt unjustly singled out joined in the demands for equal enforcement throughout the land.[52]

USOE's first effort to enforce Title VI in a northern city occurred in 1966. Acting on a complaint that the school board had intentionally fostered segregation, USOE attempted to delay the flow of $30 million in aid to Chicago. The threat to withhold federal funds mobilized the entire Chicago political organization, and Mayor Daley appealed directly to President Johnson. The showdown with the powerful Chicago political organization, which had been so influential in the president's election, had serious political repercussions. President Johnson was placed in an intolerable political position, and USOE was forced to retreat and to reevaluate its power to cut off funds. As this incident reveals, the legal power to withhold federal funds must be used sparingly and only after all alternative actions have failed, because of the intimate relationship between politics and administration.[53]

Despite USOE's fiasco in Chicago, administrative and legal pressures have steadily increased on northern city schools to desegregate. USOE continues to monitor the expenditures of federal funds by city school systems and is able to apply pressure through such administrative devices as affirmative action plans. Of even more significance have been the federal court decisions narrowing the distinction between de facto and de jure segregation.[54]

Federal judges have become increasingly impatient with the delays of school districts and have spelled out in specific terms actions required of schools. In May 1968 the U.S. Supreme Court in *Green* v. *County School Board* struck down the "freedom of choice" approach to school desegregation. Furthermore, the Court held that school authorities were charged with the affirmative duty to do whatever was necessary to eliminate discrimination "root and branch." The *Green* decision in unequivocal terms said: "The burden on a school board today is to come forward with a plan that promises realistically to work . . . now . . ."[55]

---

[52]Orfield, *Reconstruction of Southern Education*, pp. 102–18; Katherine Montgomery, *Historical Summary of School Desegregation Since 1954* (Washington, D.C.: Library of Congress Research Service, 1973).

[53]*Ibid*, p. 117; *cf.* Hughes and Hughes, *Equal Education*, pp. 62–66; Benjamin C. Willis and Harold Howe II, "Federalism, Race, and the Chicago Schools" (Letter and Report), in *Cooperation and Conflict: Readings in American Federalism,* ed. Daniel J. Elazar *et al.* (Itasca, Ill.: F.E. Peacock Publishers, Inc., 1969), pp. 593–602.

[54]Paul R. Dimond, "Segregation, Northern Style," *Inequality in Education*, Center for Law and Education (Harvard University, August 3, 1971), pp. 17–23; *cf.* John C. Hogan, "School Desegregation—North, South, East, West: Trends in Court Decisions, 1849–1973," *Phi Delta Kappan*, September 1973, pp. 58–63; Thomas A. Shannon, "The Denver Decision: Death Knell for De Facto Segregation?" *Phi Delta Kappan*, September 1973, pp. 6–9.

[55]Green v. County School Board, 391 U.S. 413 (1968).

Since the *Green* opinion, a spate of decisions have held school segregation actionable in many "northern" cities: South Holland (Michigan), Pasadena, Las Vegas, Los Angeles, Pontiac (Michigan), Benton Harbor (Michigan), Denver, San Francisco, Oxnard County (California). The courts, in their determinations as to whether school boards have intentionally utilized powers at their disposal to perpetuate segregation, are increasingly looking at such administrative practices as faculty hiring and assignments, equalization of facilities and resources, school attendance zones, and school construction. The legal distinction between de facto and de jure segregation has been greatly narrowed by these decisions.[56]

It has become evident in city school systems that segregated housing patterns make it impossible to desegregate schools without the busing of black and white students. After the courts ruled that "freedom of choice" was out and that school authorities were charged with an affirmative duty to eliminate racial discrimination in schools, busing became about the only option available to city schools.[57]

Busing and School Desegregation.   The issue of busing for the purpose of desegregating schools came before the U.S. Supreme Court in the case of *Swann* v. *Charlotte-Mecklenburg Board of Education.*[58] The school district involved in this case had been operating under a 1965 district court-approved desegregation plan when black students sought further relief from segregated schools on the basis of the *Green* decision. They alleged that the district's use of geographic zoning—the so-called neighborhood concept—with a free transfer provision had not resulted in integration of the schools, and that fourteen thousand of the twenty-four thousand black students in the district were still attending all-black schools. The district court held that the schools were indeed operating in an unconstitutional manner and gave the school board at least three opportunities to come forth with an acceptable plan. The final plan adopted by the district court utilized pairing of schools, noncontiguous zoning, grouping, cross-busing and other techniques that would result in a completely desegregated school system.

The school district appealed to the circuit court which overruled the district court order. The Supreme Court then agreed to hear the case, and it handed down its decision in May 1971.

The Supreme Court concurred with the conclusion of the federal district court that assignment of children to the school nearest their resi-

[56]Dimond, "Segregation," p. 17.

[57]Nathan Glazer, "Is Busing Necessary?" in *The Great School Bus Controversy*, ed. Nicolaus Mills (New York: Teachers College, Columbia University, 1973), pp. 196–97.

[58]402 U.S. 1 (1971).

dence would not produce an end to the dual school system. School desegregation plans, therefore, could not be limited to the "walk in" school. Furthermore, the Court held that bus transportation of students had been an integral part of the public education system for years and was a permissible technique to achieve desegregation. In its decree, the Supreme Court struck down North Carolina's antibusing law and reinstated the district court plan including that portion requiring busing for the purpose of desegregating schools.

Although the Supreme Court in the *Swann* decision ruled that it was not deciding the matter of de facto segregation, its strong language on faculty assignments, equalization of facilities and resources, and school construction lent support to many northern desegregation suits. States outside the South at first did not feel the busing issue because of the distinction between de jure and de facto segregation, but with the falling away of such distinctions in lower courts, busing for the purpose of desegregation has become a national issue.[59]

Metropolitan-wide Desegregation. "White flight" to the suburbs has been one means of avoiding school desegregation. The suburbs with their own separate and predominantly white school districts have been sanctuaries for whites, offering escape from school integration. Because of the racial isolation between central and suburban school districts, substantial integration can be accomplished only if the area encompassed by a court-ordered desegregation plan is larger than the city itself.

Early in 1972 this means of avoidance of integration was challenged. Federal District Judge Robert R. Merhige ordered the merger of Richmond, Virginia's predominantly black school district, with two predominantly white suburban county districts. Several months earlier, Federal Judge Stephen Roth in Detroit ordered Michigan officials to submit a desegregation plan for the Detroit metropolitan area. These cases rested on legal principles and factual findings which makes them applicable throughout the country.[60]

The court's reasoning in these cases was based on the following premises:

[59]Dimond, "Segregation," pp. 17–20; cf. Christopher Jencks, "Busing—The Supreme Court Goes North," in *The Great School Bus Controversy*, ed. Mills, pp. 14–26.

[60]William L. Taylor, "Metropolitan-wide Desegregation," *Inequality in Education,* Center for Law and Education (Harvard University, March 1972), pp. 45–50; cf. "Civil Rights—Judicial Consolidation of Public School Districts to Achieve Racial Balance," *Vanderbilt Law Review*, May 1972, pp. 893–909; Owen M. Fiss, "Racial Imbalance in the Public Schools: The Constitutional Concepts," *Harvard Law Review*, January 1965, p. 573; and Daniel U. Levine, "Integration in Metropolitan Schools: Issues and Prospects, *Phi Delta Kappan*, June 1973, pp. 651–57.

1. Public education is the responsibility of state government, which must make it available to all on equal terms.
2. Political subdivisions, including school districts, are creatures of the state and will be altered when necessary to meet the overriding demands of the Constitution.
3. De jure school segregation is established by demonstrating that school assignment policies are based upon segregated housing policies.
4. The state had no compelling interest in maintaining separate school systems within a single biracial metropolitan community.

In both Richmond and Detroit, these holdings were supported by massive evidence of officially sanctioned housing segregation, and the court held in effect that state-created local school districts were being used to wall black and poor families into central cities.[61]

These decisions refueled the furor over busing, since the Richmond court ordered into effect a city school board plan that consolidated the three districts into one district of 104,000 students governed by a single board and superintendent. Some 78,000 children were to be bused under the plan accepted by the district court.[62] The Fourth Circuit Court, however, overruled the district court's decision in the *Richmond* case, citing the Tenth Amendment provision that reserves all "nondelegated" powers to the state. It further stated that a federal court had no business reorganizing the internal structure of a local government unless invidious state action were found that violated the Fourteenth Amendment.[63]

The U.S. Supreme Court heard the Richmond case in the summer of 1973, but its decision was not decisive since it ended in a tie, a four to four vote with Justice Lewis Powell, a former Richmond school board president, abstaining. In effect, this decision upheld the circuit court and left Richmond's district intact under state law. But it did not settle the issue.[64]

Meanwhile, on December 8, 1973, the Sixth Circuit Court of Appeals upheld Judge Roth's finding that a metropolitan desegregation plan was required in order to provide an adequate remedy for Detroit's de jure segregated schools. In the summer of 1974 the Supreme Court overruled the circuit court in a five to four decision, which for the moment removed the pressure for cross-district busing.[65]

The import of the metropolitan-wide desegregation issue was obvious throughout the country. Other suits appeared on the courts' dockets,[66]

[61]Taylor, "Metropolitan-wide Desegregation," pp. 45–46.

[62]Bradley v. School Board of the City of Richmond, Virginia, 338 F.Supp. 67 (E.D. Va. 1972).

[63]462 F.2d. 1058 (1972).

[64]School Board of the City of Richmond, Virginia v. Bradley, 412 U.S. 92, 36 L.Ed.2d 771 (1973).

[65]Milliken v. Bradley, 94 S.Ct. 3112 (1974).

[66]Taylor, Metropolitan-wide Desegregation," p.47: *cf.* Lumpkin v. Miskell, C.A. No. 13, 716 (D. Conn., Feb. 1970).

and it is obvious that a major judicial revolution would have developed if the Court had not ruled as it did in the *Detroit* case. The Supreme Court's ruling on metropolitan-wide desegregation was certainly a landmark decision.

Reaction to Busing. Desegregation of the public schools has undoubtedly become one of the most volatile political and social issues this nation has ever had to face. The heat and vibrations from the conflict over busing have affected the entire political process. Public opinion polls indicate that 76 percent of the nation's people oppose busing for the purpose of desegregating schools. Many parents have withdrawn their children from city schools either by moving to the suburbs or by enrolling them in newly created private schools, the so-called segregation academies which have sprung up in all kinds of facilities, including many churches. Organized resistance has supported legal and political opposition and has led to violence in some instances. Candidates from the lowest office to the highest have been forced to take a stand on the busing issue. Like people generally, politicians usually are careful not to oppose desegregation, only the question of "forced busing."

The political issue of busing has become a major factor in all elections from the school board to the presidency. In the presidential campaigns of 1968 and 1972, busing to desegregate schools was a dominant issue. A number of state conventions enacted resolutions calling on Congress to halt "forced busing," and in the Florida primary election of 1972 a resolution calling for the amendment of the U.S. Constitution barring busing was overwhelmingly approved. While potential Democratic candidates were divided or indecisive on the issue, the so-called Southern Strategy of the Republican party capitalized on the fears and hostilities of southerners and suburbanites.[67]

Actions of the federal government have also been influenced by the political opposition to busing. The Nixon administration took a number of steps to slow down desegregation. By far the most important was the appointment of four "conservative" judges to the U.S. Supreme Court, resulting in the creation of the so-called Nixon Court. Also, the administrative arm of the government eased up on enforcement of the civil rights laws. In fact, a federal lawsuit brought against Secretary Elliott Richardson and the director of the Office for Civil Rights (OCR), Department of Health, Education, and Welfare, in 1972 found that actions of the OCR

[67]"The Wayward Busing Issue," *Phil Delta Kappan*, May 1972, pp. 537–38; *cf.* Alexander M. Bickel, "Untangling the Busing Snarl," in *The Great School Bus Controversy*, ed. Mills, pp. 27–37.

changed radically after 1969 with few enforcement proceedings being initiated and no funds being withheld from school districts for refusing to integrate.[68] Similarly, in a lawsuit against Secretary of the Treasury John B. Connally in 1971, the federal court issued an injunction against the Treasury Department preventing it from granting tax-exempt status and deductibility of contributions to private schools discriminating against black students.[69]

In 1972 after the Supreme Court unanimously upheld busing for the purpose of desegregating schools in the *Swann* decision, President Nixon appeared on national television to inform America that he had put before Congress bills to impose a moratorium on all new busing orders by federal courts and to provide $2.5 billion in federal aid to improve the quality of education for the poor and disadvantaged.[70]

Congress responded by passing as a part of the Educational Amendments of 1972 a measure that would delay court-imposed busing orders until all appeals have been exhausted or until time for such appeals has expired. The provision was to become void after December 31, 1973. In addition, financial aid was provided for desegregating school districts under a $2 billion authorization, much of it earmarked for special purposes such as bilingual programs, metropolitan desegregation plans that involve a city and its suburbs, and educational television.[71]

School desegregation and busing to accomplish it, like the slavery issue in the pre–Civil War period, present us with a most difficult problem to resolve. Debate continues over such diverse proposals as a constitutional amendment to outlaw "forced busing" or the creation of educational parks with superior educational facilities to which all students would be bused. But there is no consensus, and conflict continues to rage. None of the normal adaptation processes—identification, bargaining, or legal or administrative rules—has been able to effectively contain this conflict. Force and coercive actions, therefore, often have to be relied upon to enforce the law and preserve peace.

[68]Adams v. Richardson, 351 F.Supp. 636 (1972).
[69]Green v. Connally, C.A. No. 1355–69 (1971).
[70]Richard M. Nixon, "A Message to Congress on School Busing, March 17, 1972," reproduced in *The Impact of Supreme Court Decisions*, 2d ed., ed. Theodore L. Becker and Malcolm M. Feeley (New York: Oxford University Press, Inc., 1973), p. 43; *cf.* "The Wayward Busing Issue," pp. 537–38; and "Washington Report: Compensatory Education Given New Lift by Nixon," *Phi Delta Kappan*, May 1972, p. 598.
[71]"Washington Report: House Tops Nixon with Antibusing Bill," *Phi Delta Kappan*, October 1972, p. 136. The Equal Educational Opportunity Act (EEOA) of 1972 was followed by the more expansive Emergency School Aid Act (ESA), which authorized $2 billion in aid to schools that were desegregating or attacking the effects of racial isolation

Policy Outputs

We have examined to this point the determinants of federal educational policy and the policymaking process. Although all levels of government are involved in educational policymaking, the policy output of the federal government differs from local or state policies because of the differences in federal politics. Since some groups that are unable to affect policies at the state or local levels may influence federal policies, the federal government may become a source of change, as it did in the 1960s. Such periods of change, however, are infrequent. The separation of powers between the various branches of government makes a concurrent majority in all branches essential before change can be effected. Furthermore, the strong parochial nature of American political parties, coupled with the constitutional provisions of federalism, protects local values and views. The reaction of the late 1960s to the federally induced changes demonstrates how sensitive federal policy is to state and local positions.

The problem of school desegregation shows how difficult it is for the federal government to act when there is no basic agreement on public policy. The limits of legal rules and coercive actions by the federal government are readily apparent in the history of this issue. As in state and local governments, the resolution of conflict over school desegregation presents a tremendous challenge to the federal government.

chapter twelve

Interstate and Regional Influences in Educational Policymaking

Sectionalism has been a characteristic of American politics from the earliest days of the Constitution, which itself owes much to the sectional forces that shaped it. Distinctive geographic, economic, social, and cultural characteristics result in regional or sectional awareness, which is in turn reflected in politics at all levels of government. Although the region or section does not have a formal legal place in the political system, it gains its institutional character by federal, interstate, or joint federal-interstate action, as well as through voluntary, nonofficial, nongovernmental organizations. The purpose of this chapter is to examine the regional influences on educational policymaking and the network of governmental and nongovernmental institutions through which these interstate forces work.

Sectionalism or multistate regionalism differs from localism in that it is the expression of common interests that extend beyond the borders of a single state, interests that unite one "section" of the country against the rest. These regional interests are often economic, but not wholly so. The South presents the most dramatic sectional grouping in which economic and other social, cultural, and historical factors mix to produce an impressive solidarity on certain issues.

In the policy model shown in Figure 12–1, the sectional or regional "community" is represented by the circle labeled "Interstate and Regional Community." It also represents the host of cooperative interactions between regional institutions, many of which are voluntary, nonofficial, and nongovernmental.

The second circle in the policy model, labeled "Educational Commission of the States" represents the institutionalized channels for interstate cooperation. A number of interstate compacts, including the Educational Commission of the States, have been created to achieve certain educational purposes across state lines. These and other horizontal relationships

Figure 12–1   System of Interstate and Regional Influences on Educational Policymaking

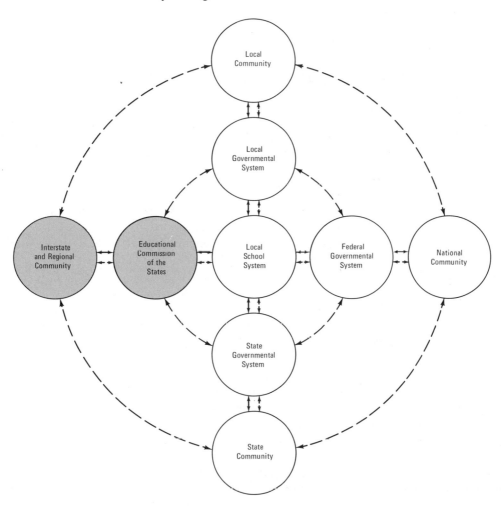

in our federal system, that is, the relationships between state and state, are considered here.

Regional Influences on Educational Policies

Sectional differences in politics and public policies are one of the most obvious aspects of American politics. The intraregional uniformity in politics and public policies suggests that decision makers are aware of their

constituents' cultural attachments in the region. Furthermore, it shows that regionalism is influential in shaping policies at all levels of government.[1]

The awareness of the cultural similarities in a region are often the basis for cooperative action in the political process. Governors and other governmental officials and administrators frequently organize on a regional basis to propose actions to, or resist actions of, the federal government. Organizations such as the Southern or Western Governors' Conference have a significant influence on federal policies and actions, since they are viewed as spokesmen of regional attitudes and opinions. In turn, the federal government recognizes the sectional groupings and organizations and uses them as an informal communication network.[2]

At the federal level, sectional conflict has been a major factor since the earliest days of the Constitution. Although nationalization of the economy, urbanization, and the development of modern communications have tended to diminish the intensity of sectional feelings on some issues, sectionalism remains an important ingredient of political life.[3]

The solidarity of southern congressmen against civil rights legislation throughout the post–World War II period is a well-known example of sectionalism in federal politics. Southern congressmen resisted civil rights legislation and defended exclusive state control of the schools in order to preserve sectional values. Through the use of such legislative weapons as the filibuster or the threat of a filibuster, the control of committee chairmanships, and the formation of alliances, they were long able to prevent civil rights legislation from being considered or acted upon by Congress.

Sectional conflict has affected numerous federal educational proposals. Federal aid-to-education bills, as previously seen, were opposed by southerners throughout most of the post–World War II period because of fear that aid would break down the segregated pattern of southern schools. Only after the courts had held unconstitutional the separate but equal doctrine, and an overwhelming national consensus had developed in the 1960s that something had to be done to ensure the rights of blacks, was the southern resistance overcome in Congress.

The influence of regionalism is also evident in such policy issues as the proposals to distribute federal aid on the basis of need in order to equalize educational opportunity between states, the proposals to aid parochial schools, and the so-called tideland oil issue, which was hotly debated dur-

[1]Ira Sharkansky, *Regionalism in American Politics* (Indianapolis: The Bobbs-Merrill Co., Inc., 1970), pp. 3–16; *cf. Multistate Regionalism* (Washington, D.C.: Advisory Commission on Intergovernmental Relations, April 1972), pp. 1–9.

[2]Daniel J. Elazar, "Federalism-Without-Washington," *Compact*, April 1970, pp. 4–7.

[3]M. J. C. Vile, *The Structure of American Federalism* (New York: Oxford University Press, Inc., 1961), pp. 91–98.

ing the 1940s and 1950s. In debates over interstate equalization, the "rich states" rallied against the "poor states," whereas on the issue of federal aid to parochial schools, the sections with many Roman Catholics opposed sections with few Roman Catholics. In the tideland oil issue, representatives of inland states saw a threat to their taxpayers' interests in this "raid on natural resources" by coastal states with tidelands. The perception of regional interests was a major factor in shaping all of these federal policies.[4]

State policies are also influenced by regionalism, as is evident by sectional similarities in politics and policies. State and local leaders are more inclined to acquire their service and tax norms from neighboring states, since their problems are considered to be similar to their own. Adapting one's program to those of nearby governments is considered to be more legitimate than following governments in other sections of the country. Furthermore, the structure of officials' organizational affiliations puts them into frequent contact with counterparts in neighboring states.[5]

Regional Accreditation Agencies.   Standardization of education within regions is encouraged by the voluntary regional accreditation agencies. Although the American education system is not a system at all in the sense of a centralized organization, American education is very much the same from one end of the continent to another, with certain similarities within the various regions. Emulation and custom exert no small influence upon educational practice, but the most direct force for uniformity comes from the voluntary accreditation agencies.

There are six regional accreditation agencies—the New England Association of Colleges and Secondary Schools, North Central Association of Secondary Schools and Colleges, Middle States Association of Colleges and Secondary Schools, Southern Association of Colleges and Schools, Northwest Association of Secondary and Higher Schools, and Western Association of Schools and Colleges. In addition to the regional accreditation agencies, a number of national professional accreditation agencies, such as the National Council for Accreditation of Teacher Education (NCATE), also influence public education policy. These organizations not only set scholastic standards but also regulate general administrative policies within schools and colleges throughout the nation.[6]

Regional accreditation agencies developed as voluntary, nongovernmental organizations mainly since the turn of the century to "accredit" or certify that schools and colleges maintained or surpassed a prescribed

---

[4]*Ibid.*, pp. 110–20.

[5]Sharkansky, *Regionalism in American Politics*, pp. 12–15.

[6]Louis G. Geiger, *Voluntary Accreditation: A History of the North Central Association, 1945–1970* (Menasha, Wis.: The North Central Association of Colleges and Secondary Schools, George Banta Company, 1970), pp. xxi–xxii.

or desirable standard. The focus in accreditation is on the quality of graduates. Assigning the rating "accredited" to a school signifies that its graduates are prepared for the next stage of education endeavor.[7]

As voluntary, nongovernmental organizations, accreditation agencies are free to set whatever standards they choose, and it is assumed that when members join they agree to support and uphold the rules and regulations. These associations may deny membership to anyone they feel does not meet the criteria for admission and may expel any member that does not maintain the standards set by the association. Because of their powers to set scholastic standards as well as general administrative policies, these voluntary, self-generating bodies of educators shape the nation's schools.[8]

Voluntary accreditation by associations of schools and colleges is a procedure unique to the United States. Its development can be attributed to (1) the absence of federal control over educational institutions, (2) the weakness of official state agencies that charter and prescribe standards for public schools and colleges, (3) the high degree of independence of nonpublic institutions from governmental control, and (4) the marked variations in the quality of educational programs from state to state. To bring out of such divergence minimum standards of quality, reputable schools and colleges—both public and nonpublic—have voluntarily joined to form accrediting associations. The process of accrediting and the minimum standards employed to determine which institutions could be accepted into associations have been controlled, typically, by member institutions.[9]

Accreditation agencies have great power over schools and colleges, since accreditation is essential if their graduates are to be admitted to higher institutions of learning. Graduates of secondary schools that are not accredited normally cannot be admitted to accredited colleges and universities. Similarly, colleges with teacher education programs must be accredited if their students are to be accepted into graduate schools or into the profession. Accreditation represents prestige for those who are members and a lack of prestige for those excluded. Thus the power to give or withhold accreditation is considerable.[10]

---

[7]*Ibid.*, pp. 101–18; *cf.* Lindley J. Stiles, "Reorganizing Accreditation for Teacher Education," *Phi Delta Kappan,* October 1963, pp. 31–37; William K. Selden, *Accreditation* (New York: Harper & Bros., 1960), pp. 30–34; and William K. Selden, "Nationwide Standards and Accreditation," *Journal of American Association of University Professors,* Winter 1964, p. 312.

[8]Mary G. Wiley and Mayre N. Zald, "The Growth and Transformation of Educational Accrediting Agencies: An Exploratory Study in Social Control of Institutions," *Sociology of Education,* Winter 1968, pp. 36–46.

[9]Stiles, "Reorganizing Accreditation," pp. 33–34.

[10]Phillip Hunter and William Kaplin, "The Legal Status of the Educational Accrediting Agency: Problems in Judicial Supervision and Governmental Regulations," *Cornell Law Quarterly,* Fall 1966, pp. 104–31; *cf.* L. Oleck, "Judicial Control of Actions of Private Associations," *Harvard Law Review,* February 1963, pp. 985–

Accreditation organizations not only have power over schools and colleges, they also have a great deal of political influence. They have not hesitated to threaten withdrawal of accreditation when public officials have acted in what appears to them to be an improper manner as far as the schools are concerned.

The North Central Association (NCA), for instance, in 1947 voted to drop all high schools in Chicago, the second largest city in the country, from its list until political appointees were eliminated from the school board and a state law repealed which divided the authority of the school administration into a triumvirate, each member of which was responsible only to the board of education. As a result of the threat of disaccreditation, NCA's conditions were substantially met. Similarly, the NCA in 1950 threatened Kansas City when the school board reduced the length of the school term because of a shortage of funds. Again the board of a major city complied rather than face disaccreditation. In effect, the NCA compelled a school board—and its constituency—to finance its school more adequately.[11]

Two other well-known cases where regional accreditation agencies have conflicted with state political officials took place in Mississippi and North Carolina. Insistence upon integrity of operation led the Southern Association of Colleges and Schools to threaten disaccreditation of all state colleges and schools in Mississippi when the governor of the state became involved in the 1962 racial problems of the Mississippi schools. The same demand for operational integrity led the Southern Association to threaten disaccreditation of North Carolina University in 1965, after the state legislature had passed a statute forbidding any subversive or Communist-affiliated individual, or anyone pleading the Fifth Amendment in governmental investigations into subversive activities, from speaking on campuses. Disaccreditation is obviously a potent threat even against state and local political officials.[12]

Interstate Relationships. Until recently there was relatively little interstate cooperation in matters pertaining to education. States newly admitted to the Union often "borrowed" or adapted some constitutional and legal provisions from the older states. Occasionally a few representatives from one state would visit another to confer on some matter of mutual interest. But state departments of education were largely isolated from

---

1099; L. Oleck, "Law Making by Private Groups," *Harvard Law Review*, Spring 1937, pp. 201–2; and Zechariah Chafee, "The Internal Affairs of Associations Not for Profit," *Harvard Law Review*, May 1930, pp. 993–1029.

[11]Geiger, *Voluntary Accreditation*, pp. 50–51.

[12]Hunter and Kaplin, "Legal Status of the Educational Accrediting Agency," p. 107.

each other. They rarely if ever initiated, and seldom participated in, interstate educational projects.[13]

A number of developments during the past quarter of a century have accelerated cooperation between the states, and especially between states sharing a sense of regional identity. The increasing national interest in education and federal financing has been a major stimulus to interstate cooperation. The growth of metropolitan areas crossing state lines, the pervasive nature of educational problems (like integration) that cross state and school district boundaries, the establishment of research and development groups over wide geographical areas, and the formation of regional and national educational-industrial complexes to furnish better educational materials are other factors forcing state departments of education to seek solutions on an interstate basis.[14]

The growing influence of interstate activities on educational policies is evident from the fact that the Council of Chief State School Officers, a division of the Council of State Governments, has become an influential organization both with educational professionals and with state and federal political leaders. It has been active in matters of national concern to the states and has helped to develop a number of cooperative interstate programs, such as the Interstate Certification Project for Teachers. Over half of the states have enacted legislation adopting the interstate agreement on qualifications of educational personnel.[15]

Interstate cooperation between state departments of education was encouraged by federal grants under ESEA Title V (Strengthening State Departments of Education). Cooperative programs on such problems as the education of migrant children, school district consolidation, educational assessment, and strengthening state-local relations in urban education have led to new patterns of interstate cooperation between state departments of education.

Federal-state regional commissions are another dimension of the evolving intergovernmental relations. Regional commissions were formed during the 1960s in economically depressed regions to undertake comprehensive economic development planning and to help set priorities for the expenditures of both state-local and federal funds in these areas. Regional commissions were established for Appalachia, the Ozarks, the Four Corners, the Coastal Plains, New England, and the Upper Great Lakes, plus the Federal Fields Committee for Development in Alaska. The seven

[13]Jack D. Gordon, "Overcoming a Curious Sense of Isolation," *Compact*, April 1970, pp. 24–25.

[14]*Ibid.*, pp. 25–27.

[15]Alvin P. Lierheimer, "Red-Faced over Red Tape: Progress in Interstate Certification of Teachers," *Compact*, April 1970, pp. 28–30.

regional commissions, which involve thirty-one states or portions of states, are shown on the map in Figure 12–2.[16]

These intergovernmental commissions represent a unique venture in partnership between states and the federal government. Composed of representatives from state, local, and federal governments, the commissions initiate plans, set general priorities and goals, and determine how funds are to be allocated in the region. Primary responsibility for deciding what specific programs and projects are to be undertaken in a state rests with the governors. Governors of the states elect a cochairman from among themselves who serves along with a federal cochairman. Each of the cochairmen (state and federal) has a veto over commission decisions so that neither party has clear dominance.[17]

Education is recognized by the federal-state regional commissions as a most important factor in the economic development of the regions. Through educational advisory committees, state and local educational agencies are closely involved in the regional planning process. Numerous

Figure 12–2 Economic Development Regions

Source: Hawkins, "Federal-State Regional Commissions," Compact, April 1970 p. 14.

[16]James E. Hawkins, "Federal-State Regional Commissions: A New Partnership, *Compact*, April 1970, pp. 18–19; *cf. Multistate Regionalism* (Washington, D.C.: Advisory Commission on Intergovernmental Relations, 1972), entire issue.
[17]*Ibid*, p. 18.

cooperative educational programs have grown out of these planning efforts, such as construction of badly needed vocational and technical facilities required to broaden the opportunity for this kind of education, additions in the curriculum of schools within the region to better meet regional and national manpower requirements, and creation of regional networks of educational television to serve schools of all the states.[18]

The interstate compact, the most formal institution for cooperation between states, is still another intergovernmental development in education. Three regional educational compacts—the Southern Regional Education Compact (1947), the Western Interstate Commission for Higher Education (1951), and the New England Compact of Higher Education (1956)—were created to promote cooperation in higher education. Some thirty-five states are covered by these compacts, which undertake studies of higher education needs of the region and make recommendations concerning the most efficient use and distribution of specialized programs, paticularly at the graduate and professional levels. Through cooperative interchange of students, the states attempt to ensure that all students in the region have an opportunity for higher education without duplication of efforts within the region's institutions of higher education. Student exchange programs make it possible for students from any state within the region to enroll at a college or university without paying out-of-state tuition.[19]

Education Commission of the States

The most ambitious interstate effort to shape educational policies was the Education Commission of the States (ECS). States were quick to discern that a major shift in the locus of educational policymaking was occurring as a result of the numerous federal programs enacted in the 1960s. To counter the rapid growth of federal influence in education, they acted upon a proposal by Dr. James B. Conant for the creation of a new body to coordinate planning at all levels of education.[20]

In September 1965, soon after the Elementary-Secondary Education Act was passed, state governors, legislators, and educational representatives from all fifty states met in Kansas City to create an interstate com-

[18]*Ibid.*, pp. 18–19; *cf.* Robert E. McNair, "The Appalachian Regional Commission," *Compact*, April 1970, pp. 20–22.

[19]Robert H. Kroepsch, "Regional Cooperation in Higher Education," *Compact*, April 1970, pp. 35–38; *cf. Multistate Regionalism*, Advisory Commission on Intergovernmental Relations, pp. 146–47.

[20]James Bryant Conant, *Shaping Educational Policy* (New York: McGraw-Hill Book Company, 1964).

pact for education. Although its founders stated that they were not opposed to federal participation in education, it seemed to owe its existence to fear of the new federal power.[21]

The goals of the compact, according to former Governor Terry Sanford, one of the leading proponents of the compact, were not to set policy, but merely to be the means of developing alternatives for policy decisions, which were to be made by local and state policymaking bodies. It was to furnish the state with the best available information and suggest appropriate goals. According to Governor Sanford, the compact was to provide for a partnership between the state political and professional forces in education and stimulate cooperation between the two.[22]

The creation of the compact, however, was not universally supported by the various political and educational groups in the states, and many felt threatened by it. One effect of the compact was to strengthen the position of state politicians, and particularly the governor, in educational policymaking. This explains, in part, why the compact received overwhelming endorsement from the nation's governors, and at the same time why fears and suspicions arose among many of the professionals.[23]

The marriage between the politicians and the professionals has been difficult to pull off. Many of the professionals who participated in Kansas City were less than enthusiastic about the idea. Members of the National Association of State Universities and Land-Grant Colleges, who have strong political alliances both in their own state legislatures and Congress, expressed their collective misgivings about the compact. State university presidents were generally apprehensive of the powers of the compact. Similarly, the National Education Association (NEA) and many of its state affiliates had qualms about creating another agency led by state politicians with potentially greater influence than the teachers' organization.[24]

The compact's potential for increasing the influence of the state over local districts also raised some fears. As we have seen, many of the urban districts have had closer political ties with Washington than with the state capitals, and they did not relish the thought of losing their influence to a state compact which potentially could monopolize the processing of articulating educational needs to Congress.

[21]Allan M. Cartter, "The Shaping of the Compact for Education," in *Cooperation and Conflict: Readings in American Federalism*, ed. Daniel J. Elazar *et al.* (Itasca, Ill.: F.E. Peacock Publishers, Inc., 1960), pp. 389–402.
[22]Terry Sanford, "The Compact for Education—A New Partnership in the States," *School Boards Chart a New Course: Proceedings, 1966 Conference of the National School Boards Association* (Evanston, Illinois, 1967), pp. 30–32.
[23]Nicholas A. Masters and Lawrence K. Pettit, "Some Changing Patterns in Educational Policy Making," *Educational Administrative Quarterly*, Spring 1966, pp. 81–82.
[24]*Ibid.; cf.* Cartter, "Shaping of the Compact," pp. 391–92.

Relationships of other interstate agencies dealing with education were also changed by the compact. Such agencies as the Western Interstate Commission for Higher Education, the New England Board of Higher Education, and the Southern Regional Board also had reason to suspect that the national compact would lessen their influence as multistate spokesmen for education.[25]

Despite these internal divisions, the Education Commission of the States has developed into a major forum for consideration of educational problems. Its principal efforts have been devoted to examining and analyzing the problems of education and making recommendations that look toward its betterment. It has also become a major forum for carrying on the political dialogue on federal-state relations in education. Political leaders from all levels of government have been involved in ECS programs dealing with the growing problems of education.

ECS has provided leadership on such issues as the financial dilemma raised by the now famous *Serrano* and *Rodriguez* cases, the controversies over public aid to private schools, and the debate over the nature of federal aid programs and federal administration of education programs generally. ECS has also assumed responsibility for conducting the national assessment program.[26]

The proposal by the United States Office of Education in the mid-1960s for national assessment of education raised violent political opposition. Because of the fears and controversies over this proposal, there appeared to be no way that an assessment could be made. The deep conviction that education is a local and state responsibility discouraged the superimposition of a national assessment program based upon criteria that might minimize the local and state decision-making powers in determining curriculum content and emphasis. It was only after the ECS in July 1969 agreed to undertake the program that state and local educational groups did an about-face in regard to national assessment.[27]

National assessment such as that being conducted by ECS is designed to give a national and regional picture of educational attainment broken down eventually by size and type of community, sex, color, and parents' educational level. It will not provide state and school comparisons, al-

---

[25]Masters and Pettit, "Some Changing Patterns," pp. 81–82; *cf.* Cartter, "Shaping of the Compact," pp. 392–93.

[26]Robert W. Scott, "Leadership during Changing Times," *Compact*, August 1972, p. 2; Winfield Dunn, "A Partnership in Critical Times," *Compact*, August 1972, p. 3; James B. Conant, "Five Years of a Developing Partnership," *Compact*, April 1970, pp. 8–11; and L. W. Newbry, "A Legislator Looks at the Compact," *Compact*, April 1972, pp. 12–14.

[27]Wendell H. Pierce, "Accountability through National Assessment," *Compact*, October 1970, p. 4; *cf.* "ECS Takes on National Assessment," *ECS Bulletin*, June 1969.

though ECS hopes to encourage states to make their own state assessments. Unlike standardized tests, there are no scores, norms, or standards. Assessment is not trying to state what people should know, but what they do know. The objectives of national assessment are (1) to obtain census-like data on educational attainment of major portions of our national population and (2) to measure the growth or decline in educational attainment that takes place over time in key learning areas. Despite these limited objectives, it seems evident that through this program ECS will greatly influence curriculum decisions in the future.[28]

The Education Commission of the States has the potential to help shape a nationwide system of education if the political forces in the states can unify and support alternatives for providing solutions to mounting educational demands of our people. Its greatest source of power is that state political leaders are involved along with educators from all levels of education. The political affiliations of state leaders help to give ECS greater access in the political arena than professional educators alone would have. Potentially, ECS could become the main spokesman for education at the federal level.

The weaknesses of ECS are also apparent. Interstate compacts in the American governmental system have not proved to be means of solving difficult political problems. Furthermore, the divisions in its constituencies loom larger than do the unifying forces that could give it political strength. The differences and fears of the various groups of educators prevent ECS from speaking for education generally. The influence the compact will have on educational policy in the future depends on the ability of professionals to live and work with state political leaders.

In Summary

The purpose of this book has been to make a macroscopic analysis of educational policymaking in the United States. An attempt has been made to develop a heuristic model that would help to identify the multitude of actors and factors influencing educational policies and could be used to study the social dynamics of the policy process. In concluding, several points should be emphasized.

---

[28]Leonard J. DeLayo, Chairman, "Assessment Programs—Implication for Education," Panel Session, *Compact*, Special Edition of 1971 Annual Meeting of the Commission of the States, July 7–9, 1971, p. 16; James A. Hazlett, "Looking Forward to National Assessment Results," *School Administrator*, June 1970, p. 11; George B. Brain, "Some Values of Assessment," *Compact*, February 1972, pp. 5–6; and Carmen J. Finley, "Not Just Another Standardized Test," *Compact*, February 1972, pp. 9–12.

First, education is a social enterprise that exists neither in splendid isolation from society nor in direct conflict with other components of society. It exists as a part of the overall fabric of society and is related to all other components. American education reflects American society with all of its diversities and complexities. The educational policymaking process, therefore, is a complicated matrix of differential inputs and outputs among a vast array of decision makers within all levels of government, a process in which no clear point of orchestration exists.

The complexity of educational policymaking is in part caused by the structure and spirit of American federalism, which shapes the entire policy process. The foremost characteristic of American federalism today is the interdependency of the various levels of government, not their mutual independence. Governments at all levels are linked into a "system of systems," which allows the whole and its constituent parts to retain their respective integrities. Politics at each level differs; each responds differently to political demands because of the various structural, cultural, and situational factors affecting each level. But policymaking in this decentralized system is highly interrelated. What any one level of government does, or does not do, in turn affects the other levels of government.

As a result of federalism, there are no simple answers to how educational policies are made. All levels of government share in the making of all the fundamental educational policies, such as who will attend school, what will be taught and who will teach, and how the educational system will be administered and financed.

Three main strands of American politics—localism, sectionalism, and pluralism—are also major factors influencing educational policies. Each has helped shape the institutional structure of education, and the interplay of these forces in educational politics is a source of dynamics on the policy process.

A unique feature of educational policymaking is the major role played by educational professionals and the voluntary, nonofficial, nongovernmental organizations created by them. It is frequently averred that an almost monolithic structure of professional educators controls education and that educational policies in the United States have been determined in the past by the more or less haphazard interaction of (1) leaders of public school teachers, administrators, (2) state educational authorities, (3) a multitude of state colleges and universities, and (4) private colleges and universities.

The looseness of the formal governmental structure has influenced the development of education in the United States. It may be hypothesized that this system has stimulated education to develop more rapidly than other areas of social policy. A comparison between twentieth-century

United States and Western European allocation patterns and priorities shows that in other social policy areas, such as social insurance or health care, America lags about one generation behind Europe. Education, by contrast, is a striking exception to the "Europe leads, America lags" social policy thesis.[29]

We found that the educational policymaking system has been remarkably adaptive despite the frequently made assertions that it cannot meet the dynamic changes challenging the nation. The educational system has met many of the major demands placed upon it in recent years. Within our generation the number of local districts has been reduced from 125,000 to approximately 15,000, the curriculum has been remodeled, the system for financing schools has been modified, numerous pedagogical innovations have been introduced, and a major assault has been made on inequality of educational opportunities. The educational policymaking system itself has been modified in such a way as to permit broader participation. There has been a significant shift in the power affecting the control and support of schools and colleges, a shift characterized primarily by the vigorous entrance of the federal government into educational policymaking, but also involving important changes in the relationships of all parts of the system and the political patterns supporting education. Local systems have been opened to greater participation by parents and other community groups, and state politics of education has changed and is more pluralistic, resembling American policymaking generally. The development of intergovernmental relationships between the states, especially the development of the Education Commission of the States, has opened the process of education policymaking to other groups, particularly to state politicians. In addition, there has been a growing pluralism among groups speaking for education or placing demands on the educational system.

Major resistance to change has occurred in those political areas where we have not been able to resolve the conflict in our society. The urban school controversies, particularly the issue of school integration, are and long have been America's dilemma. Education alone cannot solve the nation's problems. It is hoped that schools can help ease the urban crisis, but all institutions in society must share in these problems and their solutions.

[29]Arnold J. Heidenheimer, "The Politics of Public Education, Health and Welfare in the U.S. and Western Europe: How Growth and Reform Potential Have Differed," Paper presented at the 1972 Annual Meeting of the American Political Science Association, Washington, D.C.: Sept. 5–9, 1972 (mimeographed).

Bibliography

Books

ABRAHAM, HENRY J., *The Judiciary: The Supreme Court in the Governmental Process.* Boston: Allyn & Bacon, Inc., 1965.

AGGER, ROBERT E., *et al., The Ruler and the Ruled: Political Power and Impotence in American Communities.* New York: John Wiley & Sons, Inc., 1964.

ALFORD, ROBERT R., "The Comparative Study of Urban Politics," in *Urban Research and Policy Planning*, Urban Affairs Annual Reviews, Vol. I, ed. Lee F. Schnore and Henry Fagen. Beverly Hills, Calif.: Sage Publications, Inc., 1967.

ALTSHULER, ALAN A., *Community Control: The Black Demand for Participation in Large American Cities.* New York: Pegasus, 1970.

BAGDIKIAN, BEN H., *In the Midst of Plenty: A New Report on the Poor in America*, New York: Signet Books, 1964.

BAILEY, STEPHEN K., *The Office of Education and the Education Act of 1965*, Interuniversity Case Program #100. New York: The Bobbs-Merrill Co., Inc., 1967.

————, AND EDITH K. MOSHER, *ESEA: The Office of Education Administers a Law.* Syracuse, N.Y.: Syracuse University Press, 1968.

BAILEY, STEPHEN K., *et al., Schoolmen and Politics: A Study of State Aid to Education in the Northeast.* Syracuse, N.Y.: Syracuse University Press, 1962.

BARR, W. MONDORD, *et al., Financing Public Elementary and Secondary School Facilities in the United States.* Bloomington: Indiana University, National Education Finance Project, Special Study, 1970.

BECKER, THEODORE L., AND MALCOLM M. FEELEY, eds., *The Impact of Supreme Court Decisions.* New York: Oxford University Press, Inc., 1973.

BELL, WENDELL, *et al., Public Leadership.* San Francisco: Chandler Publishing Co., 1961.

BENDINER, ROBERT, *Obstacle Course on Capitol Hill*. New York: McGraw-Hill Book Company, 1964.

BENSON, CHARLES, *Education Is Good Business*. Washington, D.C.: American Association of School Administrators and National Boards Association, 1966.

BERUBE, MAURICE R., AND MARILYN GITTELL, eds., *Confrontation at Ocean-Hill–Brownsville: The New York School Strikes of 1968*. New York: Frederick A. Praeger, Inc., 1969.

BIDWELL, CHARLES, "The School as a Formal Organization," in *Handbook of Organizations*, ed. James G. March. Chicago: Rand McNally & Co., 1965.

BLAIR, GEORGE S., *American Legislatures: Structure and Process*. New York: Harper & Row, Publishers, 1967.

BLOOMBERG, WARNER, JR., AND MORRIS SUNSHINE, *Suburban Power Structures and Public Education: A Study of Values, Influence, and Tax Effort*. Syracuse, N.Y.: Syracuse University Press, 1963.

The Book of the States, 1970–71. Lexington, Kentucky: Council of State Governments, 1970.

CAMPBELL, ROALD F., GERALD E. SROUFE, AND DONALD H. LAYTON, eds., *Strengthening State Departments of Education*. Chicago: University of Chicago, 1967.

CARTTER, ALLAN M., "The Shaping of the Compact for Education," in *Cooperation and Conflict: Readings in American Federalism*, ed. Daniel J. Elazar, *et al.* Itasca, Ill.: F.E. Peacock Publishers, Inc., 1969.

CAYO, PATRICIA, *The American School: A Sociological Analysis*. Englewood Cliffs, N.J.: Prentice-Hall, Inc., 1967.

COLEMAN, JAMES S., *Community Conflict*. Glencoe, Ill.: The Free Press, 1957.

CONANT, JAMES BRYANT, Shaping Educational Policy. New York: McGraw-Hill Book Company, 1964.

CONN, PAUL H., *Conflict and Decision Making: An Introduction to Political Science*. New York: Harper & Row, Publishers, 1971.

CORWIN, RONALD G., *Militant Professionalism: A Study of Organizational Conflict in High Schools*. New York: Naiburg Publishing Corporation, 1970.

————, *A Sociology of Education: Emerging Patterns of Class, Status, and Power in the Public Schools*. Englewood Cliffs, N.J.: Prentice-Hall, Inc., 1965.

COUNTS, GEORGE S., *The Social Composition of Boards of Education; A Study in the Social Control of Public Education*. Chicago: The University of Chicago, 1927.

CRAIN, ROBERT L., *The Politics of School Desegregation*. Garden City, N.Y.: Anchor Books, 1969.

CRANE, WILDER, JR., AND MEREDITH W. WATTS, JR., *State Legislative Systems*. Englewood Cliffs, N.J.: Prentice-Hall, Inc., 1968.

DAHL, ROBERT A., *Modern Political Analysis*. Englewood Cliffs, N.J.: Prentice-Hall, Inc., 1963.

DALY, CHARLES U., ed., *The Quality of Inequality: Urban and Suburban Schools*. Chicago: University of Chicago Center for Policy Study, 1968.

DAWSON, RICHARD E., AND KENNETH PREWITT, *Political Socialization*. Boston: Little, Brown and Company, 1968.

DEVEREUX, EDWARD C., JR., "Parsons' Sociological Theory," in *The Social Theories of Talcott Parsons: A Critical Examination*, ed. Max Black. Englewood Cliffs, N.J.: Prentice-Hall, Inc., 1961.

DYE, THOMAS R., "Urban School Segregation: A Comparative Analysis," in *The Politics of Urban Education*, ed. Marilyn Gittell and Alan G. Hevesi. New York: Frederick A. Praeger, Inc., 1969.

EASTON, DAVID, *A Systems Analysis of Political Life*. New York: John Wiley & Sons, Inc., 1965.

EDWARDS, NEWTON, *The Courts and the Public Schools*. Chicago: University of Chicago Press, 1955.

EIDENBERG, EUGENE, AND ROY D. MOREY, *An Act of Congress: The Legislative Process and the Making of Education Policy*. New York: W. W. Norton & Company, Inc., 1969.

ELAZAR, DANIEL, *American Federalism: A View From the States*. New York: Thomas Y. Crowell Company, 1966.

EPSTEIN, JASON, "The Politics of School Desegregation," in *Politics of Urban Education*, ed. Marilyn Gittell and Alan G. Hevesi. New York: Frederick A. Praeger, Inc., 1969.

FANTINI, MARIO D., "Community Control and Quality Education in Urban School Systems," in *Community Control of Schools*, ed. Henry M. Levin. Washington, D.C.: The Brookings Institution, 1970.

———, "Community Participation," in *Politics of Urban Education*, ed. Marilyn Gittell and Alan G. Hevesi. New York: Frederick A. Praeger, Inc., 1969.

———, *et al.*, *Community Control and the Urban School*. New York: Frederick A. Praeger, Inc., 1970.

FEIN, LEONARD I., *The Ecology of the Public Schools: An Inquiry into Community Control*. New York: Pegasus, 1971.

FENNO, RICHARD F., JR., "The House Appropriations Committee as a Political System: The Problem of Integration," *American Political Science Review*, June 1962, pp. 310–24.

FITZGIBBON, THOMAS, *The Use of Standardized Instruments with Urban and Minority-Group Pupils*. New York: Harcourt Brace Jovanovich, 1971.

FORRESTER, JAY W., *Urban Dynamics*. Cambridge, Mass.: The M.I.T. Press, 1969.

FOX, DOUGLAS M., "Federal Urban Policies Since 1945," in *The New Urban Politics: Cities and the Federal Government*, ed. Douglas M. Fox. Pacific Palisades, Calif.: Goodyear Publishing Co., Inc., 1972.

FRANCES, WAYNE L., *Legislative Issues in the Fifty States: A Comparative Analysis*. Chicago: Rand McNally & Co., 1967.

FROMAN, LEWIS A., JR., *People and Politics: An Analysis of the American Political System*. Englewood Cliffs, N.J.: Prentice-Hall, Inc., 1962.

GALLAGHER, JOHN, *School Board Politics in Los Angeles County*. Los Angeles: University of California, 1962.

GEIGER, LOUIS G., *Voluntary Accreditation: A History of the North Central Association, 1945–1970.* Menasha, Wis.: The North Central Association of Colleges and Secondary Schools, George Banta Company, 1970.

GITTELL, MARILYN, "Community Control of Education," in *Urban Riots: Violence and Social Change*, ed. Robert H. Connery. New York: Random House, Inc., 1969.

————, *Participants and Participation: A Study of School Policy in New York City.* New York: Frederick A. Praeger, Inc., 1969.

GLAZER, NATHAN, "Is Busing Necessary?" in *The Great School Bus Controversy*, ed. Nicolaus Mills. New York: Teachers College, Columbia University, 1973.

GOLDHAMMER, KEITH, *The School Board.* New York: Center for Applied Research in Education, Inc., 1964.

GRAVES, W. BROOKE, *American Intergovernmental Relations: Their Origins, Historical Development, and Current Status.* New York: Charles Scribner's Sons, 1964.

GRODZINS, MORTON, *The American System: A New View of Government in the United States*, ed. David J. Elazar. Chicago: Rand McNally & Co., 1966.

————, "The Federal System," *Goals for America.* New York: The American Assembly, Columbia University, 1960.

GROSS, NEAL, *Who Runs Our Schools?* New York: John Wiley & Sons, Inc., 1958.

————, AND ROBERT E. HERRIOTT, *Staff Leadership in Public Schools: A Sociological Inquiry.* New York: John Wiley & Sons, Inc., 1965.

HAGAN, CHARLES, "The Group in a Political Science," in *Approaches to the Study of Politics*, ed. Roland Young. Evanston, Ill.: Northwestern University Press, 1958.

HANSEN, KENNETH H., "State Organization for Education: Some Emerging Alternatives," in *Emerging State Responsibilities for Education*, ed. Edgar L. Morphet and David L. Jessen. Denver, Colo.: Improving State Leadership in Education, 1970.

HARRINGTON, MICHAEL, *The Other Americans: Poverty in the United States.* Baltimore: Penguin Books, Inc., 1962.

HAVIGHURST, ROBERT J., *Education in Metropolitan Areas.* Boston: Allyn & Bacon, Inc., 1966.

HEARD, ALEXANDER, *State Legislatures in American Politics.* Englewood Cliffs, N.J.: Prentice-Hall, Inc., 1966.

HOWE, HAROLD, II, AND BENJAMIN C. WILLIS, "Federalism, Race, and the Chicago Schools," in *Cooperation and Conflict: Readings in American Federalism*, ed. Daniel J. Elazar *et al.* Itasca, Ill.: F.E. Peacock Publishers, Inc., 1969.

HUGHES, JAMES F., AND ANNE O. HUGHES, *Equal Education: A New National Strategy.* Bloomington: Indiana University Press, 1972.

HUNTER, FLOYD A., *Community Power Structure.* Chapel Hill: University of North Carolina Press, 1953.

HYMAN, HERBERT, *Political Socialization*. New York: The Free Press, 1959.

IANNACCONE, LAURENCE, *Politics in Education*. New York: Center for Applied Research in Education, Inc., 1967.

————, AND FRANK LUTZ, *Politics, Power, and Policy: The Governing of Local School Districts*. Columbus, Ohio: Charles E. Merrill Books, Inc., 1970.

JEWELL, MALCOLM E., AND SAMUEL C. PATTERSON, *The Legislative Process in the United States*. New York: Random House, Inc., 1966.

JOHNS, R. L., "The Economics and Financing of Education," in *Emerging Designs for Education: Program, Organization, Operation and Design*. Denver, Colo.: Designing Education for the Future, 1968.

JOINER, CHARLES A., *Organizational Analysis: Political, Sociological, and Administrative Process in Local Government*. East Lansing: Michigan State University, 1964.

KAUFMAN, HERBERT, *Politics and Policies in State and Local Governments*. Englewood Cliffs, N.J.: Prentice-Hall, Inc., 1963.

KEPPEL, FRANCIS, "Education Lobbies and Federal Legislation," in *Challenge and Change in American Education*, ed. Seymour Harris and Alan Levensohn. Berkeley, Calif.: McCutchan Publishing Corp., 1965.

KEY, V. O., JR., *Politics, Parties, and Pressure Groups*. New York: Thomas Y. Crowell Company, 1955.

KNIGHT, DOUGLAS M., *The Federal Government and Higher Education*. Englewood Cliffs, N.J.: Prentice-Hall, Inc., 1960.

KOERNER, JAMES D., *Who Controls American Education?: A Guide for Laymen*. Boston: Beacon Press, 1968.

KRISLOW, SAMUEL, *The Supreme Court in the Political Process*. New York: The Macmillan Company, 1965.

LATHAM, EARL, "The Group Basis of Politics: Notes for A Theory," in *Readings in Political Parties and Pressure Groups*, ed. Frank Munger and Douglas Price. New York: Thomas Y. Crowell Company, 1964.

LEVIEN, ROBERT E., *National Institute of Education: Preliminary Plan for the Proposed Institute*. Rand Corporation, 1971.

LEVINE, NAOMI, AND RICHARD COHEN, *Ocean-Hill–Brownsville: A Case History of Schools in Crisis*. New York: Popular Library, 1969.

LINDBLOM, CHARLES E., *The Policy Making Process*. Englewood Cliffs, N.J.: Prentice-Hall, Inc., 1968.

LOCKARD, DUANE, *The Politics of State and Local Government*. New York: The Macmillan Company, 1963.

LUTZ, FRANK W., AND LAURENCE IANNACCONE, *Understanding Educational Organizations: A Field Study Approach*. Columbus, Ohio: Charles E. Merrill Books, Inc., 1969.

MARSH, PAUL E., AND ROSS A. GORTNER, *Federal Aid to Science Education: Two Programs*. Syracuse, N.Y.: Syracuse University Press, 1963.

MCDONALD, NEIL A., *The Study of Political Parties*. New York: Random House, Inc., 1963.

MARTIN, ROSCOE C., *Government and the Suburban School*. Syracuse, N.Y.: Syracuse University Press, 1962.

MASTERS, NICHOLAS A., "The Politics of Public Education," in *Perspectives on Educational Administration and the Behavioral Sciences*. Eugene: University of Oregon, 1965.

————, "Some Political Problems Involved in Educational Planning," in *Planning and Effecting Needed Changes in Education*. Denver, Colo: Designing Education for the Future, 1967.

————, et al., *State Politics and the Public Schools: An Exploratory Analysis*. New York: Alfred A. Knopf, Inc., 1964.

MERANTO, PHILIP, *The Politics of Federal Aid to Education in 1965: A Study in Political Innovation*. Syracuse, N.Y.: Syracuse University Press, 1967.

————, *School Politics in the Metropolis*. Columbus, Ohio: Charles E. Merrill Books, Inc., 1970.

MONSEN, R. JOSEPH, JR., AND MARK W. CANNON, *The Makers of Public Policy: American Power Groups and Their Ideologies*. New York: McGraw-Hill Book Company, 1965.

MORGAN, JAMES N., et al., *Income and Welfare in the United States*. New York: McGraw-Hill Book Company, 1962.

MORPHET, EDGAR L., AND DAVID L. JESSEN, eds., *Emerging State Responsibilities for Education*. Denver, Colo.: Improving State Leadership in Education, 1970.

MOSHER, FREDERICK C., AND ORVILLE F. POLAND, *The Costs of American Governments*. New York: Dodd, Mead & Co., 1964.

MUNGER, FRANK J., AND RICHARD F. FENNO, JR., *National Politics and Federal Aid to Education*. Syracuse, N.Y.: Syracuse University Press, 1962.

MURPHY, WALTER, AND C. HERMAN PRICHETT, *Courts, Judges and Politics: An Introduction to the Judicial Process*. New York: Random House, Inc., 1961.

ORFIELD, GARY, *The Reconstruction of Southern Education: The Schools and the 1964 Civil Rights Act*. New York: John Wiley & Sons, Inc., 1969.

PARSONS, TALCOTT, AND EDWARD A. SHILS, *Toward a General Theory of Action*. Cambridge, Mass.: Harvard University Press, 1951.

PFAUTZ, HAROLD W., "The Black Community, the Community School, and the Socialization Process," in *Community Control of Schools*, ed. Henry M. Levine. Washington, D.C.: The Brookings Institution, 1972.

POLSBY, NELSON W., *Congress and the Presidency*. Englewood Cliffs, N.J.: Prentice-Hall, Inc., 1964.

POST, C. GORDON, *An Introduction to the Law*. Englewood Cliffs, N.J.: Prentice-Hall, Inc., 1963.

RAPAPORT, ANATOL, "Some System Approaches to Political Theory," in *Varieties of Political Theory*, ed. David Easton. Englewood Cliffs, N.J.: Prentice-Hall, Inc., 1966.

REAGAN, MICHAEL D., *The New Federalism*. New York: Oxford University Press, Inc., 1972.

RICHARDSON, ELLIOT, "Educational Lobbies and Federal Legislation," in *Challenge and Change in American Education*, ed. Seymour Harris and Alan Levensohn. Berkeley, Calif.: McCutchan Publishing Corp., 1965.

ROSENTHAL, ALAN, "Pedagogues and Power," in *Governing Education: A Reader on Politics, Power, and Public School Policy*, ed. Alan Rosenthal. Garden City, N.Y.: Anchor Books, 1969.

———, *Pedagogues and Power: Teacher Groups in School Politics.* Syracuse, N.Y.: Syracuse University Press, 1969.

ROSSI, PETER H., "Theory, Research and Practice in Community Organization," in *Social Science and Community Action*, ed. Charles R. Adrian. East Lansing: Michigan State University, 1960.

ROURKE, FRANCES E., *Bureaucracy, Politics, and Public Policy.* Boston: Little, Brown and Company, 1969.

RUBIN, LILLIAN B., *Busing and Backlash: White against White in an Urban School District.* Berkeley: University of California Press, 1972.

SAPP, CARL R., "Executive Assistance in the Legislative Process," in *Public Administration and Policy*, ed. Peter Woll. New York: Harper & Row, Publishers, 1966.

SAYRE, WALLACE, AND HERBERT KAUFMAN, *Governing New York City.* New York: Russell Sage Foundation, 1960.

SCHLESINGER, JOSEPH A., "The Politics of the Executive," in *Politics in the American States*, ed. Herbert Jacob and Kenneth Vines. Boston: Little, Brown and Company, 1971.

SCHWARTZ, LETA LINZER, *American Education: A Problem-Centered Approach.* Boston: Holbrook Press, 1970.

SEIDMAN, HAROLD, *Politics, Position, and Power: The Dynamics of Federal Organization.* New York: Oxford University Press, Inc., 1970.

SELDEN, WILLIAM K., *Accreditation.* New York: Harper & Bros., 1960.

SEXTON, PATRICIA CAYO, *The American School: A Sociological Analysis.* Englewood Cliffs, N.J.: Prentice-Hall, Inc., 1967.

SHARKANSKY, IRA, *Public Administration: Policy-Making in Government Agencies.* Chicago: Markham Publishing Co., 1970.

———, *Regionalism in American Politics.* New York: The Bobbs-Merrill Co., Inc., 1970.

SOMERS, HERMAN M., "The President as Administrator," in *Public Administration and Policy,* ed. Peter Woll. New York: Harper & Row, Publishers, 1966.

TIEDT, SIDNEY W., *The Role of the Federal Government in Education.* New York: Oxford University Press, Inc., 1966.

TRUMAN, DAVID B., *The Governmental Process.* New York: Alfred A. Knopf, Inc., 1948.

———, "The Group Concept," in *Introductory Readings on Political Behavior*, ed. S. Sidney Ulmer. Chicago: Rand McNally & Co., 1961.

TRUMAN, HARRY S, *Memoirs*, 2 vols. Garden City, N.Y.: Doubleday & Company, Inc., 1956.

TUTTLE, EDWARD, *School Board Leadership in America*. Danville, Ill.: Interstate Printers and Publishers, 1958.

USDAN, MICHAEL D., *et al.*, *Education and State Politics: The Developing Relationship between Elementary-Secondary and Higher Education*. New York: Columbia University Press, 1969.

VILE, M. J. C., *The Structure of American Federalism*. New York: Oxford University Press, Inc., 1961.

WAYS, MAX, "Creative Federalism and the Great Society," in *Cooperation and Conflict: Readings in American Federalism*, ed. Daniel J. Elazar *et al.* Itasca, Ill.: F.E. Peacock Publishers, Inc., 1969.

WEIDNER, EDWARD W., "Decision-Making in a Federal System," in *Cooperation and Conflict: Readings in American Federalism*, ed. Daniel J. Elazar *et al.* Itasca, Ill.: F.E. Peacock Publishers, Inc., 1969.

WIGGIN, GLADYS A., *Education and Nationalism: An Historical Interpretation of American Education*. New York: McGraw-Hill Book Company, 1962.

WILDAVSKY, AARON, *The Politics of the Budgeting Process*. Boston: Little, Brown and Company, 1964.

WOOD, ROBERT C., *Suburbia*. New York: Houghton Mifflin Company, 1958.

WRIGHTSTONE, J. WAYNE, THOMAS P. HOGAN, AND MURIEL M. ABBOTT, *Test Service Notebook 33: Accountability in Education and Associated Measurement Problems*. New York: Harcourt Brace Jovanovich, 1968.

ZEIGLER, L. HARMON, *The Political Life of American Teachers*. Englewood Cliffs, N.J.: Prentice-Hall, Inc., 1967.

———, M. KENT JENNINGS, WITH G. WAYNE PEAK, *Governing American Schools: Political Interaction in Local School Districts*. North Scituate, Mass.: Duxbury Press, 1974.

———, AND KARL JOHNSON, *The Politics of Education in the States*. New York: The Bobbs-Merrill Co., Inc., 1972.

Articles

"Accountability '70," *Compact*, October 1970, entire issue.

"Accountability through National Assessment," *Compact*, October 1970, pp. 4–13.

ALESHIRE, ROBERT A., "Power to the People: An Assessment of the Community Action and Model Cities Experience," *Public Administration Review*, September 1972, pp. 428–43.

ALSEN, JAMES, "Challenge of the Poor to the Schools," *Phi Delta Kappan*, October 1965, pp. 79–84.

"The Assessment Debate at the White House Conference," *Phi Delta Kappan*, September 1965, pp. 17–18.

ATCHLEY, ROBERT C., "Can Programs for the Poor Survive in Middle-Class Institutions?" *Phi Delta Kappan*, December 1971, pp. 243–44.

BAIN, HELEN, "The Argument for a Department of Education," *Phi Delta Kappan*, September 1971, pp. 11–12.

BARNES, CRAIG S., "Who Cares about Education?" *Compact*, April 1971, pp. 3–4.

BARRO, STEPHEN M., "An Approach to Developing Accountability Measures for the Public Schools, *Phi Delta Kappan*, December 1970, pp. 196–205.

BEBOUT, JOHN E., AND HARRY C. BREDEMEIER, "American Cities as Social Systems," *American Institute of Planners Journal*, 29, No. 2 (1963), 64–76.

BENSON, CHARLES S., "The Bright Side and the Dark in American Education," *Phi Delta Kappan*, September 1965, pp. 8–12.

BERKE, JOEL S., "The Current Crisis in School Finance: Inadequacy and Inequity," *Phi Delta Kappan*, September 1971.

BESVINICK, SIDNEY L., "Universities and Sponsored Research Policy," *Phi Delta Kappan*, October 1966, pp. 72–74.

BILLINGS, CHARLES, "Community Control of the Schools and the Quest for Power," *Phi Delta Kappan*, January 1972, pp. 277–78.

BLASCHKE, CHARLES L., "The DOD: Catalyst in Educational Technology," *Phi Delta Kappan*, January 1967, pp. 208–14.

BLOOMFIELD, NEIL JON, "Equality of Educational Opportunity: Judicial Supervision of Public Education," *So. Cal. Law Review*, 43 (1970), 275–306.

BONJEAN, CHARLES M., AND DAVID M. OLSON, "Community Leadership: Direction of Research," *Administrative Science Quarterly*, December 1964, 278–300.

BOONE, RICHARD W., "Reflections on Citizen Participation and the Economic Opportunity Act," *Public Administration Review*, September 1972, pp. 444–55.

BOWLES, B. DEAN, "The Power Structure in State Politics," *Phi Delta Kappan*, February 1968, p. 337.

BRADDOCK, CLAYTON, "Project 100,000," *Phi Delta Kappan*, May 1967, pp. 425–28.

BRADEMAN, JOHN, "Education and the Military: A Diversified Partnership," *Phi Delta Kappan*, May 1967, p. 423.

BRAIN, GEORGE B., "Some Values of Assessment," *Compact*, February 1972, pp. 5–6.

BROWN, JULIUS S., "Risk Propensity in Decision Making: A Comparison of Business and Public School Administrators," *Administrative Science Quarterly*, December 1970, pp. 473–81.

BUNZEL, JOHN H., "Pressure Groups in Politics and Education, *National Elementary Principal*, January 1964, pp. 12–16.

CAMPBELL, ALAN K., "Inequities of School Finance," *Education Review*, January 11, 1969, pp. 44–48.

————, AND PHILIP MERANTO, "The Metropolitan Education Dilemma: Matching Resources to Needs," *Urban Affairs Quarterly*, September 1966, pp. 42–63.

CAMPBELL, ROALD F., "Federal Impact on Board's Decisions," *School Board Journal*, March 1967, pp. 38–43.

———, "The Folklore of Local School Control," *School Review*, Spring 1959, pp. 1–11.

———, AND DONALD H. LAYTON, "Thrust and Counterthrust in Education Policy Making," *Phi Delta Kappan*, February 1968, pp. 290–94.

CARTER, RICHARD F., "Voters and Their Schools," *Phi Delta Kappan*, March 1961, pp. 245–49.

CASS, JAMES, "Profit and Loss in Education," *Saturday Review*, August 1971, pp. 39–40.

CATALLOZZI, JOHN, "Accountability and Responsibility in Education," *Journal of Education*, December 1971, pp. 21–29.

CHAFEE, ZECHARIAH, "The Internal Affairs of Associations Not for Profit," *Harvard Law Review*, May 1930, pp. 993–1029.

CHARTERS, W. W., JR., "Social Class Analysis and the Control of Public Education," *Harvard Educational Review*, Fall 1953, pp. 268–83.

CHASE, FRANCIS, "R & D in the Remodeling of Education," *Phi Delta Kappan*, February 1970, pp. 299–304.

———, "Some Effects of Current Projects on Educational Policy and Practice," *School Review*, Spring 1962, pp. 132–47.

"Civil Rights—Judicial Consolidation of Public School Districts to Achieve Racial Balance," *Vanderbilt Law Review*, May 1972, pp. 893–909.

CLARK, BURTON R., "Interorganizational Patterns in Education," *Administrative Science Quarterly*, September 1965, pp. 225–37.

"The Coleman Report: Controversial Report on Education; What It Really Means," *U.S. News and World Report*, December 1968, pp. 44–45.

CONANT, JAMES B., "Five Years of a Developing Partnership," *Compact*, April 1970, pp. 8–11.

"Free Choice in Desegregating Public Schools," *Congressional Record*, December 4, 1967, p. S17785.

Congressional Quarterly, Weekly Report, April 4, 1970, p. 2992.

Congressional Quarterly, Weekly Report, February 5, 1971, p. 358.

Congressional Record—House, August 1, 1968, pp. H8087–88.

Congressional Record—Senate, December 15, 1967, p. S18953.

COONS, JOHN E., WILLIAM H. CLUNE III, AND STEPHEN D. SUGARMAN, "Educational Opportunity: A Workable Constitutional Test for State Financial Structures," *California Law Review*, April 1969, pp. 307–421.

COREY, ARTHUR F., "Educational Power and the Teaching Profession," *Phi Delta Kappan*, February 1968, pp. 331–34.

"Crisis in Finance and Governance," *Phi Delta Kappan*, September 1971, entire issue.

CRONIN, JOSEPH M., "The Politics of School Board Elections," *Phi Delta Kappan*, June 1965, p. 508.

CRONIN, THOMAS E., "The Presidency and Education," *Phi Delta Kappan*, February 1968, p. 295.

CROSBY, MARIEL, "Who Changes the Curriculum and How?" *Phi Delta Kappan*, March 1970, pp. 385–88.

CUNNINGHAM, LUVERN L., "A School District and City Government," *American School Board Journal*, December 1960, pp. 9–11.

DEJNOZKA, EDWARD L., "School Board Members: Their Opinions, Status, and Financial Willingness," *Journal of Educational Sociology*, January 1963, pp. 193–98.

DELAYO, LEONARD J., Chairman, "Assessment Programs—Implications for Education," Panel Session, *Compact*, Special Edition of 1971 Annual Meeting of the Education Commission of the States, July 7–9, 1971, p. 16.

DERSHIMER, RICHARD A., "Will the Bureaucrats and Engineers Ruin NIE?" *Phi Delta Kappan*, December 1971, pp. 250–51.

DEWITT, NICHOLAS, "Investment in Education and Economic Development," *Phi Delta Kappan*, December 1965, pp. 197–99.

DIMOND, PAUL R., "Reform of the Government of Education: A Resolution of the Conflict between 'Integration' and 'Community Control,' " *Wayne Law Review*, Summer 1970, pp. 1005–45.

DOLL, RONALD C., "The Multiple Forces Affecting Curriculum Change," *Phi Delta Kappan*, March 1970, pp. 382–84.

DUNN, WINFIELD, "A Partnership in Critical Times," *Compact*, August 1972, p. 3.

EASTON, DAVID, "The Function of Formal Education in a Political System," *School Review*, Autumn 1957, pp. 309–10.

ECKER-RACZ, L. LASZLO, "Federal-State Fiscal Imbalance: The Dilemma," *Congressional Record*, 89th Cong., 1st sess., Vol. III, No. 143.

ELAZAR, DANIEL J., "Federalism-Without-Washington," *Compact*, April 1970, pp. 4–7.

———, "Fiscal Questions and Political Answers in Intergovernmental Finance," *Public Administration Review*, September-October 1972, p. 471.

ELIOT, THOMAS H., "Toward an Understanding of Public School Politics," *American Political Science Review*, December 1959, pp. 1032–50.

ENGLISH, GARY, "The Trouble with Community Action," *Public Administration Review*, May-June 1972, pp. 224–31.

FANTINI, MARIO D., "Alternatives for Urban School Reform," *Harvard Educational Review*, Winter 1966.

"Federal Government's Remaining Job in Education," Conversation between Harold Howe II and Samuel Halpern, *Congressional Record*, January 15, 1969, pp. E205–56.

Federal Role in Education, Congressional Quarterly Service, Washington, D.C., 1965.

FENNO, RICHARD F., JR., "The House Appropriations Committee as a Political

System: The Problem of Integration," *American Political Science Review*, June 1962, pp. 310–24.

FINLEY, CARMEN J., "Not Just Another Standardized Test," *Compact*, February 1972, pp. 9–12.

FINN, CHESTER E., "What the NIE Can Be," *Phi Delta Kappan*, February 1972, pp. 347–51.

FISHER, JOHN H., "Our Schools: Battleground of Conflicting Interests," *Saturday Review*, March 21, 1964, p. 66.

FISS, OWEN M., "Racial Imbalance in the Public Schools: The Constitutional Concepts," *Harvard Law Review*, January 1965, pp. 564–617.

FOSKETT, JOHN, "Social Structure and Social Participation," *American Sociological Review*, August 1955, pp. 431–38.

FREEBORN, ROBERT, "Local School Boards and Superintendents," *Phi Delta Kappan*, February 1968, pp. 346–48.

GITTELL, MARILYN, "Professionalism and Public Participation in Educational Policy-Making: New York City, A Case Study," *Public Administration Review*, September 1967, pp. 245–46.

———, "Teacher Power and Its Implications for Urban Education," *Educational Digest*, November 1965, pp. 25–27.

GLENNAN, THOMAS K., "OEO Experiments in Education," *Compact*, February 1971, pp. 3–5.

GOLDHAMMER, KEITH, "Community Power Structure and School Board Membership," *School Board Journal*, March 1955, pp. 23–25.

———, "The School Board and Administration in the American Perspective of Government," *School Board Journal*, December 1954, pp. 29–31.

GOLDWATER, BARRY, "In Place of Federal Aid," in *American Education: A Problem-Centered Approach*, ed. Leta Linzer Schwartz. Boston: Holbrook Press, 1970, pp. 145–56.

GORDON, JACK D., "Overcoming a Curious Sense of Isolation," *Compact*, April 1970, pp. 24–25.

GREEN, DONNA, "The Candidates Equivocate on Seven Education Issues," *Phi Delta Kappan*, April 1972, pp. 472–75.

GREEN, JOSEPH, "The Media Centers Reviewed," *Clearing House*, January 1970, pp. 319–20.

GREGG, RUSSELL T., "Political Dimensions of Educational Administration," *Teachers College Record*, November 1965, pp. 118–28.

HAND, HAROLD C., "National Assessment Viewed as the Camel's Nose," *Phi Delta Kappan*, September 1965, pp. 8–13.

HARVEY, JAMES C., AND CHARLES H. HOLMES, "Busing and School Desegregation," *Phi Delta Kappan*, May 1972, pp. 540–42.

HAWKINS, JAMES E., "Federal-State Regional Commissions: A New Partnership," *Compact*, April 1970, pp. 18–19.

HAZLETT, JAMES, "Looking Forward to National Assessment Results," *School Administrator*, June 1970, p. 11.

HOGAN, JOHN C., "School Desegregation—North, South, East, West: Trends in Court Decisions, 1849–1973," *Phi Delta Kappan*, September 1973, pp. 58–63.

HOROWITZ, HAROLD W., AND DIANA L. NEITRING, "Equal Protection Aspects of Inequalities in Public Education and Public Assistance Programs from Place to Place within a State," *UCLA Law Review*, April 1968, pp. 787–816.

"How Education Groups View Contracting," *Nation's Schools*, October 1970, pp. 86–87.

HUGHES, LARRY W., "Know Your 'Power' Structure," *School Board Journal* May, 1967, pp. 33–35.

HUNTER, PHILLIP, AND WILLIAM KAPLIN, "The Legal Status of the Educational Accrediting Agency: Problems in Judicial Supervision and Governmental Regulations," *Cornell Law Quarterly*, Fall 1966, pp. 104–31.

JENCKS, CHRISTOPHER, "Who Should Control Education," *Dissent*, March-April 1966, pp. 150–55.

JENNINGS, M. KENT, "Parental Grievances and School Politics," *Public Opinion Quarterly*, Fall 1968, pp. 363–78.

JORDAN, K. FORBUS, "A Workable Plan for Full State Funding of Public Education," *American School Board Journal*, March 1971, pp. 66–68.

KELLY, JAMES, AND MICHAEL D. USDAN, "Urban Politics and the Public Schools: Myth, Reality, and Response," *Perspectives on Education*. N.Y.: Columbia University, Teacher's College, 1968, pp. 18–32.

KENT, JAMES K., " 'The Coleman Report,' Opening Pandora's Box," *Phi Delta Kappan*, January 1968, pp. 242–44.

KERR, FREDERICK H., "Politics and Schools," *National Civic Review*, April 1966, pp. 193–98.

KERR, NORMAN, "The School Board as an Agency of Legitimation," *Sociology of Education*, Fall 1964, pp. 34–59.

KROEPSCH, ROBERT H., "Regional Cooperation in Higher Education," *Compact*, April 1970, pp. 35–38.

KURLAND, PHILIP B., "Equal Educational Opportunity: The Limits of Constitutional Jurisprudence Undefined," *University of Chicago Law Review*, Summer 1968, pp. 583–600.

———, "Politics and the Constitution: Federal Aid to Parochial Schools," *Land and Water Review* (1966), pp. 476–94.

LAND, WILLIAM G., "Can Federal Programs Be Coordinated?" *Phi Delta Kappan*, March 1965, pp. 347–48.

———, "The Shakeout in USOE," *Phi Delta Kappan*, September 1965, pp. 31–33.

LA NOUE, GEORGE, "Political Questions on the Next Decade of Urban Education," *The Record*, March 1968, pp. 517–30.

LANTOS, THOMAS P., "The Economic Value of Education," *California Teachers' Association*, May 1965, pp. 10–14.

LAUX, DEAN M., "A New Role for Teachers?" *Phi Delta Kappan*, February 1965, pp. 265–69.

LEVINE, DANIEL U., "Integration in Metropolitan Schools: Issues and Prospects," *Phi Delta Kappan*, June 1973, pp. 651–57.

————, "The States Run Scared," *Phi Delta Kappan*, November 1965, pp. 134–35.

LIERHEIMER, ALVIN P., "Red-Faced over Red Tape: Progress in Interstate Certification of Teachers," *Compact*, April 1970, pp. 28–30.

LOREN, PARKE B., AND IRA A. ENGLAND, "Florida Education: Running a Political Obstacle Course," *Phi Delta Kappan*, September 1968, pp. 27–32.

LUTZ, FRANK, "Power Structure Theory and School Board Decision Making Process," *Educational Theory*, January 1965, pp. 19–25.

MACKLER, BERNARD, AND NANCY BORD, "The Role of the Urban Mayor in Education," *The Record*, March 1968, pp. 531–39.

MCMORRIS, ROBERT F., "National Assessment: Coming in 1968–69?" *Phi Delta Kappan*, June 1968, pp. 599–600.

MCNAIR, ROBERT E., "The Appalachian Regional Commission," *Compact*, April 1970, pp. 20–22.

MASON, ROBERT E., "Decline and Crisis in Big-City Education," *Phi Delta Kappan*, March 1967, pp. 306–10.

MASTERS, NICHOLAS A., "Committee Assignments in the House of Representatives," *American Political Science Review*, June 1961, pp. 345–57.

————, AND LAWRENCE K. PETTIT, "Some Changing Patterns in Educational Policy Making," *Educational Administration Quarterly*, Spring 1966, pp. 81–98.

MEAGHER, JOHN K., "Why a Department of Human Resources Is Needed Now," *Phi Delta Kappan*, September 1971, pp. 8–10.

MENACKER, JULIUS, "The Organizational Behavior of Congress in the Formulation of Educational Support Policy," *Phi Delta Kappan*, October 1966, p. 79.

MINAR, DAVID W., "Community Politics and the School Board," *School Board Journal*, March 1967, pp. 37–38.

MONAT, LUCIA, "U.S. Schools Fight Fiscal Pinch," *Christian Science Monitor*, Chicago edition, January 4, 1969, p. 1.

MORRIS, VAN CLEVE, "Grassroots-ism and the Public School," *School and Society*, June 1957, pp. 217–19.

MYERS, WILL S., "Fiscal Balance in the American Federal System," *State Government*, Winter 1968, pp. 57–64.

"National Assessment: Measuring American Education," *Compact*, February 1972, entire issue.

NEWBRY, L. W., "A Legislator Looks at the Compact," *Compact*, April 1972, pp. 12–14.

NORTON, GAYLE, "The Florida Story," *Phi Delta Kappan*, June 1968, pp. 555–59.

OLECK, L., "Judicial Control of Actions of Private Associations," *Harvard Law Review*, February 1963, pp. 985–1099.

————, "Law Making by Private Groups," *Harvard Law Review*, Spring 1937, pp. 201–2.

PARKER, FRANKLIN, "Federal Influences on the Future of American Education," *School and Society*, October 27, 1967, pp. 383–87.

PARSONS, CYNTHIA, "Schools, Parents at Odds: Harlem's Embattled Schools," *Christian Science Monitor*, July 10, 1968, p. 1.

PIERCE, WENDELL H., "Accountability through National Assessment," *Compact*, October 1970, p. 4.

"Problems of Urban Education," *Phi Delta Kappan*, March 1967, entire issue.

PULLEN, THOMAS G., "Superintendents' Authority Underminded?" *American School Board Journal*, November 1966, pp. 12–15.

REDDICK, THOMAS L., "National Institute of Education: An Open Door to the Future," *School and Community*, November 1972, p. 84.

REICHLEY, A. JAMES, "The States Hold the Key to the Cities," *Fortune*, June 1969, p. 134.

RICE, ARTHUR H., "Federal Guidelines Actually Control Public School Policy," *Nation's Schools*, June 1966, pp. 10–104.

ROSENTHAL, ALAN, "Pedagogues and Power," *Urban Affairs Quarterly*, September 1966, pp. 83–102. Reprinted in *Governing Education: A Reader on Politics, Power, and Public School Policy*, ed. Alan Rosenthal. Garden City, N.Y.: Anchor Books, 1969.

ROSSI, PETER, "Community Decision Making," *Administrative Science Quarterly*, March 1957, pp. 415–43.

RUDIGER, CHARLES W., AND RUBEN POLLACK, "Full State Funding: An Idea Whose Time Has Come," *School Management*, November 1971, pp. 18–20.

SALISBURY, ROBERT H., "School and Politics in the Big City," *Harvard Educational Review*, Summer 1967, pp. 408–24.

SCHER, SEYMOUR, "Congressional Committee Members as Independent Agency Overseers: A Case Study," *American Political Science Review*, December 1960, pp. 911–20.

SCOTT, ROBERT W., "Leadership during Changing Times," *Compact*, August 1972, p. 2.

SCRIBNER, JAY D., "A Functional-Systems Framework for Analyzing School Board Action," *Educational Administration Quarterly*, Autumn 1966, pp. 204–14.

SELDEN, WILLIAM K., "Nationwide Standards and Accreditation," *Journal of American Association of University Professors*, Winter 1964, p. 312.

SHANNON, THOMAS A., "The Denver Decision: Death Knell for De Facto Segregation?" *Phi Delta Kappan*, September 1973, pp. 6–9.

SHARKANSKY, IRA, "The Utility of Elazar's Political Culture: A Research Note," *Polity*, Fall 1969, pp. 66–83.

SILARD, JOHN, and SHARON WHITE, "Intrastate Inequalities in Public Education: The Case for Judicial Relief under the Equal Protection Clause," *Wisconsin Law Review*, 1 (1970), 7–34.

SINGER, IRA, "A Regional Complex of Supplementary Educational Centers," *Phi Delta Kappan*, November 1965, pp. 142–46.

"State Aid to Private Education," *Compact*, February 1970, entire issue.

STERNER, JACK, "Accountability by Public Demand," *American Vocational Journal*, February 1971, pp. 33–37.

STILES, LINDLEY J., "Reorganizing Accreditation for Teacher Education," *Phi Delta Kappan*, October 1963, pp. 31–37.

STREET, PAUL, "Compensatory Education by Community Action," *Phi Delta Kappan*, February 1970, pp. 320–22.

"Teachers Warn Boards: You Haven't Seen Anything Yet," *American School Board Journal*, October 1968, p. 31.

THACKERY, RUSSELL, "National Educational Organizations and the Changing Politics of Education," *Phi Delta Kappan*, February 1968, pp. 312–15.

TYLER, RALPH W., "Assessing the Progress of Education," *Phi Delta Kappan*, September 1965, pp. 13–16.

VONTRESS, CLEMMONT E., "Our Demoralizing Slum Schools," *Phi Delta Kappan*, November 1963, pp. 77–81.

VOSE, CLEMENT E., "Interest Groups, Judicial Review, and Local Government," *Western Political Science Quarterly*, March 1966, pp. 85–100.

———, "Taxpayers' Suits: A Survey and Summary, *Yale Law Journal*, April 1960, pp. 895–924.

WALLACE, ROBERT, "The Battle for Urban Schools," *Saturday Review*, November 16, 1968, pp. 5–7.

"Washington Report: Compensatory Education Given New Lift by Nixon," *Phi Delta Kappan*, May 1972, p. 598.

"Washington Report: House Tops Nixon with Antibusing Bill," *Phi Delta Kappan*, October 1972, p. 136.

"Washington Trends," *American School Board Journal*, June 1971, p. 6.

WAYS, MAX, "The Deeper Shame of Cities," *Fortune*, January 1966, pp. 132–35.

WAYSON, W. W., "The Political Revolution in Education, 1965," *Phi Delta Kappan*, March 1966, pp. 333–39.

"The Wayward Busing Issue," *Phi Delta Kappan*, May 1972, pp. 537–38.

White House Memorandum, "The Ship of Integration Is Going Down," *Harper's Magazine*, June 1972, pp. 66–67.

WILEY, MARY G., AND MAYRE N. ZALD, "The Growth and Transformation of Educational Accrediting Agencies: An Exploratory Study in Social Control of Institutions," *Sociology of Education*, Winter 1968, pp. 36–46.

WILSON, CHARLES H., "Local Pressures in Education," *National Elementary Principal*, January 1964, pp. 32–35.

"With All Deliberate Speed: The First Ten Years," *Phi Delta Kappan*, 1964, entire issue.

WOOD, W. W., "What's *Right* with PTA?" AND ALAN A. SMALL, "What's *Wrong* with PTA?" *Phi Delta Kappan*, June 1964, pp. 456–57.

ZIMMER, BASIL G., AND AMOS H. HAWLEY, "Factors Associated with Resistance to the Organization of Metropolitan Area Schools," *Sociology of Education*, Fall 1967, pp. 334–47.

Public Documents

Adams v. Richardson, 351, F.Supp. 636 (1972).

Adams v. Richardson, 356 F.Supp. 92 (1973).

Adler v. Board of Education of City of New York, 342 U.S. 485 (1952).

Advisory Commission on Intergovernmental Affairs, *Who Should Pay for Public Schools*. Washington, D.C.: Government Printing Office, 1971.

BEACH, FRED F., *The State and Education: The Structure and Control of Education at the State Level*. U.S. Department of Health, Education, and Welfare, 1955.

Bradley v. Milliken, 345 F.Supp. 914 (1972).

Bradley v. School Board of the City of Richmond, Virginia, C.A. No. 3353 (E.D., Va., Jan. 5, 1972); 40 USLW 2446 (Jan. 18, 1972).

Brown v. Board of Education of Topeka, Kansas, 347 U.S. 483 (1954).

Budget of the United States. Washington, DC.: Government Printing Office, 1973.

CARTER, RICHARD F., AND WILLIAM G. SAVARD, *"Influence of Voter Turnout on School Bond and Tax Election*. U.S. Department of Health, Education, and Welfare, 1961.

CHASE, FRANCIS S., *The National Program of Educational Laboratories: An Independent Appraisal of Twenty Educational Laboratories and Nine University Research and Development Centers*. U.S. Office of Education, Department of Health, Education, and Welfare, 1968.

Cochran v. Louisiana State Board of Education, 281 U.S. 370 (1930).

Contemporary Issues in American Education, Consultant's papers prepared for use at the White House Conference on Education. U.S. Department of Health, Education, and Welfare, July 20–21, 1965.

Cooper v. Aaron, 358 U.S. 78 (1958).

Deal v. Cincinnati Board of Education, 369 F.2d 55 (1966); cert. den., 387 U.S. 935; on remand, 419 F.2d 1387 (1970).

Downs v. Kansas City, 336 F.2d. 988 (1962); cert. den., 380 U.S. 914.

Emergency School Aid Act (ESA).

Engel v. Vitale, 370 U.S. 241 (1962).

Equal Educational Opportunity Act (EEOA), 1972.

Everson v. Board of Education of Ewing Tp., 330 U.S. 1 (1947).

Federalism in 1971: The Crisis Continues, 13th Annual Report, Advisory Commission on Intergovernmental Relations. Washington, D.C., 1972.

Fiscal Balance in the American Federal System, Advisory Commission on Intergovernmental Relations, Vol. I. Washington, D.C., 1967.

Green v. Connally, C.A. No. 1355–69 (1971).

Green v. County School Board, 391 U.S. 413 (1968).

Green v. County School Board of New Kent, Virginia, 88 S.Ct. 1689 (1968).

HALL, MORRELL, *Provisions Governing. Membership on Local Boards of Education.* U.S. Office of Education Bulletin 13, Department of Health, Education, and Welfare, 1957.

Hamilton v. Regents of the University of California, 293 U.S. 245 (1934).

HEW and Civil Rights. U.S. Department of Health, Education, and Welfare, no date.

HEW and Title VI: A Report of the Organization, Policies, and Compliances of the Department of Health, Education, and Welfare under Title VI of Civil Rights Act of 1964. Washington, D.C.: U.S. Commission on Civil Rights, 1970.

Illinois ex rel. McCollum v. Board of Education, 333 U.S. 203 (1948).

JAMES, H. THOMAS, *et al., Determinants of Educational Expenditures in Large Cities of the United States.* U.S. Department of Health, Education, and Welfare, 1966, pp. 68–69.

KEESECHER, WARD W., *State Boards of Education and Chief State School Officers.* U.S. Department of Health, Education, and Welfare, 1950, pp. 7–10.

LUMPKIN V. MISKELL, C.A. No. 13, 716 (D. Conn., Feb. 1970).

McInnis v. Shapiro, 293 F.Supp. 327 (1969).

MINAR, DAVID, "Educational Decision-Making in Suburban Communities." Evanston, Ill.: Northwestern University, U.S. Office of Education Cooperative Research Project No. 2440 (1966), p. 42.

Minersville School District v. Gobitis, 310 U.S. 586 (1940).

Multistate Regionalism. Washington, D.C.: Advisory Commission on Intergovernmental Relations, April 1972.

NAACP v. Alabama ex rel. Flowers, 12 L ed 2d. 325 (1963).

NAACP v. Button, 83 S.Ct. 328, 336 (1963).

Parental Involvement in Title I, ESEA. U.S. Department of Health, Education, and Welfare, No. OE 72–109, 1972.

Pierce v. Society of Sisters, 268 U.S. 510 (1925).

Policies on Elementary and Secondary School Compliance with Title VI of the Civil Rights Act of 1964. U.S. Department of Health, Education, and Welfare, 1968.

Racial Isolation in the Public Schools, U.S. Commission on Civil Rights, Vol. I. Washington, D.C., 1967.

Rodriguez v. San Antonio Independent School District, C.A., No. 68-175-SA (W.D., Tex., Dec. 1971).

San Antonio School District v. Rodriguez, 411 U.S. 1, 93 S.Ct. 1278 (1973).

State and Local Finances and Suggested Legislation, Advisory Commission on Intergovernmental Relations. Washington, D.C., 1970.

State and Local Finances: Significant Features 1967 to 1970, Advisory Commission on Intergovernmental Relations. Washington, D.C., 1969.

Swann v. Charlotte-Mecklenburg Board of Education, 403 U.S. 912, 91 S.Ct. 1267 (1971).

Taylor v. Board of Education of New Rochelle, 294 F.2d 36 (1961); cert. den., 368 U.S. 940.

Urban America and the Federal System, Advisory Commission on Intergovernmental Relations. Washington, D.C., 1969.

Urban School Crisis, Urban Education Task Force. U.S. Department of Health, Education, and Welfare, 1970.

U.S. v. Texas, 321 F.Supp. 1043; 330 F.Supp. 235; aff. mod., 447 F2d. 441; stay den., 404 U.S. 1206; cert. den., 404 U.S. 1016.

Van Dusartz v. Hatfield, No. 3-71 Civ. 243 (D. Minn., Oct. 12, 1971).

WALKER, DAVID B., "State Legislatures in a Changing Federal System," Address before the Southeastern Assembly on State Legislatures in American Politics, Atlanta, March 31, 1967. Printed in *Congressional Record*, 90th Cong., 1st sess., May 11, 1967, Vol. 113, No. 74.

West Virginia State Board of Education v. Barnette, 319 U.S. 624 (1943).

WHITE, ALPHEUS L., *Local School Boards: Organization and Practice*. U.S. Department of Health, Education, and Welfare, 1962.

Wieman v. Updegraff, 344 U.S. 183 (1952).

WILL, ROBERT F., *State Education: Structure and Organization*. U.S. Department of Health, Education, and Welfare, 1964, pp. 7–11.

Zorach v. Clauson, 343 U.S. 306 (1952).

96 Cal. Rept. 601; 487 P.2d 1241 (1970).

402 U.S. 1 (1971).

462 —F.2d 1058 (1972).

Reports and Publications
of Learned Organizations

AASA Convention Reporter, highlights of 1972 Annual Convention, February 12–16, 1972, pp. 2–3. Prepared by the editors of *Education, U.S.A.*

Addresses and Proceedings, NEA, Annual Meeting, Detroit, 1971.

Annual Conference Proceedings, National Education Association, Washington, D.C., June 26–July 2, 1971.

BAIN, HELEN P., "Report of the President." *Annual Conference Proceedings*, National Education Association, Washington, D.C., June 26–July 2, 1971.

BEARD, CHARLES, *The Unique Function of Education in American Democracy*. Educational Politics Commission, 1937.

CAMPBELL, ROALD F., "State Organization and Responsibilities for Education: Supplementary Statement," *Implications for Education of Prospective*

Changes in Society. Conference Report, Designing Education for the Future, Denver, 1967, pp. 270–71.

CONNER, FORREST E., *The Realities of School Finance*. Washington, D.C.: American Association of School Administrators, 1971.

DIMOND, PAUL R., "Segregation, Northern Style," *Inequality in Education*. Center for Law and Education, Harvard University, August 3, 1971.

"ECS Takes on National Assessment," *ECS Bulletin*. Published by the Education Commission of the States, June 1969.

Educational Administration in a Changing Community, Thirty-seventh Yearbook, 1959, American Association of School Administrators.

"Federal Officials Plug Revenue Sharing but Schoolmen Aren't So Sure," *1973 AASA Convention Reporter*. Prepared by the editors of *Education, U.S.A.*

Financial Status of the Public Schools. Washington, D.C.: Committee on Educational Finance, National Education Association, 1970, p. 54.

GREEN, EDITH, "The Role of the School Board in Society," *School Boards: A Creative Force, Proceedings of the 1967 Convention of the National School Boards Association*, pp. 9–12.

HECKINGER, FRED M., "Superintendent and Board-Staff Relations: Changing Dimensions of Education Roles," *School Boards Chart a New Course: Proceedings of the 1966 Convention of the National School Boards Association*, pp. 247–54.

Improving State Leadership in Education, Annual Report of the Advisory Council on State Departments of Education. U.S. Department of Health, Education, and Welfare, 1966.

JAMES, H. THOMAS, "Interdependence in School Finance: The City, the State, and the Nation," *Proceedings: National Conference on School Finance*, Dallas, 1968.

JOHNS, R. L., "The Economics and Financing of Education," *Emerging Designs for Education*. Conference Report, Designing Education for the Future, Denver, May 1968, pp. 193–94.

————, "State Organization and Responsibilities for Education," *Implications for Education of Prospective Changes in Society*. Report, Designing Education for the Future, Denver, 1967, pp. 245–66.

JUDD, CHARLES H., "Staff Study Number 19," *Research on the United States Office of Education*. Washington, D.C.: Advisory Committee on Education, 1939.

KELLY, JAMES D., AND MICHAEL D. USDAN, "Urban Politics and the Public Schools: Myth, Reality, and Response," *Proceedings: New York Teachers' College Conference*, 1968.

KEYSERLING, LEON H., *Progress or Poverty: The United States at the Crossroads*. Washington, D.C.: Conference on Economic Progress, 1964.

LAMBERT, SAM M., "Report of the Executive Secretary," *Annual Conference Proceedings*, National Education Association, Washington, D.C., June 26–July 2, 1971.

Regional Educational Service Prototypes, Operational Statutory Arrangements and Suggestions for Implementation. Washington, D.C.: National Education Association, 1967.

Reinforcing the Role of States in Education, Second Annual Report of Advisory Council on State Departments of Education. U.S. Department of Health, Education, and Welfare, 1967.

SACKS, SEYMOUR, "Central City Educational Systems: Economic and Fiscal Aspects of Their Current Dilemmas," *State School Finance Workshop,* National School Board Association, Detroit, March 28–31, 1968, pp. 17–26.

SANFORD, TERRY, "The Compact for Education—A New Partnership in the States," *School Boards Chart a New Course: Proceedings, 1966 Conference of the National School Boards Association,* Evanston, Illinois, 1967.

SCHULTZ, THEODORE, "Education and Economic Growth," *Social Forces Influencing American Education,* Sixtieth Yearbook, National Society for the Study of Education. Chicago: University of Chicago Press, 1961.

SPENCER, DAVID, "The Anatomy of Conflict: Claims of the Parties at Interest," *The Struggle for Power in the Public Schools: Proceedings of the Sixth Annual Conference, National Committee for Support of the Public Schools,* Washington, D.C., March 17–19, 1968, pp. 25–28.

State Educational Assessment Programs, Princeton, New Jersey, 1971 p. ix.

TAYLOR, WILLIAM L., "Metropolitan-wide Desegregation," *Inequality in Education,* Center for Law and Education, Harvard University, March 1972, pp. 45–50.

TYLER, RALPH W., "A Program of National Assessment," *National Education Assessment: Pro and Con.* Washington, D.C.: American Association of School Administrators, 1966.

UNRUH, JESSE M., "The Politics of Education," *Proceedings of the National Conference of State Legislators,* December 4–6, 1966, pp. 17–21.

WADSWORTH, HOMER C., "A Basis for Cooperation between School Districts and Municipal Governments in Metropolitan Areas," *Proceedings: First Annual Seminar on Intergovernmental Relations.* Lawrence: University of Kansas, 1966.

WEBB, HAROLD V., "Role of the State and National School Board Association," *Facing Challenges to the Public Schools, Proceedings of the 1962 Convention of the National School Boards Association,* pp. 30–34.

Unpublished Materials

BOWLES, DEAN, "Educational Pressure Groups and the Legislative Process in California, 1945–66." Ph.D. dissertation, Claremont Graduate School, 1966.

"Emergency Committee for Full Funding of Education Programs," Stanley J. McFarland, Chairman. Washington, D.C., no date.

HEIDENHEIMER, ARNOLD J., "The Politics of Public Education, Health and Welfare in the U.S. and Western Europe: How Growth and Reform Po-

tentials Have Differed," paper read before the American Political Science Association, Washington, D.C.: September 5–9, 1972.

HOWE, HAROLD, II, "Change and American Schools." Address before the American Association of School Administrators, Atlantic City, New Jersey, February 13, 1967.

————, "National Policy for American Education." Address before the 71st Annual Convention of the National Congress of Parents and Teachers, Minneapolis, May 22, 1967.

————, "Objectives for Federal Funds." Address at Morehead State University, Morehead, Kentucky, July 21, 1967.

————, "Unfinished Work for the States." Address before a panel on "Education: The Federal-State Relationship," at the Annual Convention of the National Conference of State Legislative Leaders, Washington, D.C., November 18, 1966.

KLAMIE, ROBERT A., "A Comparison of the Desirability and Feasibility of Accountability Measures as Perceived by Public School Administrators and Teachers." Ph.D. dissertation, North Texas State University, 1973.

McFARLAND, STANLEY J., "The Emergency Committee for Full Funding of Education Programs—What Is It?" mimeographed. Washington, D.C., no date.

President Nixon's Message to Congress, "The National Institute of Education: A Brief Outline of Its History, Status, and Tentative Plans." NIE staff, March 3, 1970.

RICHBURG, JAMES R., "The Movement for Accountability in Education." Paper read before the Annual Convention, National Council for the Social Studies, Denver, November 1971.

ROSENTHAL, ALAN, "Community Leadership and Public School Politics: Two Case Studies," Ph.D. dissertation, Princeton University, 1960.

STARKEY, A. E., "State-Level Educational Decision-Making." Ph.D. dissertation, University of Texas, 1966.

"The U.S. Office of Education as a Part of the Problem," Commissioner's Conference 1971. U.S. Department of Health, Education, and Welfare, Dallas, March 12, 1971.

WADSWORTH, HOMER C., "A Basis for Cooperation Between School Districts and Municipal Governments in Metropolitan Areas," *Proceedings: First Annual Seminar on Intergovernmental Relations.* Lawrence, Kansas: University of Kansas, 1966.

WEBB, HAROLD V., "Role of the State and National School Board Association," *Facing Challenges to the Public Schools.* Proceedings of the 1962 Convention of the National School Boards Association, 1962, pp. 30–34.

WEBER, RONALD E., AND WILLIAM SHAFFER, "The Costs and Benefits of American State-Local Government Policies." Paper delivered at 1972 Southwestern Political Science Association, San Antonio.

WITHROW, FRANK B., "The U.S. Office of Education as a Part of the Problem." Presentation given at the Conference on the Consolidation of Special Revenue Sharing Educational Legislation, Dallas, March 12, 1971.

Index

Department of Justice, United States, 187
Department of Labor, United Staes, 157, 187, 195; manpower administration, 195; women's bureau, 195
Department of State, United States, 185, 187
Department of Transportation, United States, 187
Depressed regions, economically, 235
Desegregation of schools, 52, 79, 80, 81, 85, 114, 116, 140, 141, 143, 154, 157, 175, 176, 178, 179, 186, 193, 207, 216, 220, 221, 226, 227, 228; cases, 175, 178, 196, 216; conflict over, 193; political resources for dealing with, 80, 81; (see also School desegregation)
Desegregation plans and administrative practices, 223, 224; cross-busing, 223; equalization of facilities and resources, 224; faculty assignments, 224; noncontiguous zoning, 223; pairing of schools, 223; school construction, 224; "walk-in" school, 224
Detroit, Michigan, cross-district busing, 87, 224, 225
Developing a curriculum (See Curriculum)
Devereux, Edward C., Jr., 38
Dimond, Paul R., 222, 223, 234
Direct federal participation to change schools, 217; (see also Federal government, role in education; Federal educational programs)
Disaccreditation, 234; (see also Regional accreditation agencies)
Disciplinary action against teachers, 34
Discipline, student, 53, 56
Discrimination, 192
Dismissal of teachers, provisions for, 92, 101
Distinctive features of American education, 22, 23, 24; decentralization, 22; Federalism, 22; localism, 23; sectionalism, 24
Distribution of Burdens and Bounties to different units of government, 164; (see also Public finance)
District consolidation (See School district consolidation)
Doll, Ronald C., 11
Donation or sale of public domain to private parties, 88
Downs v. Kansas City, 221
Draft resistance, 207; (see also Resistance to military draft)
Dress and hair codes, 19
Drop outs, 53, 66, 92, 157
Dual federalism, 19
Dual school system, 140, 176, 220, 221
Due Process of Law, 87
Dunn, Winfield, 239
Dye, Thomas R., 69

Easton, David, 1, 14, 15
Easton's model of the political system, 14, 15
Ecker-Racz, L. Laszlo, 70, 100, 163
Economic development regions, 236
Economic functions (roles) of education, 2, 89
Economic interest groups, 110: (see also Interest groups)
Economic Opportunity Act of 1965, 207, 218; community action agencies (CAA's)) 218; training programs, 187
Educational Amendments of 1972, 227
Educational assessment, 235; (see also National assessment)
Educational bureaucracy, 39, 45, 51; communications between, 49, 50, 51, 52; control over information by, 39; power of, 39
Educational centers (See Educational media centers)
Education clientele groups, 195
Educational committees in Congress, 183, 184; (See also Congress); educational bills in other committees, 185; House Committee on Education and Labor, 184, 185; Senate Committee on Labor and Public Welfare, 184, 185
Educational conflict, character of, 141; comprehensive-incremental, 141; ideological-pragmatic, 141
Educational demands (See Demands on local, state, and federal governments)

Education exchange programs, 185
Educational finance, 82, 83, 242; traditional patterns, 140
Educational goals of the states, 154
Educational interest groups, 98, 100, 117, 120, 170, 185, 186, 206, 211, 238, 239; state and local, 239; weaknesses of, 169, 170
Educational Issues in Congressional Campaigns, 185
Educational Laboratories, 191, 192
Educational Media Centers, 70, 205
Educational parks, creation of, 227
Educational Policy Commission, 47
Educational policymaking, 237, 240, 241; changes in, 215; federal actions to open, 218; at the federal level, 199; model, 36; in state government, 137; traditional view of, 38
Educational politics, a new era of, 217
Educational problems, 137, 154
Educational professionals, 75, 93, 98, 101, 132, 139, 218; in school elections, 75; role of, 241;
Educational programs: for the disadvantaged, 206, 227; in the military service, 157; for the retarded and disabled, 187; research, 187, 190
Educational revenue sharing (See Educational special revenue sharing)
Educational special revenue sharing, 193, 208, 210
Educational technology, 215
Educational television, 205, 227, 237; regional networks, 237
Educational Testing Service, 91
Education as a campaign issue, 113; in congressional campaigns, 185; for governors, 113, 114; in presidential politics, 177, 178
Education as a national function (priority), 89, 206; a social enterprise, 240; a tool to solve national problems, 157, 160, 196, 202
Education as a state responsibility, 123, 165
Education Commission of the States (ESC), 91, 191, 229, 237, 239, 240, 242; influence of, 240; role, 239; source of power, 240; weakness, 240
Education of migrant chidren, cooperative programs for, 235
Education Week, 57
Edwards, Newton, 87
Eidenberg, Eugene, 161, 170, 174, 178, 180, 204
Eighteen-year-old vote, 186
Eisenhower, President Dwight D., 176, 178, 188
Elazar, Daniel, 19, 20, 24, 25, 26, 34, 64, 160, 217, 222, 231 238
Election of 1968, presidential, 207
Elections (See School Board Elections)
Elementary and Secondary Education Act of 1965 (ESEA), 91, 157, 168, 188, 190, 191, 192, 217, 218, 221, 237; administration of, 205, 208, 209; formula, 208; funding of, 205, 206; passage of, 204; National Advisory Council on the Education of Disadvantaged Children, 209: reaction of state and local agencies to USOE's administration, 210; Title I, 205, 206, 209; Title II–V, 205; Title V (strengthening SDE's), 235
Elementary-Secondary education groups, 167, 168; American Association of School Administrators (AASA), 168; American Federation of Teachers (AFT), 168; National Congress of Parents and Teachers Association, 168; National Education Association (NEA), 5, 6, 101, 102, 105, 106, 134, 145, 167, 169, 170, 182, 188, 193, 202, 238; National School Boards Association, 167, 169
Eliot, Thomas H., 2
Emergency Committee for Full Funding of Educational Programs, 206
Emergency School Aid Act of 1972 (ESA), 177, 227
Eminent domain, 88
Employment, unequal opportunity, 67
Engel v. Vitale, 197
England, Ira A., 104
English, Gary, 214
Environmental changes, 15, 212; increasing U.S. military requirements, 15; internationalization, 157, 212; nationalization of economy, 157, 165, 212; population growth, 15, 28, 61, 159, 199, 215; scientific and technological revolu-

273

Segregated academies, 195, 226
Segregated housing (*See* Housing patterns, segregated)
Segregation cases, 85; (*see also* Desegregation of schools; and School desegregation)
Segregation of schools, 201, 220; all-black and all-white schools, 221; de facto, 224; de jure, 221, 222, 225; distinction between de facto and de jure segregation, 223, 224; (*see also* Desegregation of schools; and School desegregation)
Seidman, Harold, 180, 182
Selden, William K., 233
Selection of teachers (*See* Conflict over School Administration)
Senate of the United States: power of confirmation, 182
Separate but equal doctrine, 201, 231
Separation of church and state clause of the Constitution, 88, 201
Separation of powers, 170, 173, 175, 228; effect on policymaking, 174; (*see also* Basic features of American government)
Serrano v. Priest, 86, 100, 239
Sex education (*See* Curriculum)
Sexton, Patricia, Cato, 6, 167
Shaffer, William, 154
Shannon, Thomas A., 222
Shared taxes (*See* Public Finance, system of)
Shared-time educational programs, 85, 205
Sharkansky, Ira, 25, 28, 131, 181, 182, 231
Shils, Edward A., 37
Silard, John, 71, 86
Singer, Ira, 70
Situational factors (*See* Inputs)
Slavery issue, 227
Small, Alan A., 58
Smallpox, examination requirements, 87
Smith-Hughes Act, 188
Smithsonian Institution, 187
Smoley, Eugene R., 6
Social conflict (*See* Conflict)
Socialization of youth (*See* Political socialization)
Social legislation in 1960's, 194
Social policy areas, 242; health care, 242; social insurance, 242
Social science analysis evaluating educational performance, 189
Societal charges (*See* Environmental factors)
Southern Governor's Conference, 231
Southern Regional Board, 239
Southern Regional Education Compact, 237
Southern State Industrial Council, 167
Southern Strategy (*See* Republican party)
South Holland, Michigan, 223
South (southern states), 176, 207, 220, 221, 222, 226, 229; position on federal aid-to-education, 200, 201; Southern Congressmen, 201, 231; Southern schools, 210; 224, 231; Southern solidarity (Solid South), 179, 207, 231
Special district governments, 38, 67, 69, 70
Special interest (*See* Interest groups; and Pressure groups)
Special revenue sharing for education *(See* Revenue sharing)
Spencer, David, 53, 82
"Spill over" effect of education, 164; of local educational policies, 90
Sputnik, 14, 138, 139, 212, 213
Sroufe, Gerald E., 123, 129, 130, 150
Standarized tests, 240
State administrative agencies, 133, 134; bureaucracies, 117, 118, 122; clientele groups, 133, 134; competition between, 133, 134
State Administrator's Association, 105,, 106, 107
State-aid formulas for financing education, 85; funds for education, 66
State assessment of education, 240
State attorney general, 136
State board of education, 116, 123, 124, 127, 131, 149; communication linkage with politicians, 131; method of selection, 123, 124, 125, 127, 131
State budgets, 20, 113, 115, 116, 117, 135
State bureaucracies (*See* State administrative agencies)
State capitol, 238

State constitutions, 95, 117; consitutional powers of state, 97; control of education, 231
State department of education (SDE), 123, 127, 129, 130, 131, 133, 145, 149, 187, 205, 212, 234, 235; federal grants to strengthen, 205; roles, 129, 130; rules and standards, 212
State education agencies, 112, 122, 123, 124, 125, 127, 128, 129, 130, 131, 132, 134, 149; clientelle groups, 134; communications with politicians and public, 130, 131; fragmenation, 125, 130; functions, 128, 129; major activity areas (roles), 128, 129, 130; method of selection, 123, 127; new demands on, 128, 129; political influence, 122; political weakness, 130; state board, 123, 127, 128, 129, 130, 131; state department, 123, 127, 129, 130, 131, 133, 145, 149, 187, 205, 212, 234, 235; state superintendent (chief state school officer), 116, 122, 123, 131, 149; state support of, 132; structure, 124, 125; system, 190; weaknesses, 133; withholding of state funds, power to, 136, 150
State education associations, 101, 116, 124, 125; activities of, 101
State educational assessment programs, 91
State educational politics: changes in, 98, 99, 242; common factors shaping, 96; fiscal factors influencing, 99; legal and functional factors influencing, 97; political factors influencing. 97
State executives, 134
State expenditures on education, 110, 111, 132, 138, 139, 141, 143, 152, 153, 164, 199; ability to finance, 164; financial formula, 143; funds for, 66, 104, 128, 199, 212; as percentage of personal income, 153; percentage of state income spent on, 164; per pupil, 152, 153, 164; range of teachers' salaries, 164
State finances (*See* State tax system; State revenues; State expenditures)
State financial formula for supporting schools (*See* State expenditures on education)
State goals, 66
State government, 157, 158, 210, 217, 236; authority over the individual, 196; policymaking bodies, 238; resistance to federal programs, 218; response to urban problems, 216; responsibility for education, 225, 239; support for education, 100; within puts, 112, 122, 127
State highway departments, 122
State inputs on local education (*See* inputs)
State judicial process, 134
State legislative politics: legislative districts, 118; legislators, 97, 98, 101, 108, 122; legislators, visibility of, 121; mal-apportionment, 216; one-party control, 118; two-party competition, 118; (*see also* Legislative politics)
State legislatures, 97, 112, 117, 118, 120, 130, 131, 132, 133, 134, 149, 155, 197, 234, 237, 238; appropriation bills, 118; classification according to degrees of party competition, 119; influence of political parties on, 118; power over education, 117, 231; Ways and Means Committees, 117, 118; weaknesses, 117
State-local relations in urban education, 235
State officials ,81, 97, 147, 219; (*see also* State executives)
State plans, federal grant requirements for, 210; (*see also* Federal grant administration)
State political parties (*See* Political parties)
State politicals and education (*See* politicians)
State political system, 95, 220; (*see also* State government)
State politics of education (*See* State educational politics)
State regulatory provisions pertaining to education, 111; certification of teachers, 97, 111; compulsory attendance laws, 87, 97; minimum standards for operation of schools, 97; selection of text books, 97, 135, 141, 212
State revenues (*See* State tax system)
State's rights, 19, 143, 160, 184, 200, 203
State School Board Associations, 107, 108
State schools for the deaf and blind, 97
Statesman (*See* Politician)
State superintendent, 116, 122, 123, 131, 149, 202; methods used to select, 128
State tax system, 97, 99, 104, 110, 114, 116, 138, 141, 199; constitutional limitations, 38; con-